HARVARD STUDIES IN BUSINESS HISTORY

1. JOHN JACOB ASTOR, BUSINESS MAN

BY KENNETH WIGGINS PORTER

2. JAY COOKE, PRIVATE BANKER

BY HENRIETTA M. LARSON

3. THE JACKSONS AND THE LEES: TWO GENERATIONS OF MASSACHUSETTS MERCHANTS, 1765–1844

BY KENNETH WIGGINS PORTER

4. THE MASSACHUSETTS–FIRST NATIONAL BANK OF BOSTON, 1784–1934

BY N. S. B. GRAS

5. THE HISTORY OF AN ADVERTISING AGENCY: N. W. AYER & SON AT WORK, 1869–1939

BY RALPH M. HOWER

6. MARKETING LIFE INSURANCE: ITS HISTORY IN AMERICA

BY J. OWEN STALSON

7. HISTORY OF MACY'S OF NEW YORK, 1858–1919: CHAPTERS IN THE EVOLUTION OF THE DEPARTMENT STORE

BY RALPH M. HOWER

8. THE WHITESMITHS OF TAUNTON: A HISTORY OF REED & BARTON, 1824–1943

BY GEORGE SWEET GIBB

9. DEVELOPMENT OF TWO BANK GROUPS IN THE CENTRAL NORTHWEST: A STUDY IN BANK POLICY AND ORGANIZATION

BY CHARLES STERLING POPPLE

HARVARD STUDIES IN BUSINESS HISTORY
IX

EDITED BY N. S. B. GRAS
STRAUS PROFESSOR OF BUSINESS HISTORY
GRADUATE SCHOOL OF BUSINESS ADMINISTRATION
GEORGE F. BAKER FOUNDATION
HARVARD UNIVERSITY

LONDON : HUMPHREY MILFORD
OXFORD UNIVERSITY PRESS

A MAP OF THE METROPOLITAN AREA OF THE TWIN CITIES

DEVELOPMENT OF TWO BANK GROUPS IN THE CENTRAL NORTHWEST

A Study in Bank Policy and Organization

CHARLES STERLING POPPLE, D.C.S.

CAMBRIDGE, MASSACHUSETTS
HARVARD UNIVERSITY PRESS
1944

PRINTED AT THE HARVARD UNIVERSITY PRINTING OFFICE
CAMBRIDGE, MASSACHUSETTS, U.S.A.

To
MY MOTHER

CONTENTS

APPENDICES

CHARTS

ILLUSTRATIONS

EDITOR'S INTRODUCTION

THE AUTHOR of this book has dealt with men and firms as he has seen them. His theme is the struggle of business men in the Central Northwest to create banks, to keep them going, and to give them strength. There may have been banking principles at work, and other metaphysical forces, driving men onward, but the author is interested in the forms that the efforts have taken and the services that have resulted.

In unfolding the evolution of banking in the Central Northwest, the author has been confronted with cross-currents and strife that give color to the story but at times obscure the main issue of a struggle for a banking system that could best serve the region. At first, the conflicting interests were those of creditor and debtor. Then, the country districts and the Twin Cities were at odds. Soon, the interests of the Twin Cities were in conflict with those of outside financial centers. And, running through all these conflicts, at least one political party has been pitted against the financial organization centering in the Twin Cities.

Dr. Popple has written the latest, though possibly not the last, chapter in the history of metropolitan economy in the Central Northwest. To be sure, much remains to be done in unfolding details, but the main story seems now to have been sketched. In reading Dr. Popple's book, we might well have before us the parallel but still broader treatment (1925) of the economic development of the region by the late Dr. Mildred L. Hartsough, which, however, is now quite incomplete, particularly on the side of finance.

The growth of different forms of capitalism is illustrated within the field of banking — petty capitalism, industrial capitalism, financial capitalism, and the dawning national capitalism. The climax of the book is reached in the banking structure created chiefly in 1929, in accordance with the policy of financial capitalists but without involving control by investment bankers. The New Era is shown in its strength and weakness; and the New Deal is observed to enter at an embarrassing time, though its coming is recognized as far from disastrous. Indeed, the New Deal may have saved the banking structure of the United States (which the New Deal leader had also helped to shatter), but the solid construction work in the Central Northwest had already been accomplished under the aegis of financial capitalism. In fact, in the Central Northwest we see a significant duality in the sphere of commercial banking. On the one hand, there are two large bank groups, strategically located throughout the area, with a combination of central direction and local management and, on the other hand, a large, undifferentiated group of unit banks, operating under guidance from Washington and at the same time under local management. History seems to indicate that in such competitive situations there is greatest promise of efficiency.

The chief contribution of this book is the history of the two big banking groups of the Twin Cities, which were created by the more conservative bankers of the metropolis of the Central Northwest. Together, these two groups have provided the expert banking direction, the efficiency of operation, and the safety and stability long needed in the region. Moreover, these bank groups, combining strong central direction and alert local management, have made no effort to impair or destroy the remaining unit banks scattered throughout the region. Indeed, as the author says, the two big groups have really held an umbrella over the smaller banks, a circumstance which has been the chief factor in making the groups politically acceptable in the region.

The author has had distinct advantages in the study he has undertaken. He knows the region as the home of his family for three generations. As a student he has been interested in banking development. His actual experience in the First Bank Stock group has served him well. His contacts with the other group, growing up around the Northwestern National Bank, have been indispensable. His conversation with bank executives has given him insight into developments otherwise not clear. His use of bank records has provided a familiarity with the working of both the large and the small banks, that constitutes a necessary background for judgment and perspective. And, then, a certain liveliness of style has enabled the author to drive the story home to his readers.

Many a reader will observe that the author has preferences, such as every mature person is likely to develop while studying a field of conflicting interests. He sees, for these times, more merit in the specialized metropolitan bankers (industrial capitalists) who created the big unit banks than in the preceding petty capitalists who just ran banks, often ran them into a hole. He sees more merit in the work of financial capitalists creating the big bank groups than in the work of industrial capitalists who could, of course, rightly be proud of their big unit banks. He has the point of view of the banker somewhat more than of the user of the bank, though, of course, banks exist to serve the user. He emphasizes the long-time consideration as against short-time interests, though he would admit that a business man must survive the short-time in order to enter the long-time period of his work. He is tremendously impressed with the strong start and great strength of the particular bank groups which he knows so well. In other words, he has the point of view of the Street, of the Group, that has been successful in a field of almost despairing struggle. And, finally, in order to present the subject as a rounded whole, he has had to cover a field which is almost too broad for treatment in one volume.

This study of banking in the Central Northwest was suggested by the material which came to the author's attention while at work in the bank. Since the experience of one bank, even though the center of a large group, was too one-sided, the second group was brought in. The two groups have given information and encouragement but have not financed research. They have jointly assisted, however, in the publication of the volume, particularly in the interest of a wider distribution at a lower price. Final decisions in matters of generalization and in statement of facts have been made by the author.

The editor cannot help wondering whether, in the possible future restoration of financial capitalism to leadership in a much chastened and scorched nation, these two big banking groups and also that "far-off region" of the Central Northwest may not play a distinguished part. If such a possibility as this arises, that is, for a center other than New York to play a strong rôle, we may think of America as having begun to grow up economically. In the past, American business has had to bow to one banking center after another —

London, Philadelphia, and finally New York. When all the metropolitan centers of the United States have attained financial strength, the country will have come of age. Of course, in this connection, we can only welcome parallel studies of banking in other metropolitan regions, particularly on the Pacific Coast, in the Southwest, and in the Old South.

N. S. B. Gras

May, 1943

AUTHOR'S PREFACE

THIS IS A STUDY of financial development in a region which crammed into less than a century what often filled hundreds of years in older parts of the world. Within that crowded span, banking in the Northwest quickly left behind its first simple function, supplying a medium of exchange. It progressed to the point of supplying capital through debtor banking by capitalizing the debts of the community, a great service in many respects, but darkened by bankruptcies and desolation. It came at last to the position of protecting capital by a creditor system of banking which analyzed its own weaknesses and tried to remedy them without sacrificing the benefits of unit banking or taking on the rigidities of branch banking.

During the past thirteen years, group banking has come upon the scene to make a valiant stand for strength and service, not without some mistakes, but with a generous measure of success. It has been supported by a process of evolution, by intelligent, capable management, and by the approaching maturity of the region, all of which have collaborated in strengthening the general banking system.

Because the present is always imperceptibly evolving into the future, it is a truism to say that banking in the Ninth Federal Reserve District will continue to evolve: in fact, it is plastic and will shape itself to changing circumstances. The possible questions which now confront us are whether some form of *group banking* will survive; whether the system will disintegrate into *unit banking* with extensive government control; or whether *branch banking*, with its attendant strength and rigidity, will finally emerge. Down one of these paths lies the future.

In this study I have taken a broad approach, concerning myself with broad trends rather than personal details and statistical minutiae. I have preferred the qualitative to the quantitative. Yet, through it all, run the bright threads of names, personalities, and stories. I have felt that generalizations are best understood through specific illustrations. I have not hesitated to give names, to cite actual examples, to supply figures, and to quote pertinent data in support of my conclusions.

My obligations to Professor N. S. B. Gras are very great; without his constant encouragement and advice this book would neither have been undertaken nor completed. Professors J. Franklin Ebersole, R. L. Masson, and Pearson Hunt have examined the manuscript and given valuable advice. Professor Henrietta M. Larson has been most helpful with both criticism and advice.

Messrs. J. Cameron Thomson and A. H. Kennedy, presidents of the Northwest Bancorporation and of the First Bank Stock Corporation, respectively, have encouraged the writing of this history. They have facilitated the use of private records and have been generous with their wide information and their comments.

In addition, the manuscript has had the advantage of being read throughout by Messrs. C. T. Jaffray, Lyman E. Wakefield, L. B. Hogue, Julian B. Baird, Robert F. Mactavish, and John B. Faegre. I have gained from their comments and may have erred in not always following their advice. To many others, too numerous to mention, I owe a debt of gratitude which is rather difficult to repay.

I am indebted to Miss Catherine Newton for her caustic but constructive criticism of both form and subject matter. Mrs. Madeleine Cummings Casey has supervised the typing of the manuscript; to her my thanks. To Mrs. Elsie Hight Bishop I am indebted for expert assistance in putting the manuscript through the press and for making the index.

The Minnesota Historical Society has been most kind in permitting me access to their collections and in giving me permission to reproduce certain pictures. I am grateful to the Society and especially to Mr. Willoughby Babcock.

This work is not an official history; I alone am responsible for facts and opinions.

Charles Sterling Popple

February 15, 1943

CHRONOLOGY

1852 Borup and Oakes commenced business in St. Paul.
1853 Parker Paine and Company commenced business in St. Paul.
1857 Sidle, Wolford and Company commenced business in Minneapolis.
1859 Parker Paine and Company became Thompson, Paine and Company.
1861 Thompson, Paine and Company became Thompson Bros.
1862 Thompson Bros. became the Bank of Minnesota.
1863 The Bank of Minnesota became the First National Bank of St. Paul.
1864 Sidle, Wolford and Company became the Minneapolis Bank.
1865 The Minneapolis Bank became the First National Bank of Minneapolis.
1872 The Northwestern National Bank of Minneapolis was founded.
1872 The Merchants National Bank of St. Paul was founded.
1873 The beginning of a depression.
1874 The Farmers and Mechanics Savings Bank of Minneapolis was founded.
1878 The Security Bank of Minneapolis was founded.
1883 The Minnesota Loan and Trust Company was founded.
1887 James B. Forgan joined the Northwestern National Bank.
1887 E. W. Decker and C. T. Jaffray joined the Northwestern National Bank.
1888 The Minneapolis Trust Company was founded.
1893 A panic followed by a depression.
1903 The Union Investment Company was founded.
1905 The Northwestern established the first savings department in the Twin Cities.
1907 The Currency Panic occurred.
1909 The Northwestern and the Minnesota Loan and Trust Company became affiliated through stock ownership.
1912 James J. Hill bought the First National Bank of St. Paul.
1913 The Minneapolis Trust Company became affiliated with the First National Bank of Minneapolis through stock ownership.
1915 The First National Bank of Minneapolis and the Security Na-

tional Bank were merged as the First and Security National Bank.

1917 Beginning of the war boom.

1920 Beginning of the postwar collapse.

1921 The revival of the War Finance Corporation.

1922 The Minneapolis Trust-Joint Stock Land Bank was founded.

1922 Two groups of banks were organized in Minneapolis.

1923 The Minnesota Rural Credits Bureau was established.

1923 The beginning of urban prosperity.

1923 A prosperous business in securities developed in the Twin Cities.

1925 The Minneapolis Trust Company absorbed the Wells-Dickey Trust Company.

1927 The Minneapolis Trust Company absorbed the Hennepin County Savings Bank.

1929 Organization of the Northwest Bancorporation.

1929 Merger of the Merchants National Bank and the First National Bank as the First National Bank of St. Paul.

1929 Organization of the First Bank Stock Corporation.

1929 Stock-market crash in New York.

1930 Organization of the BancNorthwest Company.

1930 Organization of the First Securities Corporation.

1931 Defaults, repudiation, and bankruptcies became common.

1932 Banks raced for liquidity.

1932 Widespread closing of banks developed.

1933 The Bank Holiday occurred.

1933 All members of both groups reopened immediately.

1933 The Emergency Bank Act was passed.

1933 The Minnesota Loan and Trust Company was merged with the Northwestern National Bank as the Northwestern National Bank and Trust Company.

1933 The First Securities Corporation was liquidated.

1933 The BancNorthwest Company was liquidated.

1933 The First National Bank was merged with the First Minneapolis Trust Company as the First National Bank and Trust Company of Minneapolis.

1934 A temporary deposit insurance system was established.

1934 The member banks of the Bancorporation sold preferred stock.

1934 The country banks of First Bank Stock Corporation sold a small amount of preferred stock.

1934 The Moorhead Trial was held.

1934 The Minneapolis Trust-Joint Stock Land Bank was liquidated.
1935 A permanent deposit insurance system was established.
1935 A period of convalescence began.
1936 The member banks of the First Bank Stock Corporation retired the last of their preferred stock.
1940 The member banks of the Northwest Bancorporation retired the last of their preferred stock.

DEVELOPMENT OF TWO BANK GROUPS

CHAPTER I

A PROLOGUE TO BANKING IN THE NORTHWEST

Financial Development a Phase of Economic Development

The covered wagons that rolled into the Central Northwest — that immense area which now embraces Minnesota, North and South Dakota, and Montana — and the boats that plied its streams brought men with hope in their hearts. They found a land that stirred their pulses. There were great forests of pine; rushing waterfalls; gold, copper, and iron ores; and, far more important, fat acres to farm and a long, mild growing season. The territory lay untouched, offering to the strong opportunities and riches to compare with the treasures of Peru — but not without toil. Perhaps a few of those lean pioneers visualized the great regional empire to come, but probably most men saw only their own little opportunities to find a nook and to achieve some degree of economic security, wealth, and fame.

The early pioneers, those who came between 1849 and 1872, found profitable opportunities innumerable. There were fortunes in fur trading, and steamboats on the Mississippi made their owners prosper. Other lucrative occupations were cutting timber, sawing logs into lumber, milling wheat into flour, building railroads and factories, and developing productive farms. The abundance and the quality of the raw materials, the demand of the settled areas for cheap goods, the constant influx of population, and steadily rising property values all combined to support the efforts of the aggressive business man.

One thing the wilderness did not provide, and that was capital. While a few pioneers brought money with them, the overwhelming majority had little besides their two strong hands. Whatever capital came from settled areas of this and foreign countries was rapidly expended in the construction of mills, factories, lumber camps, and power sites, and in the clearing of farm land. When their own slim funds had been expended and they attempted to borrow, the pioneers discovered that money could be obtained only from the East.

These attempts to secure loans involved almost insurmountable difficulties because to eastern capitalists the Central Northwest might well have been Timbuktu. There were profitable investment opportunities nearer home; moreover, eastern business men had had unfortunate experiences with other pioneer areas, and very high interest rates were needed to overcome their reluctance. But because it was the obtaining of money that mattered and not the interest, the pioneers cheerfully paid high rates if only they could obtain adequate funds. It mattered little to a man if he paid 36 per cent a year on his loans if he could make annual profits of 72 to 100 per cent; the more he borrowed, the more profits he made. Nevertheless, only a few pioneers were so situated that they could obtain funds in the East — to do so required good credit, collateral, and connections, and occasional eastern trips, prerequisites which eliminated the great majority. It is small wonder that to the pioneers, thus shut out of the Elysian Fields, this problem became so vital. Capital would develop the land, build for them, and create fortunes, but any quick solution of the problem had to be of local origin, contrived out of the materials at hand.

To obtain capital with which to finance local ventures the early settlers tried all the devices which had been perfected earlier in other frontier areas. Most successful were the creation of a debtor-banking system and the application of short-term commercial capital to long-term investment purposes.

A frontier bank was rarely established by a capitalist who foresaw profitable employment for his excess funds. More often, a few ambitious business men in dire need of money to finance local enterprises found they could not obtain funds from established institutions and decided to set up their own bank. They pooled their means to supply the required capital; applied for a charter when one was needed; reserved space for a banking-room, often in a local store, hotel, or real-estate office; and bought a ledger and a safe. Then they elected one of their number managing officer. The first series of transactions usually was the loan of the entire capital to the stockholders. Then the bank took in on deposit what local money there was, loaning it immediately to members of the community. The demand for money was endless; every business man, farmer, and land speculator, especially the last, thought that he could make a fortune if only he could borrow enough. As a result, the bank was barely founded before it had loans in excess of capital.

The ease with which local banks could be established, the flow of capital they supplied to local business interests (especially to the stockholders), and the profits they earned were all factors favoring their mushroom growth. Every thriving crossroads had at least one such bank. Where towns were larger, rival groups formed rival banks. Anyone who felt there was a shortage of banks was free to organize another one.

These banks performed very real services. The most important was loaning to borrowers who could have obtained money from no other source. Pioneer bankers were optimistic; their faith was in the future of the community. They believed that values would rise and that local business men would succeed, and with these convictions they financed projects which professional bankers would have scorned. They made local real-estate loans from their own funds and sold them to eastern farm-mortgage dealers, thus bringing in a large volume of outside capital. They performed other services, too. One of the most important, but probably the least recognized, was providing exchange between two men in a community, between two towns in an area, and between one area and another. This service was accomplished so well that few people were aware of the difficulties and expense involved. Also, the banks issued certificates of deposit, paid interest on funds, held items for safekeeping, supplied an occasional safety deposit box, and extended many miscellaneous courtesies.

The primary demand in a frontier community was for capital to pay either the government or the railroad for land. Then the settlers borrowed to meet living expenses while they broke the land; to pay for clearing, ploughing, and fencing, for raising barns and other buildings, and for buying cattle and financing crops. In the towns business men borrowed small sums to buy inventory and to finance the purchase of farm crops. The bulk of their borrowing, however, was poured into the construction of mills, elevators, warehouses, stores, and dwellings, and into speculation in land.

Even where the volume of loans was small, banks were organized by prospective borrowers. Because they supplied a common need, they sprang up everywhere. As the territory was settled, farms were wrested from the wilderness, roads and schools were constructed, and towns developed. Small farmers and business men made large profits and acquired valuable properties; within a single generation they found themselves transformed from poverty-stricken pioneers to petty capitalists.

Wherever the community grew rapidly and steadily, as business men succeeded in their ventures and values increased, local banking worked to the benefit of both the community and itself. The banker was repaid, with high interest, for granting loans which others would have refused. The availability of local credit promoted a speedy accumulation of capital, which grew like a snowball rolling downhill. The development of the community and the creation of local fortunes proceeded far more rapidly than would have occurred under a conservative banking system.

Debtor banking, as it developed, was fluid in the extreme, it supplied credit wherever it was demanded, and it loaned to men, companies, and localities as long as they did not fail. It was this system which financed the rapid development of the territory economically tributary to the Twin Cities. The financial history of any territory is but a record of efforts to finance its development. In the Central Northwest this history encompasses feverish efforts to import eastern capital, the slow process of capital accumulation, the creation of a debtor-banking system designed to create loanable capital funds out of the debts of the community, the recurring ravages of panic and failure, and the patient building of a strong creditor-banking system. Since banking is but a phase of general economic development and can be understood only as a part of the whole, it is necessary to sketch in the broad outlines of economic growth in the region before considering banking in detail.

Economic Development of The Twin Cities, 1819–1915

In the year 1819 a detachment of soldiers was sent up the Mississippi River to establish at the mouth of the Minnesota a post known first as Fort St. Anthony and later as Fort Snelling.[1] In 1823 the steamboat *Virginia* nosed up the river loaded with supplies, and thereafter passengers and freight arrived and departed by river steamer. Immigrants, however, were few, and when the Minnesota Territory was organized in 1849, its population numbered only 4,680.[2]

The primary business of this northern frontier territory was hunting and trapping. Furs found their outlet in St. Louis and the East. Goods to barter for them were imported, and the territory abounded in traders. Goods coming into the territory and furs going out traversed one of two main routes, either north and east via the Grand Portage and the Great Lakes, or south by way of the Mississippi to St. Louis.

Boats ascending the Mississippi found the head of navigation below St. Anthony Falls, and that became the focal point of a mushroom community. There trails converged; traders amassed pelts in return for knives and blankets, and during the navigable season frequent boats from the South brought their wares for exchange.[3] This community was named St. Paul. It overshadowed St. Anthony and by 1853 felt quite metropolitan, despite the fact that in that year Indians raided the town and a massacre occurred on the main street. As the citizens pointed out, soldiers from Fort Snelling arrived in a short time. Although people were killed and the Indians escaped, the prompt appearance of the troops certainly indicated a degree of civilization.[4]

St. Paul made little progress in developing manufactures, for it had neither cheap power nor plentiful raw materials; however, it was a natural distributing point, and under the old rule, "where bulk breaks, trade makes," business grew rapidly. All goods moving into the country by river boat landed first at St. Paul. Their quantity was immense, for the soldiers at Fort Snelling consumed large amounts, the white settlers were growing more numerous, and there were the Indians. Some of the incoming goods unloaded at St. Paul were carried away by pack train or by Red River carts, and every year pack trains and canoes arrived loaded with furs for sale. This commercial promise induced many traders to import goods and offer them for sale, and to buy furs and export them to St. Louis and other points. At the same time, the tide of population was toward the Northwest, and after 1849 settlers poured into the territory. Many were farmers and homeseekers who settled as near to Fort Snelling as possible. Their growing number increased the demand for goods imported from the East and multiplied the volume of exports.

At first the Village of St. Anthony developed more slowly than St. Paul, partly because the government land survey there was not completed until 1848.[5] Thereafter, however, a clear title could be obtained to land on the east shore of the river. One of the first to obtain land at the Falls was Franklin Steele, a sutler at Fort Snelling. He acquired riparian rights but did not have the capital necessary to develop the power.[6] On July 10, 1847, he sold nine-tenths of his water power to a Boston syndicate for $12,000 and immediately commenced to build a dam and a mill, which sawed its first lumber on September 1, 1848. Unfortunately, the syndicate did not pay the much needed cash, and Steele had to settle his debts by transferring an interest in his property to his creditors.[7] Because a substantial demand for lumber existed, and both power and logs were readily available, the first lumber mills were profitable from the beginning. In 1850 Ard Godfrey, who had constructed Steele's mill and acquired an interest in settlement, withdrew from the firm to build his own mill at the west end of the dam.[8] Other lumber and shingle mills followed in rapid succession. Steele sold a portion of his water power to New York capitalists, who in 1856 organized the St. Anthony Falls Water Power Company. Since the old dam was not entirely satisfactory, the company constructed a new one to connect with the dam of the Minneapolis Mill Company, which had been chartered in February, 1856, for the purpose of developing the power on the west side of the river. The new dam was completed in 1857, together with a canal to carry water to the mills built on the west shore.[9]

CURRENCY ISSUED BY THE NORTHERN OUTFIT BEFORE 1853

ST. PAUL, MINNESOTA, LOWER LEVEE, FALL OF 1856

By 1854 St. Anthony had a school, a hotel, churches, and several lumber and shingle mills. In that year a sash, door, and blind factory was opened and shortly thereafter a furniture factory. Blacksmith shops appeared at a very early date; toolmakers followed; and soon foundry and machine shops were also in operation. The town developed a lively business in mill furnishings and cooperage. Thus St. Anthony, soon to be merged with Minneapolis, was not a trading center like neighboring St. Paul, but a community active in all types of manufacturing. Back of this development was the seductive source of cheap power, the immense area of fine timber lands tributary to the location, and the ease with which logs could be floated down the river. The commercial activities of the town were subsidiary to its manufacturing.[10] The original mills at St. Anthony were primarily lumber mills. Since ample power was available, and wheat could be grown in the territory, and because a local demand for flour existed, flour-milling developed at an early date. In 1851 Richard Rogers built a grist mill at St. Anthony, obtaining his power from Steele's dam; in 1852 he formed a partnership with Franklin Steele and enlarged his operations. October, 1854, brought into operation the Minnesota Mill, owned by John W. Eastman, Captain John Rollins, and R. P. Upton. William W. Eastman, a brother of John W., in partnership with Paris Gibson, constructed the Cataract Mill in 1859.[11] From that time on, the number of flour mills grew steadily.

Cadwallader C. Washburn, who with Dorilus Morrison had been active in lumbering and logging, erected a flour mill in 1866, taking George H. Christian as his active partner.[12] Three years later William Hood Dunwoody left Philadelphia for Minneapolis, where he was soon employed to buy Minneapolis flour for eastern wholesalers. In 1879 he joined the Washburn firm.[13] In the year 1877 John Crosby, a man of some means who had been engaged in various business activities in the State of Maine, came to Minneapolis and formed a partnership with Cadwallader C. Washburn for the operation of the Washburn "B" Mill and assumed its management. In 1889 the firm of Washburn-Crosby was incorporated with J. S. Bell, W. H. Dunwoody, John Washburn, and John Crosby, Jr., on the board of directors.[14] John S. Pillsbury came to St. Anthony in

1855. He first established a hardware business and then bought a small flour mill. The venture was profitable and its expansion steady.[15] Flour-milling in Minneapolis continued to grow in importance. Eventually it passed lumbering, which declined with the exhaustion of the timber. The change, however, had little effect on the growth of the city.

Before the development of the railroads, St. Paul, being the head of navigation on the Mississippi, was the natural center of transportation and commerce in the territory. Passengers and goods bound for Minneapolis usually came through St. Paul.[16] Roads supplemented the river at an early date, providing transportation by stage line and wagon teams. As early as 1847 a regular packet line was established between St. Paul and St. Louis, and in 1849 ninety-five steamboats docked at St. Paul.[17] A daily line of wagons between St. Paul and St. Anthony brought goods for sale. By 1855 a wire suspension bridge crossed the Mississippi, linking St. Anthony and Minneapolis.[18]

In 1854 the Chicago and Rock Island Railroad connected Chicago with the Mississippi, and thereafter goods from St. Paul descended the Mississippi by steamboat and were transported from the river to Chicago by rail.[19] From the first settlement, considerable effort was made to finance and construct railroad lines in Minnesota, but early efforts met with little success and no roads were operated before 1862. Since the Minnesota pioneers, like all others, believed that the railroad was the key to unlock the fabulous riches of the Northwest, a grass-roots demand for the promotion and construction of railroads existed. Despite this all-pervading belief, no progress was made before 1857. True, Minnesota Territory previously had chartered some fifteen railroad corporations, and that year saw nearly as many charters granted; [20] nevertheless, primarily because of a lack of capital, not a single foot of track had been laid. The pioneers were in a dilemma; they could not build railroads without capital, yet the territory could not acquire capital without railroads. A way out of the cul-de-sac appeared on March 3, 1857, when the United States Congress passed an act designed to encourage railroad-building by the grant of public lands.[21]

The Minnesota railroad promoters, grouping the proposed roads into four systems, the most prominent of which was the Minnesota and Pacific Railroad Company, applied for land grants.[22] Although their application met with a cordial response from the legislature, it was not introduced independently but was added as an amendment to a measure intended to encourage the destruction of gophers and blackbirds.[23] Despite this peculiar teaming of subjects, the bill passed by an overwhelming majority. The railroads were to receive six alternate sections on each side of the track for each mile surveyed, and an additional amount when the road was ready for operation.[24] Even after such liberal grants, railroads were not constructed, for the land was almost unsalable. The Transit Railroad Company attempted to sell its land at $1.00 an acre but found no buyers.[25] It became apparent that, if Minnesota was to have railroads, more drastic action would have to be taken.

Because the Minnesota constitution forbade the legislature to borrow over $250,000 or to loan the State's credit,[26] embryonic plans for the State subsidy of railroad construction appeared destined for oblivion. On February 24, 1858, however, a bill to permit the State to subsidize railroad construction was introduced in the legislature. This act, passed March 5 and ratified by the people April 15, authorized the issuance of $5,000,000 of State bonds, which were to be exchanged for the bonds of railroad companies.[27] Since the State bonds bore a 7 per cent interest rate, the issue was commonly known as "Minnesota Sevens." Although the bonds were a general obligation of the State, the railroads were to pay both principal and interest out of their earnings and the proceeds from the sale of their land grants.[28] The bonds would finance the construction of the railroads, which would increase the value of the lands, making them readily salable at a price sufficient to repay the cost of railroad construction. It was a fair sample of frontier financial philosophy; the only trouble was that it did not succeed. The act provided for the issuance of $10,000 of bonds per mile of graded road and a like amount upon the completion of the tracks, but no roads were brought into operation.[29] The absence of operating railroads effectively stopped the sale of railroad lands and the acquisition of funds.

Meanwhile, another difficulty arose. Investors, wary of the Minnesota Sevens, were loath to purchase them. From a desire to provide both a market for the bonds and more currency, the Free Banking Act of 1858 permitted Minnesota Sevens to be used at their market value as collateral for the notes of State banks.[30] The provision for the use of the bonds at market was theoretically conservative; actually no definite market price existed, for the bonds had not sold. They were nominally quoted at 95 in 1858, a price which seems a trifle high. Since by July 1, 1859, contractors had received $2,275,000 of these inactive bonds,[31] they were anxious to develop a market; accordingly, they encouraged the organization of banks of issue. The banks were able to absorb only $509,000 of the total; the others were dumped on the market with unfortunate consequences. The bonds sold as low as 16¼.[32] By this time, although the railroads had graded 239 miles of roadbed, they still had laid not a single mile of rail. They were unable to make any payments, and the bonds were defaulted.

When the public realized that the State might levy a tax to pay the bonds, it became frightened, and on November 6, 1860, a constitutional amendment was passed forbidding the levy of any tax to retire the Minnesota Sevens unless it was approved by a majority of the voters.[33] The amendment also barred the railroads from the further use of public credit.

Since the banks of isssue had used $509,000 principal amount of the Sevens as collateral, the default of the bonds and the prohibitive tax legislation hit them hard. By the end of 1860 seven had failed; only two survived until 1863.[34]

Though the Minnesota and Pacific failed, it was reorganized as the St. Paul and Pacific Railroad and construction of the road was started. In July, 1862, the first train ran from St. Paul to the Falls of St. Anthony.[35] In 1864 the road reached Anoka and in 1867 Sauk Rapids. By 1870 it extended to Breckenridge. Eventually it passed into the hands of a receiver and was reorganized by James J. Hill.

The Chicago, Milwaukee and St. Paul connected St. Paul with Chicago in 1868.[36] Eventually a group of other lines connected St. Paul with the East and South. These other lines included the Chicago, St. Paul, Minneapolis and Omaha, the Burlington and Northern, and the Rock Island.[37]

The period up to 1872 in the Twin Cities had been one of pioneer beginnings. The Panic of 1873 brought railroad-building nearly to a stop and slowed city development. Nevertheless, business continued to grow, though at a slower pace, and the population continued to increase. Conditions turned for the better in the late 'seventies and continued to improve in the 'eighties. From 1882 to 1892 Minneapolis had ten years of prosperity which exceeded anything in its previous history.[38]

The major portion of growth in Minneapolis came from flour-milling or lumbering or allied industries. The production of spring wheat in the area west of Minneapolis increased from year to year, and the spreading network of western railroads brought an ever-swelling flow of grain. Minneapolis' numerous mills, elevators, cheap power, and advantageous location fostered this development.[39] In 1879 Minneapolis was ninth among the primary wheat markets of the country; by 1881 it ranked third; in 1885 it took first place.[40] In 1912 the receipts for the first time reached 100,000,000 bushels. Elevator capacity did not exceed 1,000,000 bushels until 1879, but it increased to 12,500,000 bushels in 1887, and to nearly 30,000,000 in 1900.[41]

The distribution of harvesting machinery began to assume importance shortly before 1880, and within a decade Minneapolis claimed recognition as headquarters in the Northwest for this business.[42] By 1900 the Deering Harvester Company, the McCormick Harvesting Machine Company, Deere and Webber Company, and the J. I. Case Implement Company had all set up sales agencies and warehouses there.[43] The Minneapolis Harvester Works and the Monitor Plow Works were established by 1883, and the Minneapolis Threshing Machine Company followed in 1888.[44]

The lumber industry had been of major importance in the early history of Minneapolis. The rise of wheat and flour reduced lumber's relative importance in the town but did not precipitate an actual decline. The cut of lumber had increased steadily: in 1870, 118,000,000 feet were sawed; in 1880, 190,000,000 feet; in 1890, 343,000,000 feet; and the high of 594,000,000 feet was reached in 1899.[45] By that time the best timber in the area tributary to Minneapolis had been logged, and actual lumber production in Minneapolis had begun to slacken steadily. Its slump in relative importance was much more rapid. By 1915 it was a minor industry, and what remained was destined soon to disappear.

From the beginning, miscellaneous manufacturing in the Twin Cities was extensive, and over a period of years these enterprises grew both in actual volume and in relative importance. By 1910 they aggregated in Minneapolis just under 50 per cent of the total value of manufacturers' products.[46] Among these miscellaneous plants were the machine shops, the foundries, and numerous factories. Their output included railroad machinery, agricultural implements, mill machinery,[47] furs and hides, woolen products, sandpaper, abrasives, and many other products.

The packing industry was established in St. Paul in 1882 with the organization of the Union Stock Yards Company.[48] Before this time packing had been a local enterprise. Now packers bought hogs and cattle from a wide area and marketed their products on a national scale. In 1887 the Union Stock Yards Company moved to South St. Paul.[49] This organization owns and operates the yards, while the packing companies, notably Swift, Armour, and several smaller ones, own and operate the actual packing plants. The volume of cattle and hogs handled by the Union Stock Yards Company tended upward steadily until in 1916 South St. Paul took its place among the five largest packing centers in the United States.[50]

St. Paul's earliest traders were the fur-traders, followed by retailers and by the wholesalers who supplied the merchants of the interior. Jobbing continued to grow with the years. In Minneapolis during this early period the jobbing business developed primarily out of the marketing of local manufactures. In 1883 St. Paul's wholesale business was estimated at $67,907,800, while that of Minneapolis was valued at $48,138,000; by 1890 Minneapolis had passed St. Paul, the figures being $111,000,000 and $109,000,000, respectively.[51]

Just after 1900 the Twin Cities gained a new business: the distribution of automobiles, automobile supplies, and tractors.[52] Starting with only a few dealers, they soon became the center of this activity in the Northwest. With the growing popularity of motoring this business assumed increasing importance.

These items are details, and we can summarize by saying that the history of the Twin Cities from their settlement to 1915 is a tale of surging, eager growth. Industry and commerce prospered, and the population increased steadily and rapidly. True, there were setbacks, but these were only temporary and speedily surmounted. They caused a depression in manufacturing and trade, and some bankruptcies, but they did not last long. The Cities were in a period of strong growth which panics might slow down but could not stop. Optimistic business men, making use of the periods of depression to purchase property from distressed or discouraged owners, to found new business ventures, or to map plans of expansion for those already in existence, laid the foundations of many a Twin City fortune.

The Twin City area in this period was the paradise of the petty capitalist — profitable opportunities went begging. Since capital was scarce, the small man did not have to compete with aggressive organizations of overwhelming strength. Rising values were normal, and if the petty capitalist could make a living from his business, the growing population, increasing volume, and rising prices produced long-term speculative profits. Under these circumstances there was a steady demand from small capitalists for long-term capital loans. By 1915 the territory was so far advanced that many petty capitalists had accumulated fortunes.

Economic Development of Minnesota, 1852–1915

The rapid rise of St. Paul and Minneapolis was only a part of the development of the Northwest. The growth of both cities was possible only because the hinterland provided a source of raw materials and a market.

In 1852 the Sioux Treaties had been completed, opening to settlement the best farming district in Minnesota.[53] Settlers had poured in during the boom of the 'fifties. During the Civil War the rate of immigration declined, but after its close in 1865 the influx became increasingly strong.

The early farmers clung to the neighborhood of the navigable rivers for two reasons: usually they came to the State by river, and a river afforded the most convenient transportation of produce to market. The earliest agricultural settlements, therefore, were around the various river towns: Hastings, Red Wing, Wabasha, and

Winona.[54] By 1857 Minnesota was producing a surplus of agricultural products, and thereafter these towns did a brisk business in exporting foodstuffs.[55]

During the late 'sixties, the tide of immigration covered southeastern Minnesota and a large area in the south-central part of the State; the remaining farming areas were fully settled during the 'seventies. Long before Minnesota was well populated, some settlers passed it by for the Dakotas and Montana. These western areas, however, did not receive much immigration until the 'eighties.[56]

As settlers arrived in increasing numbers, hamlets and villages appeared to supply multitudinous services to their areas. General stores dispensed the household necessities; post offices distributed mail; blacksmiths plied their trade; carpenters and masons constructed buildings; churches and schools catered to religious and educational needs; and doctors and lawyers hung out shingles. Since transportation was vital to economic life, it was the hamlets strategically located with respect to the low-cost assembly and distribution of goods that grew most rapidly into villages, towns, and cities. Convenient to river transportation were all the earliest settlements of note in Minnesota.

In the hinterland "the iron horse" substituted for navigable rivers, and the rails were beaded with stations struggling to become villages and towns. Bursting with civic enthusiasm and ambition, if not with civic virtue, each shipping point claimed to be the prospective metropolis of the Northwest. The accoutrements of shipping dominated the local scene: sidetracks, freight cars, a water tower, cattle-pens, the loading platform, bawling cattle, bleating sheep, two grain elevators, one drab depot, and perhaps a lone, depressed-looking traveler. In the eastern part of the district the towns were surrounded by tree-covered hills, but in the western section the flat, monotonous prairie was unbroken except by the grain elevator and the water tower of the next town, ten miles down the tracks.

Towns often sprang up in anticipation of railroad construction. Railroads were projected, charters and land grants obtained, and the prospective route mapped. Wherever the plans called for freight stations, towns appeared before the railroad had reached the designated point. Speculators rushed ahead to acquire corner lots, while business men, in order to participate in the future prosperity, established stores, hotels, and harness-shops. For instance, the rich, productive farming region of Martin County, located in southern Minnesota, received its first settlers in 1856.[57] No towns developed, however, until 1858, when a post office was established at Fairmont. Since this location marked the center of the settled area and was at the junction of main roads it was a logical site for a town. After the establishment of the post office, a general store, a blacksmith's shop, and a hotel were opened. The influx of land-seekers provided the hotel with a brisk business. Tales are still told of five men in a bed, and the bed not too good to start with.

Fairmont grew slowly until 1861, when, owing to the Civil War, immigration nearly stopped. However, a few settlers came in during this period, the most notable of whom was A. L. Ward, who arrived in April, 1864. He was a poor Yankee farm boy of great intelligence and ambition, who reputedly had suffered from very poor health. Upon his arrival in Fairmont, Ward filed upon a homestead adjoining the village. Not content with farming, he soon had a finger in many ventures. He managed to be admitted to the bar, and combined the practice of law with the sale of real estate and insurance. In January, 1865, in partnership with R. M. Ward, he opened a general store, later to be known as Ward and Cadwell.

Following the close of the Civil War, the discharged soldiers of the Northern armies began to descend upon the area to homestead the free land. In 1872 H. F. Sherman organized a land colonization company and went to England to interest prospective pioneers. He was so successful that in 1873, 1874, and 1875 a horde of English settlers poured into the county and bought land. Since land was cheap and fertile and the English had some capital, they believed they could live like country gentlemen. They began to raise beans with hired labor. Unfortunately, the Rocky Mountain locusts are especially fond of tender young beans; they feasted bounteously. Since many of the settlers raised their own tobacco, piteous tales have been handed down of how the locusts dined on beans, helped themselves to a chew of tobacco, and then sat on the fence, chewed, and spat tobacco juice.

Although the railroad was momentarily expected in Fairmont, it did not reach there until 1878. It found the village already thriving and most impatient for its arrival. Time, however, had not hung too heavily on the settlers' hands. The English colonists danced all night, hunted coyotes with hounds at dawn, mellowed themselves with suitable liquid refreshments, and had some hell-raising horse races on the Sabbath. The Yankee settlers enjoyed themselves vicariously, cursing the grasshoppers, the cutworms, the English, and other disturbers of the public peace.

Nearly all the pioneer farmers raised wheat as their money crop, but those in the southeastern and central areas early tended toward diversified agriculture. The western part of Minnesota was primarily a wheat-producing area.

In 1884 the mining of iron ore was begun on the Vermillion range in northern Minnesota, and in 1890 and 1891 the much larger deposits of the Mesabi range were discovered.[58] Mining formed the basis of industrial development and prosperity, but the area never became an integral part of the Central Northwest. The ore mined in Minnesota has always been shipped from Duluth and Two Harbors to Pittsburgh and other points for smelting and manufacturing. Consequently, the area has always looked east to Cleveland and Pittsburgh and has had much closer contacts with those cities than with Minneapolis and the rest of the territory.

Economic Development of North Dakota, South Dakota and Montana, 1859–1915

Hostile Indians discouraged permanent settlement in this territory until in 1863 and 1864 they were driven west of the Missouri. The first railroad reached the eastern border of North Dakota in 1871, and thenceforth settlement was rapid.[59] In 1873 the Northern Pacific Railroad reached the Missouri River at Bismarck, opening additional territory.[60] Settlers poured into the Red River Valley in the wake of the railroads. West of the Missouri the country was made safe for settlers and most hazardous for Indians by campaigns from 1876 to 1891. This area was immediately occupied by cattlemen. From a handful in 1870, the population rose to 36,909 in 1880; 190,983 in 1890; 319,146 in 1900; and 577,056 in 1910.[61]

The early settlers found the eastern portion of the State ideally suited to the growing of wheat. Some of them pioneered in raising cattle, but the wheat farmers gradually forced them into the arid regions of the West.

The first permanent settlements in South Dakota were made at Bon Homme and Yankton in 1859.[62] The railway reached the eastern boundary in 1868. In 1872 the first railroad in South Dakota, the Dakota Southern Railroad, was built from Sioux City to Yankton.[63] The discovery of gold in 1874 by the men of Custer's expedition precipitated a gold rush.[64] By March, 1876, the town of Custer, in the Black Hills, had a population of at least 6,000. In 1877, Moses and Fred Manuel located the famous Homestake lode, a discovery which gave the region stability and made the towns of Deadwood and Lead important.[65] After the gold strike the tide of population turned to cover the prairies in the eastern part of the State, and by 1886 the better portions were settled. The population increased from 98,268 in 1880 to 348,600 in 1890 and 401,570 in 1900.[66]

The earliest settlers in the eastern part of the State, around Sioux Falls and Yankton, were farmers who engaged primarily in raising wheat. The Black Hills were settled by gold miners, and mining has remained an important industry. The intervening area was given over to wheat farmers and cattlemen. Gradually the homesteaders forced the cattlemen west of the Missouri and for a few years bade fair to drive them out of the State. Since constant drought made it difficult to grow wheat successfully west of the Missouri, eventually most of the wheat farmers were liquidated, and the cattle and sheep raisers repossessed the land. In the northeast corner the settlers found excellent farming land; in the territory east of the Missouri, fair wheat land; in the Black Hills, gold; and, in the remainder of the State, grazing land.

The earliest settlements in Montana resulted from the discovery of precious metals, but previously the area had been explored by fur traders. In 1807 a trading post on the Yellowstone at the mouth of the Big Horn River was established.[67] Manuel Lisa's traders made regular trips into the country. The Missouri Fur Company, organized in St. Louis in 1808, built a trading house on the upper Missouri.[68] For the next half-century the fur trade dominated the region. The eastern slope was monopolized by the American Fur

Company, while the trade west of the divide was controlled by British interests. The real rush of immigration came shortly after the discovery of gold in 1857.[69] For the next few years one discovery followed another. Silver was found early, but the great copper deposits were not developed until the 'eighties.[70]

For many years the eastern part of the State was sparsely settled. Although cattle-raising was prosperous from an early date, agriculture did not thrive except where there were railroads which could carry the crops to distant markets.[71] The first drive of cattle from Texas to Montana was made in 1869. Cattle were first driven from Montana to the Union Pacific in 1874.[72] The Northern Pacific completed its crossing of the State in 1883.[73] This stimulated both cattle- and sheep-raising.

Before 1890 farming was not important in Montana. Only a little land in the Bitter Root and Gallatin valleys was cultivated. By 1900 farming had crept eastward, and considerable irrigated agriculture had developed.[74] The completion of the railroad gave it some stimulus by providing a way to market. Wheat could be raised in some areas by dry farming, but these lands were settled slowly. Farms numbered 1,519 in 1880, 5,603 in 1890, 13,370 in 1900, and 26,214 in 1910.[75] Over half the improved acreage was irrigated in 1900. From 1900 to 1915, dry-land farmers poured into eastern Montana, and by 1920 only 15 per cent of the cultivated land was irrigated.[76] In 1870, Montana had 20,595 inhabitants; in 1880, 39,159; in 1890, 142,924; in 1900, 243,329; and in 1910, 376,053.[77] Before 1890 the population was engaged in fur-trading, mining, cattle- and sheep-raising, and a very little farming. Some wheat-farming developed in the decade between 1890 and 1900. Thereafter, most of the immigrants raised wheat on dry farms.

By 1915 the period of pioneer settlement was over in the Central Northwest. It must be noted that the areas within the territory did not develop simultaneously. Southeastern Minnesota was well developed by the 'seventies, the Twin Cities kept pace, and certain other agricultural sections were fairly well settled by that time. Others, opened much later, lagged behind. While there was a continuous overlapping, the time finally came when all the areas were well settled: farms had been developed, towns had sprung up, and roads and railroads connected the settlements. Since the period before 1915 was affected by the forces of colonization and that after 1915 by agricultural inflation induced by the First World War, 1915 forms a logical line of demarcation between the period of settlement and the period of maturity.

CHAPTER II

A HISTORY OF BANKING IN THE NORTHWEST DURING THE PERIOD OF SETTLEMENT 1851–1915

Rise of Banks in the Twin Cities, 1851–1872

The very earliest period in the history of the Central Northwest was marked not only by the complete lack of specialized banking facilities, but also by a great scarcity of currency. Indeed, a large portion of the fur trade was carried on by means of barter, and a portion of the transactions among the early settlers was also accomplished by this primitive method. The American Fur Company in early days bought furs, sold goods, and carried on certain banking transactions. It sold exchange, cashed drafts, granted some loans, and carried credit balances for its customers.[1] In addition, some of its employees conducted a private banking business.

As early as May 1, 1851, Charles W. Borup, who worked for the American Fur Company, began dealing in bills of exchange and drafts on all parts of the United States.[2] His office was in the building of the Minnesota Outfit, St. Paul. In January, 1852, Charles H. Oakes, also of the fur company, advertised that he had money to loan. Borup and Oakes formed a partnership in June, 1852, as general commercial bankers.[3] This firm developed a good business and soon was making substantial profits, but it was not long without competition. A year after its opening, in May, 1853, Parker Paine of Anson, Maine, arrived in town, and, although his advent coincided with a local Indian massacre, he decided to stay. With the small amount of capital which had accompanied him, he founded the banking house of Parker Paine and Company.[4] He was a very aggressive man, but since the community was growing rapidly, he did not hurt Borup and Oakes. By the spring of 1854 a third competitor had appeared. This was the firm of Mackubin and Edgerton, the partners being Charles M. Mackubin and E. S. Edgerton.[5]

PARKER PAINE, PRIVATE BANKER, ST. PAUL

NOTES OF THE PEOPLES BANK, ST. PETER, MINNESOTA
Undated

In 1856, H. Meyer and Ferdinand Willius started in business in St. Paul as Meyer and Willius, Private Bankers.[6] Meyer died in 1857, and Ferdinand Willius' younger brother Gustaf entered the firm, which thereafter operated as F. and G. Willius.[7]

In Minneapolis the first banking firm was that of Richard Martin, opened in 1854.[8] In the same year Sumner W. Farnham and Samuel Tracy entered the banking business, followed in 1855 by the firm of Snyder and McFarlane.[9]

The business of these early bankers was not highly specialized. They engaged in such miscellaneous ventures as selling insurance and real estate, dealing in mortgages, acting as brokers, buying and selling goods, serving as wholesalers, and taking partnership interests in all kinds of projects. To be sure, they accepted deposits, made loans, and dealt in exchange, but this was only one division of their heterogeneous activities. From 1853 to 1857 they apparently made large profits, but the latter year bankrupted most of them.[10]

In 1857, Rufus J. Baldwin opened a private bank in Minneapolis at Washington Avenue and Cataract Street, which is now Sixth Avenue South.[11] In the same year the firm of Beede and Mendenhall opened a bank.[12] Richard J. Mendenhall was a Quaker who had been well educated and had worked as a surveyor, a land agent, and a florist. He came to the Northwest with some capital, looking for a promising business opportunity; he stayed, convinced that Minneapolis had a great future and that banking ought to be very profitable. He had known Cyrus Beede for some time and wrote urging him to come to Minneapolis. Upon his arrival, they opened a successful private bank.[13]

The firm of Sidle, Wolford and Company was also organized in 1857 by Jacob K. Sidle and Peter Wolford.[14] Sidle was a native of York, Pennsylvania, who had just come overland to Minneapolis. Once there, he decided to found a bank and persuaded Peter Wolford to join in the venture. Their capital was $10,000 which they brought from Pennsylvania in specie, and their original office was on the west shore of the river, just above the falls, on Hennepin Avenue.[15]

The earliest firms in Minneapolis were extremely short-lived. Richard Martin's company survived the Panic of 1857, but closed in 1858.[16] Martin paid off his depositors in full and had only real estate left. S. W. Farnham and Company, Snyder and MacFarlane, and Curtis H. Pettit and Company were all out of the banking business by 1859, and Beede had withdrawn from the firm of Beede and Mendenhall.[17] The firm of Borup and Oakes had failed on October 21, 1857.[18] In 1858 Mackubin withdrew from the firm of Mackubin and Edgerton, which then became the Peoples Bank, with E. S. Edgerton as president and D. A. Monfort as cashier.[19]

The central part of the Northwest Territory was relatively free from the currency troubles which had beset much of the United States. The people were suspicious of any issue of bank notes and loath to allow banks the privilege of issuing paper money. A few scattered attempts at an early date made little headway and disappeared in a short time.

The early bankers in St. Paul and Minneapolis were not especially interested in issuing paper money; they were commercial bankers and dealt in domestic exchange. They stood ready to buy or sell exchange on St. Louis, New Orleans, Chicago, New York, and other eastern and southern points. When a merchant sold a shipment of goods in the East, he drew a draft on the purchaser, accompanied it with the bill of lading, deposited it with one of the local banks, which credited him with the proceeds and then collected the draft, usually depositing the amount collected with its correspondent bank. If a merchant wished to pay a bill in a distant town, he bought from the local bank a draft drawn on its correspondent at the distant point. At the time they were dealing in exchange, these banks also developed the business of financing local merchants, loaning them money to import goods and purchase furs. From the beginning they served as banks of deposit, holding funds subject to the order of their depositors.

Most of the early Twin Cities banks carried on a brisk business in bank notes. The entire United States was flooded with notes put out by banks in various parts of the country. Those issued by some banks were as good as gold and redeemable in specie on demand. Others were nearly worthless. The bulk ranked somewhere between the two extremes. It was expedient to exercise great care in accepting notes, for even those of entirely solvent banks depreciated as they radiated away from their place of redemption. Bank notes came into

Chart I. Genesis of The First National Bank of St. Paul

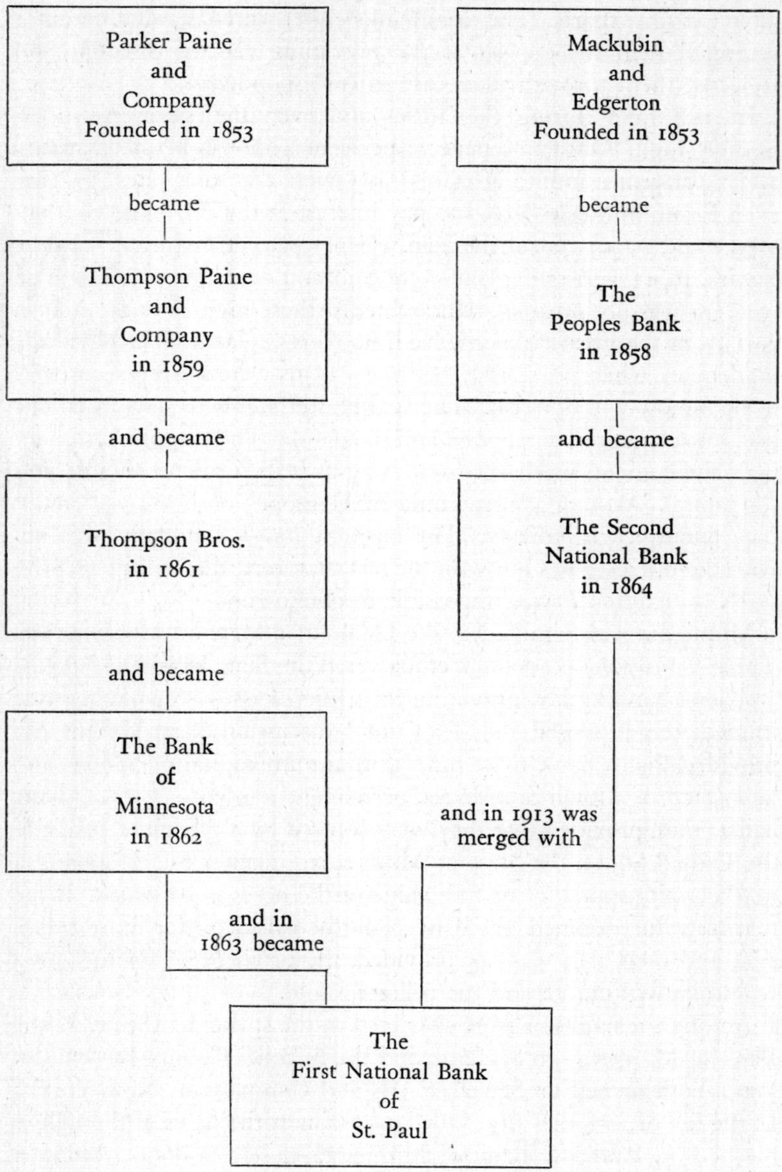

the Central Northwest either in the pockets of immigrants or as payment for exports. The local banks either purchased the notes, or accepted them for deposit at the prevailing rate of discount and collected them through their eastern correspondents.

Interest rates during the 'fifties and even the 'sixties were extremely high. On prime paper 3 per cent a month before maturity and 5 per cent a month after maturity were common rates. In 1855 even Franklin Steele agreed to pay interest at the rate of 20 per cent a year and 25 per cent if the loan was not paid at maturity.[20] In the 'sixties, 10, 12, and 15 per cent were common on prime paper, and 20 per cent was not unusual. Undoubtedly, these high rates resulted in part from the great risks involved, but this explanation is obviously inadequate when we realize that many loans were so well secured as to be almost without risk. The real reason seems to have been the usual explanation of supply and demand. The supply was limited; the demand was large, stemming as it did from profitable uses for capital. As long as men could make money on borrowed funds, they attempted to borrow. The business man's complaint was not with the interest rates but with the fact that, regardless of the security or the rate, often it was impossible to obtain funds.

Minnesota was admitted to the Union as a State on May 11, 1858. The constitution, as adopted, empowered the State legislature to pass a general banking law providing for banks of issue. Such a law was immediately proposed and, after much discussion, passed. This Act provided that a bank must have a minimum capital of $25,000 and be located in a town of over 200 permanent residents. It could issue bank notes, provided that they were secured by a pledge of bonds of the United States, the State of Minnesota, or other States, having a market value equal to the face value of the notes to be issued. If the market value declined, the bank could be called on for more collateral, and then, if it was not provided, the privilege of issuing notes would be withdrawn and the collateral sold.[21]

Among the banks of issue chartered in the spring of 1859 were the Bank of Minnesota in St. Paul, and the Nicollet County Bank at St. Peter, both owned by Sewell, Ferris and Company of New York.[22] In the fall of 1859 that firm failed. As soon as the news of the failure reached St. Paul, the Bank of Minnesota closed its doors. Monfort

H. Thompson, *Cashier.* — J. E. Thompson, *Pres't.*

FIRST NATIONAL BANK

—OF—

SAINT PAUL,

PAID UP CAPITAL, $600,000.

GOVERNMENT BONDS, COIN, LAND W
RANTS AND HALF-BREED SCRIP

BOUGHT AND SOLD.

Prompt attention given to the collection of Qurter-master Vouchers. Agency for the sale of

PASSAGE TICKETS

From Liverpool and Amsterdam to New York and Saint Paul.

Drafts on England, Ireland, Germany, France, Spain and Norway.

January 4, 1866.

ADVERTISEMENT OF THE FIRST NATIONAL BANK OF ST. PAUL, 1866

of the Peoples Bank had drafts and bank notes on the Nicollet County Bank, and he immediately raced to St. Peter to present them. He outran the news, arriving in time to collect $5,000 in specie, which aided in keeping the Peoples Bank open during the ensuing run.[23] The only three banks surviving in St. Paul were Parker Paine and Company, the Peoples Bank, and F. and G. Willius. In Minneapolis by 1859 the banks had been reduced to Rufus J. Baldwin, Mendenhall's Private Bank, and Sidle, Wolford and Company.

In that year J. E. Thompson, a merchant of Americus, Georgia, visited the town of St. Paul. Attracted by the profitable possibilities in banking, he formed a partnership with Parker Paine.[24] Thompson contributed considerable money to the firm, which became known as Thompson, Paine and Company. In 1861 Thompson's brother Horace became a partner in the firm.[25] The partnership with Paine was dissolved, and the business was carried on under the title Thompson Bros.[26] The following year Thompson Bros. took out a State charter and changed its name to the Bank of Minnesota.[27] It had a capital of $100,000. In 1863 the National Banking Act was passed, and the Thompsons, quick to take advantage of it, applied for a national charter. This was issued, and on December 8, 1863, the Bank of Minnesota became the First National Bank of St. Paul, with a capital of $250,000.[28] From the first its business was substantial, and in September, 1864, the First National Bank doubled its capital to $500,000.[29] In 1865 this was increased to $600,000.[30]

Edgerton's bank — that is, the People's Bank — applied for a national charter shortly after the Bank of Minnesota, and in December, 1864, it received the title of The Second National Bank of St. Paul.[31]

In 1861 a new banking firm by the name of Holland, Berry and Dawson made its appearance in St. Paul.[32] When Holland withdrew the next year, the firm became Berry, Dawson and Company. In 1865 Berry also withdrew, leaving the title Dawson and Company, Bankers.[33] It took out a State charter in 1882, becoming the Bank of Minnesota.[34]

The firm of F. and G. Willius took in Lewis L. Dunbar as a partner in 1863.[35] The firm's name then became Willius Bros. and Dunbar. It operated with a capital of $20,000.[36]

THOMPSON BROS., BANKERS, ST. PAUL, PRIOR TO 1864
The bank in question is just behind the carriage and horses

Chart II. Genesis of The Merchants National Bank of St. Paul

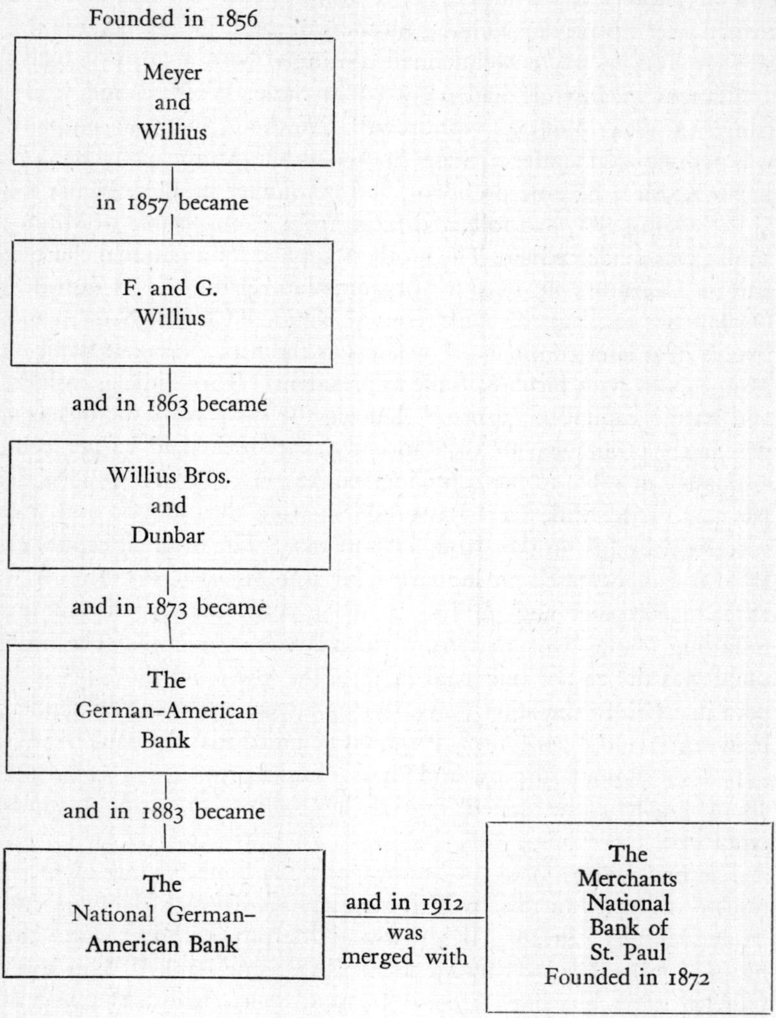

In Minneapolis, in November, 1862, Rufus J. Baldwin and Richard J. Mendenhall purchased the State Bank of Minnesota at Austin and in January, 1863, moved it to Minneapolis.[37] Rufus Baldwin turned over his private-banking business to the firm and became the active manager, while Mendenhall continued with his private bank.

Changes meanwhile had occurred in Sidle, Wolford and Company; in 1864 Wolford withdrew.[38] At that time the company was reorganized under a State charter as the Minneapolis Bank.[39] Jacob K. Sidle became president, and a younger brother, Henry G. Sidle, who in 1863 had followed Jacob from Pennsylvania to Minneapolis, was made cashier. The brothers applied for a national charter, and on December 12, 1864, the organization certificate was signed.[40] On January 12, 1865, the bank received National Charter No. 710 and twelve days later commenced business as the First National Bank of Minneapolis with Jacob K. Sidle as president, Henry Sidle as cashier, and with a capital of $50,000.[41] During the early years the business was fairly profitable. In 1866 and 1867 the bank paid 12 per cent annually; in 1860, 10 per cent; in 1869, 12 per cent; and in 1870, 24 per cent. J. K. Sidle served as president from 1864 to 1888 and was succeeded by his brother from 1888 to 1894. The original capital of $50,000 was increased on January 1, 1874, to $100,000; on October 1, 1877, to $600,000; and on July 1, 1885, to $1,000,000.[42] From the founding of the bank to 1894, dividends were generous. The high point was the 24 per cent paid in 1870, the low point the 4 per cent paid in 1888. In the other years payments were about evenly divided between 12 and 8 per cent.[43] It should be noted that the bank always had a substantial surplus, and these rates represented a return of about one-half the stated rate if figured on the capital funds employed.

The first savings bank in Minneapolis, the State Savings Association, was formed in 1866 by R. J. Mendenhall, Rufus J. Baldwin, and T. A. Merphy. In 1873 Baldwin and Merphy withdrew, and the business was taken over by Mendenhall's Private Bank.[44] This bank failed in 1877, but since it paid out most of its claims, Mendenhall was discharged from bankruptcy.[45]

The Hennepin County Savings Bank was founded in 1870 with Edwin S. Jones as president and a capital of $50,000, which was im-

FIRST NATIONAL BANK OF MINNEAPOLIS

Washington at Nicollet Avenue, Minneapolis, about 1880

NOTES OF THE BANK OF RED WING, MINNESOTA
Undated

mediately increased to $100,000.[46] Jones had studied in the law offices of Isaac Atwater and had been admitted to the bar in April, 1855. In 1856 he became a judge, and during the Civil War he served in the army and returned a major. Upon his return to Minneapolis, he practised law, but his interests were in banking. He was active in organizing the new savings bank, which was a privately owned institution. Eventually, he became its head, remaining active until his death in 1890, when he was succeeded by John E. Bell. He in turn was succeeded by William Henry Lee.[47]

The period 1853–1872 had been one of pioneer beginnings in Twin City banking characterized by a scarcity of currency, capital, and loanable funds. Methods of transferring money were primitive and unsatisfactory. Growing business created a demand for funds for both short- and long-time investment far beyond the ability of local financial organizations to supply. Outside business organizations did not come in, nor did settlers ordinarily bring capital funds substantial enough to establish banks. The demand for banks was supplied by petty capitalists.

Most of the early bankers of the Twin Cities possessed neither ample capital nor banking experience. Their skills were in various lines of business, and their capital consisted of a very few thousand dollars. Many early bankers regarded banking only as a side line to such activities as real estate, insurance, lumbering, and wholesaling. A few, however, confined themselves to a banking business from the first. Prominent examples are Sidle, Mendenhall, Paine, Edgerton, the Williuses, and the Thompson brothers.

In the course of years, part-time bankers tended to be eliminated either by bankruptcy or by voluntary withdrawal. Moreover, the bankers still active in 1872 had acquired a great deal of practical experience. The large profits accruing from pioneer banking aided capital growth. General business also had been profitable, and the community had accumulated some capital. By 1872, it would have been sufficient in the Twin Cities to supply local commercial needs if funds had been applied only to that use, but not nearly enough for long-term capital purposes.

NEW BANKS ARE FOUNDED AS NEW LEADERS APPEAR IN OLD BANKS, 1872–1899

By 1871 Minneapolis had grown so large that a profitable opportunity seemed to exist for another bank, especially one which would actively serve the entire Northwest. Many local lumbermen and flour millers who felt that they were not receiving satisfactory service from Sidle, Wolford and Company had discussed the organization of a competitor. Prominent in local discussions were the following: Dorilus Morrison, Henry T. Welles, S. E. Neiler, C. B. Heffelfinger, C. H. Pettit, J. S. Pillsbury, S. W. Farnham, Franklin Steele, Thomas Lowry, S. C. Gale, C. M. Loring, and Paris Gibson.[48] Tentative plans for the new bank were drawn up, and it was decided to approach the builders of the Northern Pacific. These men, when asked to coöperate, subscribed liberally; the bank's records show fourteen out-of-town subscribers among whom were the following officers of the railroad: J. Gregory Smith, president; R. D. Rice, vice-president; Samuel Wilkison, secretary; and A. H. Barney, treasurer.[49]

The organization meeting was held on April 23, 1872, at the Nicollet House. The articles of incorporation were adopted and the capital was placed at $200,000.[50] The name of the new organization was the Northwestern National Bank of Minneapolis. A board of directors was elected; Dorilus Morrison was chosen president, and S. E. Neiler cashier.[51]

On June 28, 1872, the Comptroller of the Currency, John Jay Knox, granted the Northwestern National Bank of Minneapolis National Charter No. 2006.[52] On September 1, 1872, the bank opened its doors for business in a banking-room at the corner of Washington and First Avenues South. S. E. Neiler, cashier, who had previously been with the West Philadelphia Bank, Philadelphia, Pennsylvania, was given active control of the bank's operations. W. H. Dunwoody was the first depositor. The average deposits for 1872 were $50,400. There was an ample demand for loans, and they kept pace with deposits. The bank immediately became profitable, and on June 24, 1873, it paid its first dividend at the rate of 5 per cent. Since that date the bank has never passed a dividend date, although the amount has

FIRST NATIONAL BANK OF ST. PAUL
Building Erected in the 1880's

INTERIOR OF THE FIRST NATIONAL BANK OF ST. PAUL
In the 1880's

Chart III. Genesis of The First National Bank of Minneapolis

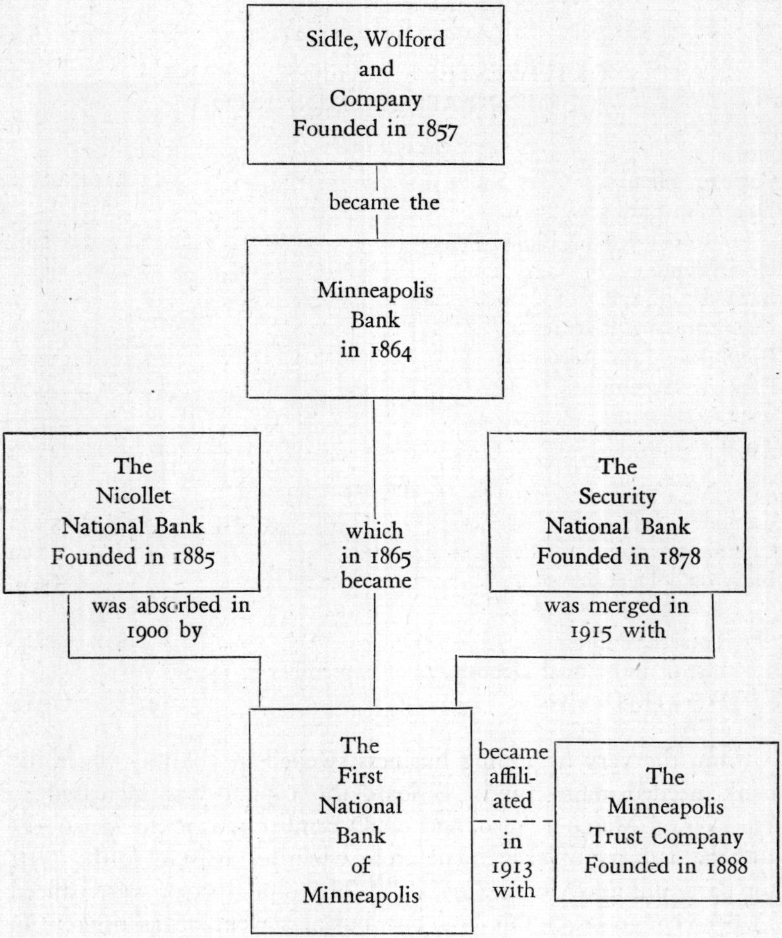

varied, the average return being 8 per cent.[53] A copy of the Northwestern's first balance sheet follows:

STATEMENT OF CONDITION
(As of Sept. 7, 1872)

NORTHWESTERN NATIONAL BANK
OF MINNEAPOLIS, MINNESOTA

Resources

Cash on Hand	$113,200.71
Due from Banks	
Jay Cooke & Co., Phila., Pa.	2,065.33
U. S. Bonds	50,000.00
Bank Building	24,080.22
Furniture and Fixtures	1,881.63
Bond Premium Account	6,437.50
Expense Account	2,299.61
Total resources	$199,965.00

Liabilities

Capital	$152,650.00
Circulation	45,000.00
Individual Deposits	2,315.00
Total Liabilities	$199,965.00
List of Individual Deposits as of September 7, 1872	
WM. H. DUNWOODY	$ 2,315.00

From the very beginning business swelled in volume. Since the bank needed more funds to loan, the capital was increased to $300,000 on March 1, 1876, and on December 1, 1876, to $500,000.[54] In 1879 a flurry of excitement arose when an assistant cashier left for parts unknown with $127,000.[55] The capital stock was reduced 20 per cent to cover this loss, and business went on as usual. On March 30, 1880, the capital was restored to $500,000, and on July 1, 1882, it was increased to $1,000,000, the new stock being sold at 105.[56]

In St. Paul a new bank was organized by a group of merchants headed by Maurice Auerbach of Auerbach, Finch and Scheffer, wholesale dry goods. Since all the original incorporators were St.

Paul merchants, the bank adopted the title of the Merchants National Bank.[57] It commenced business July 24, 1872, with a capital of $250,000, which in July, 1873, was increased to $500,000, and in 1880 to $1,000,000.[58] Maurice Auerbach was president from 1872 to

CHART IV. GENESIS OF THE NORTHWESTERN NATIONAL BANK OF MINNEAPOLIS

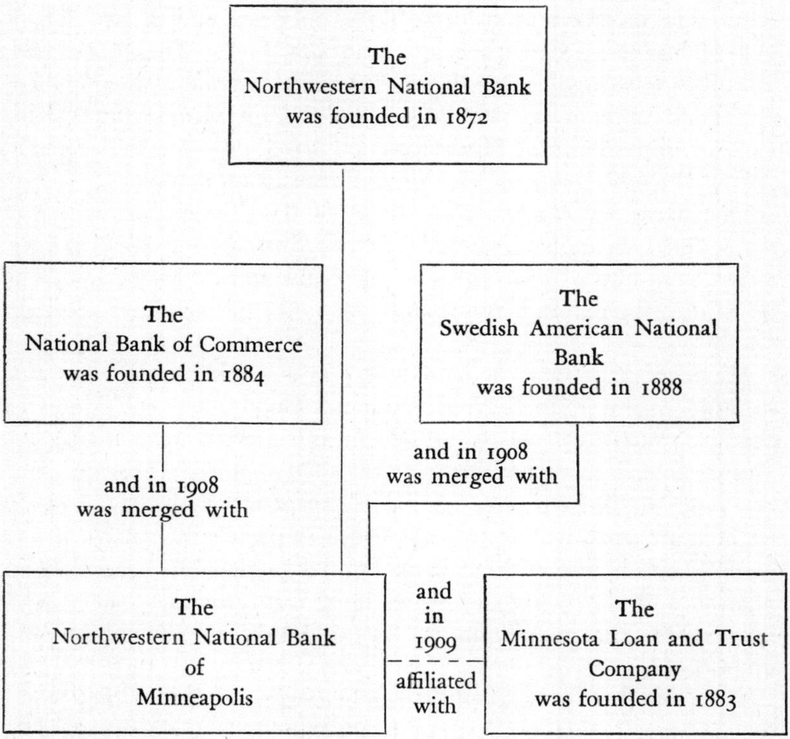

1880; John L. Merriam, 1880 to 1884; and his son, William R. Merriam, 1884 to 1897. Kenneth Clark succeeded Merriam.[59] This bank was extremely aggressive in developing local business, a policy which proved successful, making the bank an important factor in the city. It also proved very profitable, for the bank's earnings were substantial.

In 1873 Willius Bros. and Dunbar took out a State charter as the German-American Bank, which in January, 1883, became the National German-American Bank, with a capital of $2,000,000.[60]

In September, 1873, the closing of the New York banking office of Jay Cooke and Company precipitated a panic which spread throughout the United States. In the Northwest, railroad building ceased, and a general depression set in which lasted for several years. Real estate became almost unsalable at any price, and the volume of general business declined sharply. The banks in the Twin Cities had an amazingly good record during this period; none of them closed and none of them assessed its stockholders. A vicious run on the First National Bank of Minneapolis occurred, but with the coöperation of the other banks it met all withdrawals on demand.[61] Fortunately, the run was short-lived. In a few days the tide turned, and the withdrawn money was redeposited. Business activity was very low. As industrial concerns sold their inventories, they paid their notes at the banks, and, as a result, both assets and liabilities declined steadily.

Much of the trouble in the country as a whole sprang from the inelastic nature of the currency system. Good assets could not be changed into cash, and even solvent institutions were unable to acquire money to replenish their exhausted supplies. Consequently, everyone hoarded currency. As people spent money locally, it went to the merchants, who in turn applied it to paying their notes at the bank. The absence of local bank failures tended to maintain confidence, and the fact that the territory was growing also helped matters, for the population was continuously augmented by immigration.

The panic had so little effect that in 1874 a mutual savings bank was organized in Minneapolis by E. H. Moulton and Clinton Morrison, the son of Dorilus Morrison.[62] This bank was known as the Farmers and Mechanics Savings Bank.

So far we have discussed banks in the Twin Cities. We shall now mention some early banks in the rural area. Though the first settler arrived in Martin County, Minnesota, in 1856, and the post office of Fairmont was founded in 1858, the real tide of immigration came after 1865. The county was settled rapidly. Business was profitable,

DORILUS MORRISON
First President of the Northwestern National Bank, Minneapolis

BUILDING IN WHICH THE NORTHWESTERN NATIONAL BANK, MINNEAPOLIS, STARTED BUSINESS, 1872

but capital scarce. Despite high interest rates and a strong demand for funds, no banks were organized until 1874 when the Exchange Bank of Fairmont was established by two pioneer settlers, H. A. Munger and William Viesselman.[63] This bank soon changed its name to the Bank of Fairmont.

Because banking appeared profitable, A. L. Ward, that homesteader, merchant, lawyer, insurance and real-estate salesman, and mortgage dealer, decided to open a rival institution. He usually lacked capital to finance his diverse operations, and this need, plus the possibility of substantial profits in banking, apparently influenced his course of action. In 1875 he hung out the sign "Martin County Bank" and announced that he would receive deposits and make loans.[64] Since capital was scarce, deposits were modest in amount; the demand for loans was consistently in excess of available funds. All loans were local in nature and made mainly to farmers. They included loans to carry farmers over until they could market their crops and loans to buy machinery, horses, cattle, sheep, and hogs. Interest rates were high, and each borrower had to be well insured, a prerequisite which greatly simplified Ward's insurance business. In order to raise funds to loan, Ward borrowed from his major correspondents by pledging the bank's assets as collateral for his notes. He was able to borrow in Chicago at rates from 6 to 8 per cent; he loaned money locally at rates from 12 to 14 per cent.[65] Since this spread provided a handsome profit, he endeavored to borrow as much as he could obtain. His local loans were secured by chattel mortgages on growing crops, cattle, machinery, or any other assets possessed by the borrowers.

There was a great demand for farm-mortgage money, and although interest rates were high, they usually were somewhat below those on short-term loans. To some extent this was owing to the ease with which farm mortgages could be sold in the East. The local demand for short-term money exhausted Ward's capital, deposits, and borrowing capacity so that he had no capital available for mortgage lending. He made mortgage loans, however, disposing of them immediately through the metropolitan mortgage dealers or to insurance companies and private capitalists in the East. Even had he been able, he probably would not have sold them locally, for distant purchasers employed him to service the mortgages, watch the property, collect the interest, and see that the buildings were insured and the taxes paid. In due time, this phase of his business also became lucrative. The bank fitted in well with Ward's other operations to produce substantial profits.

The Bank of Fairmont carried on a business very similar to that of the Martin County Bank. It too made substantial profits and soon decided to erect suitable quarters. The original plans somehow got out of hand, and the result was the Occidental Hotel Building.[66] It was very elaborate for the time, and it housed both the bank and a hotel. The building cost more than had been originally estimated, and it tied up much of the bank's capital. In 1879 the Bank of Fairmont was assigned to A. L. Ward for liquidation.[67]

Meanwhile many eastern investors had turned envious eyes toward the West. From a very early date, houses had sprung up which made a specialty of selling western mortgages in the East. The most permanent of these was the Wells-Dickey Company, organized in 1878 by Edward Payson Wells and Alfred Dickey at Jamestown, North Dakota. Wells was a flour-miller and commercial banker, while Dickey had served in the infantry during the Civil War, taught school, and run a bookstore. The partners had been interested in a chain of banks around Jamestown. They sold farm mortgages for themselves and then gradually commenced to purchase mortgages from country banks for resale to eastern investors. Since this type of business was growing, they established a specialized company to handle it. A considerable portion of this business originated in the homestead settlements in the Dakotas.

It was in the 'eighties that the County of Richland in southeastern North Dakota was settled and the village of Lidgerwood became locally important.[68] Among the settlers the Movius family played a prominent part. They had come to the United States in 1867 and had lived in various localities; finally the children had moved to Richland County. The dominant member of the family was Emil A. Movius. Since grain farmers were swarming into the area and the demand for farm machinery was strong, Movius obtained the dealership for various lines, including the McCormick reaper. From the first, this business was successful; in fact, the volume was embarrassingly large. Most equipment was sold on credit, and the dealer was forced to carry the notes of his customers. As a result, Emil Movius was constantly hampered by having to borrow money and sell his accounts receivable, an awkward and costly procedure. To make matters worse, he started a general store, handling all lines of goods. He attempted to operate on a cash basis; the fact that his customers had little money until they had harvested their crops made this impossible. Since building was very active, Emil Movius also started a lumber yard, and here, too, he was constantly required to extend credit. His most pressing problem was credit; fortunately the answer was simple.

In the early 1890's, Movius took out a State charter for the Movius State Bank of Lidgerwood. Its capital was $10,000; the cashier was his brother, J. B. Movius, and the assistant cashier was his sister Mary. At first the bank's main function was to carry the credit lines of the Movius enterprises, which in due course included the farm-equipment business, the general store, a furniture store, the lumber yard, a farm-loan company, and a flour mill. These concerns operated primarily on a cash basis. When customers approached him for credit, E. A. Movius took them gently but firmly by the arm and led them to his brother or sister in the bank. His instructions to his sister relative to loaning money are interesting. He advised her never to loan beyond the farmer's ability to repay with a fair crop. Notes were to be secured by chattel mortgages on machinery, horses, cattle, growing crops, and/or wheat in storage. Above all, notes should be secured by a real-estate mortgage, a first if possible, a second if there was an equity in the land. This would guarantee against loss, for land, which was always valuable, formed the foundation of all credit.

The bank was successful from the beginning, and its earnings were substantial. In the latter part of 1900, a rival bank applied for a national charter under the title First National Bank. This perturbed Emil Movius, for he regarded this title as both distinguished and valuable. Since applications lapsed if they did not comply with regulations within six months, he decided to wait and watch. Sure enough, the other bank did not comply, and its application lapsed. The Movius State Bank immediately applied for the coveted name and in 1901 became the First National Bank of Lidgerwood, with a capital of $50,000.[69]

Despite the early prosperity of the county, capital was scarce and deposits were small. In 1901 the First National Bank of Lidgerwood had capital and surplus of $55,150 and deposits of only $90,530.[70] As was customary, it borrowed from its correspondent bank, in this case the National German-American Bank in St. Paul, in order to provide funds for local loans. It also did a brisk trade in farm mortgages and insurance.

While the early bankers in both the country communities and the Twin Cities arose from the petty capitalist class, a few professional bankers appeared at an early date in the Twin Cities. Prominent among these were the Prince brothers.

The Prince family has left a deep imprint on Twin City banking. Frank Moody Prince was born in Amherst, Massachusetts, July 23, 1854, the eldest of four brothers. The family was in moderate circumstances, and although the boys were sent through high school, thereafter they were obliged to earn their living. When his schooling was completed, Frank Prince left Massachusetts for Stillwater, Minnesota, where in 1876 he became a clerk in the First National Bank of Stillwater. Two years later he left the Stillwater bank for a similar position in the First National Bank of Minneapolis.[71] The vacancy at Stillwater was filled by his next younger brother, George Harrison Prince.[72] In 1882 Stillwater needed a cashier and rehired Frank Prince for that position. He remained until 1892, when he became first secretary and then treasurer of the Minnesota Loan and Trust Company, and later vice-president of the First National Bank of Minneapolis.[73]

Frank Prince was of an extremely conservative disposition; he was gifted with exceptional ability to get along with men and lead them to do and see things his way. George Prince was very aggressive and possessed an abundance of vital energy; he valued accomplishment for its own sake and drove both himself and his associates to the limit of endurance. While these two were getting under way, the youngest Prince brother, Walter, left Massachusetts and, like the others, entered the employ of the First National Bank of Stillwater. Eventually, he became its president.

Another family which left an enduring mark on northwestern banking was the Harrisons. The father was a Scotch-Irish, circuit-riding Methodist minister whose home was in Belleville, Illinois, near St. Louis. Since he had nine children and his salary as a minister was nominal, he operated a small flour mill in order to eke out a living. While his children were small, life was very hard; but as they grew older and took their places in the mill, conditions improved. By the time the younger ones were grown, milling profits were substantial, and at the death of the father, the family realized that it was relatively well-to-do.[74] In 1859 Hugh Harrison and his sister decided to take a vacation. A river steamer brought them to St. Paul. Here Hugh Harrison was fascinated by the growing activity, but his milling experience told him that the real future lay in St. Anthony with its water power. His optimism concerning the future of Minneapolis ran so high that he succeeded in persuading his brothers to sell the family mill and move to Minneapolis. In 1860 the three brothers, Thomas, Hugh, and William, went into partnership with Joseph Dean in a lumber business which included a mill at St. Anthony and logging camps up the river.[75] Conditions in the lumber business at that time were prosperous. The Harrisons built large homes in the vicinity of Fourth Avenue and Eighth Street, and in a few years each of them accumulated a fortune. In 1877 they retired from active business, selling their mill and logging camps. With the proceeds they immediately organized the Security Bank, which opened on January 2, 1878, with a capital of $300,000.[76] In its entire history it had only three presidents: Thomas A. Harrison, 1878 to 1887; Hugh G. Harrison, 1887 to 1891; and Francis A. Chamberlain, 1891 to 1915.[77]

F. A. Chamberlain was born April 20, 1855, at Bangor, Maine, the son of James T. and Caroline Emery Chamberlain.[78] The father was a merchant who moved from Bangor to Red Wing, Minnesota, when F. A. Chamberlain was two years old. Shortly after their arrival, James T. Chamberlain died, and his wife married Professor James Thorpe of Hamline University, which at that time was located in Red Wing. Professor Thorpe died within a short time, and his widow taught school to support her family. Chamberlain attended Hamline for two years and the University of Minnesota for two years. Upon leaving college he went to work for the Merchants National Bank of Minneapolis as a collector, or what would now be called a messenger.[79] The year 1880 found him working as a clerk for the Harrisons at the Security Bank.[80] Chamberlain was well liked by his employers, and their friendship for him was fostered by the fact that they were all very active in the Methodist Church. Even without this tie, Chamberlain's progress in the bank would have been rapid. He was the best-educated employee, hard working, and possessed of a keen sense of values and a knowledge of character. The bank had few employees, and Chamberlain passed rapidly through clerical positions to the offices of cashier, vice-president, and eventually president.

Chamberlain entered the business world just as the boom of the 'eighties got under way. Business continually improved, and real-estate values mounted constantly. Beginning in a small way, mainly on capital supplied by outside partners on a profit-sharing basis, Chamberlain commenced to speculate in real estate. Each transaction was profitable, and he steadily broadened his operations. His capital was limited, but his credit was good, and he borrowed increasingly large sums of money. Rising prices aided his advance, and by 1892 he was the possessor of a small fortune, most of which was invested in thin real-estate equities and lumber ventures. During his long career he had a constructive record in banking and he died possessed of a substantial fortune.

The number of banks in Minneapolis grew so rapidly that in 1880 a clearing-house was organized. Operations began on January 2, 1881. The members were the Merchants National Bank, the Citizens Bank, the City Bank, the Commercial Bank, Valentine G. Hush & Co., the Bank of Minneapolis, the Security Bank, the Hennepin County Savings Bank, and the Northwestern National Bank.[81] Since Sidle was unwilling to accept any of the established rules and regulations, his bank did not join.

Up to this time Minneapolis had not had a corporate trust company to handle estates and trusts. The need for such an institution was recognized by business men in general and by lawyers in particular. Koon, Merrill and Keith, a law firm with offices at Nicollet and Washington, engaged in estate work and, in addition, carried on a lively and profitable business in real-estate mortgages. These men spent much time discussing the advisability of organizing a trust company. Eventually, E. A. Merrill persuaded Edmund J. Phelps, a local capitalist, to join him in organizing the Minnesota Loan and Trust Company. This company began business on May 1, 1883.[82]

During its early months the company did not have an office of its own but occupied a room in the law office of Koon, Merrill and Keith. In 1883 it bought a lot at 311–313 Nicollet Avenue and immediately constructed a seven-story skyscraper with an elevator.[83] This elevator, the first in the territory, was a thing of wonder. People traveled from afar to view it, and a few of the braver souls even rode in it. The company did not have any estate business at the beginning, nor did it do any banking. Its first undertaking was an intensification of the mortgage-loan business formerly carried on by Merrill. By the end of the first year, however, it had acquired a few estates in trust, and thereafter its trust business grew steadily. The advisability of accepting general deposits was debated from the beginning, and by 1887 the company was accepting time deposits.[84] On November 5, 1887, its authorized rates of interest on time deposits were:

60 days — 2 per cent
90 days — 3
6 months — 4
Under restriction, 6 months — 5

In September, 1887, the Northwestern National Bank had sixteen employees, and Harris, the cashier, was looking for a new clerk. Among the applicants was Mr. Edward Williams Decker, a farm boy from the vicinity of Austin, Minnesota. The Decker family, which was Holland Dutch, had arrived in New York in the seventeenth century. The father, Jacob Smith Decker, left his home in New Jersey in 1855, traveling by train to Chicago and thence to Prairie du Chien. There he bought a team of oxen and a cow, and drove north to what is now Austin, Minnesota, where he bought 160 acres of land at $1.75 an acre. The land was fertile, and in due course Jacob Smith Decker prospered.

In 1869 Edward Williams Decker was born.[85] He was graduated from the local high school in June, 1887, and in the fall of that year was sent to Minneapolis to attend the State University. Unfortunately for his schooling he met a teller of the Northwestern National Bank, who told him that the bank needed a messenger. Since the bank interested young Decker more than the University, he applied for the job and was hired for the sum of $15 a month.

A few days later Mr. Clive Talbot Jaffray, arriving from Berlin (now Kitchener), Ontario, also heard that there was a vacancy at the Northwestern. He applied for the position, and although Mr. Decker had been hired, he, too, was employed. Mr. Jaffray was of Scotch ancestry. He was born July 1, 1865, had been educated in the high school of his native town, and had served his apprenticeship in the Merchants Bank of Canada.[86]

Shortly after these two boys started work, James B. Forgan, who came from the Bank of Nova Scotia, became cashier; thus, both received their training from one of America's most capable bankers. Forgan was born on April 11, 1852, at St. Andrews, Scotland. When he was sixteen years of age, he was indentured for three years as an apprentice to the Royal Bank of Scotland at a salary of £10 the first year, £15 the second year, and £20 the third year. In March, 1873, Forgan went to work in Montreal as a clerk for the Bank of British North America. His salary increased to $700 a year. Two years later he made another change, this time joining Dun, Wiman and Company, the Canadian branch of R. G. Dun and Company, for $1,000 a year. He had been there about that long when the Bank of Nova Scotia hired him as paying teller at $1,200. However, he did not continue in that capacity for long. He was assigned to auditing the branch offices. After some months of this, he commenced to review assets and methods of operation, reporting his impressions of management efficiency and chances of success among the branches. Eventually, as a specialist in reorganization, he was sent out to overhaul unsuccessful branches.

Some years before this a Bank of Nova Scotia branch in Winnipeg had become involved in a local real-estate boom and collapse. Forgan went out to look over the situation. Since Winnipeg had intimate business relations with Minneapolis, Forgan in the course of his examination became familiar with conditions in the latter town. Impressed with the prospects, he recommended that an agency be established there, and in 1885 he came to Minneapolis for that purpose. This agency proved very successful from the start. Forgan himself and his methods made a lasting impression upon the officers and directors of the local banks, and it was natural that he should, for he was the only one among them who had been highly trained in banking.

In 1887 Henry T. Welles retired from the presidency of the Northwestern, and S. A. Harris, the cashier, succeeded him. Harris' first act was to hire Forgan as cashier at double his former salary and give him complete control of clerical work. Forgan was horrified when he examined the methods used in the bank. There was little formal organization; duties, responsibilities, and privileges were not clearly defined; the bookkeeping system was obsolete. Accordingly, he called in Mr. C. T. Jaffray, the bookkeeper, and with his help revised the bookkeeping and clerical records. Next he studied the bank's operations, breaking them down into component parts. Then he wrote out an instruction sheet which fixed each employee's responsibilities and carefully defined his duties. After he had established and explained the new system, Forgan set about enforcing it. Forgan was a strict disciplinarian, a hard worker himself, a driver who never accepted an excuse for failing, and a man of terrific tempers. Within a year the new system was functioning smoothly. Despite Forgan's ruthlessness, he was reputed to be absolutely fair and he rewarded achievement with a free hand.

It was in this school that Mr. Decker and Mr. Jaffray cut their banking teeth. They absorbed Forgan's Scotch-Canadian methods; they learned to fix responsibility, to exact efficiency, to be ruthless if necessary, to revere achievement, and, above all, to demand success. Because, next to the Prince brothers and James B. Forgan, these two men probably were the most influential in affecting the course of Twin City banking, some consideration of their personalities is in order. Both were capable and aggressive and rapidly moved into positions of importance. Men instinctively felt their reliability and trusted their judgment.

Mr. Decker has a genial, optimistic personality. He is imaginative and enthusiastic, instinctively looking on the bright side of life. He is a dreamer of great dreams, but behind this ability to visualize achievements there is a driving, practical nature. No sooner does he lay his plans than he has tackled them with practical effort. Thought and action are so synchronized that in the course of the years he has accomplished many things.

Mr. Jaffray is of a somewhat more serious disposition. Life to him is no light matter — perhaps his Scotch background is responsible. He loves his work and works for the sake of working. He is noted for his conservatism and his inability to view a proposition in a buoyant frame of mind. He makes few mistakes. His relaxation he takes as seriously as his work. He is devoted to hunting, and his golf game has long been a Twin City legend. His work and his play have been equally serious and successful.

On June 30, 1890, Mr. Jaffray was appointed assistant cashier of the Northwestern, and on July 14, George A. Pillsbury was elected president.[87] On November 19, 1891, James B. Forgan resigned as cashier to become vice-president of the First National Bank of Chicago.[88] He was succeeded at the Northwestern by his brother, David R. Forgan, who in turn left in 1896 to become vice-president of the Union National Bank of Chicago.

The Minneapolis Trust Company was organized in 1888 by Samuel Hill, a son-in-law of James J. Hill. The company's original capital was $500,000, of which James J. Hill subscribed $100,000 and Samuel Hill, $25,000.[89] Prominent among the early stockholders were H. A. Harrison, Perry Harrison, William H. Dunwoody, T. B. Janney, F. F. Semple, C. H. Pettit, and Clarkson Lindley.[90] This company's business was somewhat similar to that of the Minnesota Loan and Trust Company. It concentrated on the administration of estates, avoiding the general banking business. Not until it had been active in business for many years and was being severely pressed by competitors did it accept time deposits and engage in a general banking business. For a long time it carried on a brisk farm-mortgage business with country banks.

In the Northwest the 'eighties were marked by good business and a steady increase in local land values. The boom, however, came to an abrupt end in 1893, and a panic set in. The currency system was still inelastic, and the depression rapidly destroyed values. As a result, even solvent banks were hard pressed, and the worst series of bank failures in the history of the Twin Cities ensued.

On May 20, 1893, the Farmers and Merchants State Bank failed. No dividends were ever paid to depositors. On June 22 the State Bank of Minneapolis closed its doors. Eventually, depositors received a liquidation of 19 cents on the dollar. On July 1 the American Exchange Bank failed, paying out at 24 cents on the dollar. It was followed on July 8 by the Citizens Bank, which paid 29 cents on the dollar. The Bank of New England held out until July 16 and paid slightly over 42 per cent of its deposits.

The Northwestern National Bank of Minneapolis by July 1, 1892, had increased its capital to $1,250,000 and this tended to strengthen its position during the troublous 'nineties. Mr. Decker's progress there was smooth and uneventful. In 1895, however, he resigned to become an assistant cashier at the Metropolitan Bank and the following year he was advanced to cashier and managing officer. In 1900 he returned to the Northwestern as cashier.

The First National Bank of Minneapolis under the management of Jacob Sidle had been aggressive, building up its deposits rapidly and loaning to all local enterprises. On his death in 1888, Sidle was succeeded by his brother Henry, under whose management the bank became even more liberal in its loaning policy. The other banks were severe in their criticism, for they regarded the First National as a disturbing element in the local credit situation. They alleged that it stole customers, underbid its competitors, and made many undesirable loans; also, it was not coöperative in the matter of hours and services. Within the bank it was felt that Henry Sidle was arbitrary, a disconcerting trait, to say the least, for he refused to delegate authority, even insisting on answering all correspondence himself. The spindles of his desk were always cluttered with unanswered letters. Despite their disapproval of his policies and personality, the other officers and the minority stockholders made no immediate effort to remove him.

In 1893, however, it became evident that the First of Minneapolis was experiencing heavy going, and a steady drain of deposits set in. The directors realized that, because assets were not in the best condition, drastic action was necessary in order to bolster confidence. Early in 1894 Henry G. Sidle's removal from the presidency necessitated the selection of a successor.[91] The directors desired a man of unquestioned character and reputation, regardless of his experience, and the choice fell on Captain John Martin, a director since the organization of the bank and one of the most highly respected men in the territory. Captain Martin was not a practical banker and he took the job only on the condition that he might hire a manager to take full charge of the bank's operations. For this responsibility he selected Frank Moody Prince, who became cashier July 31, 1894, and vice-president on January 8, 1895.[92] Prince chose as his assistant Mr. Clive Talbot Jaffray of the Northwestern National Bank, who assumed the title of cashier when Prince became vice-president.

The change in management did much to restore confidence, and the new officers, with the coöperation of the directors, labored to improve the character of the bank's assets. Wherever possible, payments were obtained, even though small, and additional collateral was acquired. Despite the success of this policy, losses and charge-offs were such that the bank decided to assess its stock. On July 15, 1894, a 30 per cent assessment was levied, and on April 5, 1895, an additional 50 per cent.[93] These assessments caused difficulty for the stockholders, most of whom were already financially embarrassed. Some made no attempt to pay, and their stock was sold to meet the assessment. The amount of cash realized by the bank was enough to offset the realized losses, and operations continued. In fact, on an operating basis moderate profits were continuous during the 'nineties.

The Panic of 1893 was followed by a partial recovery, but conditions took another bad turn in 1896. On January 14 the Irish-American Bank and the City Bank of Minneapolis closed. On December 28 the Scandia Bank failed, paying 62 cents on the dollar. On December 20 both the Northern Trust Company and the Washington Bank failed, the Northern paying 40 cents and the Washington 52 cents on the dollar. Conditions were serious in 1897. On January 14 the Columbia National Bank and the Bankers Exchange Bank closed. On March 20 the Union National closed, paying 96 cents, and on August 27 the Bank of Minneapolis, paying 86 cents on the dollar. On February 17, 1899, the Minneapolis Savings Bank failed.

St. Paul experienced little trouble in 1893. No bank failures occurred until 1896. Then, on January 28, the Ramsey County Savings Bank closed. It was involved in frozen real-estate mortgages, and the final recovery was only 25 per cent. On December 22 the Bank of Minnesota (Dawson and Company) closed. The final recovery was 90 per cent. On July 7, 1899, the State Savings Bank of St. Paul failed; recoveries amounted to 80 per cent. On July 17 it was followed by the Germania Bank, the recoveries of which amounted to 71 per cent.

Banking in the 'nineties had a chaotic setting. Values were falling rapidly, and there was no market for even the best collateral. Banks were numerous and usually over-extended. Many soon became insolvent and closed their doors. This put additional strain on those remaining open. Even perfectly solvent banks were in distress. Their customers demanded money, and there was no means of obtaining it. The banking and currency mechanism was faulty: there was no surplus strength, for each bank held fast to its cash, and each survived or failed by itself. The Chicago and New York banks, involved in difficulties of their own, were unable to aid the situation. Even normal borrowing from correspondent banks ceased. Necessity made it a matter of every man for himself. The Twin City banks were refused aid in the eastern cities; they refused it to country banks. Even the large Twin City banks were unable to help one another.

This period was the hardest ever experienced by Twin Cities bankers, and only the greatest effort kept the remaining banks open. The First National Bank of Minneapolis had received such a complete overhauling in 1894 and 1895 that it met the crisis of 1897 as well as any of the Twin City banks. When the padlocks were all counted, the leading survivors in Minneapolis were the Northwestern National, the First National, the Security, the Minnesota Loan and Trust Company, the Minneapolis Trust Company, the Hennepin County Savings Bank, and the Farmers and Mechanics Savings Bank. In St. Paul they were the First National, the Merchants National, the Capital National Bank, the Capital Trust and Savings Bank, and the National German-American Bank. By 1900 conditions began to thaw somewhat, and general business was resumed in fair volume.

The character of the management of the city banks had changed entirely during the 'nineties. All the old-time pioneer bankers had disappeared, and with them the last of the petty capitalists who had entered banking without experience. They had been replaced by a new school of young men who had served their apprenticeship in the industry and who could be termed professional bankers. As a class they had entered the banks without capital or good connections and had come up the hard way. They had worked in every clerical position, had won promotions because of outstanding ability, efficiency, and good judgment, and had reached the position of second in command by 1890. The depressions of 1893 and 1897 and the passage of time forced the older men out of the way, making room for the younger.

These new men assumed command during trying times: values were falling and banks closing. They had little time to think of anything but remedying the mistakes caused by the optimism of their predecessors. The most immediate problem was to keep their banks open from day to day. They were repeatedly impressed by the troubles that grew out of a too liberal loan policy, and the objectives which they came to revere were liquidity and solvency. It is possible that this period wielded a strong hand in molding the characters of the men who controlled Twin City banking for the next forty years.

With the removal of Henry G. Sidle from the presidency of the First National Bank, the domination of Twin City banks by individual stockholding officers approached an end. This prototype was replaced by the professional banker. The stock of the large banks was now owned by outsiders on an investment basis; the management was in professional hands.

The depressions and panics of the 'nineties were not entirely detrimental to the Twin City banks that survived. True, sizable losses had occurred, but many competitive banks had been eliminated. The ones that closed had, in general, been optimistic and liberal in their loaning policies. They had provided an unrestricted competition difficult for the conservative banks to meet. Since their closing left only conservative banks, the competitive situation was improved. In addition, much of the business and deposits of the closed banks eventually went to the survivors. The hard times of the 'nineties tended to improve the character of bank management and to increase earnings during the following period.

Growth and Mergers in the Twin Cities, 1900–1915

By 1900 the First National Bank of Minneapolis was in excellent shape, having cleared up its doubtful paper and retained part of its income during the 'nineties. At the end of that year, which marked the beginning of a long period of growth, it absorbed the Nicollet National Bank with deposits of $1,400,000, paying the former stockholders par for their stock, a total of $250,000.[94] Deposits of the First National Bank passed the ten-million mark for the first time in 1901. Their growth is shown below:[95]

1900	$ 5,068,956
1905	12,233,962
1910	18,255,775
1915	65,910,114

In 1903 Captain John Martin retired. He was succeeded by Judge John B. Gilfillan. Two years later Judge Gilfillan became chairman of the board, and Frank Prince was advanced from vice-president to president.[96]

Until 1905 the commercial banks in the Twin Cities had not operated savings departments. This possibility had been discussed, however, and on December 1 of that year the Northwestern opened a savings department with Mr. Lyman E. Wakefield in charge.[97] The interest rate allowed was 3 per cent. Other banks followed immediately. The Panic of 1907 found the Northwestern with about $7,000,000 in deposits. The banks of the country had agreed that no actual cash should be paid out, and that all payments should be in clearing-house certificates. In the late summer and early fall, the Twin Cities had shipped out about $50,000,000 in currency to country banks to finance the movement of the crop. Normally, this currency would have flowed back to the Twin Cities within a few weeks, but because the city banks suspended currency payments, the country banks held on to this cash. Thus, since the entire system was frozen, no liquidation appeared imminent. When the pressure on the Northwestern was greatest, William H. Dunwoody deposited $1,000,000.

In December of that same year, Mr. Decker visited Chicago to confer with his former chief, James B. Forgan, and to discuss with the Chicago Clearing House the resumption of cash payments. It was decided that the best way was simply to resume, and in January, 1908, all the banks in the Northwest did so. Some anxious days followed, for there was always the danger of a run, but depositors brought in cash instead of taking it out, and once more the entire system began to function smoothly. The currency panic was over.

On June 9, 1908, the Northwestern assumed the assets and liabilities of the National Bank of Commerce,[98] and on July 10 it increased its capital to $2,000,000 and added $1,000,000 to surplus.[99] On November 28 it purchased the Swedish-American National Bank.[100] Thus, it began the year with deposits of $12,900,000 and ended it with $25,500,000.

The drive toward mergers was stimulating, and during 1908 the Northwestern cast appraising eyes at the Minnesota Loan and Trust Company. The national banking laws did not permit a national bank to conduct a trust business, and hence a genuine merger was impossible. However, eastern banks had already worked out an ingenious method of affiliation which it was decided to adopt. On September 25, 1909, an agreement was signed with the stockholders of the Minnesota Loan and Trust Company to purchase their stock.[101] The funds to pay for it were supplied by the Northwestern through a special dividend to its stockholders, who turned over their pro rata share to trustees with instructions to buy and hold the Trust Company stock. Their pro rata interest in the Minnesota Loan and Trust Company stock was indicated by an endorsement on the Northwestern's stock certificates.[102] Thus the ownership of the two companies was knit together so that one company could not be separated from the other. At the time of the affiliation the Northwestern increased its capital from $2,000,000 to $3,000,000.

On January 11, 1910, Mr. Lyman E. Wakefield was appointed assistant cashier of the Northwestern, and on January 9, 1912, Mr. E. W. Decker was elected president.[103] By 1915 the average daily deposits had reached $36,071,600, a new high. The Northwestern was fortunate in possessing not only strong but also well-balanced management. Forgan was only one of the capable officers who had managed its affairs, but his influence was so strong that it affected succeeding generations of bankers. Mr. Decker had been trained by Forgan, but his own personality, too, was of great value — enthusiastic, visionary, yet practical, he was filled with an exuberant drive and a love of accomplishment for its own sake. He helped to keep the Northwestern always in the forefront of every movement. Perhaps this energy and enthusiasm might have caused trouble had it not been restrained by more cautious heads. For this, William H. Dunwoody and Judge M. B. Koon were noted. Dunwoody had been a director since 1876, and Judge Koon since 1881. Both were intelligent, shrewd, level-headed, and more than a trifle cautious. They knew that developments often proved disappointing; they insisted on conservatism. Together, the Dunwoody-Koon-Decker combination produced great results. Decker originated and activated ideas; Dunwoody and Koon winnowed them, eliminating the impractical, approving the sound. The death of Judge Koon in 1912 and that of William H. Dunwoody in 1914 represented a great loss to the Northwestern as well as to the community.

James J. Hill had been connected with the First National Bank of St. Paul since January 21, 1880, when he had acquired a small block of stock, and since May 12, 1880, he had been a director. During his active days in railroading he had never shown a great interest in banking and had represented very little stock. However, he had thrown his business, as well as a considerable volume from his companies, to the First National Bank, which had come to lean on his support. Upon his withdrawal from active railroading, he attempted to buy the First National Bank, but the stockholders, who desired a high price, rejected his offer.[104] Apparently the matter was dropped. Then, on October 10, 1912, Hill bought the Second National Bank of St. Paul, paying $1,240,000 for its stock, which represented a book value of approximately $900,000. Since the threat of losing the railroad business was too much for the stockholders of the First National Bank, Hill was able to buy the First National Bank of St. Paul on December 31, 1912, for $3,350,000 in cash.[105] Early in 1913 the First National and the Second National were merged, James J. Hill becoming the sole owner.[106]

It would be interesting to know exactly the motives which prompted Hill's activities. Of course, they can never be accurately determined, but the explanations of his associates are interesting. According to these gentlemen, Hill always had dreamed of a great railroad empire which would embrace several roads, supplemented by land-owning, iron-mining, and development companies, all unified by a holding company and served by a large bank. Its physical hulk was to be housed in one great office building, every tenant of which was to be Hill-controlled and an integral part of the whole. Since this dream was already on its way to fulfillment by 1911, it is logical to assume that Hill was looking for a bank to fill his waiting niche. Acquiring the Second National was only a part of his campaign to secure the First National. He used it as a lever to force the sale of the bank he actually wanted, and proceeded to merge the two. The merged institution moved into the banking quarters prepared for it in Hill's new office buildings.

From the beginning, although they were not controlled by the same individuals, the First National Bank of Minneapolis and the Minneapolis Trust Company had worked in close harmony. In fact, after the early 'nineties there was not a dominant stockholder in either organization, the stock being widely scattered and held in small blocks, primarily by the bank's customers. By April, 1913, it was decided that the First National should purchase the Minneapolis Trust.[107] The First's stated capital was $2,000,000. The procedure in purchasing the Trust Company was both intricate and devious. The bank declared a cash dividend of 25 per cent to stockholders, at the same time giving them the right to purchase 1 share of stock for each 4 shares held. Then the stockholders endorsed their dividend checks back to the bank, accepting the new stock but returning it to the bank with a power of attorney authorizing its exchange for stock of the Minneapolis Trust Company. As soon as the exchange had been effected and the stock of the Trust Company acquired, the pro rata interest in the Trust Company was endorsed on the back of each share of the bank's stock.[108]

Originally the First National Bank had been located on Hennepin Avenue down by the river. Then it had moved to Nicollet and Washington Avenues, and later to the Phoenix Building at Marquette Avenue and Fourth Street. In 1906 it had built a one-story building at Marquette and Fifth, and in 1911 it bought the

FIRST NATIONAL–SOO LINE BUILDING
Minneapolis, 1916

adjoining New York Life Building. In 1915 it collaborated with the Minneapolis, St. Paul and Sault Ste. Marie Railroad in the construction of the First National–Soo Line Building. This structure, gaped at by all Minneapolis, towered to the dizzy height of 20 stories. The lower floors were to be occupied a portion by the railroad and the remainder by the bank; the balance was to be for rent. The plans announced by Mr. Prince astounded everyone. A great deal of critical comment developed among the officers when they realized the spaciousness of the banking-rooms. Why, it was entirely too large for any reasonable use. One officer said that it looked like a railroad station. The more reflective commenced to wonder and to look about for two and two. After all, Mr. Prince and Mr. Jaffray were not given to doing foolish things. They always objected to spending money ostentatiously, especially for such luxuries as bank buildings — bricks were too difficult to convert into cash when customers demanded money.

In spite of attempts to keep the secret, eventually it leaked out. The First National Bank and the Security National Bank were to merge as the First and Security National Bank, and the consolidated organization was to occupy the new building. This was a basic consolidation, for it resulted in a merger not only of business, but also of capital, officers, and employees. At this time the First National had a capital of $2,500,000. On March 19, 1915, the directors voted to buy the Security National Bank for $5,000,000 cash and to assume all its assets and liabilities.[109] This was done by increasing the capital of the First National to $5,000,000 through an issue of 25,000 additional shares at $250 a share, $100 to be assigned to capital and $150 to surplus. Of these, 1,250 shares were to be sold to the stockholders of the First National; 3,750 shares were to be sold at the option of the board of directors; and 20,000 shares were to be sold to the stockholders of the Security National Bank.[110] At a special meeting, stockholders of the Security National Bank voted to dissolve the bank and sell its property to the First National for $5,000,000.[111] They then exercised their rights to buy First National Bank stock.

The banks were merged March 29, 1915, and moved into the new building. In the consolidated organization Frank M. Prince became chairman of the board, and Francis A. Chamberlain, who since 1892 had been president of the Security National Bank and its predecessor, the Security Bank, became president. Mr. Jaffray was made senior vice-president. When the assets of the two banks were being merged, a considerable difference in policy came to light. Both banks were sound and solvent and had produced good earnings. The Security's assets, however, included a large number of charged-off items, while the First National had practically none. These had come into existence through loans which had gone bad, for the Security had been liberal in its loan policy whereas the First had been so conservative that it seldom had a loss. However, these charge-offs were more than balanced by the bank's earnings. The new bank continued to care for the customers of both its predecessors.

CHAPTER III

COUNTRY BANKING AND AGRICULTURAL INFLATION, 1915–1920

COMMERCIAL BANKS, THEIR NUMBER AND POLICIES, TO 1920

DURING the period of settlement, the number of banks in existence increased steadily. In 1900, Minnesota had 267, North Dakota 155, South Dakota 207, and Montana 35.[1] By 1911, Minnesota had 997, North Dakota 707, South Dakota 631, and Montana 175.[2] Their establishment, for the most part, had been in close relationship with the growth of the country.

During the war boom, banks were organized in large numbers in the district. In 1911 there were 2,510 banks in the States of Minnesota, North Dakota, South Dakota, and Montana; by 1920 the number had increased to 3,551.[3] On the basis of population, the Ninth Federal Reserve District was the most "over-banked" section in the country. In the East figures varied from one bank for every 5,000 population to one for every 10,000 population. The average for the United States was one bank for every 3,520 population, but in 1921 Minnesota had one for every 1,590 people, Montana one for every 1,370, South Dakota one for every 921, and North Dakota one for every 768.[4] Even under the most favorable conditions many of these banks would not have been justified. Their multiplication had been fostered by lax banking laws and the small amount of capital required.[5] It actually cost less to start a bank than it did to buy a good farm.

An examination of Minnesota bank figures for 1920 shows that out of 1,518 banks, 1,383 had total balance-sheet footings of less than $1,000,000; a substantial majority of these had footings under $300,000. Banks to the number of 118 had assets between $1,000,000 and $5,000,000, and only 17 had assets in excess of $5,000,000. All of the latter group were located in Minneapolis, in St. Paul, or in Duluth. North Dakota had 898 banks, of which 880 had assets under

$1,000,000; 16 were between $1,000,000 and $5,000,000; and only 2 topped $5,000,000. One was the First National Bank of Fargo; the other was a public institution, the Bank of North Dakota at Bismarck.[6] South Dakota had 704 banks including 659 with assets below $1,000,000; 44 were between $1,000,000 and $5,000,000; and only one, the Sioux Falls Savings Bank, in excess of $5,000,000.[7] Montana had 431 banks, of which 392 had assets under $1,000,000; 36 were between $1,000,000 and $5,000,000; and only three, W. A. Clark and Brother of Butte, the First National Bank, and the Metals Bank and Trust Company of Butte, were over $5,000,000.[8] An average of all State banks in Minnesota in 1920 indicates footings of $459,000, loans and discounts of $335,000, and investments of $60,000.[9] In North Dakota the average State bank had total footings of $214,000, including $172,000 of loans and discounts and $12,000 of investments.[10] In South Dakota the average had footings of $364,000, including $284,000 of loans and discounts, and $9,000 of investments.[11] In Montana footings were $433,000, including $309,000 of loans and discounts and $40,000 of investments.[12] As a matter of fact, the median bank in each of the four States was well below the average.

Figures for loans and discounts on country-bank statements were somewhat misleading, for on published statements this item was a catch-all which included many types of miscellaneous loans as well as real-estate mortgages. In the cities bona fide commercial loans existed, but in the country districts loans were based almost entirely on agricultural collateral. Nor does this mean that banks were loaning primarily on real-estate mortgages. In general, the so-called country commercial loans were not intended to apply to real estate. They were made to farmers for the raising of cattle or crops and were designed to be paid off out of the sale of the product. Usually they were secured by a lien on the products by chattel mortgage and often also by a first or second mortgage on the land. Thus, in many cases a real-estate mortgage served only as additional collateral to secure a supposedly self-liquidating loan. It is true that banks continuously made real-estate loans, but these the local bankers intended to sell through the mortgage dealers. They were, in fact, readily salable and in many cases were considered a secondary reserve. It was believed that they could always be liquidated. Holding them against demand deposits was merely a temporary procedure, and, whenever the demand for so-called commercial loans in the territory increased, the banker sold real-estate mortgages to raise funds for local loans.

Throughout most of the territory in this period the demand for short-term agricultural credit was so extensive that few banks had enough money available to carry permanently any large volume of real-estate mortgages. So insistent was this demand for local credit that banks were often completely loaned up and were obliged to borrow money from their city correspondents. Borrowing was stimulated by the fact that they could obtain money in the city at a rate considerably below what they were getting in the country. The city banks, however, demanded and got excess collateral for their loans.

In their interest in real-estate mortgages there was little difference between national and State banks. Originally, national banks had been forbidden to hold real-estate mortgages, but the Federal Reserve Act permitted them to make loans for not more than five years on farms or longer than one year on city property.[13] The funds employed were to aggregate not more than one-fourth of capital and surplus or one-third of time deposits, whichever was greater. This gave the national banks sufficient leeway to deal in real-estate mortgages, and the difference existing between State and national banks in this respect seemed more closely correlated with their size than with their charter. Most banks held some bonds in their portfolios, but these were used not so much for a secondary reserve as for collateral to secure deposits from townships, cities, counties, and the State. Bonds were not a popular country-bank investment, and they were purchased only to the extent necessary for collateral, because yields on bonds were not so high as on readily available local paper.

A further examination of the bank statements of this period (1920) brings out another interesting fact, the importance of time or savings deposits. While there was considerable individual variation, time or savings deposits in country banks tended to constitute approximately two-thirds of total deposits, and demand deposits one-third or less. In the larger city banks the situation was reversed: time deposits seldom aggregated more than one-third of total deposits and in some instances amounted to less than 20 per cent.

The history of the Northwest had been marked by a steady increase in the number of banks. By 1920 the territory was covered by an extensive network. These banks were not only numerous but also profitable, and they supplied their communities with a multitude of services. Nevertheless, strong, well-managed institutions which restricted their operations to legitimate commercial banking were somewhat rare in the country regions.

The Operations of a Country Bank

Since the country banks in the wheat areas of the Ninth Federal Reserve District differed considerably in their operations from metropolitan city banks serving an industrial and commercial district, it is advisable to consider two typical situations in some detail. Let us consider a fair example of a bank entirely dependent upon the success of the wheat crop. The Farmers Bank in a small rural center obtained a State charter on July 17, 1905, with an authorized and paid-up capital of $10,000.[14] The president was Adam Hannah, a Minneapolis chain banker who had started his career as a green grocer but soon had gone into real-estate mortgages.[15] He represented Scottish capital and purchased western real-estate mortgages for his principals. In the course of this business, he became interested in a chain of little banks. Most of the banks were profitable, and since they supplied Hannah with mortgages for sale, they fitted well into his plans.

This Farmers Bank was, as usual, very short of funds. Its statement as of December 31, 1911, showed total footings of $69,500 divided as follows: capital $10,000, surplus $3,800, individual deposits $26,700, demand certificates $3,900, and time certificates $24,900. Assets consisted of loans and discounts $37,700, overdrafts $800, bonds $2,600, banking house $4,500, other real estate $3,000, due from banks $18,900, and cash $1,800.[16] The loans and discounts included a small amount of first mortgages on real estate, but the major portion consisted of farmers' notes in amounts ranging from $50 to $500 and secured by chattel mortgages on horses, equipment, machinery, cattle, sheep, or pigs. It was generally understood that no payment would be demanded until after the next crop season, and most farmers expected further loans. This bank never had the slightest intention of levying on the pledged chattels; it was willing to wait for a good crop. The banker felt justified in extending credit to the farmer because as a last resort the farmer usually had a good equity in his farm. True, there might be a first mortgage held by others, but it was seldom for the full value of the land.

Since the bank was loaded with farm paper which could not be collected until a good crop had been harvested, its condition was far from liquid. Some cash could be raised by the sale of first mortgages, but little could be squeezed out of loans and discounts. This situation did not bother Hannah. If his country banks needed cash, they borrowed it from their city correspondents. The city banks normally carried the burden of liquidity for the country, and the country banks kept themselves fully invested. Their loans were normally carried as bills payable, although sometimes country banks showed them as certificates of deposit. The city banks normally demanded a margin of collateral.

On January 6, 1917, the cashier of the Farmers Bank wrote as follows to Paul J. Leeman, vice-president of the First National Bank of Minneapolis: [17]

> Our balance with you will be getting bigger every day from now on as we are getting returns on our farm loans. We made nearly $100,000 in farm loans (real-estate mortgages) this fall and had all the way from 30 to 40 thousand of our money tied up every day and as a result our account went down to nothing. We employed our money in the farm loan field this fall and as we have now sold nearly all of them, we expect returns and will get them every day from now on and you will get the balance as we are highly pleased with the service you render.

On October 17, 1918, the cashier wrote: [18]

> Kindly advise if you are disposed to carry some cattle paper for us. We have at present about $6,000 worth of good cattle paper with the Stock Yards National Bank that is due and they charge us 7½% on it. Thought if you would be interested we would submit them to you as we figure you might give us a better rate.

Leeman replied on October 20, 1918:[19]

Do not know of any reason why we shall not be very glad to rediscount this amount of paper for you for 6 months at 6%. Only difficulty of our carrying a line of cattle paper for you is fact we cannot handle paper which runs for longer maturity than 6 months, which at times is not long enough for this class of paper. However, in view of your statement the paper is already placed in South St. Paul, anticipate it will not run any longer than this length of time so you may be able to avail yourselves of this offer.

The cashier wrote on November 26, 1918:[20]

Kindly let us have 30 days extension of our $5,000 C/D or we might be able to pay it before that time but cannot stand the pressure on our account just now.

Leeman replied November 27, 1918:[21]

Glad to renew this C/D for this length of time and would appreciate your sending us a new C/D to replace the old one.

The cashier wrote on July 29, 1919:[22]

We might need a little money for 90 days to assist during the harvest, and until they can market their grain.

The cashier wrote to Leeman on November 3, 1919:[23]

I am taking the liberty of sending you our C/D in the amount of $5,000 for which kindly give us credit. We will not need this for over 30 days but I have made it for 60 days. Kindly let us know what collateral you want. We are not so very hard up but we expect a call and like to look respectable. We paid off quite a few certificates yesterday and it pulled our cash reserve down.

Leeman commented on November 12, 1919:[24]

. . . was in. All they owe at the present time is the $5,000 we are carrying and $3,000 carried by the Stockyards National Bank of South St. Paul, and $3,000 paper purchased by the Farmers and Merchants Bank of Minnesota.

The cashier wrote again on May 4, 1920:[25]

We are compelled to send you another $10,000 for credit as we had an unexpected withdrawal today from one of our customers. We are only making this for 30 days when it will be paid back as we have warrants and farm loans in amount of $25,000 to sell and we will begin to clean house so that we will not be such heavy borrowers. The demand for feed has been terrific on us and it is the only thing we have been loaning money for, which was absolutely necessary.

Let us consider another example of a country bank. This bank filed articles of incorporation May 23, 1910, and commenced business two days later with a capital of $10,000.[26] Control of the stock was in the hands of two business men of North Dakota.[27] Active control of the bank was in the hands of the cashier. The bank was moderately successful from the beginning, and during its first 10 years of existence earnings are reported to have approximated 15 per cent annually.[28] By May, 1915, capital amounted to $10,000, surplus to $500, and deposits to $54,700; loans and discounts were $50,800, cash $9,200, and banking house $3,100.[29] There was only $1,500 of other real estate. Loans and discounts were entirely local and made almost exclusively to farmers.

The area was non-competitive from a banking point of view, and local farm loans bore a rate of 12 per cent. In addition, the bank wrote fire insurance. The situation was ideal from the cashier's viewpoint. Loans mounted in volume during the spring and summer and they were cleaned up in the fall. Complete crop failures were rare, and to some extent they even benefited the bank. Then loans held up in volume during the winter and increased throughout the following crop seasons; the new crop paid both years' loans. While it placed a great strain on the bank, this situation tended to increase earnings. In common with most western banks, this one issued certificates of deposit and sold them in the East. The bank was successful in this venture, placing its certificates with Minneapolis and eastern capitalists and with insurance companies.[30]

A crop failure in 1917 placed considerable strain on the bank, and loans and discounts increased from $102,300 in September, 1916, to $131,700 in September, 1917.[31] Even in 1916, collections had not been satisfactory. Business was increasing in volume, and the bank was pressed for money. In May, 1917, the cashier requested his city correspondent to rediscount $15,000 of paper. This was refused, but the bank was loaned $5,000 on a note secured by $7,500 of collateral.[32]

The crop failure stopped collections, and the bank was unable to get out of debt. Since it was not too badly pressed, the loan was carried forward; additional loans were also made, but the directors were required personally to guarantee the notes.[33]

On December 14, 1918, the cashier wrote to Leeman:[34]

Collections have been coming in so slow this fall it will be necessary for us to renew our C/D for $5,000 due on the 20th. We are expecting a remittance of over $60,000 on Federal Loan applications sent in from this district, and a very large amount of this will be paid to us and we will then be in a position to take up the obligations with you. Had fully expected to take this up by the 20th of this month and if this renewal is not satisfactory kindly advise the first of the week.

On January 18, 1919, the cashier wrote:[35]

Find we are obliged to renew our C/D expiring on the 20th and enclose C/D for $5,000 due in 60 days at 6%. The writer is secretary-treasurer of the local National Farm Loan Association and has been expecting for the past 30 days or more to have remittances on over $70,000 worth of these loans which have been approved by the Federal Land Bank but so far our hopes have been futile. It does not appear we will receive these during this generation so if you will kindly renew this for us another 60 days will see what success we have in instilling a little more speed in remitting on the Federal Loans we are to receive. A very considerable amount of these loans will be left with us on either payments or deposits, and we should not need to avail ourselves of the borrowing privilege which you are asked to extend to us.

Apparently the bank was not successful in obtaining the federal funds: deposits continued to shrink and loans remained stationary.

A field man's report to Paul J. Leeman on this bank, dated April 20, 1920, read as follows:[36]

. . . said the only time they carry anything to speak of at Washburn is when they are flush with funds, which is far from being the case at the present time. As you know . . . and . . . of North Dakota are interested here and are men well thought of and of considerable means. They also own some stock in the Capital Security Bank of Bismarck. Of their time deposits about $40,000 consists of money from outside of the State and none of it due until about July or August. . . . figured they would get along without borrowing to any extent but a deposit of $11,000 was withdrawn and used in meeting a payment on Iowa land the depositor had purchased. We are carrying them for $13,000 at present and they anticipate they will need another $5,000. . . . of North Dakota was offered some 6% money by the Citizens Commercial Trust Company of Buffalo and this bank has their arrangement to let them have $5,000 at 6%.

Land values average about $35 an acre around . . . . The farmers are hard up so far as cash is concerned but with one fair crop they will be able to reduce their obligations to quite an extent. I checked over the collateral we have from this bank and feel that it is of fairly good value. All the makers except . . . are land owners and reported to be good farmers. . . . 's wife owns a quarter section of land, free of encumbrance. This bank carried an account with the Merchants National Bank but it has been closed for some time. They report being very well satisfied with our service and had no complaint to make whatsoever. I am inclined to believe . . . is doing everything in his power to hold down loans and told me they are not making any loans at all, except in cases of extreme necessity and then only for feed and seed. The crops in this section were not a total failure as flax averaged very close to 7 bushels and some of the wheat went as high as 9 to 10 bushels. Higgins agreed to send in new statements of the directors and to send in a guarantee signed by them for $20,000. I think the old guaranty is for $10,000.

Since farming in this district during 1917, 1918, 1919, and 1920 was characterized by partial crop failures, the cashier had made every effort to secure his loans further. He had taken second mortgages, and when farmers became too deeply involved, he foreclosed. As a result, the bank had acquired title to real estate subject to existing first mortgages. Other real estate amounted to $1,500 in 1915; it was charged off in 1916; thereafter, it grew to $1,600 in 1917 and 1918; $2,100 in 1919; $6,600 in 1920; and $11,300 in 1921,[37] the banking house being carried at $5,200 in that year. The combination of other real estate and banking house was approximately equal to capital, surplus, and undivided profits. The bank was over-extended, loans were poor, and capital funds had been absorbed into other real estate.

Bank Chains

Although the country bank was primarily local in capitalization, as well as in deposits and loans, it always coöperated closely with its city correspondent. This correspondent performed various services, chiefly holding the country bank's balances and supplying it with loans. In general, this was purely a service relationship. There was no community of stock interest.

From the very beginning, however, bank chains sprang up in the territory. These chains purchased stock in existing banks and often founded new banks. The chains had a controlling interest in some banks, a minority interest in others. Where the chain was built around a city bank, the city bank acted as correspondent, holding the members' reserve balances, rediscounting their paper, making them short-term loans, and acting as sales agent for their real-estate mortgages. The city bank purchased securities and investments from member banks which had an excess and sold them to those which had a deficiency. If all the members had an excess, it sold them to other organizations.

Prominent among the bank chains in 1920 were Adam Hannah and Company; Ulland, Mealey, Carley Company; John F. Sinclair Company; Isaac Hazlett; Thomas Beiseker; John Birkholz; Leon N. Bolter Company; John W. Black Company; Sheldon Brothers; Ross-Davidson Company; and the Union Investment Company.[38]

It was common for a successful banker or business man, either directly or through a company, to establish or buy a small bank in some other town. In this manner one group often acquired interests in numerous banks. In fact, only a small proportion of the local banks were 100 per cent home-owned institutions. This interlocking stock ownership often existed strictly on an investment basis, the only activity of the outside stockholder being the reading of the annual report and the election of directors.

A more complex type of bank chain, however, developed at an early period. This was a company or partnership which purchased an interest in a chain of banks, established a city office, and, in addition to close business relations, exercised some degree of supervision over the member banks. To be sure, the fiction of local independence was preserved, and in many cases, as far as local business went, the apparent independence was actual.

An unfortunate example of a bank chain was Ulland, Mealey, Carley Company, organized in 1919 by J. S. Ulland of Fergus Falls, Minnesota, S. J. Mealey of Monticello, Minnesota, and J. R. Carley of Grand Forks, North Dakota. The original capital of $100,000 was contributed by the three incorporators, by C. B. Mills and G. L. Heegaard of Minneapolis, and by Otto Bremer of St. Paul.[39] The company eventually acquired control of 13 small country banks. The original capital, proving insufficient, was subsequently increased by contributions from the stockholders until by February, 1920, it had reached $250,000.[40] The company did not prove profitable and never paid a dividend.[41] By 1921 the members of the firm were ready to get out of the banking business. A portion of the banks was sold to Otto Bremer's Dakota Corporation and the remainder to other purchasers. In effect, the purchase price was paid to the unit banks in cash, and Ulland, Mealey, Carley received payment in poor assets taken out of the banks. Thus, the company went from banking to the liquidation of defaulted notes, second mortgages, and real estate.[42]

The company's next step was to buy control of the Farmers and Merchants State Bank of Savage, Montana. This venture cost the firm most of its remaining good assets. One of its deposits was made by the local county, against which county officials demanded that the bank pledge bonds as collateral, and since the bank had no such securities, it satisfied the county with the guaranty bond of a surety company. Before the surety company would write the bond, it insisted that the Ulland, Mealey, Carley Company guarantee it against loss by pledging its miscellaneous assets as security. When the bank failed as a result of an agricultural depression caused by a crop failure arising from a drought, the surety company paid the county and demanded payment from Ulland, Mealey, and Carley, and their unfortunate firm finally settled the matter by turning over all its assets to the surety company in return for a release.[43]

A very different tale is that of the Union Investment Company, which was organized by Dr. F. H. Wellcome of Granite Falls, Minnesota.[44] Dr. Wellcome was a man of some means. He had been trained in medicine and had opened a general practice in

Granite Falls.[45] From the beginning he took care of his own investments, and rumor had it that he would go just as far to make a loan as he would to answer a sick call. He was said to be a good doctor and a better banker. From his experience as a stockholder and officer in the bank run by Bert Winter at Granite Falls, he came to the conclusion that there should be money in operating a chain of banks, and he interested others in the idea. Thus, the Union Investment Company came into being late in 1903. Associated with him in this venture were the following: E. C. Warner of the Midland Linseed Oil Company; F. E. Kenaston, president of the Minneapolis Threshing Machine Company; S. A. Harris, president, and A. A. Crane, vice-president, of the National Bank of Commerce in Minneapolis; F. W. Lyman, in the terminal-elevator business; Bert Winter, a banker at Granite Falls; Porter J. McCumber, United States Senator from North Dakota; S. H. Bowman of the Bowman Lumber Company of Minneapolis; and Gilbert G. Thorne, vice-president of the National Park Bank of New York City. The president was Dr. Wellcome himself; the secretary and treasurer was Bert Winter.[46] The company started with a paid-in capital of $50,000 which was rapidly increased to $155,000. During the first year the company acquired an interest in 16 small country banks and by 1908 it had increased the number to 31. Capital, surplus, and undivided profits then aggregated $369,301. The total capital of the member banks was $662,500, of which the company owned $266,100.

By this time the Union Investment Company was conducting a general investment business of its own, buying bonds and warrants from dealers, making direct customer loans, and purchasing all types of paper from member banks. A part of these investments was resold on the open market; a part, where denominations and maturities were satisfactory, was sold to member banks; and a part was pledged as collateral for note issues which were sold to banks.[47] In such cases the collateral was held by the Union Investment Company, as trustee. Mr. Theodore Albrecht, who for some years had been the managing officer of the Citizens National Bank of Wahpeton, North Dakota, became secretary of the company on October 1, 1911, and a director in February, 1912. In February, 1918, he became vice-president and treasurer, and on February 1, 1921, president.

At the close of 1919, the company had a capital of $500,000, and surplus and undivided profits of $145,500. It was interested in 33 banks — 23 in Minnesota, 7 in Wisconsin, 2 in North Dakota, and 1 in Michigan.[48] A consolidated statement as of December 31, 1920, showed capital and surplus of $1,287,750, individual deposits of $3,869,000, time deposits of $9,698,900, and rediscounts of $87,800. Assets included local loans and discounts, $6,523,300; loans and discounts purchased from the Union Investment Company, $3,516,300; bonds, $2,415,400; liberty bonds, $320,000; due from banks, $1,713,800; cash, $409,500; and banking houses, $232,100.

The banks paid the company a service fee, which in 1920 amounted to $35,400. This fee, the management stated, never covered the costs involved, and the company never made a profit on investments sold to affiliates.[49] The deficit was covered by profits from dealings with non-member banks and from dividends received on bank stocks owned by the company. Under the conditions prevailing from 1903 through 1920, the company and its affiliated banks normally made profits and dividend payments were substantial.[50]

From its organization the Union Investment Company did not necessarily control its member banks; often it had only a small interest. Under such circumstances it was unable arbitrarily to determine uniform policies. In most cases the local management had complete control of the local business, although the company, through close attention and contact, stood ready to call to the attention of the local owner any dangerous tendencies. The general result was satisfactory, and the public received an excellent type of banking service.

There seems little question that the Union Investment Company was fortunate in possessing capable, conservative management. The central treasury possessed assets in addition to its bank stocks, and it acted to strengthen rather than to weaken its member banks. In addition, the location of its banks probably had much to do with its record. They were situated not in the specialized one-crop areas with their high risks, but in the diversified farming areas which normally had ample rainfall.

War-Time Agriculture, 1915–1920

The outbreak of the first World War did not immediately affect the situation in the Northwest, but eventually it resulted in an increasingly heavy demand for all types of products, both manufactured goods and raw materials, and an insistent call for larger and larger quantities of food. Prices started on a steady upward climb. Wheat prices in Minneapolis fluctuated from $0.89 to $1.66 in 1915; in January, 1917, they went to $2.00, and by August had reached $3.05 per bushel.[51] At this time the government stepped in and controlled wheat prices from September, 1917, to June, 1920. The price for No. 1 dark northern wheat was fixed at $2.21 a bushel in Minneapolis.[52]

The high price, plus the theory that it was patriotic to raise more wheat, caused a determined effort on the part of farmers to increase production. Government officials, bankers, business men, and farm leaders added their pleas to the cause. A conference was held on April 15, 1917, at Fargo, North Dakota, for the purpose of urging a greater acreage.[53] It was estimated that out of this conference grew another million acres of wheat in North Dakota alone. Such results encouraged other conferences. Many were held during 1917 and 1918, and the wheat acreage became steadily larger.

In 1917 production in the four wheat States — Minnesota, North and South Dakota, and Montana — amounted to 170,374,000 bushels; in 1918, 277,459,000 bushels; in 1919, 132,340,000 bushels; and in 1920, 143,648,000 bushels.[54] The value of all North Dakota farm products increased from $260,000,000 in 1915 to $638,000,000 in 1918.[55] That year the average per capita wealth in the entire United States was $1,956, whereas in North Dakota it was $2,966.[56]

Pressure to increase the raising of pork and its companion product, corn, was exerted with considerable success. In the same four States the production of corn in 1917 amounted to 191,922,000 bushels; in 1918, 229,484,000 bushels; in 1919, 225,692,000 bushels; and in 1920, 244,369,000 bushels.[57] This increase resulted from a larger acreage in the better farming regions where ample rainfall was assured. Many of the additional fields came from pasture lands which were plowed and cultivated. In the four States there were 59,566,142 acres of improved land in 1910; by 1920 the number had increased to 75,251,416 acres.[58] As we have seen, this increased acreage did not produce proportionately larger crops; but the soaring price of agricultural commodities sharply increased farm income.

The rapid rise in the price of farm products brought about a change in the methods of agriculture. Emphasis came to rest on the cash crop; side lines were abolished. The farmers thought that, with the price for wheat high, they could afford to rent land and to borrow money from the local bank to finance their operations. They could hire land plowed and prepared, buy the seed, and pay their bills in cash, and when the transactions were over, they would have a substantial profit.

There were two important technical developments during this period: the widespread use of the tractor and the growing popularization of the automobile. Both these developments added sharply to cash expenditures. The use of power equipment necessitated money for gasoline and oil and repairs. A large portion of this equipment was bought on credit. Spurred on by their own eagerness to make sales and by the competitive situation, the equipment companies offered machinery on liberal terms. With an eye to prospective profits as well as to their patriotic duty, farmers revolutionized their methods and became mechanized producers. The first result was entirely beneficial: the production per worker rose, total crop production increased moderately, and prices were high. The farmer who raised a hundred acres of wheat, reaped twenty bushels to the acre, and sold it at a price based on $2.21 a bushel found himself suddenly prosperous. True, he owed for his machinery and his automobile, and he had heavy cash operating costs, but he also had a cash surplus. This was something new in his experience.

The discovery of a cash profit in agriculture pushed land values into an upward spiral. Farmers became less anxious to sell their land; some, desiring to enlarge their operations, attempted to purchase land. This induced a steady increase in price, which for a period of time caused what may have been a reasonable capitalization of potential earning power. Eventually, speculators came into the picture. They purchased land with no intention of operating it and with no regard for its actual value, but merely with the idea of reselling it at a profit. Increasing land values created an illusory picture of prosperity. Many conservative farmers sold their land, taking a cash payment and a mortgage for the balance. Often, to secure funds for other ventures, they sold these mortgages to local banks or to dealers. Eventually those conservative farmers who had sold early in the period, becoming convinced that they had made a mistake, bought new lands at highly inflated prices. In the four States land values aggregated $2,878,860,211 in 1910; by 1920 they had increased to $6,952,986,047.[59]

Rising land values and the increasing turnover of land swelled the amount of farm mortgages. In Minnesota in 1910, farm mortgages amounted to $77,866,000, and to $254,475,000 by 1920; [60] in North Dakota they amounted in 1910 to $48,841,000 and in 1920 to $108,825,000; [61] in South Dakota they increased from $32,771,000 to $90,082,000; and in Montana, from $10,741,000 to $77,950,000. For the four States the total increase was from $169,221,000 to $530,-792,000.[62] Mounting mortgages added heavily to the load of the farming industry and burdened debtor farmers.

The period was marked by still another development, the steep climb of taxes. Most subdivisions of the government carried on local improvement programs financed by borrowed money, a procedure which benefited the immediate situation and postponed the inevitable day of payment. The farmers' tax burden soon became two or three times as heavy as in the prewar era.

The progress of the war boom in American industry caused a rapid, steady rise in the prices of the things which farmers purchased.[63] Manufactured foods, clothing, and supplies advanced. Farm machinery, automobiles, furniture, gasoline, oils, and binder twine became more expensive. Pressed on first by competition among the farmers themselves and then by the competitive demand of the cities, farm wages increased from the $16 to $20 a month, prevalent before the war, to $40 or $50.[64] Occasionally as much as $100 a month was paid in addition to room and board. Meanwhile, as we have seen, interest charges increased and taxes mounted.

THE DEMAND FOR MORTGAGE MONEY, 1915–1920

The demand for additional credit facilities did not become vociferous until the outbreak of the first World War. It became politically popular to "damn" the bankers and to urge political action, and various political groups sponsored the movement. In 1916 the Federal Farm Loan Act was passed, authorizing the establishment of twelve federal land banks and an indefinite number of joint stock land banks.[65] In 1915 Montana established a rural credit system, and South Dakota followed suit in 1917;[66] both plans provided for the sale of State bonds to provide funds for loans on mortgages.

There was a constant demand that local banks advance mortgage money, but the scarcity of deposits made it impossible for them to do this to any extent. In their attempts to obtain outside deposits they were handicapped because of the East's suspicions regarding the solvency of the local banks. In order to solve this problem a movement developed looking toward the State guarantee of bank deposits. While this was not approved by the majority of bankers, it was strongly favored by country bankers who desired to obtain outside deposits. The matter was bitterly debated on the lecture platform and in the newspapers. Most conservatives were violently opposed to it, but the liberals and the rural elements were devoted to it. It was overwhelmingly popular in the drought areas of the West.

On March 10, 1917, the State of North Dakota passed a law guaranteeing the deposits of State banks.[67] Under its provisions all deposits not otherwise covered by specific pledges of collateral were guaranteed by a Depositors Guaranty Fund Commission, which assured all depositors that they would receive 100 per cent of their money, according to contract. To this end, banks were assessed an annual fee of 1/20 of 1 per cent of their deposits.[68] Upon the closing of a bank, all deposits were to be paid immediately, as far as possible out of the liquid assets of the bank, and then, where necessary, out of the guaranty fund. When the cash in the fund was not sufficient, depositors were to receive 5 per cent warrants, which would be paid out of the first available income of the guaranty fund.[69] The country banks exploited this guaranty fully, and we find their advertisements in papers of the time offering 6 per cent on 6 to 12 months' certificates of deposit.[70] The advertisements state in large type that the banks were fully guaranteed.

The State of South Dakota also had a depositors' guaranty fund law, effective January 1, 1916.[71] This was similar to the North Dakota law, except that it provided for annual assessments of ¼ of 1 per cent.[72] The history of the South Dakota law up to 1920 shows it to have been relatively satisfactory. There were very few failures, and in all cases the depositors were paid 100 per cent.[73] Little strain was placed on the fund because in nearly every case of failure the bank was able to repay the fund. There were even certain nominal refunds to stockholders. It seemed as though the liberals and the farmers had been wiser than the conservatives and the financiers.

Although the country banks were heavy borrowers on balance from the city banks, there was a constant popular outcry in the country that the city banks instead of lending were draining money out of the country. This was a prevalent political philosophy and one of the tenets of the Non-Partisan League in North Dakota. In answer to this clamor the Non-Partisan League pledged itself to organize a State bank in North Dakota which would retain funds locally and which would loan sufficient amounts of money to farmers on real-estate mortgages. Early in 1919 the State Legislature authorized the incorporation of a bank with a capital of $2,000,000 to be subscribed by the State.[74] In order to raise the necessary funds, the State was to sell $2,000,000 in bonds, which were to be a direct obligation.[75] The interest and principal were to be paid from the earnings of the bank; if these were not sufficient, the State was to levy a tax to meet the deficit. The State Treasurer was authorized to supply cash out of general funds to meet any deficiency. An advance was to be repaid out of either the State tax or the excess earnings of the bank.

The idea of a State bank was nothing new in American history. The Vermont State Bank was functioning in 1806, the Bank of the State of South Carolina in 1812, the State Bank of Illinois in 1821, the Bank of Alabama in 1823, the State Bank of Indiana in 1834, and the Bank of the State of Arkansas in 1836. These are only samples; nearly every State at one time or another established or considered establishing a State bank.

When the bonds appeared, investors, suddenly wary of the political theories prevalent in North Dakota, ignored them. The Bank of North Dakota opened for business as planned and, because the law required the deposit of all township, school district, village, and county tax funds, its deposits were soon substantial.[76] Next the bank purchased the bonds from the State out of its deposits, thus supplying the State with funds.[77] The State cheerfully subscribed the $2,000,000 to the bank, and its operations continued, although there were those who alleged that it still had no capital.

The position of the Bank of North Dakota was not enhanced by the difficulties of the Scandinavian-American Bank of Fargo, control of which had been purchased by individuals associated with the Non-Partisan League.[78] This bank had a capital of $50,000 and a surplus of $10,000. Its stock had been bought by Leaguers and paid for out of funds borrowed from the Exchange National Bank of St. Paul on a pledge of stock of the Scandinavian-American Bank.[79] The Exchange Bank soon called the loan, which was thereupon transferred to the Mercantile State Bank of Minneapolis, which accepted it on the same basis.[80] It has since been rumored that the Mercantile received State funds for deposit as a reward for making this loan. At any rate, the loan eventually was taken out of the Mercantile and placed elsewhere. In spite of assistance and deposits from the Bank of North Dakota, the Scandinavian-American bank failed disastrously in February, 1921.[81]

Political feeling ran high over the question of the State Bank, and it developed into a political storm.[82] A law was initiated and passed by the voters, which specifically authorized the audit of the bank's books and permitted political subdivisions to carry their funds with private banks if they wished.[83] The division of the law permitting the withdrawal of funds from the bank took effect on November 2, 1920. An outflow of deposits commenced, and immediately the State Industrial Commission ordered the bank officials not to permit the withdrawal of money deposited before November 2, 1920.[84] However, they instructed the bank to permit the withdrawal of funds to meet current expenses. The result was that many political sub-divisions paid their current expenses out of funds on deposit with the bank and deposited incoming money in private banks.[85] As a combative measure, the State Industrial Commission then ordered the Bank of North Dakota to refuse to pay checks drawn by treasurers who were not making new deposits with the bank.[86]

When the bank was finally audited, it was disclosed that it had loaned to hard-pressed farmers and to favored banks on terms which could not be defended as wise and prudent. Past-due loans as of December 2, 1920, amounted to $1,405,438.[87]

The Non-Partisan League lost control of the State in October, 1921. Under the incoming administration the bank lost its importance and engaged in the farm-loan business, raising its funds through the sale of long-term, farm-loan bonds. Since the administration was then in conservative hands, a loud outcry soon proclaimed that farm loans in North Dakota were more difficult to obtain from the State Bank than from private banks.

A Foretaste of Trouble, 1920

Although during the early part of 1920 all surface indications pointed to continued prosperity, the Cassandras already were forecasting trouble. Articles in newspapers and periodicals directed attention to the fact that it was impossible to make money on farm land which cost between $300 and $400 an acre, and that farmers formerly prosperous on $1.00 wheat were now losing money on $3.00 wheat.[88] The blame was placed on land prices. It was argued that land could not be worth from $250 to $400 per acre when equally good land in other sections of the country was selling at much lower prices.[89] While the greatest rise in land values had occurred in Iowa and southern Minnesota, the Dakotas and Montana also had experienced sharp increases. Ignoring variations within each State, and taking 1912–1914 as 100, we find that the average value of farm land in 1920 in Minnesota was 213; in North Dakota, 145; in South Dakota, 181; and in Montana, 126.[90]

On January 10 it was reported that the Federal Farm Loan Board was giving attention to inflated land values.[91] At about the same time James B. Forgan came out with the warning that we were facing a depression.[92] F. M. Prince was quoted as saying, "We look for a reaction some time during the coming year of the activity of our industrial business. It will be necessary for commodities to get onto a lower level of prices before business conditions can be stable."[93] George M. Reynolds of the Continental and Commercial of Chicago said that now was the time to curb speculation, even if

FEDERAL RESERVE BANK OF MINNEAPOLIS, 1916

our foreign trade did suffer a decline.[94] Joseph French Johnson, dean of New York University's School of Commerce, stated that it was quite possible, if not probable, that within a year or two the country would be facing a period of painful and exasperating and disconcerting deflation and falling prices.[95] Mindful of forecasts, the city banks set about strengthening their position, but the country banks were unable to follow their example.

This fact in itself foreshadowed trouble, and already certain conditions were moving toward a crisis. The base price of No. 1 dark northern wheat was fixed at $2.21 a bushel, but the farmers were dissatisfied. They claimed that their costs were above this figure. The politicians, making use of this fact, took $5.00 wheat as a political slogan and encouraged farmers to hold out for that price.[96] There were other factors, too, which forced the farmers to hold their crops. Although, as we have seen, drought had thinned out the 1919 crop, the railroads, even under government control, were so short of rolling stock that the Ninth Federal Reserve District could not marshal enough freight cars to move the wheat to market.[97] Local elevators bulged with it, and the bulk of the crop had to stay on the farms. The same shortage of transportation curtailed the supply in the milling centers. Agricultural loans had to be carried forward.[98] Since there were no future sales available until June 15, 1920, the banks could not protect themselves. The 1920 wheat crop was only moderate in size, although it exceeded that of 1919. Because of the transportation tie-up, the 1920 crop came onto the market before the 1919 crop had been moved.

In its bulletin for February, 1920, the Minneapolis Federal Reserve Bank reported that the unfavorable transportation situation was the outstanding feature of current conditions.[99] It stated that 400 country elevators were closed to farmers because of their inability to move the grain, and that bank loans, 50 per cent greater than six months before, were not being liquidated. By April it reported that bank loans were rising and that the demand for credit was heavy.[100]

One factor contributing to the rising loans in country banks was the weather conditions in the winter of 1919–20. The cold was unusually severe, and stockmen were forced to buy feed for their cattle. It is estimated that during the winter more than $45,000,000 was expended in the Ninth Federal Reserve District for cattle feed.[101] A large proportion of the money was borrowed from the banks with cattle as security.

By September there was a national shortage of 250,000 box cars, and the grain carriers did not have a fair percentage of their own cars, for only 72 per cent of them were on their own tracks.[102] Moreover, repairs and maintenance on the railroads had been held at a minimum, and many of the existing cars were unfit for service.

Coincident with the rising volume of loans, there was a steady withdrawal of funds from banks in order to meet the customers' expenses. In October the Minneapolis Federal Reserve Bank reported that member banks' deposits were shrinking moderately.[103] On July 15, 1920, future trading in wheat was resumed.[104] In June, 1920, cash wheat sold at $3.10, and in September cash wheat sold at $2.68.[105]

In the face of the fact that wheat was not selling, the farmers were dissatisfied with the price. Farm organizations set $2.75 a bushel as the cost of raising wheat in most areas.[106] Interesting articles pointed out the statistical shortage of wheat in relation to previous demand, alleging that wheat prices must advance. During this period only a few people realized that export conditions prevailing before the war and in 1919 might not continue and that exports of foodstuffs in April, 1920, amounted to only $145,000,000, compared with $292,000,000 in April, 1919.[107] In September, meetings held in the Kansas City area urged farmers to hold their wheat for $2.77 a bushel.[108] Despite this publicity, wheat prices tended lower. In October, cash wheat's high price was $2.28¼, and in December it was $1.82⅛.[109] The lows were $1.97½ and $1.54.

A steady drain of cash forced the country banks to seek credit in the cities. Federal Reserve member banks borrowed heavily from the Federal Reserve Bank. Non-member banks called on their correspondents for accommodations. By November, Twin City bank loans to their country correspondents were $40,000,000 above normal, and country-bank deposits in city banks were $35,000,000 below normal.[110]

By May, 1920, general business in the cities had reached its peak and a recession developed.[111] While cessation of demand was almost complete, readjustment was rapid. When goods were not sold, factories closed and laid off their workers. Storekeepers who attempted to hold up their prices found that their competitors were marking everything down. Industrial prices fell into a rapid decline; widespread unemployment caused wage rates to fall; and by the close of the year costs were being brought into line with selling prices.

This city depression was accompanied with a choking-off of output, and by the very end of 1920 bank loans to city customers were dwindling.[112] The city banks were comparatively well fortified, since, in effect, their commercial deposits served to offset their commercial loans. They had loaned their customers funds to manufacture goods, and for the system as a whole these loans represented deposits. As business receded, customers, although they ceased borrowing, continued to manufacture their raw materials into salable goods. During this time deposits were drawn down, but as the goods were sold notes at the bank were paid. The net result was an automatic reduction of both assets and liabilities. Although the sales volume of industrial goods declined, it always remained substantial enough to create a mechanism for the liquidation of bank credit. At the same time, city firms continued to insist upon collections for goods sold in the country. Cash, therefore, flowed from the country districts to the cities, but little returned to the country in payment for crops.[113] The city banks found the strain most severe during the summer and fall of 1920. Extended to their utmost, they were forced to go to the Federal Reserve for money.

On September 12, 1919, the First National Bank of Minneapolis had rediscounted with the Minneapolis Federal Reserve Bank $2,101,000 in paper; by November 15, 1920, this figure was $27,509,482.[114] The Northwestern National Bank on the former date had rediscounted $1,931,000; by November its figure was $16,637,000.[115] The Federal Reserve Bank likewise had felt the strain. On August 1, 1919, its loans to members amounted to $13,000,000, and to the other Federal Reserve Banks, $17,000,000.[116] By August 1, 1920, loans to members had increased to $90,000,000, and the Bank itself had borrowed $13,000,000 from other Federal Reserve Banks.[117] The whole Federal Reserve System was hard pressed, for in 1920 its gold reserves fell below 42 per cent.[118]

During the summer and fall of 1920, the agricultural depression deepened. By July the market for raw wool was practically non-existent, and there were large stocks in the United States, England, Australia, and New Zealand.[119] The mills, faced with canceled orders, ceased buying raw materials. Cattle and hog prices decreased; and, despite transportation difficulties, all grain went down steadily.

Nevertheless, banks experienced few losses in 1920, largely because they did not force the collection of loans. In North Dakota, South Dakota, and Montana a few banks closed, but, considering the number of banks in the Ninth Federal Reserve District, failures were not excessive. A total of only 35 closed their doors during the year, and they were small institutions with a combined capital of $1,151,000 and combined deposits of $11,704,000.[120] That rapid deflation in the face of inability to market crops was causing severe losses still was not recognized.

In the East industrialists became perturbed. It was pointed out that the prosperity of the past few years had been based on European buying, which had been financed by borrowed funds. It was recognized that Europe could not continue to buy unless the United States was willing either to buy foreign goods in exchange or to continue its loans abroad. Since the idea of lowering tariffs and permitting the import of European goods was not popular, most plans to revive trade centered in some loan scheme. George M. Reynolds, president of the Continental and Commercial National Bank, in discussing the problem, stated that while the general public was lukewarm toward foreign loans, business men realized their necessity. If foreign loans were not made, our foreign trade would break down with unfortunate results.[121] To be sure, a few hardy souls pointed out that a loan was not the final answer to any problem. The banks of the Northwest, however, were not immediately concerned with theoretical discussions of foreign trade. All they were trying to do was to stay open and serve their customers.

During the latter part of the year continuous pressure was exerted by the decline of deposits. On September 12, 1919, total deposits in the First National Bank of Minneapolis amounted to $80,085,000; by November 15, 1920, they had declined to $62,626,000.[122] The Northwestern National Bank on September 12, 1919, had deposits of

FIRST NATIONAL BANK OF MINNEAPOLIS, 1912

$57,209,000; by November 15, 1920, $50,355,000.[123] City-bank deposits reached their depths and loans their peak late in the fall of 1920. Then city customers commenced to repay loans, and the general decline of activity lessened the demand for funds. At the same time, some pressure was put on the stronger country banks to reduce their loans. Few country banks, however, were in any condition to make payments, for their customers had not sold their crops and transportation was still far from satisfactory. While the country-bank situation was acknowledged to be dangerously extended, the year ended with only a few bank failures. No one seemed to realize how perilous was the future.

CHAPTER IV

AGRICULTURAL DEFLATION 1920–1929

Beginning of Agricultural Deflation, 1920–1924

The year 1920 proved most disappointing to agriculture in the Ninth Federal Reserve District. As discussed in Chapter III, during its early months prices had been high, but inadequate transportation had kept marketings low.[1] Meanwhile, as we have seen, Europe sharply reduced her buying of agricultural produce, raw materials, and semi-manufactured goods.[2] Exports declined; agricultural surpluses developed; prices fell steadily. These conditions carried over into 1921. Again crops failed; exports dwindled; agricultural surpluses mounted. Prices scarcely met marketing costs. In fact, farmers used corn as fuel.[3] Their meager cash income had to be hoarded for the most necessary living expenses.

In 1910, 50.9 per cent of the farms in North Dakota had been mortgaged; by 1920 the percentage had increased to 75.9 per cent. In Montana it was 64.6 per cent in 1920 as compared with 21.1 per cent in 1910; in South Dakota, 63.1 per cent as compared with 38.2 per cent; and in Minnesota, 56.3 per cent as compared with 46.3 per cent.[4] This change in the number of farms mortgaged, plus a rapid increase in the size of the mortgages, put a heavy burden on operating farmers, especially since a corresponding rise had occurred in taxes.[5] Confronted with sharply declining income, farmers failed to pay their taxes and meet the payments on their mortgages. Innumerable mortgages went into default. This fact, added to a widespread realization of existing agricultural difficulties, lessened the demand for farm mortgages. The dollar value of mortgages sold in 1921 was only 58 per cent of that of 1920.[6]

Favorable weather conditions in the spring and summer of 1922 fostered good crops. In the four northwestern States — Minnesota, North Dakota, South Dakota, and Montana — yields were excellent.[7]

Unfortunately, crops in other countries were likewise bountiful. Exports of wheat dropped to about 50 per cent of their 1921 level, and prices tumbled.[8] In September, wheat was quoted at $1.08 in Minneapolis. In 1923 the crops were not large, although total farm income in the Ninth Federal Reserve District was estimated to be $68,000,000 greater than in 1922.[9] The farmers' income, however, remained pitifully small, and depression continued to haunt the country.

Meanwhile, agricultural depression was forcing farmers to cut expenses. In an attempt to minimize cash expenditures, they defaulted on interest, principal, and taxes, and refused to spend money for anything they could produce on the farm or do without. They either cut wages sharply or discharged their hired men. Farm wages decreased steadily during 1921 and 1922, but in 1923 they strengthened sharply because the revival of prosperity in the cities created a strong demand for labor at high prices.[10] This competition resulted in the freezing of rates for farm workers at a level which was not justified by conditions on the farm.

Since they had expanded their operations, the farmers were handicapped in reducing expenses. If they had land, they had either to cultivate or sell it. The market for land had practically vanished, and any sale would force the realization of a loss. They continued, therefore, to operate on a large scale and to hope for a good crop and high prices.

Agricultural conditions during the first seven months of 1924 were extremely bad. Farm purchasing power was reported to be lower than at any similar period in ten years.[11] Taxes and interest remained high, and the farmers continued to default on their bank loans and mortgages. At that time, however, a glimmer of improvement in agricultural conditions became apparent. The world-wide wheat failure and the shortage of other crops, coupled with general prosperity in the cities, forced the prices of agricultural products upward. (Wheat reached $1.77 a bushel in Minneapolis.) The Ninth Federal Reserve District was extremely fortunate in having ample rainfall and large crops to swell farm income.[12] For the first time since 1918 the average farmer had cash in his pocket. True, if he paid his taxes and some of his overdue installments, he would have nothing left, but at least this crop supplied him with the means to settle a portion of his debts. On an operating basis, farmers were prosperous in 1924, and retail trade was very active. Those who were out of debt enjoyed the full effect of this prosperity, and debtor farmers set about meeting their obligations.

FARMERS BANK, 1920–1923

The experience of the Farmers Bank during this period is typical of a majority of country banks. This community had basked in prosperity during the years 1915 through 1917, but crop failures in 1918 and 1919 had weakened the position of the farmers and created problems. On May 10, 1920, the cashier wrote to Leeman, vice-president of the First National Bank of Minneapolis:[13]

I certainly appreciate your favor of the 6th and can assure you that I will reciprocate with a big fat deposit this fall. The last week has been excellent for farming work and they have all been hitting the ball. They have from ten to one hundred acres of wheat in and with favorable weather this week, 65% of the wheat should be in the ground. It will, however, take until May 25th before it can all be gotten in. We have had another soaking rain this morning that will delay the work for to-day. It certainly is gratifying to see the moisture come so easily as it has this spring. The indications for a big crop are good, in fact, the best I have ever seen since I came here. If the promises of the spring materialize, we will collect a load of money this fall, and you may be sure that we are not going to let everybody else get their first. This is one time when we will be on the ground floor and I will do nothing but collect if given the opportunity. A credit extended again will be on a different plan altogether and we certainly are not going to set anyone up in business from now on.

On August 25, 1920, the cashier wrote the following:[14]

We are enclosing herewith our C/D for $5,000 with collateral aggregating $7,961 and will be obliged to you if you will place proceeds to our credit for 30 days as our threshing season is beginning, and we will need this amount for a few days until grain commences to come in. A few of the earlier fields have been threshed, and have turned out fully as well as we anticipated, and we feel assured that within the next sixty days that the money we have been obliged to loan to get this crop will be returned to us in at least double or triple amount. It will surely be a pleasure for us to take care of our obligations with you.

On August 30, 1920, the cashier wrote again:[15]

I know our loan is very high with you but if I did not know that we will be able to pay you back this fall I would not have asked you for another 5M the other day. We must, however, see to it that the grain is cut and harvested and it takes money to do it. The farmers are now unable to get credit with the local dealers for twine and repairs, so it is up to us to get it for them. The crop is turning out fully as well as we expected. In fact, it is better than we had hoped for. The wheat that has been threshed so far has gone 15 bu. to the acre and I know that better yields will show up when they get to threshing up north of . . . . Our south territory this year will raise a money crop for the first time since 1916 and farmers that we have carried through the last four years will be able to cut their debts to us at least one half. We will come first this year. Other years we have let them pay off their store and other bills, and in some cases they have bought automobiles or tractors. This year, however, we must be first all around and no one will be allowed to settle any bills unless we say so. We have taken good care of our customers during these years and they cannot blame us if we collect this year. If they do, they can take their business elsewhere and pay us off. We won't get sore now no matter who offers us our money. I don't want to go through another grilling like I have passed through the last four months.

The pressure on the Farmers Bank still continued to grow during the summer and fall of 1920. This territory had a better than average crop; better, in fact, than in most portions of the wheat area. This made the bank willing to extend accommodations, and its loans continued to accumulate. During the period immediately following the harvest, prices were fair, but the farmers, believing that prices were going to advance, were unwilling to sell their grain. As it happened, however, during the latter part of the year prices fell steadily.

On December 1, 1920, the cashier wrote to Leeman:[16]

We have been urging the farmers to sell their wheat but very few are willing and it is a hard matter to make them do it against their will, in fact some of them ask us to make them sell if we can. Now we have not as yet taken any drastic measures to force them but we are making it plain that we cannot allow them to hold after January 1st. If I had known, they all say that now, we would have forced collections when they threshed, so many factors were against it at that time, the farmers had to plow and help each other thresh, so that they had little or no time to haul grain and when they began wheat was dropping every day. It is going to be expensive plowing if wheat don't came back a little. I think that the farmers have made up their minds that the price will not go back to $2 and if such a thing should happen that it would go back to around $1.50 here or more, they would all sell. There is a lot of farmers who won't even sell enough to pay their taxes and interest that is due.

On December 10, 1920, the cashier wrote again:[17]

I have your favor of the 8th and appreciate very much the spirit of your letter, but if you could sit here Mr. Leeman and pay all the withdrawals we have had, you would have to be some collector to keep up with the time. We have made one mistake and that was when we let the farmers plow their ground, we should have pounded them on the back like we intended to do but the newspaper propaganda, together with the advice from the Non-partisans to hold their wheat made the situation difficult to handle without being lynched. It seems so as if everything was against us this fall, we are however going to get in some money around here this fall, and unless they draw all their deposits out of here, we will be able to pay you some the next 15 days. It is Hell all around but I don't see where it helps matters much to criticize now what could have been done, we are hogging every cent we can and trying to get in all we can without rocking the boat too much.

On December 23, 1920, the cashier wrote to Leeman as follows:[18]

We are sending you under separate cover collateral to cover our C/Ds. We have been getting in some collections but the withdrawals are so heavy that we cannot keep up with the collections and the farmers are hard to get in. You hear this talk from nearly everyone I presume so it is getting to be an old story with all of us. We have started suit against two of our best customers to see if we cannot inject some fear into the balance of our customers so that they will pay some attention to us. Most of them are willing to do what is right but there are others who think that they will just let us go the limit with them and they will stand law suits of all kinds in order to hold their grain and that doesn't get us our money and just makes matters worse but we have gone after two of them that we know can pay and there is no use trying to sue a man from whom you cannot realize some money. We have tried to impress on their minds since early this fall that we wanted our money and we have never offered any advice as to the best way in holding of wheat as nobody but a fool would come right out and say, if I know that, I would not be here in . . . . Now, we have about $50,000 in farm loans and warrants that if we could sell and get our money we could pay you at least $10,000 of our bills payable and my note for $6,050. We are unable to float loans and what we have sold, have not been paid for. I sold about $8,000 in warrants in Wisconsin but it is a drop in the bucket. I wish that you would try and see if you can place some of our warrants for me and also if you could get the Minneapolis Trust Company to take some of our loans, you could get some of your money that way. What money we collect in from grain must be kept as a reserve with you to pay our drafts. It is no easy matter to keep going when you get hit like we have the last 40 days. We have been fairly comfortable all fall till the last 40 days and thought we would be able to pay you all up but I think you know by now that we will not be able to pay you in full now or later this winter.

We are making all our farmers who have no loans (mortgages) on their farms take out loans and pay us up and they are willing to do it. We can raise quite a lot of money that way and will keep on working on it till we can get our paper in such shape that you or anyone else will be glad to take it off our hands as collateral or in payment of our debts. If I were the only one that was in bad shape at this time, I would resign my position and say that I was not made to run a bank but when I look around and see that bankers who always have been in fine shape up to the present time are in about the same shape I think that I better stay and work this matter out and with proper cooperation, I can, but it is impossible to do anything unless you can have that. You have done more for me than anyone and I won't forget, but if I get through this and can keep going, I will never be a borrower for my customers. These are times when real bankers are made and I would like very much to stay and see it through because I know now that I am not such a good banker as I thot I was or else I would not have gone out last spring and borrowed money to loan out for feed and seed. There is, however, one thing that I have not done and that is that I have never financed any deal for non-essentials such as automobiles and land deals.

Paul Leeman replied: [19]

The Minneapolis Trust Company would not be interested in taking on any loans in the . . . territory at the present time as they are having their hands full in taking care of their renewals without forming any new connections.

The Farmers Bank stayed open during 1920 only with the greatest difficulty. Individual deposits, which on May 4, 1920, had amounted to $88,100, had declined by April 15, 1921, to $67,600. Demand certificates had declined from $18,600 to $3,000. Collections were poor, and the bank was forced to increase its loans and discounts. On balance the bank had lost cash, and bills payable had increased from $30,000 to $72,500.[20]

The situation did not improve in 1921. On August 5, the cashier wrote:[21]

We are aware of the fact that our line with you is a most liberal one but we will pay this fall, and I don't see where a small amount of $2,500 should be denied; more so in view of the fact that we are putting up as collateral farm loans, not farmers' notes. We are getting time on twine but repairs and some help must be paid for in cash and we have a large clientele of farmers to look after. We are not loaning a cent to anyone for anything but twine, repairs and some hired help that comes here for a few days and then leaves again.

On October 12, 1921, he wrote again:[22]

I am certainly glad you are going to help us in getting a loan through the War Finance Corporation and I shall appreciate it if you will use it in our favor in order to get our application through as quickly as possible. Kindly see them if you will and have them send me the necessary blanks. No wheat has been sold for the last ten days owing to the dropping price. Today is the first money we will get from the sale of wheat again as it has been going up the last couple of days.

This loan from the War Finance Corporation was refused, but the bank finally obtained $22,150 from that source. It was not enough, however, to strengthen the bank, and on April 24, 1922, Leeman commented in a memorandum:[23]

At a conference with Semingson of the Bank of North Dakota, Porter of the Guaranty Commission, and Frederick and Adam Hannah, it was agreed if the Hannah interests would raise 25M to be used for their fourteen North Dakota banks carrying accounts with us, the Guaranty Commission would advance 25M and we would advance 50M, the collateral for the $75M advanced by the Guaranty Commission and this bank to be selected by either our representative or a representative of the Examiner's Department in North Dakota. We are to hold the collateral for our own bank and for the Guaranty Commission. Hannah estimates $25M will see his banks thru. . . . In addition to advances we have made to the different Hannah banks, the Market State Bank is carrying $80M paper and the State Deposit Bank $250M. Both of these banks have instructions from the Clearing House Examiner they are not to make any further advances on North Dakota paper. The money we have agreed to advance them is not to be used except in cases of emergency in paying off their time deposits.

Things went from bad to worse, and in October, 1922, the cashier was replaced.

The 1922 crop did not supply money for liquidation, and the bank's quandary grew. On November 29, 1922, the new cashier wrote to Leeman:[24]

We have your letter of the 27th inst. and your collect wire of today in regard to overdraft of $350 and unpaid drafts for $118.35 and $151. The wire arrived too late for a reply to reach you in business hours today. This overdraft was occasioned, as you know, by our entire balance with you of $5200 being applied on our Bills Payable when our account was garnisheed for $1700 C/D by Swan Sigford, attorney for Quale estate. Only a small percentage of this $5200 was represented by collections on your collateral and the taking of this amount of our reserve put us in a hole from which, so far, we have been unable to recuperate. We have repeatedly asked you people to reloan us part of this $5200 but have met with refusal in each instance. We know all about the collateral being tied up and all that, but nevertheless feel that there must be some way to adjust this in fairness to us. A few hundred dollars means a good deal to us at present, and in view of the circumstances above mentioned, we trust that you will show some leniency in the matter of this overdraft and give us a little time to recover from this blow below the belt. It is our intention to send our remittances to you again as soon as danger of further garnishments is past, but we can hardly be blamed for protecting ourselves the best we know how for the time being. As I understand it, I was put in here to keep this business going, and if possible to get it back on a firmer basis. So far we have kept going and have straightened out a good many tangles caused by mismanagement but it is plain that we need coöperation in order to continue on the path we have started upon.

C. B. Brombach, an officer of the First National Bank of Minneapolis, replied:[25]

We appreciate fully that the garnishment tied you up. However, there was practically nothing for us to do but to apply the amount on your loan rather than let someone else take the money out of the bank. As far as your being afraid of another garnishment is concerned, the account now shows an overdraft of around $650 and if you merely send in this amount there would be enough to clear the overdraft on our books and nothing left for a garnishment. Will you please give this your attention.

No progress was made by the bank in 1923. On July 30 a field examiner for the First National Bank of Minneapolis reported as follows:[26]

I don't know whether or not these fellows have reported crop conditions in vicinity to you as they pictured them to me or if you have received a report from here, but I do know they are going to be greatly disappointed. Examined wheat fields from 10 miles south of here to a point 12 miles north of Corinth. They have straw for a 20 to 25 bushel average but if I know anything about black rust at all, which I believe I do, then the wheat crops in this vicinity are, with the exception of a field now and then already matured, damaged at least from 25% to 40% and I figure this is conservative. It is possible of course that I may be mistaken and I hope I am, but right now I am satisfied that when they start threshing this 20 to 25 bushels crop the people are talking of, it will have shrunk to an average of 10 to 12 bushels, at best, rusted grain. These same conditions must extend to the north clear to the Canadian line and a considerable distance west.

When the crop was finally threshed, the yield was below even the most pessimistic forecast. Prices were low, and it was almost impossible to make collections. Until 1920 the bank's statement seldom showed "Other Real Estate," and when it did this item was quickly eliminated. In May, 1920, it had $3,000 in Other Real Estate. By September 6, 1921, primarily as a result of forcing collections, this figure had increased to $17,100; by July 30, 1923, it had reached $33,300. Notes Payable were $121,500.[27] During this entire period Capital and Surplus approximated $12,000. Toward the end of 1923 the bank closed for liquidation.

THE EFFECT OF DEFLATION ON COUNTRY BANKS

The country banks had loaned liberally to the farmer, and as we have seen, the fall of 1921 found them with three years' unpaid loans on their hands. Their most diligent efforts to collect met with scant success. All they could do was to exert pressure and occasionally squeeze out a modest payment. All too frequently the bank not only had to take notes for the interest on a loan; it even had to advance money in order to keep farmer and farm together, for where the farmer had become too involved in debt, the bank would be forced to take a loss if it closed him out. The most the bank could do was to attempt to acquire additional collateral.

At the same time, the country bank was confronted with steadily declining deposits. Solvent customers operating at a loss continually withdrew funds, and every day saw an outward flow of cash. Deposits had reached a peak in February, 1920; thereafter, in country banks in the Ninth Federal Reserve District as a whole they declined at an average rate of one per cent a month until December 31, 1921.[28] At first the banks met the withdrawals by selling marketable securities, but these soon came to an end. Next they borrowed from the Federal Reserve Bank or from their city correspondents, thus shifting part of the strain to the city banks.[29] Until the city customers started to repay loans in 1921, the city banks were forced to borrow heavily from the Minneapolis Federal Reserve Bank. Country-bank borrowings at the Federal did not slacken. The Federal Reserve tightened its requirements, taking government bonds at the market instead of at par as had been its custom.[30] Nevertheless, it had to borrow from other Federal Reserve Banks. Many country banks soon exhausted their collateral eligible for discount with the Federal Reserve. Unfortunately, most of their assets consisted of items not eligible for rediscount; and, when they were unable to obtain further funds, it appeared that many of them would be forced to close their doors.

There was a widespread feeling, however, that if the country banks could stay open and meet withdrawals, the situation would right itself. In few cases was failure due to runs; rather there was a steady shrinking of deposits and an overload of assets which were not liquid. Real runs seldom developed, except when there was reason to suspect that the bank was about to close. The nearest thing to a run was the tendency of outside money to leave the territory — a serious matter for many country banks. The stability of local deposits, however, was amazing. Citizens, seldom doubting their banks, left their deposits undisturbed. Local withdrawals were caused primarily by the fact that farmers were operating at a loss and had to withdraw funds to cover their deficits.

The country banks' most pressing problem during this period was the raising of funds to meet the steady withdrawals. This was complicated by their inability to make local collections. The banks were constantly forced to advance more money to their debtors in order to keep them operating. Although this looked like sending good money after bad, it was necessary, for the banks' only hope lay in keeping their debtors farming until they had harvested a good crop which could be sold at a fair price.

Investment Difficulties

Since few country banks during the early 'twenties had either government or other high-grade bonds in any quantity, this item was not important. If bonds were held, they usually were pledged as security and therefore were not available for conversion into cash. In addition, the bond market was so frequently depressed that even high-grade bonds often sold at a considerable discount.

In some respects, second-grade bonds were a more satisfactory investment. Improved earnings in the cities during the latter part of the 'twenties strengthened the market for second-grade bonds, many of which worked out satisfactorily. Despite the poor reputation of first mortgages as bank investments, they made a surprisingly good showing, particularly where they had been made in amounts moderate in relation to land values. In many cases foreclosure was necessary, but the ultimate realization was substantial. The main drawback was their lack of liquidity and their slow marketability.

It was the loans and discounts in the country banks that caused the most trouble. As we have pointed out, this type of investment was commercial in name only. Most of it depended for repayment on the reaping of a successful crop. Its security could not be levied upon without crippling the farmer, and too often the security proved insufficient.

Second mortgages were taken to reinforce the bank's position, a practice with disastrous consequences. After foreclosure the bank bought in the land, subject to the first mortgage, thereby becoming, instead of a creditor, an equity owner bound to apply its own funds to the payment of taxes and the interest and principal payments on the first mortgage.

THE SEARCH FOR LIQUIDITY

During this period country banks were confronted with dwindling deposits, an increased demand for loans, and complete inability to obtain repayment. They sold their few bonds and borrowed from their correspondent banks. They attempted to sell their real-estate mortgages, but to their consternation the private market had vanished. The most pressing need was a source of ready cash. Under these circumstances it was felt that every effort should be made to thaw out the banks.

By July, 1921, a pool had been organized by Twin City and eastern banks to loan funds to country banks on the security of assets not eligible for rediscount.[31] This was a step in the right direction, but it was not sufficient. Country banks, not only in the Ninth Federal Reserve District but also all over the nation, were in distress. A cry went up from both banking and farm organizations for government help, and rural politicians sponsored such a movement.

Accordingly a plan was brought forth, that of utilizing the War Finance Corporation, which had been created during the War to assist reconstruction through the financing of foreign trade. Its operations had been suspended in May, 1920, but it was now revived to meet the emergency. The Agricultural Credits Act of August 24, 1921, authorized it to sell bonds guaranteed by the government and to advance the proceeds to banks which had made agricultural loans.[32] Mr. M. O. Grangaard was in charge of the Minneapolis office.[33] The War Finance Corporation announced that its advances were to be made for not more than one year, either on the banks' notes secured by collateral or through the rediscount of endorsed paper.[34] The corporation took every precaution to secure itself against loss; it intended merely to provide liquid funds for the banks and not to absorb their losses. The first loan in this district was made on November 7, 1921.[35] By May, 1923, the corporation had advanced $20,729,685 in North Dakota alone.[36] Frozen but solvent banks rushed in to borrow. With the War Finance Corporation functioning, the pool to loan on ineligible assets organized by the bankers withdrew from active operation except to liquidate its loans.[37]

While the War Finance Corporation remedied many cases, it refused to make any loans secured by real-estate mortgages. This was a severe handicap to banks with funds invested in this type of security, for the vicissitudes of agriculture had ruined the market for farm mortgages. This situation was cared for to some extent by governmental agencies. The South Dakota Rural Credits Commission sold State bonds and loaned the proceeds on mortgages. By the end of 1920 it had some $29,000,000 in loans outstanding.[38] The St. Paul Federal Land Bank loaned $1,000,000 a month during 1921, and the Bank of North Dakota continued to loan moderately.[39]

The country banks, however, were embarrassed because, when mortgages were in good standing, they could make little effort to have them paid, and the governmental agencies insisted on making new loans direct to the farmers instead of buying farm mortgages from the banks. Most banks which had mortgages tried to make it worth while for the farmers to refinance their loans with the governmental agencies. The joint stock land banks, the federal land banks, insurance companies, and various State rural credit organizations made loans to farmers even though valuations were reduced. Thus, the banks tended to work out of first mortgages. In many cases this involved a considerable loss. When the mortgage was excessive in amount, it had to be reduced until the lender, after due consideration of the agricultural depression and reduced land values, would buy it.

If a farmer indebted to a bank on a current basis could not pay out of his income, he was urged to settle his current bills by borrowing money on his land. In this way some progress was made toward liquidation, but when, as in many cases, the existing mortgage was greater than the current value of the land, this procedure was of little use. In such cases the only alternatives were foreclosure or the voluntary waiving of interest and scaling of principal. The banker went over his loans to discover which debtors had property on which they could borrow money. Whenever he discovered a man with unpledged property, he insisted on his obtaining money from outside sources. The banks acted as agents in approaching private investors, insurance companies, trust companies, and joint stock land banks to persuade them to loan money. Eventually, they worked out means of approaching the federal and State mortgage agencies. Whenever they could float a new mortgage or obtain an increase in an old one, they applied the proceeds toward payments of the customer's notes at the bank.

The State of Minnesota had never had any State agencies to aid rural financing, but both farmers and bankers now favored the adoption of some such system. The farmers hoped that it would enable them to obtain more liberal loans at lower cost; the bankers thought that it would supply borrowers with funds to pay their bank loans. In the middle of 1923, Minnesota established the Minnesota Rural Credits Bureau. With the first issue of bonds in July, 1923, the State entered the farm-mortgage business.[40]

The activities of the multiple federal and State agencies making loans and refinancing farm mortgages tended to thaw out the situation, but in the country, contrary to frequent statements, little real progress was made. Debts were refinanced or changed from one lender to another, but they were not liquidated to any great extent. On June 30, 1920, total loans and discounts in country banks in the Ninth Federal Reserve District had amounted to $1,137,000,000; on June 30, 1923, this aggregate had been reduced to $957,000,000. At first glance this comparison indicates a considerable repayment; a closer examination reveals that $66,200,000 had been eliminated by the closing of banks, $50,000,000 had been charged off as losses by operating banks, and $23,000,000 had become Other Real Estate. Only $41,007,000 actually had been repaid.[41] In the refinancing of farm mortgages during this period the creditors so often had to take a loss by waiving interest and reducing principal that the volume of mortgages tended to decline. The numerous instances in which farmers turned over their property in settlement of their debts or lost their land through foreclosure also tended to reduce the reported indebtedness. Nevertheless, the accumulation of unpaid interest, the funding of miscellaneous debts, and the borrowing to cover operating losses evened the score. Little change was apparent in the total of the mortgage debt.

From the wave of settlements and foreclosures emerged a constantly rising percentage of tenant farmers.[42] Many an owner struggling with a heavy mortgage concluded that he could do better as a tenant, accepted foreclosure, and occupied the land during the year of redemption without even paying the taxes. Many used this right in negotiating a favorable lease on the farm.

Not until 1923 did Congress attempt to remedy a fundamental defect in the credit system, the lack of provision for intermediate loans. In that year it liberalized the Federal Reserve System and provided for 12 federal intermediate credit banks with capital subscribed by the United States Government.[43] These associations were to sell debentures guaranteed by the government and loan the proceeds to farmers for intermediate periods. The act also extended the life of the War Finance Corporation.[44]

Banks borrowed directly from the Federal Reserve Bank, their correspondent banks, and the War Finance Corporation, and indirectly from intermediate credit banks. They attempted to refund their farm mortgages with the various State and federal mortgage agencies. This program was well advanced by the end of 1923, but inevitable losses commenced to appear. Most refinancing by banks was merely a method of temporarily obtaining cash. Losses could not be avoided when loans were inadequately secured. Unfortunately, depressed farming conditions and low farm income made many farmers who had been considered perfectly solvent unable to pay their debts. The collateral — crops, machinery, cattle, and so on — was not sufficient to cover the principal.

Deflation was progressing steadily in spite of attempts to keep the situation liquid. The War Finance Corporation, the federal intermediate credit banks, the federal land banks, the joint stock land banks, and the rural credit systems in the Dakotas and Minnesota poured funds into the territory to help banks. They performed an outstanding service, but the progressive liquidation of agriculture and country banking kept forcing the weaker banks to close. Bankruptcy among the farmers soared, and innumerable compromise settlements had to be arranged between farmers and their creditors.[45]

The outlook darkened so rapidly that the elaborate machinery which had so lavishly been established to provide liquidity seemed suddenly inadequate, and new agencies were planned. Early in 1924 the Agricultural Credit Corporation was founded by a group of city bankers.[46] Mr. C. T. Jaffray was chairman of the board and Mr. Arthur P. Kemp was president. Mr. Kemp, born in Chicago in 1881, had been on the staff of the First National of Chicago, had joined the Auburn Automobile Company in 1919 as vice-president and treasurer, and had become its president in 1921.[47] The new corporation functioned by selling debentures to city banks and loaning the proceeds to solvent country banks which could not readily obtain funds from other sources.

By November 30, 1924, the federal and the joint stock land banks had loaned $181,205,000 in the four States of Minnesota, North Dakota, South Dakota, and Montana[48] without improving conditions or stopping bank failures.

The 1924 harvest was generally known as "the bankers' crop," for it served to thaw out agricultural conditions. The first effect of the bountiful crop and high prices was a rapid increase in rural deposits.[49] Country bankers began to pay current borrowings from city banks, the Federal Reserve Bank, and government agencies.[50] At the same time, the more solvent farmers settled their bank notes. As the liquidation became general, country-bank deposits piled up sharply and discounts dropped to a minimum.[51] The day of settlement was at hand, and creditors insisted on final payment.

Since an emergency no longer existed, the Agricultural Credit Corporation retired from active business. Mr. C. T. Jaffray stated that the corporation had assisted 250 banks and helped 30 to reopen during its short life.[52] It collected its loans without loss and thereafter devoted its efforts to encouraging diversified farming in the wheat areas by loaning money for cattle-raising.[53]

The War Finance Corporation, which had greatly aided banks in this area, also proceeded to liquidate and on January 6, 1925, refunded its capital to the government.[54] It still had some $62,623,000 outstanding in loans which represented profit on its national operations.[55] Both Mr. Kemp and Mr. Grangaard joined the staff of the First National Bank of Minneapolis.[56]

The satisfactory agricultural conditions in the fall of 1924 created a mechanism for final debt settlement. The banks refused to renew notes, insisting on payment. Solvent debtors paid up; legal proceedings were instituted against the others. Foreclosures multiplied; chattels were sold to satisfy judgments; and agricultural bankruptcies increased.[57] Banks were forced to realize their losses, for both State and national examiners, intent on a thorough housecleaning, insisted that realized losses be charged off and reserves established against doubtful assets.

LOSSES IN COUNTRY BANKS, 1920–1924

The country banks made little effort to collect in 1920, for they were unaware of how steadily losses were creeping up. In 1921 efforts to collect were more determined, but little cash was obtained. A few mortgages were foreclosed and the property bought in. In 1922 and 1923 Other Real Estate increased steadily. By 1924 the banks were frantically trying to collect, and Other Real Estate was mounting precipitously. Of course, losses were not immediately apparent, for Other Real Estate was carried at a high figure. In many country banks Other Real Estate not only exceeded capital funds, but often became two or three times as large. There were many poor loans which had been renewed and kept in good standing.

The bank examiners must have been in a quandary during this period. They surely realized that most of these banks were insolvent and ought to be closed. They knew, however, that a good crop would save many, and they did not want to be precipitate. The closing of one bank would adversely affect others and increase the strain. They could not shut down all insolvent banks, for that would ruin the country areas. Apparently they decided to close only those which were definitely hopeless.

The lack of ready cash threatened the entire system, but the impromptu efforts of the city banks and the government successfully met this problem. Since by 1924 banks which were even partially solvent could obtain sufficient cash for their daily needs, it was only insolvency that forced them to close.

The banks most severely shaken were those which had been short of capital funds and local deposits. They had sold certificates of deposit and had borrowed money from their correspondent banks. As distant depositors withdrew their money, these banks were forced to borrow increasing sums from other banks, and they were under constant pressure for repayment. Thus as conditions grew worse they became weaker and weaker. Banks which operated without bills payable and foreign funds were in a much stronger position. Their deposits held up better, and in the darkest days they had reserve borrowing power because their assets were not already pledged.

The record of bank failures in the Ninth Federal Reserve District through 1924 follows:[58]

1920	35
1921	73
1922	64
1923	279
1924	295

The number of banks which failed during the period from 1920 through 1924 is not surprising; the number of country banks which survived is remarkable. In the four States of Minnesota, North Dakota, South Dakota, and Montana, there were 3,551 banks in 1920. By December 31, 1924, there were 2,840 still solvent; 746 had closed. The banks which remained open had been operating under the same general conditions as those that failed.

An analysis of the closed banks brings to light several interesting facts. A large number were in the wheat areas, where all local loans depended on one crop; repeated crop failures and low prices bankrupted their communities. A large percentage had a capitalization of $25,000 or less. Another large division comprised those which were the only banks in their towns. In communities with more than one bank the strong tended to absorb the weak, where this could be done without loss, or the stockholders of weak banks contributed funds to absorb the loss and the depositors voluntarily reduced their claims to make a merger possible. The existence of many of the closed banks had never been justified, for their volume of business was not sufficient to cover expenses, much less produce earnings, except in boom times. Actual dishonesty was exceptional. A solvent bank could usually obtain funds to meet a run; or, if it did close, it reopened immediately.

Where bankers were capable, banks were solvent; and as long as banks were solvent, the newly created credit machinery kept them liquid. Where bankers were not capable, loans were poor, depending on the continued prosperity of the community. Even the utmost effort could not remedy past evils, and eventually these banks closed. After the depression had set in, it was too late to adjust conditions which had developed during prosperity. The general progress in debt payment affected bank deposits, for debtors used their balances to pay off notes. The realization of actual conditions caused many banks to close, and this, too, reduced total bank deposits. Nevertheless, the total income of the country in 1924 was so large that it offset these deflationary forces, and total country-bank deposits increased modestly.[59]

The State Guaranty of Deposits in the Dakotas, 1920–1924

The South Dakota State Guaranty Fund operated satisfactorily during 1920. Relatively few banks in its territory failed, and the depositors of those which did were paid in full.[60] Nevertheless, toward the end of 1921 it became evident that, if many more banks closed, the fund would be unable to meet payments.

In North Dakota the situation was very different. There it was alleged that most closed banks were fundamentally solvent and would reopen without loss to any depositor. Consequently, the Commission did not deem payments advisable.[61] The depositors of closed banks, agitating for the settlement of their claims, were considerably heartened when the Guaranty Fund Commission collected the assessments due from operating banks, because payment then appeared imminent.[62] The money collected was deposited in the Bank of North Dakota, which at that time desperately needed cash.[63] The Commission then stated that it would not pay any depositors who had received over 6 per cent on their certificates and savings accounts.[64] Charges were met with counter-charges, but the Commission made no payments in 1921. Despite the troubles of the

North Dakota Guaranty Fund, there was considerable sentiment in both Minnesota and Montana for the establishment of a similar guaranty of State deposits.[65]

The growing insolvency of country banks as time passed caused tremors in the State guaranty funds of both North and South Dakota. The latter had exhausted its cash and by the end of 1923 was paying claims in certificates.[66] The North Dakota State Fund was involved in a question of priority.[67] The holders of claims against the first banks to fail insisted that they had a right to be paid in full before holders of later claims received anything. Their stand was strengthened by the fact that, if the fund had functioned as had been intended, their claims would have been paid off before the later banks failed. The fund, however, had not paid; the other banks had failed, and their depositors alleged that all claims were on a parity and should be paid pro rata. To be sure, it was an academic question, for the fund was not paying anybody. The holders of the early claims sued the Commission to enforce payment, but the only decision they received was that the Commission could not be sued by an individual.[68] The situation at length became so involved that in July, 1923, a law was passed which terminated the guaranty and ordered the prorating of funds in the Commission's possession among all creditors.[69] In accordance with this law, the Commission announced that it would pay 10 per cent to the creditors of banks which had failed before July 1, 1923.[70]

The South Dakota Guaranty Fund was in serious trouble by 1925.[71] In September it was reported to be heavily in debt.[72] Its annual income amounted to only $275,000, not even enough to pay the interest on its debt.[73] In 1925 the law which had established it was repealed, and the Commission was ordered to prorate its assets.[74] Its dissolution, however, was stayed by a referendum which upheld the law. Accordingly, the guaranty remained on the statute books even though the Commission was not making any payments.[75] Although repeal of the law had proved politically impossible, repeal was for all practical purposes obtained in 1927 by an amendment providing that the assessments of each bank be held separately by the State treasurer and be available only for the liabilities of that bank.[76] The income from the fund was to be returned to each solvent bank.

Thus the fund was relieved of general liability, for, if a bank failed, the funds belonging to it held by the State treasurer were added to its assets and used to meet its liabilities. However, it had no claim on the funds belonging to other banks.

Effect of Agriculture upon Banking, 1925–1929

By 1925 the bankers of the Ninth Federal Reserve District had learned their lesson. Banking could not be safe in a one-crop town if the bank depended entirely on local loans; crop failures and low prices ruined the community and bankrupted the bank. Diversified farming offered a more secure base for operation. Total crop failures were rare, the cream check helped, and the annual sale of a few beef animals swelled the farmer's income. As a result, bankers organized to preach diversified farming and to offer loans to finance the purchase of cattle. The First National Bank of Minneapolis was a hearty supporter of the new doctrine. It emphasized the advantages of the dairy industry, urging every farmer to have dairy cattle. Under city leadership the country bankers backed the movement, which soon was enjoying moderate success.[77]

The Northwestern National Bank of Minneapolis, however, barely tolerated this campaign. It approved of the idea that wheat farmers abandon their one-crop system, but it was afraid that an emphasis on dairy products would glut the market and cause prices to break disastrously. It preached a doctrine of low costs — have cattle to be sure, but only economical producers; a few good cows are better than many mediocre ones.[78]

The zeal of the banks was abetted by nature. Continuous grain farming had harmed the land: yields were declining, the soil was becoming foul, and rust was ruining the crops. Many farmers already believed that a change of methods was expedient. Nevertheless, the transition was painfully slow.

The country banks felt that they were making some progress in strengthening their position by developing diversified farming. They also moved toward strength by changing their investment policy. No longer did they loan all their funds locally; they used a portion to buy bonds.[79] "Bonds for a secondary reserve" already was a popular banking slogan. Unfortunately, many country bankers expert in local finance were hopelessly incompetent in selecting bonds. With few exceptions, the quality of the bonds they purchased was low.

The crops of 1925 fell slightly below those of 1924, and prices declined to some extent; both, however, were fairly satisfactory. Operating conditions were mildly prosperous.[80] The drive for liquidation of the credit structure continued. Border-line and substandard loans were brought to a final settlement. Foreclosures and farm bankruptcies approximated those of 1924.

Foreclosures gave the banks of the Ninth District title to an unprecedentedly large volume of real estate. On June 27, 1918, composite Other Real Estate amounted to $9,271,000; on September 28, 1925, it was $45,323,000.[81] Regarding the increase in Other Real Estate as dangerous, examiners became very strict, urging the sale of properties which could be disposed of and the charging-off of the remainder at the rate of 10 per cent a year.[82] Real estate was difficult to sell, but some progress was made by transferring titles to individual farmers, who then obtained mortgage loans from one of the State agencies and paid the proceeds to the bank.

Considerable opposition to the rural credit law had developed in South Dakota, where the system was in financial difficulties owing to widespread defaults in farm mortgages. On July 1, 1925, a law was passed ordering the liquidation of the system, which by that time had loaned $47,000,000 to 14,400 farmers.[83] The law prohibited new loans but allowed renewals of ten years. No loan was to exceed 50 per cent of the current value of the property; previously 70 per cent had been allowed.[84]

The satisfactory agricultural conditions which had existed for two years vanished in 1926. Drought throughout the territory cut yields sharply and in many sections caused a complete crop failure; [85] low prices for the surviving crops intensified losses; and farmers who under ordinary conditions were prosperous had to borrow for living expenses or suffer actual privation. This crop failure reversed the recession of farm bankruptcies, making them mount rapidly.[86] A wave of defaults spread, and what little market there was for farm real estate vanished. The farm-mortgage lenders became more and more involved during this period as it became obvious that they had made excessive loans and could not expect payment. Defaults became common, foreclosure a daily occurrence, and the various agencies found themselves accumulating quantities of farm real estate.

Conditions during 1927 and 1928 while not prosperous were much better than those of 1926. Rainfall and other weather conditions were adequate for moderate crops throughout the entire area. The price level remained low, but farmers had revised their methods and now at least were making a living. Diversified farming had become more and more popular during the 'twenties. Some farmers had abandoned wheat for cattle and sheep or dairy farms. Where this change had occurred, improvement was progressive and prosperity general. Two obstacles hampered a whole-hearted acceptance of diversified agriculture: the amount of capital necessary, and the farmers' reluctance to engage in an occupation involving hard work the whole twelve months of the year. These drawbacks, however, did not completely stifle diversified farming, and it continued to spread in the territory.

The year 1929 brought back unsatisfactory conditions: a partial crop failure occurred in the western part of the region; [87] prices were low; the farmers' cash income declined to a little below that of 1927 and 1928. However, the steady liquidation of the debt structure of the farming industry had removed the weaker units, so that in 1929 farm bankruptcies, foreclosures, and bank failures were not numerous. During the period from 1925 to 1929, inclusive, some 771 banks closed in the Northwest. By years bank failures were as follows:

1925	168
1926	283
1927	142
1928	94
1929	84

This number, added to the 746 failures between 1920 and 1924, brought the total to 1,517. Of these banks, 226 reopened, and a few new ones were organized, with the result that on December 31, 1929, there were 2,353 banks in the territory.[88] This figure represented a decline from the 3,551 operating in 1920.

The banks which survived to 1929 were sturdy veterans of the storm; they had experienced crop failure, agricultural depression, and defaults. The weak and poorly managed ones had vanished. It should not be assumed, however, that the remaining banks were strong or ready to enter another depression. They were still licking old wounds. Many of them were loaded with submarginal paper dating in some instances from the 'teens. They were dependent for future solvency on conditions which could improve only gradually.

One definitely adverse factor was the dwindling of country-bank earnings. An important cause was the decline in the liquidity of real-estate mortgages. The rural bank had been the primary farm-loan agency prior to 1920. By 1929 this market had disappeared. Former customers refused to buy, and the remnant of the business was taken over by government agencies. Pressure from the Federal Reserve Bank had reduced income from exchange charges and from remitting below par. Moreover, having learned greater caution, banks had reduced the volume of their loans and discounts and investments, and had increased their cash reserves, reducing their income proportionately.

Those operating earnings which had survived the 'twenties had, to a great extent, been applied to writing off losses. Dividends had been small and somewhat rare. In many instances there were still losses to write off, or potential losses to be developed by the first depression or crop failure. Because of this situation, there was little optimism to space in the country-banking circles.

CHAPTER V

THE GREAT BANKS ASSUME METROPOLITAN RESPONSIBILITY AS SMALL BANKS FAIL 1920–1929

The Twin City Banking Structure and Conditions in the 1920's

During the long period of prosperity preceding 1920, banks in the Twin Cities had steadily become more numerous. In Minneapolis the two largest banks were the First National and the Northwestern National Bank. In St. Paul they were the First National Bank and the Merchants National Bank. Minneapolis also boasted four medium-sized banks: the Midland National and Trust, the Metropolitan National, the Hennepin County Savings Bank, and the Farmers and Mechanics Savings Bank. St. Paul had three: the American National, the Capital National, and the State Savings Bank.[1]

In both cities, small banks abounded. Although many of them were located on the outskirts, a surprisingly large number were crowded into the downtown financial districts. These small banks were weakly capitalized and in many cases poorly managed, but because conditions were easy they apparently were successful and profitable. They were not capable of financing the needs of large business units, but accommodated individuals and small companies. To some extent they financed consumer credit and made personal and real-estate loans. Many of them had deposits in excess of their loaning needs and were looking for investments.

In January, 1920, business conditions in the Twin Cities passed their peak and commenced to decline. The first effect of the depression on city banks was that deposits, which reached their high in February, 1920, started to shrink and temporary borrowings increased.[2] However, liquidation in the cities was rapid, for industrial concerns ceased borrowing and started to repay their loans. By May 27, 1921, the loans of city banks had declined 20 per cent from the previous year; deposits had ceased their decline.[3] Net demand deposits in city banks amounted to $187,000,000 on January 7, 1921, and declined to a low of $165,974,000 on May 4.[4] After that date they turned upward and on December 7 reached $177,983,000.[5] Time deposits, which had amounted to $69,814,000 on January 7, had increased to $72,388,000 by December 7.[6] Loans to customers, totaling $328,704,000 on January 7, had declined to $287,084,000 by December 7.[7] The net result of these transactions was that the city banks as a whole became considerably more liquid during the year, and they applied part of their excess cash to reducing their borrowings at the Federal Reserve from $54,890,000 to $21,060,000.[8]

The small banks in the Twin Cities were severely pressed during this period. Collections from small city customers slowed down, and for a short time demands for loans increased while bank deposits declined. Fortunately, this development was short-lived: deposits recovered from their slump; commercial and industrial customers began to repay their loans. Small banks with country affiliations were under severe strain, however, because the country paper they had rediscounted was frozen. To be sure, country paper was renewed and changed, but actual payment did not materialize.[9] In order to accommodate the country banks, city banks were often forced to increase their commitments.

While the Twin City banks got through 1920 and the major part of 1921 without a single failure, it had become painfully evident by the fall of 1921 that the Chicago-Lake State Bank was in trouble.[10] It was loaded with poor local paper, had too large a volume of North Dakota farm paper, and was, in general, heavily over-invested. October found it unable to meet its clearing-house obligations; [11] it was later reorganized.[12]

For a time it was thought that this would end Twin City bank failures, but on March 20, 1922, the Northern State Bank of Minneapolis failed.[13] The Western State Bank closed on April 17, 1922.[14] Two unsuccessful attempts were made to reopen but eventually the bank was liquidated. The Mill City State Bank failed early in 1922 and was taken over by the Minneapolis National Bank.[15] Toward the end of the year the Fourth Avenue State Bank closed but was reopened June 9, 1923.[16]

The Market State Bank and the State Deposit Bank, both of which were operated by Adam Hannah, then became the weak spot in the Minneapolis banking structure. As we have seen, Adam Hannah had a chain of small banks in North Dakota, which were under continuous pressure from the agricultural deflation. He used his city banks to aid those in the country. The two banks just mentioned had been warned repeatedly by the Clearing House to stop further advances and to clear up their farm paper. Hannah's country banks failed in 1922 and 1923, and by the end of the latter year it became evident that his two Minneapolis banks were insolvent. A. J. Viegel, State Superintendent of Banks, closed them on December 7, 1923.[17] Both banks had good local paper. Their losses were almost entirely on farm paper. On November 20, 1923, the Harriet State Bank of Minneapolis closed because of bad loans.[18] It was later reorganized and reopened.

The cumulative troubles of the country districts and the consequent closing of rural banks caused the bankruptcy of a majority of bank chains. The John F. Sinclair Company failed in February, 1923, and its dozen banks, located west of Minneapolis, closed.[19] Other chains followed until the only two important ones remaining were the Union Investment Company and the John W. Black Company.

During 1923 and 1924 the Republic State Bank steadily became more involved in trouble. Its deposits, which never had been large, were withdrawn until on June 15, 1924, they had shrunk to $15,029. The bank closed its doors on that date.[20] The Continental State Bank, appalled by increasing defaults, frozen paper, and losses, closed August 29, 1925. It was taken over by the Marquette National Bank.[21]

The year 1926 was even more ruinous to small Minneapolis banks, for losses had accumulated. The banks struggled valiantly to survive, but the resurgence of agricultural depression brought forth a new series of padlocks. The year got off to an inauspicious start when on February 15 the Merchants and Manufacturers State Bank on West Broadway in Minneapolis closed its doors.[22] This bank had been owned by A. M. Hovland, who also had owned the Camden Park State and a chain of banks in the Dakotas. During the early 'twenties, Hovland had sold the Camden Park to local interests but had retained the Merchants and Manufacturers. Primarily because of close connections with the Dakota chain, this bank had become laden with frozen agricultural paper. Meanwhile, Hovland had left the bank.[23] The new management worked desperately to thaw the frozen assets, but with little success, and when conditions turned for the worse in 1926, it gave up. This bank had a capital of $100,000 and claims amounting to $1,063,000.[24] Eventual recoveries totaled exactly 50 cents on the dollar.

Meanwhile, the Mercantile State Bank was looking around for some larger bank to absorb it. Allegedly it was perfectly solvent, but the lease on its bank building had expired and it wished to get out of business. It appears likely, however, that assets were not exactly liquid and that the State banking department was applying some pressure. The First National Bank made an offer but the Northwestern National topped it slightly, and on March 1 the Mercantile State was absorbed by the Lincoln Office of the Northwestern National Bank.[25] The cash involved in this transaction was paid by the Mercantile stockholders to the Northwestern.

On April 5 the Guaranty State Bank closed for liquidation.[26] This represented a total collapse. On May 4 the Nokomis State Bank failed.[27]

Stress among the small banks continued into 1927. The Liberty State Bank failed on January 13,[28] and the American State Bank closed on September 26.[29]

St. Paul did not have so many small banks as Minneapolis, nor were they so closely affiliated with the country-banking situation. Not a single St. Paul bank closed during 1921, 1922, and 1923. The worst bank failure in the city's history, however, occurred on May 3, 1924, when the Capital Trust and Savings Bank closed its door because of frozen credits and too deep involvement in farm real-estate mortgages.[30] It was evident that this failure would cause a run on its affiliate, the Capital National Bank, and that, although that bank was completely solvent, it would be forced to close its doors. Its failure, in turn, would exert a great deal of pressure on the other banks. To circumvent possible disaster, arrangements were made for the Merchants National Bank to absorb the Capital National Bank, asume its assets and liabilities, and agree to pay its stockholders 2 per cent on all accounts still with the Merchants National Bank at the end of the first year.[31] The consolidation became effective May 5 and although a moderate run ensued, the bank was able to stand all withdrawals. This speedy action undoubtedly saved the St. Paul banking system for, had the failure of the Capital National occurred, it would have been a severe blow to confidence. As it was, the failure of the Capital Trust caused considerable disturbance, although it eventually worked out fairly well. The stockholders were assessed 100 per cent, and depositors eventually received most of their money.

No further failures occurred until 1926, when, prompted by the revival of agricultural difficulties, three small banks closed. The Ramsey County Savings Bank was the first, on March 23;[32] the Broadway State Bank was next, on April 14;[33] third came the Great Northern State Bank on December 29.[34] That was the end of bank failures in St. Paul until the Second Foshay State Bank closed on November 1, 1929.

The Movement in Minneapolis toward Branches, 1922

The sharp depression in Minneapolis in 1920 and 1921 and the gradual bankruptcy of the country areas began to alarm the leading city bankers. Every effort was made to provide liquidity, and the cities' financial structure was recognized as vulnerable.

Banking leaders became disturbed by the obvious fact that, unless prompt action was taken, the Twin Cities would be confronted with a series of bank failures. Accordingly, Messrs. Jaffray, Chamberlain, Prince, Decker, Wold, Mills, Norris, and other important Minneapolis bankers considered the matter and laid plans to strengthen the banking structure. Since it was believed that competitive bidding would be unfortunate and unnecessarily costly, spheres of influence were mapped out and each large bank chose a few smaller ones for which it would be responsible. The theory was that, if control of weak banks could be obtained in time, the character of the assets could be improved and losses avoided.

In February, 1921, Mr. John Skelton Williams, Comptroller of the Currency, resigned[35] and was succeeded by Mr. D. R. Crissinger.

This change brought a new interpretation of national banking laws. Mr. Williams, as well as all former comptrollers, had held that national banks could not establish branches but Mr. Crissinger claimed that they could within the limits of their home cities. He believed that there was no restriction on the number of branch offices a bank could establish as long as they were within the city limits mentioned in its charter.[36] This was the first time that such an interpretation had been approved, and national banks all over the country were quick to take advantage of it.

On June 30, 1922, Mr. Jaffray, of the First National, stated that he felt the time was ripe for the establishment of branch offices in Minneapolis, preferably by purchasing or otherwise acquiring small banks. This method would not only provide branches with an established clientele, but also would strengthen the city's banking structure. Then, too, it would be profitable, for there were some successful banks on the market which could be purchased at a reasonable price. Other banks were in difficulties, and the stockholders would be so glad to get out that they would willingly pay an assessment to avoid further liability, and turn their banks over to the First National. Good management, Mr. Jaffray believed, could work out these situations and within a few months the banks would be in excellent shape. The continuance of high-grade management would avoid further difficulties. The acquisition of branches was preferable to their establishment, for it provided substantial deposits from the beginning, reduced costly competition, and strengthened the banking structure.

On August 15, 1922, Mr. Jaffray reported that the First had acquired the St. Anthony Falls Bank, the North Side State Bank, and the Minnehaha State Bank. It was proposed that these banks be changed into offices of the main bank.

Since the district around Plymouth Avenue and Washington Avenue North, where the North Side State Bank was located, was gradually deteriorating, the old management had decided to move the bank. Accordingly, the bank had leased space in a new building under construction at West Broadway and Emerson Avenue North.[37] When the First National acquired the North Side State Bank, it also acquired the lease on the new quarters. After much discussion it

Chart V. Foundations and Mergers of The First National Bank of Minneapolis

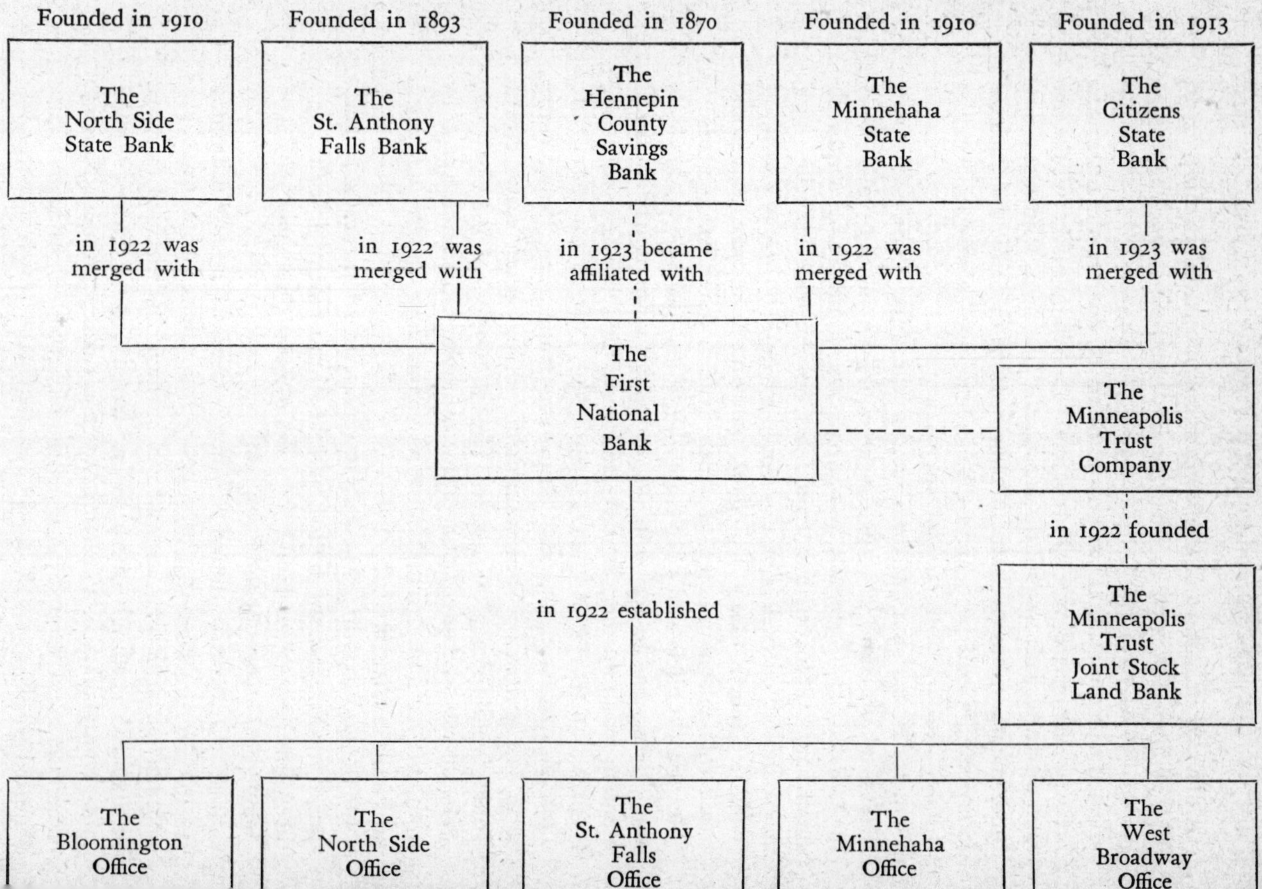

was decided that it would be poor policy to move the North Side State Bank, for in the proposed location it would lose business to the North American Bank, also located at Plymouth and Washington. The area surrounding the leased building, moreover, was becoming more populous and it was not supplied with banking facilities. Here was an opportunity for a new bank. The First National, therefore, opened a branch known as the West Broadway Office on December 19, 1922.

In the same month, as part of its movement to acquire branch offices, the Northwestern National absorbed the Lincoln National Bank, the Lincoln Trust and Savings Bank, and the South Side State Bank.[38] In November it purchased the North American Bank and in December the Northeast State Bank.[39] These banks were changed into branch offices, and in December the Minneapolis National Bank, located at Lake Street and Nicollet Avenue, became the Lake Street Office.[40]

As the national banks acquired more and more branches, the State banks became alarmed. Although they vociferously alleged that branch banking meant the end of independent banking, their first reaction was an attempt to acquire branches themselves. They consulted the attorney general on the problem, and he ruled that under the Minnesota law State banks could not acquire branches.[41] Any doubts in the matter were removed when in April, 1923, the State legislature passed a law expressly forbidding State banks to operate any type of branch.[42]

In March, 1923, arrangements were made for the First National to take over the Citizens State Bank located at Lake Street and Bloomington Avenue as its Bloomington Office.[43]

By 1925 the managements of both the First National and the Northwestern National had decided to change their method of organization by restoring certain of their branch offices to corporate independence. Pursuant to this decision, arrangements were made to acquire charters and incorporate independent banks to take over the business of the branches. In August, 1925, the charter of the Minnehaha State Bank was reinstated, and this bank commenced operations with a capital of $50,000. It took over the business of the Minnehaha Office of the First National Bank.[44] On October 23 the

Chart VI. Foundations and Mergers of The Northwestern National Bank of Minneapolis

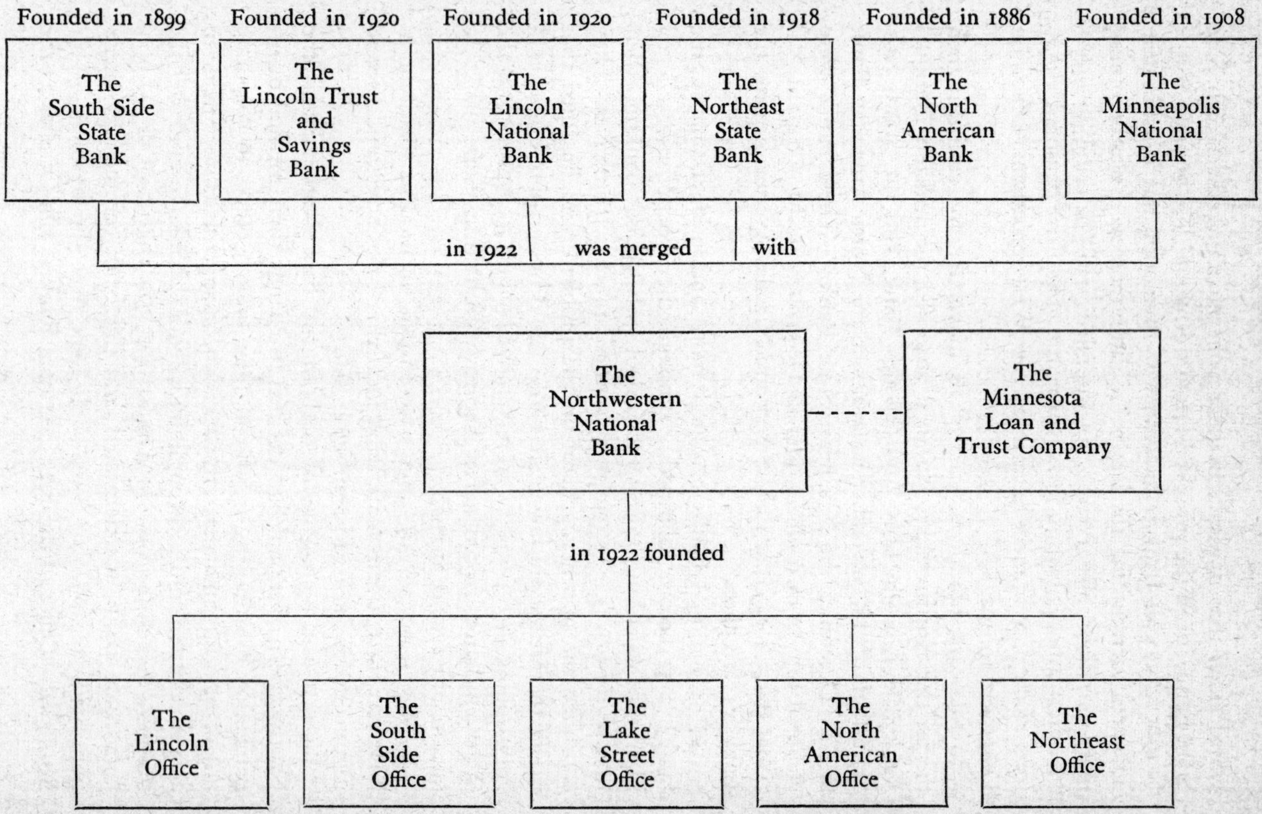

First National sold the Bloomington-Lake Office to a new bank known as the Bloomington-Lake State Bank.

In August, the business of the Northeast Office of the Northwestern National Bank was taken over by the newly chartered Second Northwestern State Bank.[45] In October the Fourth Northwestern State Bank took over the South Side Office.[46]

In May, 1927, the Fourth Northwestern State Bank took out a national charter and became the Fourth Northwestern National.[47] On June 30 the Minnehaha State Bank absorbed the Lake Street Bank and became the Minnehaha National Bank.[48] In October the Northwestern National took over the East Hennepin State Bank, changing its name to the Third Northwestern National Bank.[49] It also organized on Lake Street a new bank, with a capital of $100,000 and a surplus of $10,000, known as the Fifth Northwestern National Bank.[50]

During this period of expansion the First National had acquired five outlying banks, while the Northwestern National had acquired seven. They were strategically located to supply every area in the city with the services of a strong bank. Certain of these banks formerly had been solvent, profitable, independent organizations. They had been acquired by the big banks to distribute their services on a territorial basis and to increase the earnings of the parent banks. However, the banks which were strong and profitable had cost the big banks a high price. On the other hand, some of the banks taken over had been deeply involved and would otherwise have failed. In such cases the big banks had to restore capital funds and carry sluggish assets.

In St. Paul the banks made no effort during this period to acquire branches, perhaps because the small banks were not so badly extended as those in Minneapolis. St. Paul had fewer small banks. Moreover, they were not so closely connected with the country-bank situation as were the banks of Minneapolis.

In September, 1922, the Merchants National Bank took over the Farmers and Merchants State Bank, operating it as an independent, and in January, 1924, organized the Grand Avenue State Bank.[51] Its expansion ended there. The First National Bank of St. Paul completely ignored the branch movement.

Chart VII. Readjustments of The Northwestern National Bank of Minneapolis

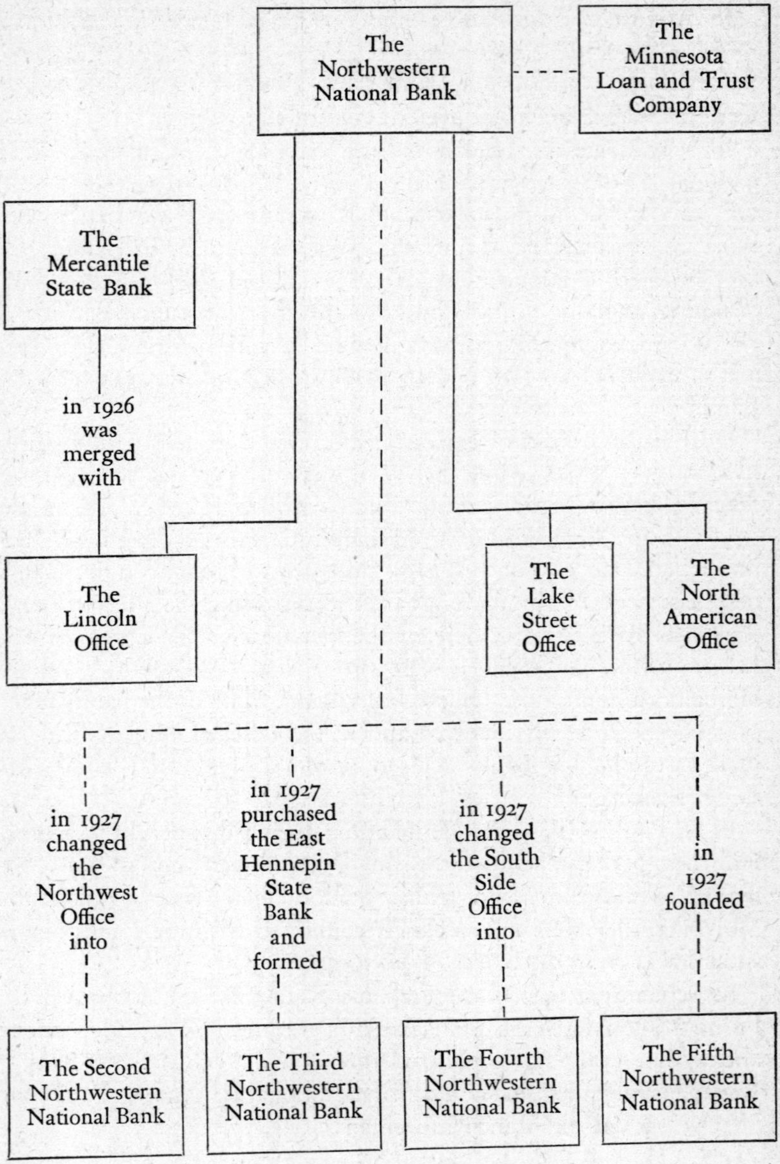

Creation of New Banks and Mergers of Old, 1920–1929

Despite the abundance of banks in Minneapolis, there were many people who wished to organize new ones. Opening a bank was still regarded as the right of any man who could comply with the minimum legal requirements.

The Payday National Bank in Minneapolis, organized early in 1920, was operating by May of that year.[52] In August, 1921, the State Institution for Savings became a trust company, adopting the name of the Marquette Trust Company.[53] Mr. Ralph W. Manuel of the Exchange State Bank was its first president;[54] he was succeeded at the Exchange State by his brother Malvern.[55] In April, 1922, the Marquette Trust Company consolidated with the Exchange State Bank, retaining Mr. Ralph W. Manuel as president.[56] In June the Payday National Bank assumed the title Marquette National Bank and took over the commercial business of the Marquette Trust Company.[57] S. M. Strand became chairman of the board, and Mr. R. W. Manuel president of both the Trust Company and the Bank.

On February 25, 1922, the Security State Bank obtained a charter and on December 9 opened an office at Eleventh Street and Nicollet Avenue.[58] In May, W. P. Kennedy applied for a charter for the Transportation Brotherhood's National Bank,[59] the stock of which was to be held by members of the Big Four Brotherhoods. This bank opened for business on December 1 in the Metropolitan Life Building. Meanwhile, G. L. Heegaard and others chartered the Sixth Avenue State Bank, which commenced operations in October with C. B. Mills as president.[60]

In August, Mr. S. G. Palmer and Mr. Sumner T. McKnight applied for a charter for the Produce State Bank.[61] The interests which owned this bank were closely affiliated with the First National. Although for some time the bank operated as an independent, it was purchased by the First National in January, 1928.[62]

On May 2, 1922, the Minneapolis Trust–Joint Stock Land Bank, a protégé of the Minneapolis Trust Company, was granted charter No. 41, and a few days later it opened for business.[63] This company sold tax-exempt bonds to investors and loaned the funds to farmers. Since this tax-exempt provision made the bonds attractive to investors, they sold readily and for a time seemed to revive the farm-mortgage business.

By the end of 1922 the new bank movement in the Twin Cities had spent itself, and the State Banking Department was reluctant to grant new charters unless a definite need could be proved. Certainly there was no lack of banking facilities in either Minneapolis or St. Paul. Opposed to the movement to create new units were the large banks which were interested not only in reducing the number of small banks in the Twin Cities and strengthening their own position, but also in consolidating the medium-sized banks in the downtown financial area.

As 1922 waned, Mr. Jaffray reported to the board of directors of the First National that negotiations were under way for the purchase of the Hennepin County Savings Bank, which was in excellent shape and had deposits of $9,000,000. A tentative plan provided that the First National declare a stock dividend of $500,000 to its stockholders, who would then return their stock to the First with instructions to exchange it for stock of the Savings Bank. Mr. Jaffray reported in detail the method of valuing both stocks and added his own recommendation to the project. The board approved the proposal. Accordingly, on February 15, 1923, an increase in capital from $5,000,000 to $5,500,000 was authorized, and a 10 per cent stock dividend was declared. The stockholders assigned the dividend and authorized the exchange of the stock for that of the Hennepin County Savings Bank. The pro rata interest in the Savings Bank was then endorsed on the stock of the First National. On May 26, 1924, the Hennepin County Savings Bank moved from the Phoenix Building to the First National–Soo Line Annex.[64]

For some time the Minneapolis Trust Company had been eyeing the Wells-Dickey Trust Company with a great deal of interest. The Wells-Dickey Trust Company had built up a very profitable volume of business by acquiring some important trust accounts. At the same time the management of the Wells-Dickey Company apparently was not genuinely enthusiastic over its venture into the trust field. The Trust Company had been incorporated in 1916, all of its stock belonging to the original Wells-Dickey Company.[65] The business made profits but caused the officers considerable worry. Meanwhile,

Chart VIII. Offices and Affiliates of The First National Bank of Minneapolis in 1925

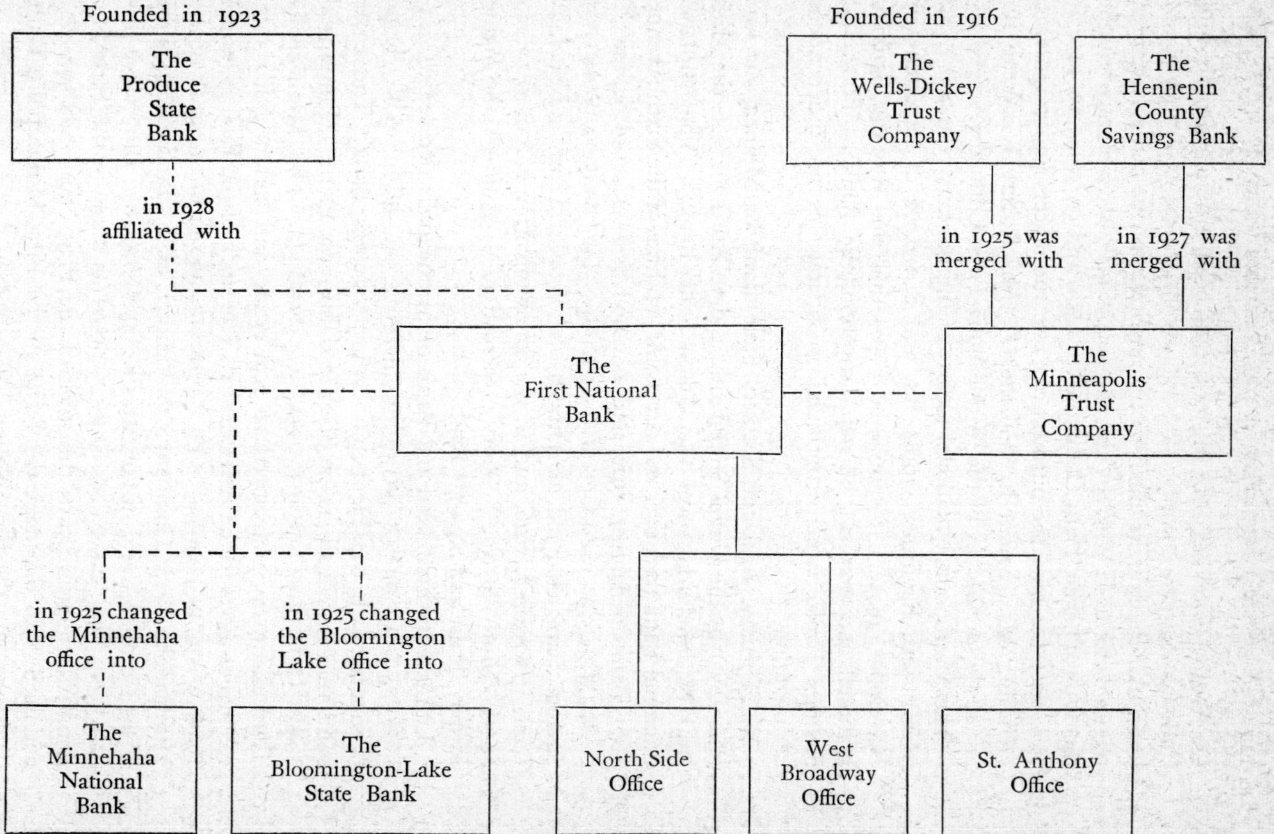

the Wells-Dickey security business had been growing rapidly and showing excellent profits. The officers began to wish they could dispose of the bothersome Trust Company. In due course, arrangements were made whereby the Minneapolis Trust Company bought the Wells-Dickey Trust Company for cash, and on April 27, 1925, it took over not only the business but also the officers and employees, including Mr. Lyman E. Wakefield.[66] Mr. Robert W. Webb retained the presidency of the Minneapolis Trust Company.

The Metropolitan National took over the Bankers National Bank — its assets, liabilities, employees, and $1,800,000 of deposits — in November, 1925.[67] It should be noted that this was the Bankers National and not its affiliated institution, the Bankers Trust and Savings Bank, which continued to operate as an independent organization.

In February, 1926, the Security State Bank of Minneapolis was taken over by the Union State Bank, and on April 26, 1926, the Midland National took over the Union State Bank.[68] The Midland National Bank took over the assets and liabilities of the Sixth Avenue State Bank in August, 1926, and assumed its $144,000 of deposits.[69] C. B. Mills was president of both banks. The Bankers Trust and Savings Bank changed its name to the Peoples Trust and Savings Bank in October, 1926, and in the following May it moved to 114 South Ninth Street.[70] Shortly thereafter, it assumed the name Foshay Trust and Savings Bank.

In 1927 the First National Bank of Minneapolis decided to simplify its corporate structure by merging the Minneapolis Trust Company with the Hennepin County Savings Bank. The latter bank transferred all its property and business to the Minneapolis Trust Company, and its stock was canceled. The Minneapolis Trust Company transferred its real estate and certain other miscellaneous assets to the Atlas Realty. The stock of the First National Bank was to be endorsed with a pro rata interest in the stock of the Minneapolis Trust Company, now known as the First Minneapolis Trust Company, and of the Atlas Realty Company. But before this had been done, the Atlas Realty changed its name to the First National Corporation; thus the stock of the First National Bank was endorsed with a beneficial interest in the First Minneapolis Trust Company and the First National Corporation.[71]

Chart IX. Offices and Affiliates of The First National Bank of Minneapolis in 1929

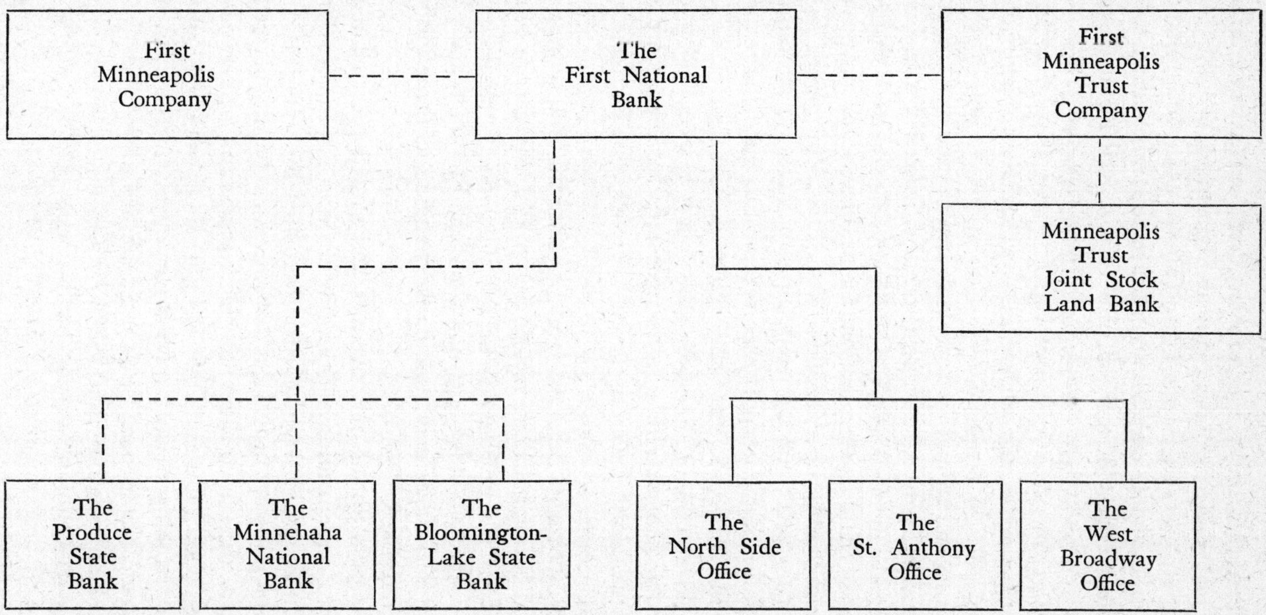

The Millers and Traders State Bank was taken over in April, 1928, by the Metropolitan National, which assumed all its assets and liabilities.[72] In August the First National assumed all the assets and liabilities of the North Commercial State Bank, merging them with its North Side Office, which was then moved from its location on Washington Avenue to 242 West Broadway, the previous home of the Merchants and Manufacturers.[73]

A meeting of the stockholders of the First National Bank of Minneapolis held in January, 1929, approved an increase in the bank's capital from $5,500,000 to $6,000,000 and the sale of the new stock at 450 per cent of par. From the proceeds $500,000 was to be credited to the bank's capital and $1,750,000 was to be turned over to the First National Corporation.[74] This organization was to take over the bond and security business of the First Minneapolis Trust Company. The par value of First National Bank stock was reduced from $100 to $20 and each old share became five new shares.[75]

At the same time the Northwestern National increased its capital from $4,000,000 to $5,000,000, issuing new stock to old stockholders at its par of $100, although the market price was $400 per share.[76] The question of lowering the par value was discussed, but sentiment was against it.

The Marquette National Bank absorbed the Transportation Brotherhood's National Bank in October, 1929.[77] Mergers in Minneapolis ended in November when the Metropolitan National absorbed the Foshay Trust and Savings Bank, and the First National group took over the Third Foshay State Bank, changing its name to the Hennepin State Bank.[78]

Evolution during the 'twenties had caused great changes in the banking organization of the Twin Cities. Numerous small and medium-sized banks had been eliminated by failures and mergers, and the great banks had labored to reduce the number of banks, to increase their own share of the business, and to avoid banking troubles and failures. Then too, they had worked to supply satisfactory banking services in every part of the Cities and to every class of people. In general they accomplished their objectives. Their satisfaction was not diminished by the fact that they had found commercial banking a profitable business.

Chart X. Offices and Affiliates of The Northwestern National Bank of Minneapolis in 1929

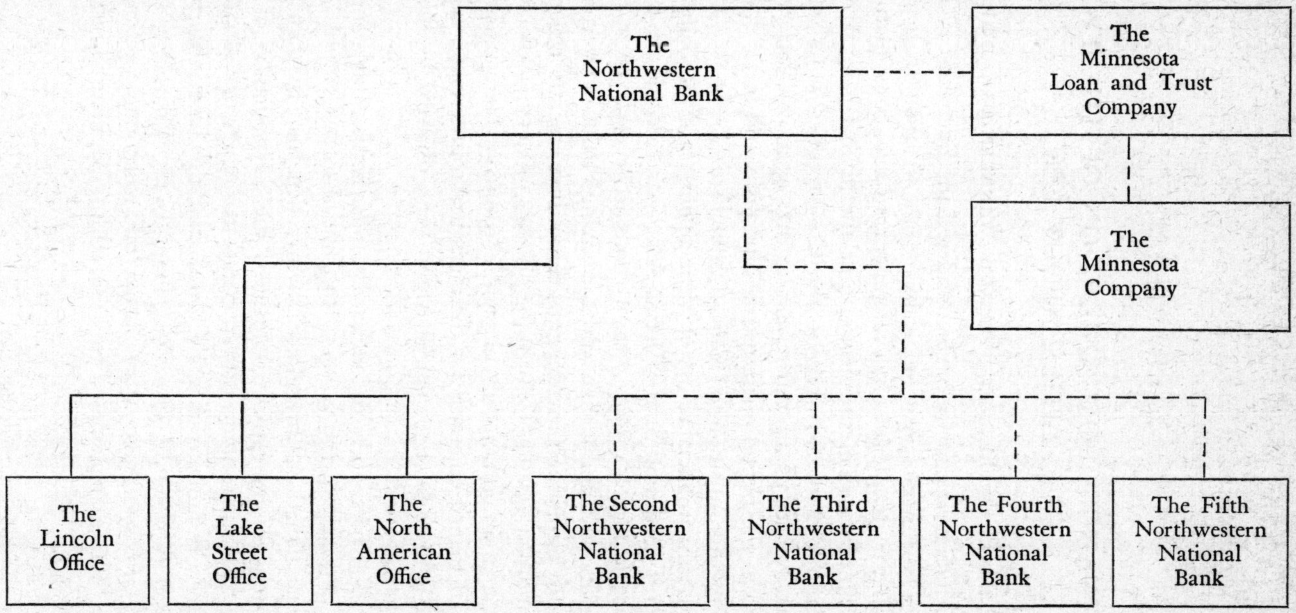

CHAPTER VI

FINANCIAL ORGANIZATION OF THE TWIN CITIES, ABOUT 1928

The Banks and Financial Areas of Minneapolis and St. Paul

In previous chapters we have considered the financial development of the Northwest chronologically, from its pioneer beginnings, through various phases of development, to a stage of maturity. In this chapter we shall stop to examine the financial organization as of a definite date. Any year in the late 'twenties would serve our purpose, but let us arbitrarily choose 1928 as most clearly marking the end of the period of industrial capitalism and being closely followed by the transition to financial capitalism.

In 1928 the financial center of Minneapolis was Marquette Avenue between Fourth and Sixth Streets. A pedestrian could walk around this area in fifteen minutes, yet it contained every type of financial organization. Commercial banks, a savings bank, trust companies, insurance companies, investment dealers, brokers, and other institutions huddled together to form the primary money market of the city and one of importance in the entire country. Here clustered the financial giants, encircled by their smaller counterparts, which, although important in their own right, were dwarfed by their proximity to the great.

The Farmers and Mechanics Savings Bank stood on Fourth Street near Marquette Avenue.[1] Organized in 1874, in the intervening years it had acquired large savings deposits. Its management, noted for conservatism, had fostered the accumulation of a large surplus and substantial reserves. Since its savings deposits were not subject to instantaneous withdrawal, and the bank therefore had little fear of a run, it invested generously in local real-estate mortgages, farm mortgages, term loans, and corporate and municipal bonds. The management was also willing to invest in long-term securities.

The Northwestern National Bank's principal business was commercial. Adjoining it on Marquette Avenue between Fourth and Fifth Streets [2] was its affiliate, the Minnesota Loan and Trust Company.[3] Though officially a trust company, this institution did a profitable business in corporate and municipal securities.

The Union Investment Company, managed by the astute Mr. Theodore Albrecht, shared the same building.[4] This company performed diverse functions. It owned a group of country banks, acted as their agent, audited their books, established investment standards, and made rules and regulations for bank operations. It also bought farm mortgages to sell in the East, sold high-grade bonds and securities to its country banks, and carried on a general securities business.

From the intersection of Fifth Street and Marquette Avenue the First National–Soo Line Building, pride of the First National Bank of Minneapolis and the Minneapolis, St. Paul and Sault Ste. Marie Railroad, rose to dominate the skyline. On the first four floors was the First National Bank; [5] a few floors above it were occupied by the Soo Line; and the balance was rented to tenants. The bank's trust affiliate, the First Minneapolis Trust Company, adjoined the First National Bank, fronting on Fifth Street between Marquette and Second Avenues South.[6] The trust company had built up two important lines of business by successful mergers. In 1925 it had absorbed the trust business of the Wells-Dickey Trust Company, and in 1927 it had acquired the Hennepin County Savings Bank. Its trust and savings business, therefore, almost equaled its profitable investment business.

The Minneapolis Trust–Joint Stock Land Bank, owned by the First Minneapolis Trust Company, had its offices in the New York Life Building, adjacent to the Trust Company and completing the block.[7] This company bought farm mortgages, pledging them as collateral behind its bonds, which sold readily despite a generally sluggish market for farm mortgages. Since the investment department of the Trust Company made a profit selling these bonds to its customers, and the Land Bank supplied a purchaser for farm mortgages, this organization was a great asset to the Trust Company and, indirectly, to the First National Bank of Minneapolis.

High up in the First National–Soo Line Building the comfortable offices of Lane, Piper, Jaffray and Company covered an entire floor.[8] This prosperous bond house had dabbled in corporate securities and after the first World War found this division expanding rapidly.[9] Another important tenant was John W. Black, who specialized in the ownership and operation of country banks.[10]

Both the First National–Soo Line Building and the New York Life Building were filled with brokerage houses, investment dealers, and fire and title insurance companies. Prominent among the latter were the Northwestern Fire and Marine Insurance Company and the Title Insurance Company of Minnesota. There was a generous sprinkling, too, of law firms specializing in corporate law and financial matters.

Directly across Marquette Avenue from the First National–Soo Line Building, the forbidding façade of the Minneapolis Federal Reserve Bank frowned down on Fifth Street.[11] Built like a fortress, strong enough to withstand mob violence, battle, siege, and storm, the massive stone walls rose to moderate height, broken only by two solid metal doors.

The Marquette National Bank and the Marquette Trust Company, affiliated institutions, lived in the shadow of the First National. Their doors were on Marquette Avenue between Fifth and Sixth Streets.[12] The two Marquettes were small companies with aggressive management. Singularly enough the organization advertised itself as the "Old Marquette," giving the impression that the bank was old, whereas it was relatively new, having been organized in 1920. To be sure, it had succeeded to the business of the State Institution for Savings, organized in 1888.

Completely apart from the financial district, but integrally an important part of the regional financial structure, was the Northwestern National Life Insurance Company,[13] its building overlooking beautiful Loring Park. As this company's volume of insurance grew, an increasing stream of premiums flowed into Minneapolis, there to augment reserves which sought investment in the local money market.

To return to the financial district, the Metropolitan National Bank at the corner of Sixth Street and Second Avenue South [14] was of medium size and did a good business with local business men. Its management was popular because of its geniality, optimism, and a sincere desire to be of service.

The Wells-Dickey Company, which by this time confined itself to the distributing of corporate and municipal bonds and stocks, was located at the intersection of Second Avenue South and Fifth Street.[15] Next door was the Minneapolis office of C. O. Kalman and Company,[16] and down the block at Fourth Street the Midland National Bank and Trust Company [17] served its many small customers and the mill and grain-elevator men who had offices in the neighboring buildings.

We have mentioned by name the outstanding leaders in the Minneapolis financial picture, but there were also innumerable persons and firms, little known individually but important collectively. The office buildings of the financial district provided headquarters for chains of country banks, for investment dealers, farm-mortgage dealers, insurance agents, loan agents, investing capitalists, an investment trust, local stockbrokers, representatives of New York Stock Exchange houses, real-estate dealers, rental agents, corporation lawyers, accountants — both local and national — promoters, and bucket shops. Nearly everyone in this district was connected with finance in at least one of its numerous aspects. There were specialists in every financial service. The commercial banks offered short-term commercial loans; the savings banks offered term loans, and would buy local mortgages and corporate and municipal bonds; local investors, capitalists, savings banks, insurance companies, and the city's one investment trust, all supplied a ready market for stocks or bonds. Capital for any purpose was therefore abundant. The entire structure was held together by a network of dealers, brokers, salesmen, agents, and bankers.

The residential parts of Minneapolis and St. Paul blended, forming one general area, but each town had a definite downtown section. In St. Paul a small plain, only a few blocks in extent, bounded on one side by the river and on others by steep hills — the area between Wabasha and Jackson Streets on the one hand and Fourth and Seventh Streets on the other — constituted the financial heart of the other Twin.

The most important financial units in St. Paul were the two great commercial banks, the First National Bank of St. Paul and the Merchants National Bank.[18] Both had strong capital funds and large deposits; after attending to the needs of local customers, they had an abundance for out-of-town use, especially for correspondent banks. Each had a trust affiliate. The First National Bank's was the Northwestern Trust Company, the Hill family owning practically all the stock of both institutions.[19] The Northwestern Trust Company conducted a substantial trust business. The Merchants National Bank was affiliated with the Merchants Trust Company,[20] which, while it did some trust and savings business, dealt actively in securities. It obtained numerous issues to sell, and, because of the volume of capital in St. Paul, it found the disposal of securities a simple procedure.

Next in size among the commercial banks came Mr. Otto Bremer's American National Bank.[21] Despite this rank, it was in comparison a small bank. In the same building with the bank itself were the offices of the Bremer chain of country banks. If anyone pictured these offices as elaborate, he would have been disappointed; Mr. Bremer employed only one secretary and a field man. Since actual operations were left to the managers of individual units, the city office did little more than audit the books.

Also important, although quite small, was the National Exchange Bank (Empire National Bank).[22] It stood on Fifth and Robert Streets and conducted a general banking business with local firms. This area offered a prime market for farm mortgages because it was the home of the St. Paul Federal Land Bank which bought quantities of mortgages. It proved of value in supplying a market when other sources of credit were frozen.

The local federal intermediate credit bank, willing to make loans for intermediate periods of time, did a considerable volume of business, for it always had funds available. Partly because of this bank's existence, and partly because of the plentiful supply of private capital, this region provided funds for term loans.

The office buildings near Fourth and Robert were sprinkled with small investment firms. The investment dealers, headed by C. O. Kalman and Company, often served as members of distributing groups, helping to dispose of New York underwritings; they also sold securities to local capitalists and institutions. There were a few local brokerage houses, which maintained markets in local securities, and several branches of New York Stock Exchange houses.

This financial area was a reservoir of commercial, entrepreneurial, and investment capital, not only for the city, but also for the entire region. Since, as in Minneapolis, there were large commercial banks, a savings bank, trust companies, fire and life insurance companies, farm and city mortgage dealers, loan agents, investment dealers, local and national brokers, corporation lawyers, promoters, and bucket shops, the St. Paul market had all the characteristics of a financial center. The casual spectator would have sensed only confusion, for the district was crowded, the units were diverse, and each seemed to have little connection with the others. All competed vigorously, and the whole group competed with its Minneapolis counterpart. The competition among individual firms was real, but actually St. Paul competed with Minneapolis no more aggressively than one unit did with another within its own boundaries. Each company wanted business — the location of its competitors made little difference. From a physical point of view there were two cities and two financial centers; from an economic point of view there were only one metropolitan center for the entire region and one financial group divided between two small areas. People spoke of the differences between the cities, but these differences became less apparent the farther away one went from the center. At a distance the two towns came into focus as one economic and financial metropolitan unit.

FUNCTIONS OF TWIN CITY BANKS

In 1928 the Ninth Federal Reserve District was covered by a network of banks comprising approximately 2,400 units. These banks conducted the routine but very important function of settling balances between individuals. The simplest form of this function was the situation in which all the individuals in a locality kept their money in one bank, paying their bills by drawing checks on it and depositing to their credit all the checks they received. The banks debited one account and credited another, adjusting exchange between individuals without the direct use of cash. This simple procedure comprised the major activity of many banks.

Country banks also had to collect items from other country banks, from city banks, and from banks in other regions. They found that the most efficient procedure was to centralize this business, using the facilities of a few city correspondents. In 1928 an overwhelming majority of the banks in the Ninth Federal Reserve District, and a substantial number in northern Iowa and in Nebraska, collected most of their out-of-town items through a few Twin City banks.

The banks in the territory, as previously discussed, varied in size. The tiniest had only $5,000 capital; a majority had less than $50,000; approximately 200 had $500,000 or over; only four had $5,000,000.[23] Since the Twin City banks, principally the big four — the First National Bank of Minneapolis, the Northwestern National Bank of Minneapolis, the First National Bank of St. Paul, and the Merchants National Bank of St. Paul — had nearly 3,000 country bank accounts, they treated them as the country banks did their local customers, crediting their accounts with items deposited and debiting them with items drawn. Thus, by coöperating the country banks and the four big city banks handled the exchange and collection operations of the region efficiently, with maximum speed and minimum expense and without the use of cash. In fact, this service functioned so smoothly that the general public was unaware of the difficulties and expense it entailed.

Sufficient time had elapsed by 1928 to permit the entire Ninth Federal Reserve District to emerge from the pioneer stage of development and amass ample commercial capital. Many areas, however, as previously discussed, were still deficient at that late date. Regardless of the amount saved, it was swallowed in some communities by the land. The Twin Cities and the industrial towns in the Ninth Federal Reserve District had accumulated commercial capital in excess of local demands. The prosperous mixed farming districts in southeastern and central Minnesota, as well as those around Fargo, North Dakota, and Sioux Falls, South Dakota, had developed, if not a surplus, at least a self-sufficiency; but the submarginal wheat lands and the drought-stricken regions apparently suffered a permanent deficiency.

In general, the banks in the area had reached a mature equilibrium. They dealt in drafts and bills of exchange and they made innumerable loans to millers, elevator men, manufacturers, wholesalers, retailers, farmers, and cattlemen. Banks in agricultural centers loaned to the farmers during the growing season; at harvest time they collected from the farmers and loaned to the elevator men, who bought, cleaned, stored, and shipped the crop. When the elevator man sold the crop to a city elevator, the seller drew a draft on the purchaser and deposited it in his local bank. In the Twin Cities the great banks loaned first to the commission men and then to the elevator men who bought and stored the wheat. Where possible, the city banks loaned to the mills to finance milling operations and the sale of the flour. The millers, however, though they could have obtained ample capital in Minneapolis, often shopped around for the lowest interest rate. The Twin City banks fared somewhat better with the miscellaneous trades. The small manufacturers, wholesalers, retailers, elevator operators, contractors, and builders had no outside contacts; they had to patronize local banks. In fact, most of them were delighted to have a dependable source of credit. Their loans, though frequently for small amounts, aggregated an important sum. The fact that most of them were almost non-competitive allowed the banks to profit from each transaction. These loans were on a permanent-customer basis, it being generally understood that a customer would not split his line of credit, and would keep an ample balance. The arrangement between the Twin City banks and their smaller customers was one of mutual advantage: the banks were to supply all the banking services their customers needed; the customers' business was to provide the banks with profitable business. Such a situation was nothing new; it had already become characteristic of New York, Chicago, and other cities. It was just good banking—banking on a stabilized basis. This type of service cost the banks money: they had to stay sufficiently liquid to be able to care for their small customers in times of depression, financial stringency, and during peak demands for credit; they had to refuse good, profitable loans from non-customers, in order to retain cash which their regular customers might demand. This service was expensive and the banks had to be paid. It was not cheap service but it was dependable.

In order to pay checks drawn on them, the country banks maintained large deposits with some of the city banks. Gradually, as we have pointed out, almost all interbank transactions for the region centered in one of four: the First National Bank of Minneapolis, the First National Bank of St. Paul, the Northwestern National Bank of Minneapolis, or the Merchants National Bank of St. Paul. These institutions competed for country-bank deposits, performing many services free of charge. While the most obvious was the collection of items and the payment of checks, the lending of funds was given more weight by the country banker.

Practically every region had a seasonal peak in its demand for credit, a time when even an actual local excess of commercial capital fell short of needs. If banks had been forced to depend entirely on their own resources they would have kept themselves very liquid, refusing many sound loans; but, preferring to keep as much of their funds as possible in use, country bankers made the loans and borrowed from their correspondents to meet seasonal demands. Fortunately for the city banks the peak demands of two or more districts rarely coincided. One area would be repaying loans and making deposits while other areas were drawing down their balances and borrowing money.

Well-managed country banks recognized the danger of runs and the importance of being able to obtain money quickly. They insisted that their city correspondents be both able and willing to supply them with any reasonable amount upon demand. This did not mean that the city banks would advance funds upon inadequate collateral to insolvent banks; it did mean that, if a solvent country bank experienced a run, it could under any circumstances obtain money from its correspondent. This arrangement permitted the country banks to maintain a fully invested position, relying upon their correspondents for emergency funds. Country-bank deposits in the city banks occasionally amounted to 40 per cent of total deposits, and loans to country banks were very large. Country business was therefore immensely important to the four big city banks.

The Minneapolis Federal Reserve Bank had been established partly to take care of bank customers during seasonal peaks and times of emergency. Since all national banks were forced to belong, this bank had been expected to have such an advantage that it would soon monopolize the country-bank business. Most of the important banks were members, and it supplied a fine type of service, holding reserve balances and clearing checks. Yet the Minneapolis Federal Reserve Bank was unwilling to displace the four Twin City banks which formed the center of country-bank activities. Although the Minneapolis Federal Reserve Bank was privately owned, all earnings in excess of 6 per cent were added to surplus and not distributed to its stockholders.[24] Thus, there was no valid reason to augment its earnings. When the city banks did not have enough money to loan, they themselves either borrowed in Chicago or New York or rediscounted with the Minneapolis Federal Reserve Bank.

Insurance in the Twin Cities

Since the Twin Cities are landlubbers, one would scarcely expect marine insurance to develop in them. Actually, this was the first type of insurance to spring up in the Northwest. From an historical point of view it is not surprising, for boat traffic on the Mississippi was vital during the early years, and valuable cargoes often were lost. To mitigate such losses a company known as the St. Paul Fire and Marine Insurance Company was organized in 1853 in St. Paul.[25] Its business became substantial and profitable, consisting first of marine business on the Mississippi and later of fire insurance. Fortunately for the company, it developed a line of fire insurance long before river traffic had disappeared. The management was conservative; for years it accumulated earnings and built up capital. Even as early as 1880 the company was known for its large business and its strength. In the course of years it broadened its lines, incorporating subsidiaries to write new types of policies. By 1928 the St. Paul Fire and Marine Insurance Company was one of the leading underwriters in the United States.[26] Its capital funds and reserves found their outlet in the investment market of the Twin Cities. The company had acquired small stock interests in a few local companies; it held some real-estate mortgages; but an overwhelming proportion of its assets was invested in municipal bonds locally purchased.

Minneapolis was considerably slower than St. Paul in producing insurance companies. Perhaps its comparative remoteness from river traffic is a partial explanation. In due course, however, fire insurance companies did appear. By 1928, Minneapolis had three of importance: the Twin City Fire Insurance Company, the Minneapolis Fire and Marine Insurance Company, and the Northwestern Fire and Marine Insurance Company.[27]

Though of little importance in volume of business and size of assets, the most interesting and distinctive insurance venture in the Twin Cities was the Underwriters at Lloyds of Minneapolis, sometimes known as the Fifty Associates. This was a limited-liability association composed of fifty financial leaders in Minneapolis. On the roll[28] we find Messrs. Shreve M. Archer, linseed oil; James Ford Bell, flour-milling; Russell M. Bennett, mining; Earle Brown, capitalist; John Crosby, flour-milling; George Nelson Dayton, merchandising; John H. Hauschild, insurance; Clive T. Jaffray, railroads; Sumner T. McKnight, real estate; John D. McMillan, grain; A. F. Pillsbury, flour-milling; John S. Pillsbury, flour-milling; Lyman E. Wakefield, banking; Willis J. Walker, lumber; and F. E. Weyerhaeuser, lumber and timber. Next to its membership the most striking thing about this company was its organization. The form was already well developed in London by the seventeenth century under the name Lloyds of London.[29] As a matter of fact, this title was misleading, for Lloyds was merely the name of the coffee house where many individual underwriters met to transact their business. These underwriters, often acting through a broker, took shares in the risks of various ventures. The same type of underwriting developed on the North American continent in the eighteenth century, especially in Boston, New York, and Philadelphia.[30] Groups of wealthy, prominent business men, acting through their brokers, underwrote sea risks. Not until the twentieth century did this form of organization penetrate to Minneapolis. The risk underwritten by the Fifty Associates was automobile liability.

There had been numerous early attempts to organize life insurance companies in the Twin Cities, but none of them had survived. The first successful company was the Minnesota Mutual Life Insurance Company, organized in St. Paul in 1880.[31] Its sales increased, its premium income mounted, and its reserves grew. These reserves were invested to some extent in farm and city mortgages, but largely in corporate and municipal bonds. The deposits of the company in St. Paul banks were large; in fact, it was one of the largest depositors in the Twin Cities.

Probably it was the success of this company that led to the organization in 1885 of its Minneapolis counterpart, the Northwestern National Life Insurance Company.[32] In 1928 this company's president was Mr. O. J. Arnold, and its board of trustees boasted representatives of both the First National Bank and the Northwestern National Bank of Minneapolis.[33] The company was successful. Its volume of insurance in force increased steadily, as did its premium income, and its growing reserves swelled both the volume of investment capital in the Twin City market and the volume of funds in Minneapolis banks.

The Title Insurance Company of Minnesota wrote policies guaranteeing the validity of titles, agreeing to defend them or to stand the loss if they were successfully attacked.[34] This corporation acquired its ample capital funds by selling stock and saving income. A purchaser of real estate, desiring to assure himself of a clear title to property, took out title insurance. The volume of this insurance had a close correlation, therefore, to the volume of real-estate transactions. The sale of title insurance was also promoted by the mortgaging of real estate, for the lender generally insisted on a clear title. Indeed, borrowers were usually obliged to insure against all hazards: fire, cyclone, windstorm, mob violence, and even death. Under these circumstances, insurance thrived as the Twin Cities grew to be a financial center.

By 1928 the Twin Cities represented a small regional insurance center. In addition to the major companies there were many small coöperative or fraternal insurance companies offering all types of insurance. To be sure, the Twin Cities did not rank with national insurance centers, but local companies provided a wide range of coverage.

The nature of the insurance business caused capital to accumulate in the home offices of companies in the Twin Cities. These funds went into the local money market. First they appeared as premium checks drawn on banks all over the region; then, as checks were collected by the banks, they reappeared as deposits. Increasing reserves were invested in every type of security: a small volume in local stocks, some money in city and farm mortgages, and a fair amount in corporate and municipal bonds. The capital, surplus, and reserves of insurance companies constituted a factor in making the Twin Cities a financial center.

Working and Investment Capital

For purposes of classification, capital can be divided into three major divisions: *working*, *risk investment*, and *non-risk investment capital*.

Working capital is usually the net current assets of business firms; it is closely related to the mechanism of production and exchange, flowing with raw materials, wages, and expenses into manufactured products, and returning to the manufacturer when the goods are sold. When business firms find their cash dwindling during the process of manufacture, they borrow from banks, agreeing to repay when the transaction is over, usually in thirty, sixty, or ninety days. The sale of the goods produces funds to repay the loan. Since companies experience alternate periods of activity and inactivity and the periods of activity vary from one unit to another, banks in effect loan the balances of temporarily inactive firms to others experiencing periods of activity. Working capital exists to finance everyday productive transactions. We have discussed the growth and accumulation of working capital in the Twin Cities in a previous section and shall merely add that by 1928 the Twin Cities and the entire region had a supply ample for their needs.

Risk investment capital is that available for investment in business ventures in return for a share of the profits. This type of capital is willing to take risks; it does not want interest, it wants profits. It is invested, not for a term of months, but indefinitely or until the termination of a venture. It is the type of capital that a man puts into his own business, advances as a silent partner in another's venture, or invests in the common stock of established corporations.

Practically every line of business — lumbering, flour-milling, manufacturing, wholesaling, retailing, banking, railroad-building and operation, public-utility promotion and operation, and real-estate speculation — had, by 1928, produced sizable fortunes. Many of these fortunes were in the hands of aggressive business men, who were willing to risk them for profits; hence they, too, should be classed as risk investment capital. While we usually think of the individual in this respect, one of the major sources of this type of capital in 1928 was the profits earned by the going concerns. A company engaged in business was always interested in new activities, the only attraction needed being the promise of moderate profits. Since many local business concerns had excess capital and perhaps were able to save reasonable amounts out of earnings, they were looking for new lines, new plants, and new territories. There were also many semi-retired business men with fortunes which they were eager to reinvest in business. Last, but possibly not least, came the little men who were willing to hazard some part of their savings in business ventures in the naïve belief that, if they persisted, some investment would reward them with a fortune.

The year 1928 revealed a large volume of risk investment capital seeking employment in the Twin Cities. The majority of promising ventures already had been developed, and only a few companies were then coming into existence. The days of tremendous profits for the average company were already a matter of history. Capital continued to accumulate as profitable opportunities for investment became more and more scarce. Perhaps it was this condition which prompted the steady appreciation of urban values, the rise in worth of operating business units, the high price placed upon good-will, and the unchecked advance in the valuation of securities so characteristic of that year. Property and security values continued to rise long after actual operating earnings had commenced to decline.

Non-risk investment capital is that which is available for long-term investment in return for a fixed rate of interest. Although occasionally it comes from individual savings, under ordinary circumstances it represents a transfer of risk capital accumulated by successful business men. These men, or their heirs, retire from the responsibilities of active business and withdraw their venture capital to place it in less bothersome, less risky, and less profitable investments. They are not concerned about liquidity or time: they want safety, a sure return, and freedom from mental exertion. The expansion of non-risk investment capital in the Twin Cities was indicated by a growing number of retired investment capitalists, a steady increase in the number and size of estates managed by corporate trust companies, and a swelling of capital in the hands of private trustees, but especially by the lengthening list of high-grade, long-term investment securities for sale by Twin City dealers between 1920 and 1927.[35]

By 1928 the Twin Cities could be classed as a small primary capital market. There was enough working and risk investment capital for all reasonable purposes. Excess non-risk investment capital was absorbed by bonds from other areas, United States Government bonds, State and municipal obligations, and foreign securities. Its accumulation was so marked that the Twin Cities became known as a market thirsty for securities.

The Investment Organization Supplies Capital to Business

The surplus of capital in the Twin Cities and the Ninth Federal Reserve District in 1928 was invested through an elaborate organization. The core was the group of commercial banks which loaned deposits directly to the business community, but it included to some extent the savings banks and trust companies. The flow of non-risk investment capital was aided by a group of professional investment dealers, individuals and organizations which purchased investment securities and sold them to commercial banks, savings banks, trust companies, insurance companies, and investment capitalists. A group of brokers developed the resale market, repurchasing and reselling securities already issued. The investment dealers of the Twin Cities were a very fluid group. Individuals operated under their own names; they formed groups, partnerships, and corporations; then they changed these formal organizations, dissolved, and reassembled. Firms shifted with great frequency, yet the leading men were the same. Regardless of combinations, individual names continued.

One of the leaders was Mr. Charles Oscar Kalman, who did business under different firm names, finally becoming simply C. O. Kalman and Company.[36] He had strong personal connections as financial adviser to Mr. Louis W. Hill and with the Northwestern Trust Company in St. Paul. Mr. Henry Thrall and Mr. David West managed the securities business of the Minnesota Loan and

Trust Company.[37] They had little to do with its trust or banking functions, concentrating their efforts on supplying the firm's customers with investments. Because of their aggressiveness and capableness, and because of their connection with the Trust Company, they were able to sell securities. Messrs. I. H. Overman and H. E. ("Hap") Atwood were in charge at the First Minneapolis Trust Company.[38] They, too, successfully disposed of a volume of investment securities to the local public. This business constituted an important source of income to the trust company.

In St. Paul the most important and prosperous investment unit was the Merchants Trust Company, the securities division of which was headed by Mr. Julian B. Baird and Mr. N. Paul Delander.[39] This company's clientele included the large local insurance companies and the first families of St. Paul.

Because the Twin Cities afforded a good volume of New York Stock Exchange business, many New York houses had established local branches, which acted as brokers for the purchase and sale of securities listed on the New York Stock Exchange. Besides the listed securities, which had to be traded in in New York, there were many unlisted local issues, which were freely bought and sold in the Twin Cities and the Northwest, and to some extent even throughout the United States. Among them were the Diamond Iron Works, Northern States Power, St. Paul Fire and Marine Insurance Company, Title Insurance Company of Minnesota, Curtis Hotel, and Nicollet Hotel, as well as innumerable real-estate ventures. The volume of trading in local and regional securities finally became so large that Twin City dealers decided to organize an exchange of their own.

We have pointed out that in 1928 the Twin Cities possessed capital and an investment-banking organization to retail securities and to act as bankers. The structure was deficient in one respect: there were no firms specializing in the issuance of large-scale local issues. Local investment banks were houses of distribution and not primarily houses of origination. To be sure, the local firms handled the small and medium-sized local issues. When a small local firm or municipality wished to sell a bond issue it negotiated a deal with a local investment house, which organized a local syndicate to sell the securities to local investors. Each issue had to be relatively small in size, but the total was large and formed a very important item in the local investment business. The local investors would purchase a moderate volume of practically any issue, and many different issues in rapid succession, but they would not absorb a large volume of any one issue without high-pressure sales methods. Most of the dealers avoided these methods; they preferred many small issues and moderate participations in large issues to large participations in large issues. When big regional firms wished to float a large issue of securities, therefore, their officials journeyed to New York to negotiate with the national underwriting firms. These firms underwrote the issue and arranged to have it sold on a national basis through regional selling houses. The Twin City dealers received their full share of these national participations.

As a matter of fact, the Twin Cities had never in any important way originated their own large issues of securities. We have only to think back to the local railroads. None of the issues of the roads which finally became the Great Northern were local in origin: the Northern Pacific was organized in the East; even the Minneapolis, St. Paul and Sault Ste. Marie, which came at a much later date, had to raise its capital in eastern Canada.

In 1910 the Eastern Railway of Minnesota wanted to borrow money, and its officers went as a matter of course to Wall Street to negotiate with Clark, Dodge and Company, Moffat and White, and Lee, Higginson and Company. They arranged for a bond issue bearing a 4 per cent interest rate and maturing in 1948.[40] Private-banking firms attended to all the details, underwrote the issue, and arranged for a syndicate to sell the bonds on a national scale.

In the following year, 1911, the Great Northern Railroad wished to issue some bonds. It conferred with its bankers, J. P. Morgan and Company, who arranged to issue the Great Northern 4¼'s of 1961, underwritten by J. P. Morgan and Company and the First National Bank of New York.[41]

In 1923, Archer-Daniels-Midland Company decided to issue a preferred stock. It negotiated with Goldman, Sachs and Company and Lehman Brothers.[42] These two firms were very active in financing promotions, mergers, and new issues in the Twin Cities during the 'twenties.

There were, of course, certain exceptions to the rule of eastern origin. The major one during the 'twenties was the Motor Transit Corporation. Mr. Glen Traer, the manager of Lane, Piper, Jaffray and Company's securities department, in coöperation with the owners of certain local bus lines, drew up the plans for the sale to the general public of equipment-trust certificates and stock to finance the companies which eventually formed the Greyhound Corporation.[43] In this instance Lane, Piper, Jaffray and Company acted as private bankers, but this activity ceased when Mr. Traer left the firm. Thenceforth the financing of Greyhound was done in other centers.

Another group of companies which developed in the Twin Cities during the 'twenties was the Foshay promotions. From a small beginning Foshay grew rapidly, financing his activities by the sale of stock to small investors, until by 1928 he was considered a leading figure in Twin City business.[44] Despite the fact that his promotions and securities emanated from Minneapolis and St. Paul, he never fitted into the accepted regional financial organization. He had few connections with the commercial banks and none with the investment distributors. His securities were thrust upon the public by his own salesmen through a campaign of promotional advertising and individual high-pressure sales which did not scorn even house-to-house solicitation. Foshay was not a part of the banking organization; he should be classed as a successful high-pressure promoter who avoided the financial machinery of the Twin Cities.

The Baker promotions fitted into somewhat the same category. Mr. Morris T. Baker, as discussed in other chapters, was a salesman of outstanding ability and a promoter of great vision and enthusiasm. Conjuring up a series of great hotels and office buildings, he sold securities directly to the public to finance their construction.[45] Although he was never fully accepted by the Minneapolis banking fraternity, he did not experience the violent opposition accorded Mr. Foshay, perhaps because his promotions enhanced the city skyline and increased local prosperity by creating building activity. Whatever happened to the bondholders, Minneapolis acquired some fine new buildings. We must conclude, however, that Mr. Baker, too, was a promoter and not a banker. He marketed his own securities by high-pressure sales methods and he made no effort either to originate or to sell securities for other companies.

Thus, we can find little trace of private banking or security origination on an institutional basis in the Twin Cities. The reason is obvious and applies to all other financial markets in the United States, except New York City. Accumulations of capital even in a large metropolitan area are not able to absorb and digest the issues of great railroads, public utilities, industrial corporations, States, municipalities, and the United States Government. Each area will absorb a moderate amount without pressure, but topping that limit requires high-pressure distribution. Thus, the sale of a large issue of securities is distinctly a national problem. Because private banking early became entrenched in New York City and because that city continued to grow in financial strength, it remains strongly centered there. It should be noted that the New York area does not itself absorb all these securities; they are distributed throughout the United States. Each metropolitan center allows its large-scale financing to originate in New York, taking only a small share of many issues to retail in its own area. Because of the many logical reasons for this arrangement, it appears likely that investment banking will remain largely a New York function regardless of the growth and maturity of other financial centers. The most to which local firms can aspire is a generous participation in New York underwritings and, of course, a larger share in the underwriting of local issues.

Competition among Friends

Employees and officers alike were filled with an almost collegiate loyalty to their own organizations and held firmly to the conviction that all competitors were inferior. This devotion finally reached the point where clerks in one bank shook their heads sadly whenever they mentioned the bank farther up or down the street. They intimated, politely of course, that their competitor might be solvent in fair weather, but just let conditions change. . . . The clerks of their competitor retaliated with implications that some bankers were so afraid of their own shadows that they refused customers reasonable accommodations. This attitude was perfectly sincere; employees believed what they said, and antagonism was very real. Salesmen, customers' men, and junior officers worked for every tag-end of business, even to the extent of taking it away from an affiliated organization. To the individual employee it made no difference; any business he could acquire added to his own prestige. Thus, at the bottom of the financial pyramid were both enthusiastic loyalty and competition.

From a casual examination the Twin City financial organization looked entirely competitive; a closer scrutiny revealed a different picture. Competition abounded, but it was not indiscriminate, however much it appeared so. There were groups of companies bound together by corporate relationships: one company owned another, and occasionally competitors jointly or severally shared the same ownership. It requires little delving to disclose many definite alignments. Behind this definite relationship lay a shadowy field of joint interest, mutual advantage, outside contact, long association, and personal friendship. Often competitors sat side by side on the board of a neutral company. Sometimes competing companies found that they had common minority stockholders who objected to cut-throat competition and insisted on friendly understanding. It is impossible to comprehend fully these inter-relationships. It is enough to point out that they existed in the Twin Cities in 1928, welding the many competitive financial units into a few distinct groups.

There was nothing unusual in this situation; it existed in every city in the country. It was well developed in Boston and New England (the family compact) early in the nineteenth century and developed in New York at about the same time. It is merely a reflection of the fact that every individual has many sides to his character — business, religious, fraternal, and social; that like tends to associate with like; and that man is basically a rational being, preferring to coöperate rather than to compete.

Any definite statement is subject to exceptions, but we can say that in 1928 there were four major groups in the Twin Cities. One centered around the First National Bank of St. Paul, which, as we have seen, had been bought by J. J. Hill as a private investment and in 1928 was owned by his heirs, a circumstance which, of course, allied the bank with the Hill railroads and miscellaneous companies. These included the Great Northern; the Northern Pacific; the Chicago, Burlington, and Quincy; the Great Northern Iron Ore Properties; and the Northwestern Trust Company.

The other group in St. Paul consisted of the Merchants National Bank, the Merchants Trust Company, the Weyerhaeuser interests, the St. Paul Fire and Marine Insurance Company, and the Minnesota Mutual Life Insurance Company.

The First National Bank of Minneapolis formed the nucleus of a third group that included the First Minneapolis Trust Company, the Minneapolis Trust–Joint Stock Land Bank, the Northwestern Fire and Marine Insurance Company, Lloyds of Minneapolis, the Title Insurance Company of Minnesota, and the Minneapolis, St. Paul, and Sault Ste. Marie Railroad.

The fourth group comprised the Northwestern National Bank of Minneapolis, the Minnesota Loan and Trust Company, the Union Investment Company, and a diverse group of flour-milling, elevator, and manufacturing companies. It is true that the Northwestern National Bank had connections with the Northwestern National Life Insurance Company; several of its directors sat on the insurance company's board. Despite this fact, the Northwestern National Life cannot be included in the Northwestern group because, for every relationship it had with the Northwestern National Bank, there was an equivalent with the First National Bank. Thus, the insurance company seems to have provided a neutral meeting ground for two competing groups. Besides the big four there were minor groups, with very indistinct edges, which blended easily into one another.

Even the groups themselves were not senselessly competitive. The leaders were commonly members of either the Minnesota Club in St. Paul or the Minneapolis Club. They played golf at the Somerset Country Club just outside St. Paul or at the Minikahda Club in Minneapolis. Their children attended the same schools and colleges and became members of the same clubs and fraternities. In many instances the young people intermarried, and bitter competitors found themselves the grandparents of the same children. Under these circumstances mutual understanding and sympathy became strong. Moreover, they all knew that cutthroat competition, if carried to an extreme, would bankrupt an industry, destroying profits. Accordingly, just as in social life, an unofficial code of ethics developed in business, and while the senior executives encouraged competition, they insisted that rules be observed.

Thus, the Twin Cities in 1928 present a conglomeration of institutions competing vigorously with one another. Within the involved structure we have noted four distinct pyramids and many vague inter-relations. Because unwritten laws, obeyed by mutual consent, were the only cohesive, there was always a danger that unusual pressure might force a mighty disintegration and that cutthroat competition would ensue.

CHAPTER VII

THE NEW ERA, 1920–1929

The Growth of Twin City Investment Business

The investment business in the Twin Cities was not highly developed before the World War, and relatively few individuals engaged in it. During the War the national government campaigned vigorously to sell government bonds to small investors, and its high-pressure methods forced them into the hands of people who had never before purchased investment securities. This greatly broadened the field of investors. Many liberty bonds were sold on installment, purchasers being induced to borrow the funds for their purchase from commercial banks and pay for them out of income. At the same time, high wages and profits fostered the accumulation of capital, and savings in the Ninth Federal Reserve District reached a large volume. At the close of the World War, local investment dealers found conditions extremely favorable for a substantial and profitable business in investment securities. Government bonds, because of their low interest rate and tax-exempt features, tended to go into the hands of wealthy individuals or of institutions, and this movement supplied the general public with a generous volume of capital for other purposes. These funds were reinvested largely in corporate securities, which yielded a considerably higher rate than governments.

During the 'twenties the volume of investment capital continued to grow, and investment dealers experienced increasing business and more profitable operations. Old-line firms abandoned other activities in order to concentrate on the distribution of securities. While Lane, Piper and Jaffray did not dispose of its business in commercial paper, the firm saw it lost in the swell of investment business. Wells-Dickey Company sold its trust business to the Minneapolis Trust Company, turned over its farm-mortgage division to the O. M. Corwin Company, and gave its undivided attention to the merchandising of securities.[1] Kalman, Matteson and Wood were very active; and in 1921, one year after Matteson retired, the firm continued as Kalman, Wood and Company.[2]

The number of men employed in distributing bonds in the Twin Cities grew rapidly; when the Twin Cities Bond Club was organized in 1921, it boasted 125 members.[3] John S. Bauman of Wells-Dickey Company was the first president; Harold Wood of Kalman, Wood and Company was vice-president; and R. C. Mees of Paine, Webber and Company was secretary and treasurer.[4]

The country banks, as we have seen, had been brought to a sorry realization of the difficulties inherent in investing all their funds in local situations. They commenced to use bonds as a secondary reserve. Many banks purchased governments and other high-grade securities, which constituted an excellent reserve. Unfortunately some bankers, extremely capable in making commercial loans, demonstrated a lamentable ignorance of corporation finance by filling their portfolios with bonds of questionable character. Many bought entirely on a yield basis. As liquidation occurred in the country-banking structure, other loans declined, but the volume of corporate securities purchased by banks tended upward. The major portion of the growing investment business, however, came from the individual buyer, who had not only accumulated capital during the war days, but also continued to amass it in ever growing amounts during the 'twenties.

Local Promotional Ventures

General conditions, which had been very depressed in the latter parts of 1920 and 1921, turned for the better in 1922 and became very prosperous in the cities, where industrial activity thrived and buildings began to go up. During the War, because of high prices and the necessity of conserving both labor and capital, little building had been done and a shortage of space had developed. Building costs declined sharply during 1920 and 1921, but, because of the scarcity of space, rents tended to hold up. As a result, construction became lucrative. Investors could put up new buildings and lease them at a profit. Industrial concerns decided that since prices were low, they could afford to build, and, as conditions improved during 1922, people began to think of new homes. The boom was supported by the large volume of savings accumulated during the previous period and by the ready market which industrial and building concerns found for their securities. In fact, since investment dealers could sell almost anything, they stood ready to underwrite and distribute issues of real-estate securities. The wave of building helped to improve general business conditions. Innumerable homes and other small buildings were constructed in the Twin Cities in 1922 and 1923, but the most outstanding venture was the new Nicollet Hotel.

The old Nicollet House had long been a landmark, located as it was in the heart of the Gateway district at the intersection of Washington, Hennepin, and Nicollet Avenues, near the river and between the city's two passenger stations. The district had tended to deteriorate. The desirable part of the downtown area was slowly moving south up Hennepin, Nicollet, and Marquette. The steady encroachment of the rundown section was tending to lower real-estate values farther up the street. In real-estate and business circles it was felt that something should be done to halt this advance, that some of the old buildings should be replaced by modern structures which perhaps would attract a more desirable type of tenant. It was also felt that Minneapolis needed a new hotel, and thus the idea of pushing the construction and financing of a hotel project as a civic duty evolved. Plans were carefully laid, and a barrage of publicity was prepared to sell the project to the general public. A bulletin describing the project stated:[5]

> The Nicollet Hotel, Incorporated, is sponsored by a group of Minneapolis business and professional men. These men have become identified with the project because they realize that it is a civic enterprise worthy of their support. This is not a private undertaking as ordinarily understood, but is a whole-hearted endeavor on the part of Minneapolis business interests to give to the city an institution which will be a real contribution to its upbuilding and at the same time will provide a safe and profitable investment for local capital.

The land for the new hotel was leased from the owners at a ground rent of $40,000 a year.[6] A new company was organized which sold $1,800,000 of first-mortgage leasehold bonds and $1,250,-000 of preferred stock to dealers for resale to the public.[7] A little booklet of questions and answers asked why the new Nicollet Hotel should be financed by local capital.[8] The answer was: "Minneapolis cannot have too many industries paying interest and dividends to Minneapolis investors. With the new Nicollet Hotel earnings going to capital, every shareholder will be a booster for the hotel and city simultaneously and, thus, will bring more money directly into Minneapolis channels. Everything that can be done to turn the savings of Minneapolis people into safe and profitable channels will eventually react to the advantage of Minneapolis as a whole."[9] It stated further, "The Minneapolis Civic and Commerce Association, an organization devoted to the interests of the city as a whole, is sponsoring this hotel project from its inception."[10] Interesting computations were made as to what the project would earn, and it was pointed out that this was an undertaking that anybody could afford to back. It was one of those lovely propositions: the investor got a high rate on his money; the city obtained a new hotel, which would tend to build up business; all business would be made more profitable; and, in this best of possible worlds, the business of every man would be improved by his pursuit of his own best interests. Of course, such excellent securities sold readily, and the hotel was soon under construction.

During the early 'twenties, as we have seen, W. B. Foshay came rapidly to the front through his public-utility promotions. His procedure was to buy small public utility companies, incorporate them, and obtain the purchase price through the sale of new securities to the general public, retaining a controlling interest. Eventually he organized a holding company and sold its securities to the public, using the proceeds to finance his public-utility activities. From a microscopic start he advanced rapidly and by the end of 1924 owned control of the Minnesota Electric Distributing Company, the Tri-State Utilities Company, the Iowa River Light and Power Company, and the Peoples Light and Power Company.[11] He made use of the latter to centralize the control of operating companies acquired during the early days. In February, 1925, the W. B. Foshay Company added $2,000,000 to its capital by selling $1,000,000 of preferred and $1,000,000 of common stock.[12] During the year Foshay's other companies also expanded. In addition to a strong market for utility securities, he met with an unusually ready response from the public, a result perhaps of his adroit advertising. For instance, he stated that he had nothing to conceal and, again, that some companies were older and some larger, but none better.[13] Whenever one of his issues paid its interest or a dividend, he published the fact boldly in the newspapers with the comment that this was added proof of the safety of securities originated by W. B. Foshay Company. Any appreciation in market price he announced with proud enthusiasm, especially to investors who had refused to buy at lower prices. His expansion was incredible; by the end of 1925 his companies were supplying power to 140 communities.[14]

Before the World War the jitney bus had a place in the transportation system of only a few cities, but bus activity increased tremendously after the War. The growing dependability of automobiles and the improvement of roads contributed to this expansion. By the early 'twenties a network of bus lines had sprung up in the northern part of Minnesota, and several lines ran regularly out of the Twin Cities. In August, 1925, the Fitzgerald brothers of Virginia, Minnesota, who had formerly operated the Range Transit Company, purchased for about $100,000 the Terminal Motor Bus Company which connected St. Paul with La Crosse.[15] They immediately announced the extension of lines to Chicago. Confronted with growing competition, the railroads had already begun to establish and acquire bus lines, and by August, 1925, the Great Northern Railroad owned the Jefferson Highway Bus Line, the Northland Transportation Company, and the Interstate Bus Lines, and was constructing a union bus depot in Minneapolis.[16] In September, 1925, Edgar F. Zelle, owner of the Red Bus Line which operated the Motor Truck Service Company, sold his lines to the Northland and purchased the southern lines of the Jefferson Highway Transportation Company.[17]

The guaranteed real-estate mortgage made its appearance in the Twin Cities in 1925. This was an arrangement by which surety companies wrote bonds guaranteeing that the principal and interest on mortgages would be paid promptly. The risk was considered insurable, for figures covering a twenty-four-year period showed that investors had experienced only nominal losses from this type of security. The development of the guaranteed mortgage increased the supply of money for real estate and plant construction, thereby adding to the boom. The Guaranteed Mortgage Company was organized in November, 1926, with H. W. White as president, E. R. Price as vice-president and treasurer, and E. C. Warner as chairman of the board.[18] The company had a capital of $250,000. The Minneapolis Trust Company was trustee, and the mortgages pledged as collateral were guaranteed by the United States Fidelity and Guaranty Company.[19] The idea of guarantees was extremely popular, and in September, 1926, there was considerable discussion of a company to guarantee land values so that real-estate purchasers would never have to worry about a decline in the market.[20]

In May, 1925, the Minnesota and Ontario Paper Company issued $16,000,000 of 6 per cent first-mortgage bonds, which were sold by the Minnesota Loan and Trust Company and Halsey Stuart and Company, Inc., of Chicago.[21] The Minneapolis Trust Company, Wells-Dickey, and the Minnesota Loan and Trust Company offered a first-mortgage issue of New England Lime Company bonds in July.[22] In February, 1926, Foshay, preparing to incorporate the Peoples Light and Power Corporation, transferred to it substantially all of his miscellaneous public utility properties.[23] A short time later he sold control of this company to G. L. Ohrstrom and Company.[24] This did not mean, however, that Foshay was leaving the utility business. He immediately laid plans for a new pyramid of companies.

By far the most amazing promotion and construction work in the Twin Cities was the Baker series. After the World War, Mr. Morris T. Baker returned from the army to Minneapolis and a successful real-estate career. He was not long content to work for somebody else, but drew up plans for a series of building promotions. In most cases he obtained an option either to purchase or to lease the land, incorporated a building company, and sold a first-mortgage leasehold bond issue and a preferred stock issue, retaining the controlling interest in the common stock himself. His most outstanding project, as discussed previously, was the Baker Block, located between

Seventh and Eighth Streets and Marquette and Second Avenues. This block was developed through the use of different building companies, each of which contributed one of the four units, namely the Baker Building, the Baker Arcade, the Baker Garage, and the Roanoke Building. He also built and/or purchased the Sheridan Hotel, the apartment house known as 510 Groveland, the Lewis Building, and the Builders Exchange Building; [25] each of these was pledged under an individual mortgage. The various operating companies had miscellaneous issues of securities outstanding, control of which was centered in the Baker Properties, Incorporated, which likewise had bonds and preferred stock outstanding. Baker Properties, Incorporated, was controlled by the Morris T. Baker Company, and its control was held by Mr. Morris T. Baker, personally. Toward the end of the 'twenties the Morris T. Baker Company was actively engaged in a general investment business, and more particularly in distributing the securities of its own companies.

Early in 1927 a new corporation was announced. It was to be known as the Minneapolis Theatre Company, and Sumner T. McKnight was to be its president.[26] This company was going to build at Ninth Street and La Salle Avenue a modern theater for the presentation of three-dimension and vitaphone pictures. The ground was leased from the Central Trust Company of New York, trustee for J. A. Andrus and the Walker-Pence Company, and the theatre was leased to Famous Players-Lasky Corporation for twenty-five years.[27] With the land acquired and the building let, the Minneapolis Theatre Company was launched. Funds were supplied by a $1,200,000 issue of first-mortgage leasehold bonds.[28] They sold readily, for simple mathematics showed that the twenty-five-year lease would provide sufficient funds to pay both the principal and the interest.

Growing Enthusiasm

Since volume of business was growing, profits increasing, promotional ventures successful, and actual accomplishments outrunning the most optimistic forecasts, enthusiasm grew until it reached hysterical intensity. Even conservative Melvin A. Traylor stated that 1926 was a year of unequaled prosperity.[29] Credits were easy and stock prices were still low. The popularity of investment securities had grown until investments had become a common dinner-table subject. Newspapers and magazines were capitalizing on this interest by running little columns which might have been entitled *Helpful Hints to Careful Investors*, and longer articles on the subject *Does Profit-Taking Pay?* These articles pointed out that the stock market tended steadily upward, and that after a minor recession each advance was greater than the last. Mathematical computations demonstrated whether or not it paid to sell on the rises and buy on the declines. The general conclusion seemed to be that this was a very dangerous business and that the average investor was better off never to take a profit, but to buy and hold indefinitely. Books and articles were devoted to the common-stock theory of investments.

The earnings of industrial corporations continued upward, and in recognition of prosperity W. B. Foshay Company in January, 1927, not only declared the regular dividend on its preferred and common shares, but also paid a bonus on these stocks in order to share the affluence the company was experiencing.[30]

The construction of theaters, hotels, office buildings, and apartments swelled to such an extent that in 1927 even S. W. Straus, than whom there was no greater real-estate promoter, said, "There should be a temporary breathing spell in new building, as we have reached the saturation point after four years of heavy construction." [31]

In March, 1927, it was announced that Lane, Piper and Jaffray had agreed to distribute, both wholesale and retail, the new bond issues of the Guaranteed Mortgage Company of Minneapolis.[32] In April the Minnesota and Ontario Paper Company offered another bond issue.[33] In the same month W. B. Foshay announced that he had engaged Magny and Tusler, architects, to plan a new 22-story office building for Minneapolis at an estimated cost of more than $2,000,000.[34] In May, Lane, Piper and Jaffray offered 5,500 shares of Motor Transit Corporation, a company organized to acquire a diverse group of motor-bus companies and to operate the Greyhound Lines.[35] In June, Foshay began the organizing of a new company called Public Utilities Consolidated Corporation to unite the utility companies acquired since his sale of Peoples Light and Power.[36] In October, Lane, Piper and Jaffray announced a new line, investment trust securities, and Lester Bigelow left the First Minneapolis Trust Company to become a partner in Kalman and Company. In November the Minneapolis Heat Regulator Company and the Honeywell Heating Specialty Company, of Wabash, Indiana, merged as the Minneapolis-Honeywell Heat Regulator Company. The following March brought the grand opening of the Minnesota Theatre, pride of the Minneapolis Theatre Company.[37]

During this period business had been growing at an accelerating rate. In March, 1928, a popular newspaper columnist and commentator on business affairs came out with the statement that the hurdles were down and there was nothing to stop the business advance.[38] He pointed out that wealth increasing at an annual rate of $10,000,000,000 was being employed in enlarging and improving our productive capacity, which, in turn, made more wealth.[39] Production was rolling like a snowball down a hill. Doubters raised their eyebrows and demanded to know why, if this could be, it had not happened before. The answer was simple. Formerly, an imperfect banking structure had caused a shortage of credit, because advancing business reduced bank reserves and caused a credit stringency. Thus, whenever business had started to advance, it had been curbed before reaching its full stride. Now that the Federal Reserve supplied an elastic currency to remedy this situation, we could never again experience a serious depression. The fundamental assumption was that demand would take goods off the market as fast as they were produced, for anyone, even a moron, could see that there was no limit to human want when it was reinforced by purchasing power, and this beneficent industrial system of ours produced the purchasing power along with the goods! Technological advances were constantly improving industrial productivity and supplying the demand for the annual $10,000,000,000 of savings. The possibilities were infinite, and the business of the 'twenties a mere beginning. Countless magazine articles reiterated the belief that the old-time economic system had passed. To be sure, some business leaders were puzzled and a little breathless, but they were acknowledged as backward in comprehending the new prosperity.

The golden era had dawned at last. This state of mind was the background against which stock-market prices mounted dizzily. Business organizations came to realize that the quicker they could merge and expand, the greater would be their opportunities.

In April, 1928, Mr. Giannini of the Bank of Italy, in California, hurdled the continent and landed in Wall Street with the purchase of the Bank of America from the Jonas Brothers.[40] He bought 32,000 shares, a controlling interest, and the news of his purchase strengthened the price of the minority stock to such an extent that market analysts pointed out a $3,000,000 appreciation of his stock in a period of a few short days. True, he could not have sold it for this price; in fact, he did not intend to sell it, but this made no difference to the statisticians. His profit was still $3,000,000.

Early in 1928 the F. H. Peavey Company bought the business of the Van Dusen-Harrington Company, and by the middle of the year Washburn-Crosby Company had organized General Mills, Incorporated, to acquire not only the Washburn-Crosby properties but also a chain of mills extending across the country.[41] Motor Transit Corporation, owner of the Greyhound Lines, continued to grow; its financing was handled primarily by Lane, Piper and Jaffray.[42] In June, the bonds of the Nicollet Avenue Properties Corporation were sold by a syndicate composed of Lane, Piper and Jaffray, Kalman and Company, and Wells-Dickey Company.[43] In November, General Mills took advantage of the strong investment demand to sell a new issue of stock for cash.[44] The investment business was becoming so important in the Twin Cities, as discussed in Chapter VI, that dealers organized the Minneapolis-St. Paul Stock Exchange, which opened for business in January, 1929.[45] In February the Morris T. Baker Company offered and sold its own issue of Class A common stock at $20 a share.[46] By this time, plans had been drawn for the Foshay Tower, which was to be modeled on the Washington Monument. In February, W. B. Foshay filed an application for a patent on the tower.[47] In March he contracted for control of the Leamington Hotel, intending to secure the necessary cash from the public but not to disturb the existing $600,000 first mortgage.[48]

The Northwest in common with the entire nation had gone mad on the subject of promotional ventures and mergers. No price was considered too high for an interest in an established operating company. In March, 1929, Morrison and Company of Minneapolis developed plans for a bank holding company.[49] It invited independent country banks to join the corporation and considered selling stock to the general public. This promotion was the exception to the rule; it never got beyond the talking stage. In April an issue of North American Creameries, Incorporated, Class A common stock was sold by the Wells-Dickey Company and the First Minneapolis Trust Company at $23 per share;[50] and Lane, Piper and Jaffray, the First Minneapolis Company, and the Minnesota Company sold a stock issue for the Title Insurance Company of Minnesota.[51] In July the First St. Paul Company helped in the distribution of the Edward Hines Western Pine Company 6% Debentures.[52]

A few hardy pessimists still survived in the country. Paul M. Warburg, in March, 1929, stated that the Federal Reserve Bank had lost control of the credit system and that stocks were terrifically overvalued.[53] He predicted a serious crash, but no one heeded him. Stock prices soared and new issues multiplied.

Meanwhile the Foshay Tower was piercing the Minneapolis skyline.[54] It was completed by the middle of the year, and a three-day celebration ensued: a famous band was imported to play before the tower; the evenings were filled with fireworks and rejoicing; the tower was offered to church groups for religious services; the celebration closed with a great dinner attended by many business leaders. Rumors were rampant concerning the interior of the building. The man in the street had heard that the top story housed a penthouse for Mr. Foshay and that its magnificence culminated in a bathroom with fixtures plated in gold. However, the only one believed to have had any use out of the penthouse was the plumber who installed the fixtures. The gleam of the gold overcame years of prejudice, and the plumber took a bath.

The high point in real-estate promotions came in May, when Mr. Morris T. Baker offered to buy the St. Paul City Hall and Court House at what the papers reported as $1,000,000.[55] Actually the deal was made in September, when he agreed to buy the property for $700,000, deposited a certified check for $20,000, and offered to escrow

$250,000 as surety that he would construct new buildings on the spot, subject to certain specifications.[56]

In August, 1929, Northland Greyhound Lines, Incorporated, was organized and its securities were sold to the public.[57] Control of Northland Greyhound was held jointly by the Motor Transit Corporation and the Great Northern Railroad.

About the same time, Mr. R. W. Manuel's group at the Marquette planned a bank holding company which emerged as the Bank Shares Corporation.[58] This company had two classes of stock, a Class A non-voting stock and a Class B voting stock. The Class A stock after a 4 per cent dividend was to share equally with the Class B in all excess earnings.[59] The stock of the Bank Shares Corporation was exchanged for the shares of the Marquette National Bank, the Marquette Trust Company, and the Chicago-Lake State Bank. Five thousand shares of Class A were to be sold for cash. When the new stock was placed on the market, it was reportedly oversubscribed 150 times. In September, Bank Shares Corporation acquired control of the University State Bank and the Camden Park State Bank.[60]

Over in Wisconsin the First National Bank of Milwaukee was planning a really large chain. It had as its nucleus nineteen banks in Milwaukee and one in Eau Claire.[61] The promoters stated that they were forced into this action against their wishes, because groups from Chicago and the Twin Cities were ready to push their way into control of their local banks. In October it was reported that the new holding company had lined up banks with assets totaling $269,906,052, but that it had not yet chosen a name. Its charter was granted on December 11, 1929, to the Wisconsin Bank Shares Corporation.[62]

On November 1, 1929, the W. B. Foshay Company failed with estimated liabilities of $12,000,000.[63] The first concern of the Twin City banks was the fate of the banks which had been acquired by W. B. Foshay. A quick audit indicated that those in Minneapolis were in fair condition. The Metropolitan National took over the Foshay Trust and Savings Bank; the Third Foshay State Bank, formerly the Gateway State Bank, was taken over by the First Bank Stock Corporation and its name changed to the Hennepin State Bank.[64] The Second Foshay State Bank in St. Paul was insolvent and closed its doors for liquidation.[65]

CHAPTER VIII

METROPOLITAN CONCENTRATION AT BAY 1920–1930

Independence of and Dependence on the Twin Cities, 1920–1928

The business organizations that operated in Minneapolis can readily be divided into two classes: firms which conducted their manufacturing operations in the city but supplied a national or international market, and firms which purchased goods from other areas and sold them in the local market. The first type was more or less independent of the locality; it was situated in Minneapolis merely because that location offered the lowest-cost manufacturing and distribution. Its market was broad, and, if any other city offered more advantages, it was both able and willing to move. The second type was firmly fixed, its future inextricably bound up with that of the local market.

Prominent examples of the first type of firm were the flour mills: notably, Pillsbury, Washburn-Crosby, and Russell-Miller. Other examples were Cream of Wheat, Archer-Daniels Linseed Company, Midland Linseed Company, Russell Grader Manufacturing Company, Minneapolis Steel and Machinery Company, Siems-Stembel Company, Minneapolis Threshing Machine Company, Minneapolis Heat Regulator Company, Munsingwear, and a group of fire insurance companies.

A good example of firms entirely dependent upon the local market was the department stores, among them Dayton's, Donaldson's, Powers', and The Leader. There were thousands of small retailers — grocery stores, hardware stores, meat markets, and specialty shops. Local real-estate owners and operators were tied to the town, and so were those who had fortunes invested in office buildings, warehouses, and apartment buildings. Even more dependent were those who owned and operated hotels. The public utilities were also strictly local: the streetcar system (Minneapolis Street Railway), and the city's purveyors of gas (Minneapolis Gas Light), electricity (Northern States Power), and telephone service (Northwestern Bell).

Still another type of firm which depended upon the local situation was the commercial bank. While the First National Bank, the Northwestern National Bank, the Scandinavian-American (later Midland) National Bank, and the Metropolitan National Bank were wealthy institutions, they were as inseparably bound to Minneapolis as was the smallest retailer. True, if local business declined permanently, these banks could extricate a portion of their capital and move to other fields, but there is a distinction between a bank's capital and its business. Capital could be transferred, but business could not. Nor could all the capital be extricated; a sizable portion was invested in bank buildings and local real estate, which had value only as long as the banks and the area continued to thrive.

Flour-Milling in Minneapolis, 1920

Though everything appeared to be thriving in the period from 1910 to 1920, certain factors were working against the success of Minneapolis. River traffic had almost disappeared a generation before, although it still was used as an argument for preferential freight rates. Far more serious was the fact that the power from St. Anthony Falls had been completely utilized, and new or expanding concerns were forced to use either steam or electric power. In neither case could Minneapolis offer an outstanding advantage. The development of electricity was, potentially at least, a blow to the city, for it permitted the cheap transference of power to a multitude of points, minimizing the local importance of water power. Another adverse factor was that the continuous production of wheat on the same land in the area tributary to Minneapolis had fouled the soil. Declining yields had reduced the production and forced a change to other crops until Minneapolis mills had to import wheat from distant areas, a fact which increased transportation costs and made it difficult for that city to retain the freight rates which gave it a competitive advantage. Moreover, the Minneapolis mills had been built years previously; the buildings were old and crowded, poorly arranged, and definitely inferior to new, modern mills. These old properties were depreciated, and, if other areas offered superior inducements, there really was no reason for the mills to remain in Minneapolis.

The blow, which had been long in the making, fell in 1920. In that year the Interstate Commerce Commission revised the freight rate structure with results disastrous to Minneapolis.[1] With one minor exception it removed the milling-in-transit privilege; it equalized the rates through Chicago and Duluth; it raised rates to destroy the differential in favor of Minneapolis; and it made the rates on manufactured goods equal to those on raw materials.[2] As a result, no outstanding advantage remained in milling grain in Minneapolis and shipping flour to the East.

The results of the rate changes made in 1920 did not become apparent until 1922. In February of that year the Washburn-Crosby Company purchased the Star and Crescent Mill in Chicago, shifting a portion of its operations to that city, although it retained all its Minneapolis mills.[3] In February it purchased the Liberty Mill in Kansas City, Missouri.[4] In May, 1922, Pillsbury acquired a mill in Atchison, Kansas, and in September started building a mill in Buffalo, New York.[5] In December, 1923, Russell-Miller sold one Minneapolis mill and started construction of a plant in Buffalo.[6] The crowning indignity came in April, 1924, when Pillsbury dismantled its Palisade Mill and shipped it to Buffalo, where it was reassembled and put into operation.[7]

These are but a few examples of a steady movement during the 'twenties. While few mills actually were moved to other points, firms did not build new mills in the old capital, and when a Minneapolis mill burned or became hopelessly obsolete, it was not rebuilt. Instead, a new mill went up in Chicago, Kansas City, Fort Worth, or Buffalo. The result of this movement can be seen in the figures of flour production in Minneapolis. Production by years is shown on page 161.[8]

This steady decline in the output of flour in Minneapolis had little effect upon the milling companies, for they were merely shifting their operations to competitive points; but it had a great effect upon the industries which, restricted to a local market, had no possibility of moving. True, the boom of the 'twenties and the general growth of miscellaneous industry in the city increased the total volume of business; nevertheless, local industries felt the shift and regretted the loss.

Year	*Barrels*
1919–20	17,117,000
1920–21	14,524,000
1921–22	14,785,000
1922–23	15,730,000
1923–24	12,191,000
1924–25	10,969,000
1925–26	12,509,000

The banks in Minneapolis had always depended upon business with the flour industry. They had loaned to country banks to finance wheat growers and local business men until the crop was harvested; they had loaned first to local elevator men as they bought wheat and then to city elevator men who bought and stored the crop until it was needed; they had loaned to the mills themselves and to the wholesalers who distributed the flour. Moreover, they had carried on multiple activities to finance the transfer and export of various products. This business had been the backbone of Minneapolis banking, and very desirable business it was. Much of it was done wholesale; there was little bother and no great risk, and though interest rates were low, the profits were very satisfying. The business done in smaller amounts (loans to country elevators and country banks) involved some bother and more risk, but competition was almost non-existent and interest rates were fairly high. As the local production of flour declined, the Minneapolis banks' loans and income from this source shrank; a part of this business had shifted to other areas. This hurt the bankers' pride, but it taught them a lesson. If their major line of business could slip away from the locality, there was no reason why other types of business could not do the same thing. Actually their loss was more than offset by the increase in miscellaneous lines, but it forced a change in methods of business.

The banks now realized that they were dependent upon the fate of Minneapolis. If business moved to other localities, they were the ones that suffered. What had happened once might recur. The idea soon crystallized in the minds of Minneapolis bankers that they could not afford to sit passively while other groups raided their territory. They must decide what types of business they wished to retain. Then they must lay plans to hold what they had and wrest what they wanted from competitive trade areas. The best defense lay in aggressive attack.

Local Firms Acquired by Eastern Capital, 1920–1929

While some Minneapolis firms had always been owned by eastern investors, the overwhelming majority had been local both in ownership and in management. During the 'twenties there was a steady attempt on the part of eastern capital to acquire profitable local enterprises. This tendency was first apparent in the fire insurance industry.

Minneapolis in 1920 had three fire insurance companies: the Twin City Fire Insurance Company, the Minneapolis Fire and Marine Insurance Company, and the Northwestern Fire and Marine Insurance Company. In February, 1921, the Hartford Fire Insurance Company (Hartford, Connecticut) bought control of the Twin City Fire Insurance Company and elected a new board of directors.[9] Two years later, in February, 1923, the Phoenix of Hartford bought control of the Minneapolis Fire and Marine.[10] Thus, two out of the three local fire insurance companies passed into eastern control.

The remaining company, the Northwestern Fire and Marine, remained independent despite the fact that eastern companies acquired a minority of its stock. Almost every one of its directors sat on the board of the First National Bank of Minneapolis.[11] They were true Minneapolitans, tied to the city by all their interests, filled with local pride and anxious to increase the importance of their city. They were interested not only in the profits of the insurance business, but also in the investment of its funds, in the prestige of having an independent fire insurance company, and in keeping Minneapolis business free of eastern domination.

The Northern States Power Company was organized in 1909 to acquire the electric distribution system in Minneapolis and certain hydroelectric plants on the St. Croix River. Local capital had an interest in it, and local men ran it despite the fact that the Standard Gas and Electric Company early acquired about 35 per cent of its stock.[12] In 1924 the Northern States Power Company's capital structure was reorganized, and the outside holding company acquired practical control.[13] This control was acquired through the simple device of dividing the common stock into two classes, "A" and "B." The stock had equal voting rights, share for share, but the A stock, owned by the local public, had a par value of $100 a share, while the B stock was sold at $10 a share. Substantially all the B stock was purchased by Standard Gas and Electric.[14] Thus the control of the company moved away from Minneapolis. On November 3, 1926, the Northern States Power Company bought control of the St. Paul Gas Light Company, which owned and operated the gas system and about 70 per cent of the electric system in St. Paul.

The Minneapolis Gas Light Company had belonged jointly to the Rand family and an eastern company. Although the business was profitable, the Rands received an offer that they could not refuse, and in 1928 ownership of this company was transferred to the American Commonwealth Power Company.[15]

The Russell Grader Manufacturing Company was a local concern which manufactured a nationally known line of dirt-moving machinery. It did not, however, make the tractors which supplied the motive power for its equipment; they were usually manufactured by the Caterpillar Tractor Company. In 1928 Caterpillar purchased the company from its local owners.[16] Since Minneapolis firms frequently were sold to outside interests, this action did not occasion much excitement. Very shortly, however, the entire city was filled with righteous indignation, for Caterpillar shut down the plant, moving the machinery and a skeleton crew of skilled workmen to Peoria. The plant remained closed and Minneapolis lost another profitable industry, while Caterpillar acquired a line complementary to its own, skilled labor, machinery, sales agencies, and dealer outlets.

A similar story is that of the Siems-Stembel Car Manufacturing Company. This was a Minneapolis concern which built railroad cars and equipment. Like all other such companies it had periods of extreme prosperity and depression, but over a number of years it was able to produce satisfactory profits. What was more immediately important to the community, it supplied employment for a group of skilled workers, and the income from its sales contributed to the secondary business of Minneapolis. This company was purchased in 1925 from its local owners by the Standard Steel Car Manufacturing Company.[17] The purchaser made arrangements to move its machinery, a few skilled workers were taken away, the rank and file were discharged, and the plant was closed.

The Minneapolis Drug Company was another old concern which had done a wholesale business in drugs and sundries with Minneapolis and regional retail druggists. In August, 1928, McKesson and Robbins was formed partly to acquire drug companies and knitted this concern into its national chain.[18] In this instance the local company was kept in existence as a division of the parent company, and as a practical measure the former local officials were left in charge, but the basic control shifted to the home office in the East. This movement was in keeping with others where local officials, although directly in charge, became subject to the decisions of eastern management. Often this control was of little importance, but certainly it was not soothing to men who prided themselves on absolute independence.

Each year saw a steady procession of Minneapolis firms pass into the control of outside capital, and toward the end of the 'twenties this tendency seemed to accelerate. To local business executives the movement appeared definitely one-sided; Minneapolis firms were acquired by outsiders, but Minneapolis capital seldom acquired control of firms in other areas. When local bankers thought about the future, it looked dark indeed. It seemed as though, in the course of time, the existing tide would sweep before it all important Minneapolis business firms, until all profitable local business would be owned abroad. This was an inauspicious future for local owners, but they, at least, would receive payment for their property. Most alarmed were the local corporation executives and the bankers, who controlled and administered without owning. These men, through many qualities — among others, personal efficiency, business efficiency, the reputation for producing profits, personal influence, the ability to obtain proxies from scattered stockholders, and coöperative action — controlled a generous slice of Minneapolis business without a substantial ownership. Despite the lack of personal wealth, they were men of the greatest influence — powerful, impressive, arbitrary, and reputedly infallible. For a generation they had swayed the business of the Northwest with a high and mighty hand. Now they saw their dominance threatened by the invasion of outside influences, and vivid imagination conjured up their subordination to insignificant hired employees by the lords of the moneyed East. This fancied threat to their prestige and influence was more than sufficient to disturb the most phlegmatic.

Growth of Retail Chains, 1920–1929

Since before the turn of the century, the volume of business done by chain organizations had been increasing, both absolutely and in relation to that done by others. The most outstanding example, perhaps, is one chain of five-and-ten-cent stores. Woolworth had started on a modest scale but by 1923 was operating 1,182 stores.[19] Several units established in Minneapolis were aggressively successful. No small part of their success came from the fact that they supplied an economic need, but local business interests saw only that they were chain stores and that they were prospering. They were controlled by strangers, bought their goods in other areas, borrowed money in other centers, and in general were independent of the local business community.

The Great Atlantic and Pacific Tea Company, which had started in a small way in the East and expanded rapidly, acquired gradually during the 'twenties an important group of stores.[20] They were efficient, hard-hitting units which supplied the public with grocery staples at lower prices than did most of the independent food stores. The consumers accepted them gratefully, but the local merchants regarded them with distaste. They were a chain, controlled and operated from without. Manufacturers complained that they drove a hard bargain; labor unions, that they overworked and underpaid their employees; financial powers, that they took profits out of the community. Many damned them vociferously, but few ceased to buy from them.

In other parts of the country, too, chains developed rapidly. In the Far West, Safeway Stores was established on a small scale in

1914; by 1926 it was operating 342 stores and acquiring more every year.[21] In New England, First National Stores was operating 1,650 stores by 1926.[22] J. C. Penney started in the dry-goods business in a small way but spread quickly.[23] No small part of Penney's success came from well-devised profit-sharing plans and practical methods of training management and establishing units. Even the great mail-order houses of Sears, Roebuck and Company and Montgomery Ward and Company, convinced that their original business was declining, organized a chain of retail stores. Many wholesalers, as difficulties in distributing their goods multiplied, expanded to acquire retail customers.

Another rapidly growing chain was that of the picture producers, who acquired thousands of local theaters in much the same way that the oil companies acquired stations. Since a production company incurs its major costs in producing an original film and can take off any number of additional films at a nominal cost, the more times it can show a film, the greater its income. The producers, therefore, wanted more outlets for their pictures and were willing to go to some lengths to obtain them.

During the 'twenties the great motion-picture production companies invaded Minneapolis. By paying high prices they induced local operators to sell their theaters. Up and down the streets they went until scarcely a downtown theater remained independent. Not content with this, they scoured the outskirts for suburban units.

Despite the fact that the Powers Mercantile Company had become a member of the Claflin chain before 1914, most of the department stores in Minneapolis remained local in both ownership and operation. Not until 1928 was Hahn Department Stores organized.[24] Immediately rumors spread that it was negotiating for a local store, rumors which soon were verified by the sale of the L. S. Donaldson Company.[25] In St. Paul the Golden Rule, one of the leading stores, succumbed, becoming Hahn's St. Paul unit.[26] These were merely the first to fall. During the remainder of 1928 and 1929 a majority of the department stores in both cities were acquired by national chains.

As a result of the increase in outside ownership and eastern investment, the growth of mergers, and the rapid expansion of chains, the position of Minneapolis as the queen city of an independent region was threatened. Those local concerns and business leaders whose future was inextricably bound up with the fate of Minneapolis were fearful; ownership, and with it potential control, was moving eastward.

The commercial banks in Minneapolis felt the pinch of this movement. Though, as we have seen, bank executives themselves had little invested in the stock of their own institutions, the ownership of the stock remained local. This was not entirely accidental. The management of the various banks wished to have them locally owned and they did not want any one investor to hold a dominant position, for, by having the stock scattered in small blocks among local investors and customers, the management could always obtain enough proxies to control annual meetings. Inasmuch as an investor generally consulted a bank officer before selling his stock, the officers were able to guide the sale into friendly hands and keep the stock from accumulating into large blocks, whence it might pass into the possession of outsiders. Among the efforts to keep the stock properly scattered were drives known as customer-ownership campaigns. Important, profitable customers, either depositors or borrowers, were given the privilege of buying on advantageous terms from one to ten shares of stock. Usually the purchase of this stock proved to be a privilege, for the stock showed substantial earnings and paid good dividends. Its ownership built up good-will, tying the customers to the bank. The constant eagerness of bank officers to buy a block of stock and resell it in small lots maintained a ready market. Thus, the local bank officers retained their dominant position by continuous vigilance.

What was most upsetting about the eastward trend was that outside organizations seemed always to expand and never to contract. Great eastern firms kept increasing the size of their plants, adding to their capital funds, broadening the scope of their operations; seemingly, they were always on the lookout for local organizations to swallow. From 1920 to 1929 the movement gained momentum, and at times it seemed to numerous bankers that the independent unit method of operation was rapidly becoming extinct. It was as though a revolution in business organization were in progress.

Reasons for the Development of Integration in Business

The movement toward expansion and the acquisition of business units was supported by a very interesting theory, that it was becoming increasingly difficult and costly to establish new firms. The number of business firms, therefore, was limited, and it was expedient to become entrenched as rapidly as possible. Moreover, the market was becoming stabilized, each firm having an area in which it had the advantage. Since it was much easier to defend a position than to invade another area, it was prudent to buy out competitors. This theory was supported by an imposing academic sponsorship. Professors of business, from crossroads colleges to the great cement campuses, gravely assured their classes that from a practical standpoint the day of new business units was almost over. Competition was too keen; customer relationships were too fixed; the launching of new firms was too costly. It was much simpler to buy an interest in a business already beyond the promotional stage.

Really intelligent business men never subscribed to the theory that it was impossible to open new business units; even subsequent developments disproved it. They did feel, however, that competition was becoming excessively keen and that the established firm had a very definite advantage over the newcomer. Good-will had become an impressive reality.

Since retention of earnings was widely adopted by American industry during the 'twenties and earnings during that period were generally good, huge corporate savings were inevitable. Eventually the management forgot the original purpose of these savings and simply regarded as a conservative policy the retention of half or more of its earnings. The money provided funds for new plants, corporate expansion, the purchase of competitive or affiliated lines of business, and general growth.

Since the steady growth of capital in the hands of actual investors created a ready market for new issues of securities, companies wishing to raise capital by the sale of stock and bonds found an ideal opportunity. The demand was greater than the supply, and new issues were avidly consumed. Under these circumstances many corporations, deciding to strengthen their financial position, sold stock to swell current assets and to pay off bonds. Thus, from a variety of sources corporate management found ample funds for all its uses.

The relative fixity in the number of companies, set by the difficulties of launching new units, the value of customer relationships and dealer agencies, and the increasing amounts of capital seeking investments combined to create a steady upward movement in the valuation of business enterprises and pushed the stock market into a spiral which rose to dizzier and dizzier heights.

There was a general movement toward expansion. Promoters found it easy to finance their schemes by the sale of stock. Their primary problem was to work out some practical merger, for mergers made securities to sell. They offered obvious economies by eliminating dual overhead, combining sales forces, consolidating advertising, shutting down unnecessary plants, and often reducing competition. Above all, mergers offered profits to the promoters who originated them and to the investment bankers who sold the securities. Needless to say, investment dealers labored to merge.

When one company expanded, it was like a stone starting an avalanche. It acquired a few competitors and some of the suppliers of its raw materials; eventually it absorbed the dealers who handled its products. Other competitors, believing their very lives to be at stake, began a feverish expansion in self-defense. It was so simple to convince management of the need to enlarge. One company in an industry had only to make a move, and many others did likewise.

This movement undoubtedly resulted, in part, from a severe attack of megalomania. Many companies wanted to be big without having any other reason for such a desire. Size was simply an end in itself. Another very potent cause of business expansion during the 'twenties was the fact that units were organized for growth — that was the normal procedure. Then there was self-seeking. Regardless of the profits involved, many an executive wished his company were larger, because increasing the size of the company made the management seem more successful.

Furthermore, regional financial leaders were afraid of New York City. Each year New York financiers moved toward financial capitalism on a national scale by buying and controlling regional units.

The regional leaders saw the control of regional industries move to New York and they became convinced that the only defense was a move toward tightening their control of the regional business structure. Thus the movement of New York toward financial capitalism caused it to develop in regional centers of which the Twin Cities were an important example.

Effect of the Move toward Integration on Minneapolis Banks

Twin City business firms felt the movement toward expansion which developed in American industry during the 'twenties, and local banks were fully aware of it. Whenever a concern became a part of some national organization, some group or chain, it made outside contacts. Quite often the local banks lost its business. While such losses existed, they usually were overemphasized in the minds of local people. Many large organizations continued, as a matter of policy, to do a portion of their business locally. In fact, potentialities caused far more worry than the actual losses justified. The real blow was to the prestige and self-esteem of local capitalists, financiers, and civic leaders. They had always been important and influential: not a deal was hatched nor a wheel turned in the region without their consent. Now an increasing percentage of business was transacted without their approval. This damaged their pride.

A disturbing possibility in the tendency of business units to lose their independence was that Minneapolis banks might be sold to eastern capitalists. We have indicated in previous chapters that, with the exception of the First National Bank of St. Paul, the ownership of local banks was widely spread among local investors. No one person had a large block of stock. With such dissemination it would be very difficult for any group to acquire control, yet it was theoretically possible. What complicated the situation was that the operating officials had only a small interest in their own banks; in many cases they were men who had little but their abilities and their salaries. They thought that they held the confidence of the small stockholders, for they had always been able to amass enough proxies to control annual meetings. Whether the stockholders would remain blindly loyal, however, if some group offered them inflated prices for their stock was a question that raised many doubts.

Twin City bankers followed with interest the success of Mr. A. P. Giannini with his Bank of Italy. Starting with one small bank in San Francisco, he had formed an organization that soon covered not only California but also surrounding States. His bank chain was successful and profitable, and it grew rapidly. In 1929 he transferred his attentions from West to East, buying a bank in Wall Street, and announced that he intended to form a national chain.[27] To most Twin City bankers this was just news, but for officers of the First National Bank of Minneapolis it sharpened a suspicion. For some time they had been watching the transfer of small blocks of stock from local owners to Mr. Giannini. Suddenly it seemed that a plan on his part was taking shape, a plan to compete for stock and eventually to achieve a dominant position. Another alarming development added fuel to local fears: the Hill heirs, at least those in the East, sold their stock in the First National Bank of St. Paul to Blair and Company of New York.[28] At this time Blair and Company was allied with Mr. Giannini. However, since a majority of the stock belonged to Mr. Louis W. Hill, who refused to sell, Blair and Company never obtained control.

The same danger also threatened the big Twin City banks from another side — their country business. Their function as bankers' banks had grown with the passage of time until it represented a very important and profitable field. As indicated in previous chapters, it was a highly competitive business. As long as country banks remained under local ownership, the Twin Cities were able to hold their share. During 1928, however, it was rumored that negotiations were under way for the purchase, by eastern capital, of certain country banks. Minneapolis bankers began to fear that banking was about to experience the developments which had affected other industries. The correspondent business of country banks was profitable enough to attract competitors. The Twin City bankers felt that something must be done to prevent this contingency.

A little consideration of expedient courses of action advanced two possibilities: that the banks continue their time-honored course and depend upon prestige, strength, and competitive efforts; or that they organize a group of banks, owned and controlled from the Twin Cities. Though many of the bankers preferred the first choice, a larger group favored the second. Furthermore, the organization of a bank group had many collateral advantages.

One argument advanced for a bank group was that it would produce superior management. A little additional thought indicated that in all probability it would be profitable to all concerned. Strangely enough, these potential profits had little to do with increased operating economies or augmented profits. They existed for a very simple reason. The stocks of country banks were bought and sold like real estate: no general market existed; the seller had to find a buyer and then, by appraisal and argument, decide upon the stock's intrinsic value. The market was limited: usually the officers and directors of a bank were willing to buy small quantities of stock, and occasionally local business men would buy a few shares. Thus, if an owner wished to sell, he usually found that all potential buyers were bargain hunters, inclined to drive a hard bargain. The stocks of country banks tended, therefore, to sell at depressed prices.

Bank stocks which enjoyed a wide market, notably those of New York and Chicago banks, were market favorites and sold at high prices. An officer of one great Minneapolis bank, preparing a study of this phenomenon, reported that the discrepancy sprang from the market situation and not from any intrinsic differences in value. He contended that, if a large group of small banks could be welded into one company; if their stocks were then exchanged for the stock of a holding company which would be widely held and well known; if a ready market were obtained for this stock through the organization of strong, active market sponsorship; and if the stock were placed on an established dividend basis, the general market would place a high value on it, and it would sell at a price greatly in excess of the total current prices of the component bank stocks. This market situation could be aided, if necessary, by advertising campaigns, favorable publicity, the constant purchase of stock coming on the market, and its resale to investors who would hold it and not sell it again just because the market advanced. Such a situation would offer an unparalleled opportunity for profits because of the difference in valuation. Country bankers would not be able to resist an offer for their banks. If they obtained the stock of a holding company, they would have a readily marketable security worth far more than the original. If they wanted cash, by selling some of their stock they could obtain all that it had been worth on the market and still have stock left. During the early stages of promotion the purchasers for cash would obtain stock which was about to advance in the market. Even the last investor would receive his money's worth, a stock which would pay regular dividends and be just as valuable as the stock of the New York banks. The situation had amazing potentialities for all concerned, a fact which would make the organization of such a company very easy.

The formation of a large banking group offered to the promoters advantages other than financial. Such an organization centering in Minneapolis would improve the position of Twin City banks and place their country correspondents forever beyond the reach of competitive centers and eastern capital. The size and strength of the group would give its officers power and prestige, and of course such a mighty organization would pay large salaries.

A group organization naturally would cover a wide geographical area serving several different industries, a factor which would give the banking structure strength and would stabilize earnings. If one territory or industry experienced failure or depression, prosperity in others would balance this adversity. Thus, in union there would be strength, stability, and profits.

CHAPTER IX

ORGANIZATION OF THE NORTHWEST BANCORPORATION, 1928–1931

Laying the Foundation, January, 1928–January, 1929

The "Roaring Twenties" were in full clamor by 1928: industrial prosperity swept steadily onward, and the stock market mounted daily to dizzier heights. In the manufacturing centers of the nation, industrialists and bankers were triumphantly jubilant. True, the year had brought a recession during which stock prices had fallen, but this interruption had been brief and the rising tide of prosperity soon wiped out all traces of deflation.

Twin City leaders, however, were swayed by conflicting emotions. Prolonged industrial success and rising profits prompted an optimistic, whole-hearted enjoyment of prosperity; but the skeleton of marginal agriculture was always at the feast, and bankers were haunted by the ghosts of closed banks. The Northwest's heavy dependence on agriculture seemed to make its banking structure peculiarly vulnerable to depression. Since under existing conditions a financial débâcle was inherent in any major business recession, Twin City bankers found themselves unable to revel freely in the prosperity of the late 'twenties.

The Northwestern National Bank of Minneapolis was a regional banker's bank, much interested in the country-banking picture. Its officers under the leadership of Mr. Edward Williams Decker, president, were vitally concerned over this situation; they gave it serious thought and sought earnestly for a remedy.[1] The official family included, in addition to Mr. Decker, Messrs. Theodore Wold, William A. Durst, Clarence Hill, C. V. Smith, Robert Macgregor, David R. West, Henry D. Thrall, J. Cameron Thomson, and Robert Forgan Mactavish.

Which of these men first conceived the idea of group banking will never be known; each attributes it to another, and he in turn to someone else; but it seems certain that together they crystallized the pattern. Credit is generally given to Messrs. Thomson, Thrall, and West. They first brought the concept to Mr. Decker's attention, but where they got it is uncertain. Mr. Thomson knew of the group-banking ideas churning in the mind of Mr. George Rand of the Marine Midland Bank, and surely all these men were aware of the developments sponsored by Mr. Giannini on the West Coast, and the Marine Bancorporation of Seattle. Whatever the source, the idea was presented to Mr. Decker, who brought it up for discussion among the officers of the Northwestern National Bank.[2]

Inasmuch as the Bank of Italy planned to expand on a national scale, affiliates of the Union Trust Company of Pittsburgh controlled 40 banks, Dillon Read and Company controlled a group of banks and were bidding for the control of the First National Bank of St. Paul, and leading banks in Fargo and Aberdeen had been made attractive offers by eastern interests, it was pointed out by Mr. Thomson that all indications were that the trend was toward greater concentration of banking control. Some form of greater concentration in banking was inevitable. If the Northwestern National did not lead the way it would be left far behind.

In heated discussions an idea was finally forged which seemed to answer all objections and afford advantages to everyone concerned. This concept has been termed group banking. It is based on the old maxim that in union there is strength.

Each member bank was to retain its unit structure and continue to operate on a local basis. The original management was to have full control of local operations; it would be replaced only in the event of gross inefficiency, dishonesty, or mismanagement. The central office was to keep in touch with the local management; it was to offer suggestions, but not to issue orders. In addition, the parent organization was to provide specialized functions and services which were too expensive for the independent banks to supply for themselves. It was to sell a substantial issue of stock to the general public for cash which it would retain to bolster member banks when they got into trouble. No member bank was to be allowed to fail, for the holding company would absorb any serious loss.

The holding company was to be built around the Northwestern

National Bank, an arrangement which would cement customer relationships between the Northwestern and its affiliates. This organization would heighten the Northwestern's prestige, increase its business, and strengthen its position. One of the main advantages accruing to small local banks would be continuity of able management. The local banker could rest assured that, in the event of his death or incapacity, he would be capably succeeded. At the same time the group, besides supplying greater financial strength, continuity of management, and marketability of stock, would diversify both the risks involved and the earnings; supply greater fluidity of credit and more continuous use of capital; and permit the handling of larger loans. Moreover, a holding-company stock which would pay immediate dividends looked attractive to the stockholders of many small banks.

Since local stockholders might be loath to allow local banks to slip out of local hands into Twin Cities' control there was a question as to the possibility of acquiring the control of any large number of country banks. Since, even as late as 1929, despite the agricultural collapse of the 'twenties and the disastrous failure of many bank chains, 100 per cent home-owned banks were the exception and not the rule, and in Minnesota alone, some 34 chains owned control of 389 banks, this problem did not present any insurmountable difficulties. Even in the so-called home-owned, independent banks, local pride and antipathy to the Twin Cities would not serve to stop a sale when the offer was financially attractive to the stockholders.

Since prospective earning power was a vital matter to all concerned, all possibilities of increased earnings were given serious thought. From this situation two schools of thought emerged: the one, that a group system permitted sufficient economies and increased earning power sufficient to more than offset the increased expense; the other, that economies and increased earnings in a group composed of small units were largely imaginary, while overhead expenses were very real. Because of the general enthusiasm for expansion so prevalent in the late 'twenties, the optimists generally were in a substantial majority. Even the most hardy pessimists felt that, since the collateral advantages of group banking in strengthening and improving the banking structure were so obvious and important, the question of just how much earnings would be increased was of only secondary importance.[3]

While country banks were selling at prices which usually represented real bargains, the stocks of the great Twin City banks enjoying a wider market often were quoted at more than 200 per cent of book value, 25 times earnings, and to yield 3 per cent on dividends. The stocks of the larger, better-known banks were considered choice investments by a large segment of the Twin City investing public. Despite the comparatively good market for the stocks of Twin City banks compared to that for country banks' stocks, the market was limited relatively to that of large eastern banks. The shares of the great Wall Street banks were known internationally, were freely bought and sold in several markets; they often sold as high as 300 per cent of book value, 30 times earnings, and to yield less than 1½ per cent on dividends.

If a large number of country banks could be brought together in a holding company under the auspices of the Northwestern National, the shares of the individual banks exchanged for those of the holding company, one consolidated balance sheet and earning statement prepared, the shares distributed over a wide territory and to a large number of people, the stock placed on a regular dividend basis, and a regular quoted market maintained on which any holder could freely buy and sell stock in any reasonable quantity at any time at the quoted price, then the new stock having a broad, active market would sell at more than the price of the stocks of the component unit banks and be a favorite with the investing public.

Since the stock market was continuously advancing, this development appeared probable. The holding company could make country bankers a proposition which, contrary to the old adage, would allow them to eat their cake and have it too. They could retain operating control of their banks, keep their position, salary, and prestige; sell a portion of their stock, obtain a substantial amount of cash, and still have part of their stock left over; and, best of all, the new development would strengthen the banking system and be of public service.

The constant consideration of these ideas by the officers of the Northwestern National Bank early in 1928 gradually smoothed out the potential difficulties and developed a plan into workable form. The next step was to discuss it with independent bankers, most of whom were correspondents of the Northwestern National. Among the first to be consulted were the officers of the First National Bank and Trust Company of Fargo, North Dakota. This was an important bank with capital and surplus of $600,000 and deposits in excess of $7,000,000. Since it had a long record of financial stability and good earnings, an affiliation with it was something to be prized. The matter of the First of Fargo's joining the Northwestern group was discussed not only with Mr. E. J. Weiser, the president, but also with Mr. F. A. Irish, the vice-president, and other men of influence in the organization. Mr. Weiser at first was not interested in joining any organization, but a series of discussions with Messrs. Decker and West convinced him that joining the new group would strengthen the position of the First National of Fargo and his own position and be very profitable. Accordingly, he agreed that his bank become one of the original members.

The next contact was with Hanford MacNider of the First National Bank of Mason City, Iowa. The situation there was similar to that of Fargo. The First of Mason City was a well-known bank, which served a wealthy territory and in normal periods operated at a profit to its stockholders. Its management and board of directors were men of wealth and personal influence. (MacNider himself was interested not only in the bank but also in the Northwestern States Portland Cement Company, which involved him in road-building and politics.) When the matter was brought to MacNider's attention in 1928, he concluded that his position would be strengthened by the development of group banking.

The next bank approached was the National Bank of La Crosse, of which G. W. Burton was president. This bank had been a correspondent of the Northwestern for many years. Its deposits were in excess of $6,000,000 and it served a large agricultural area. Both Mason City and La Crosse were debatable territory as far as the Northwestern was concerned, for their trade contacts ran not only to the Twin Cities but also to Milwaukee and Chicago. Nevertheless, the Northwestern considered it good business to tie up with its organization the banks in these areas. A series of conferences was held with Burton and his directors late in 1928. Eventually they, too, commenced to think favorably of joining the Northwestern group. Although this deal was not closed at once, progress was sufficient to justify the Northwestern officers' decision to organize a holding company. They began to discuss an exchange of stock with Messrs. Weiser and MacNider.

The first thing to be considered was the book value of the stocks of the three banks. This, however, was a small matter compared with the earnings that each bank could produce and the trend of future growth. Later on the question of growth was to cause many a dispute, but there was little argument concerning the prospects of Fargo, Mason City, and Minneapolis. All three locations seemed fundamentally strong and bade fair to grow. The directors of the three banks finally reached an agreement regarding the relative values of their stocks. It was concluded that one share of Northwestern National Bank stock was worth $400; one share of the First National Bank of Fargo was worth $310; and one share of the First National Bank of Mason City was worth $300.[4] All these figures were based on Bancorporation's stock at its par of $50.

Although these operations had engaged the senior bank officers during most of 1928, no inkling had reached the general public. The populace, therefore, was amazed when, on the morning of January 8, 1929, it was announced that a new company, known as Northwest Bancorporation, had entered the banking field and that it had arranged to acquire the Northwestern National Bank of Minneapolis, the First National Bank of Fargo, and the First National Bank of Mason City.[5] This, it was announced, was only a beginning; the company intended to acquire a group of key banks in the Twin City trade territory.[6]

The stockholders of the three banks involved were requested to deposit their stock under a deposit agreement for exchange into the $50 par shares of the new company. If the plan should not be in operation by July 1, 1929, or if a controlling interest in each of the three banks should not have been acquired, the original stock was to be returned to depositors.[7] Since the foundation had been well laid, however, the stockholders of the three banks immediately sent in their stock for deposit. Thus, the Northwest Bancorporation had acquired substantially all the stock of the three original banks by the specified date.

Because of the great flexibility and the fair tax provisions of the Delaware law, a charter for the new company was obtained in the State of Delaware.[8] As soon as the new charter had been obtained and the stock issued, arrangements were made to exchange the deposited stock of the unit banks for stock of the Northwest Bancorporation.[9] Thus a new company, which was greatly to influence the course of northwestern banking, came into being.

Successful Acquisitions and an Unsuccessful Attempt in February, 1929

The announcement of the organization of the Bancorporation precipitated matters in La Crosse. The local bank agreed to join the group and appraised its stock at $275 per share, compared with $50 for Northwest Bancorporation. Stockholders were asked to deposit their stock for exchange. The stock came in rapidly, and the National Bank of La Crosse became the fourth member.

The acquisition of one bank seemed to put in motion forces which brought in others, for each bank had close affiliations with many others. For example, Mr. Weiser had for years been in contact with the First National Bank of Deadwood and the First National Bank of Lead, South Dakota; these banks were closely affiliated with the Homestake Mining Company. Mr. Weiser, president of the First National Bank and Trust Company of Fargo, held conferences with Mr. R. E. Driscoll, cashier of the First National Bank of Lead, relative to the acquisition of these banks. The managing officer believed that the controlling stockholders had no especial desire to retain control and would cordially regard a request to transfer their banks to the Bancorporation. This proving to be the case, on February 19, 1929, the Northwest Bancorporation acquired two new members.[10] Although they were somewhat smaller than the others acquired by the Bancorporation, they were out of the small country-bank class.

Because the management of the Bancorporation was firmly convinced that its success depended upon the acquisition of key banks, it had definite designs on certain units. The most important area was Minneapolis; second in importance came St. Paul. If the Bancorporation could acquire a large bank in St. Paul, it would stand on a double foundation, firmly entrenched in both important cities. There were only two important banks in St. Paul. One of these, the Merchants National with its active management, was not for sale. The only possibility, therefore, was the First National Bank. This bank was controlled by Hill heirs, principally Mr. Louis W. Hill. Since it represented only one of Mr. Hill's varied interests — his personal interests lay in farming and good living while his business interests included railroads, iron mines, and tremendous investments, Mr. Decker felt sure that he could be persuaded to sell if a sufficiently liberal offer was made. In February, 1929, Mr. Decker opened negotiations; since Mr. Hill desired to divest himself of the responsibilities of owning the controlling interest in a commercial bank, he received Mr. Decker cordially.

An analysis of the First National Bank's assets indicated that both commercial paper and bonds were of high quality; in fact, the bank was in excellent shape. Messrs. Macgregor and Decker lost no time in working out with Mr. Hill a tentative basis of exchange. It appeared that all that remained was the formality of signing a few papers. There was wild rejoicing in the Bancorporation office; success beyond even the wildest hopes had been attained.

Meanwhile, there was gloom in St. Paul. Although every effort had been made to keep the Bancorporation plans secret, too many people were involved. The news was a blow to the Merchants National. If the Bancorporation acquired the First, it meant an end to the Merchants' long era of peace and prosperity; under more aggressive management the First would fight for business. Both banker-brother George Prince and Mr. R. C. Lilly were perturbed. Something had to be done; just what, remained to be discovered.

Mr. Lilly, noted for both his vivid imagination and his energetic ability, soon suggested a solution: the Merchants must absorb the First National Bank of St. Paul. He discussed the matter with hard-bitten George Prince, the senior officers, and the executive committee of the Merchants. The idea was cordially received and definite plans were made. Conferences lasted all night as details were ironed out.

The best way to approach Mr. Hill seemed to be through his financial adviser, Mr. Charles Oscar Kalman, who was head of the investment firm of C. O. Kalman and Company and who would be very anxious to prevent the sale of the First to the Bancorporation, because the sale would impair Mr. Kalman's influential position in St. Paul banking circles. Whatever the background, the inference proved correct. Mr. Kalman was persuaded to oppose the transfer of the First and to advocate a merger with the Merchants.

Mr. Kalman's first approach was to suggest to Mr. Hill that transferring the First to the Bancorporation was not in the best interests of St. Paul as a city. He argued that the Bancorporation was a Minneapolis organization, owned and controlled by the Northwestern National Bank group. Membership in it would reduce the First of St. Paul to the status of a branch office. He played upon the ancient antipathy of St. Paul to Minneapolis, implying that Mr. Hill was duty bound to help St. Paul maintain its independent position. As an alternative he suggested that perhaps the First could absorb the Merchants, thereby creating for St. Paul a banking institution of superior strength. He praised the aggressive management of the Merchants, intimating that it deserved a dominating position if such a merger should materialize. Mr. Hill was not slow to grasp the practicable aspects of this proposition: it would give St. Paul a great bank to strengthen the banking structure; it promised to produce large profits for the bank's stockholders; and it would add several cubits to Mr. Louis W. Hill's prestige. Mr. Kalman was authorized to approach the Merchants National group, and with both groups favoring a merger, negotiations progressed smoothly and plans were soon perfected. When the Bancorporation officers met Mr. Louis W. Hill for the signing of the final papers he was not interested in completing the deal, advising them that all negotiations were at an end and that the First National Bank of St. Paul would remain independent.

Since it was felt that the name First National carried greater prestige and its use preserved the fiction that the First had absorbed the Merchants, the charter of the First National Bank of St. Paul was used, and on March 3, 1929, the Merchants and the First merged.[11] The dominant management group, however, came from the Merchants National Bank.

The Northwestern in its ambition in St. Paul was left without a leg to stand on, for the First National was the only bank of importance in that city. The Bancorporation, therefore, had to acquire a small bank in St. Paul or organize a new one and attempt to build it up on a competitive basis. Either program presented obstacles.

Organizing a New Bank in Moorhead, 1929

Since Moorhead, Minnesota, was heavily dependent upon the potato crop, the low prices prevailing in the fall of 1928 spelled disaster for the town, despite the digging of an excellent crop. The price did not cover expenses of transportation and marketing. It was the oft-repeated story of country banking. The low prices effectively stopped payment of local loans, the banks were overextended, and there was a demand for increased loans at the same time that deposits shrank. In December, 1928, the collapse reached its climax with the failure of the First and Moorhead National Bank.

This collapse of the banking structure in Moorhead created havoc: not only did the depositors lose their money but they lost their purchasing power as well, and local business declined. Business became so bad that business men were unable to obtain funds to repay their notes. Not only was all business reduced to a cash basis but business men and farmers, who were accustomed to borrow to finance their operations, found their source of credit closed. The blocking of the free flow of credit effectively stopped the flow of liquidation and froze the entire situation. The banks could not liquidate until they could collect money from their debtors; the debtors could not pay until the banks had made at least a partial liquidation.[12] The most promising solution was to organize a new bank. Accordingly, the Northwest Bancorporation was invited to incorporate a new bank. They accepted the invitation and in January, 1929, applied for a charter for the new First National Bank in Moorhead. The Bancorporation received the charter and purchased the entire capital stock.[13]

The Bancorporation officers realized that, even after the new bank had been organized, two or three years would normally elapse before the local financial structure had thawed out and any substantial liquidation to the depositors of the First and Moorhead National Bank had materialized; thus, it was felt that more drastic action was necessary. It was decided to arrange an immediate partial liquidation of the First and Moorhead National Bank through assumption by the new First National of 50 per cent of its assets and liabilities.[14] Thus, by one operation the situation in Moorhead would be thawed out, and debtors would obtain sufficient funds to pay their creditors, who in turn would pay their debts.

When the charter had been obtained and the organization of the new bank had been completed, the bank then entered into a contract with the receiver of the First and Moorhead National Bank whereby the new bank agreed to purchase assets equivalent to 50 per cent of outstanding deposits and likewise agreed to pay 50 per cent on the receiver's certificates, which in effect was a 50 per cent dividend on all lawful claims representing deposit liabilities of the defunct bank.

When depositors had proved their claims against the defunct bank, the receiver then issued his certificates for the full amount of the deposit liability and the new bank agreed to pay in the normal course of business, after May 1, 1929, 50 per cent on each certificate presented. In return for this payment the new bank was permitted to select an equivalent amount of assets from the defunct bank. The contract further provided that there should be a right of substitution, which carried through from the date that the transaction took place to November 15, 1929. The right of substitution simply meant that, if the assets acquired in the original transaction proved to be unsatisfactory, the new bank could serve notice on the receiver and exchange the unsatisfactory assets for any satisfactory assets, including cash, in the possession of the receiver.[15]

This plan, which became known as the Moorhead Plan, was an outstanding success. The defunct bank had failed in December, 1928; the new First National Bank in Moorhead was organized early in 1929; it stood ready to pay 50 per cent on the receiver's certificates on May 1, 1929, and within a few weeks thereafter considerable progress had been made in general liquidation. It was a rapid and satisfactory settlement of a difficult situation. The immediate thawing of 50 per cent of deposits made possible the repayment of other debts and a general liquidation ensued.

When the Bancorporation established the new First National Bank, Moorhead needed a president to assume complete control of local operations. Messrs. Decker and Weiser decided to offer the position to Mr. Herbert Hallenberg, who had been educated as an attorney, had practised law, and then had organized a small bank in Carson, North Dakota. After several successful years, he sold the bank and entered the employ of the Federal Reserve Bank of Minneapolis as a bank examiner, a job which brought him into close contact with country banking in the Ninth Federal Reserve District in the 'twenties. During the latter part of the decade he left the Federal to become a national bank examiner in upper New York State. When approached by the Bancorporation, he accepted the presidency of the new First National Bank in Moorhead.

The new bank was chartered and had a capital and surplus of $150,000 but no deposits.[16] Immediately a flow of money started into the new bank as people brought in their carefully hidden and meager hoards. Mr. Hallenberg welcomed every cent, ever bearing in mind that on May 1, 1929, his bank would be liable for 50 per cent of the deposits of the First and Moorhead National Bank. Since he could borrow from the Northwestern National any amount necessary to meet withdrawals, he was not too worried but he wished to keep his borrowings as low as possible. The fateful day arrived and the new bank was prepared for difficulties. Developments were very mild: the receiver's certificates were brought in in a steady stream, but confidence had been so far restored that most of the payments were immediately redeposited. Some money was withdrawn, but it was relatively moderate in amount and the result of actual need rather than lack of confidence. Total withdrawals were enough to force the bank to borrow, but only $60,000. After the first few days the money flowed back to the bank, which paid off its note to the Northwestern.

The situation had been worked out with a minimum of disturbance and Mr. Hallenberg had amply demonstrated his ability to the officers of Northwest Bancorporation. Accordingly he was taken out of the local bank, transferred to the Bancorporation in Minneapolis, and placed in charge of the central examining force.

The men who had been active in organizing the Bancorporation were constantly looking around for desirable banks. It was Mr. David West who opened negotiations to acquire the Security National Bank and Trust Company of Faribault, Minnesota. Mr. West pursued his opportunities from a very advantageous position, for he had close contacts in the town of Faribault and was a personal friend of the bank's controlling stockholders. The bank was an excellent prospect for the Bancorporation. It had capital and surplus of approximately $300,000 and deposits in excess of $2,000,000. Mr. West made the advantages of a group organization so attractive and the possibilities of profit so enticing that the local stockholders agreed to exchange their stock. On February 20, 1929, the deal was consummated and the Security National Bank of Faribault became a part of the Bancorporation.[17]

THE FIRST SALE OF BANCORPORATION STOCK, FEBRUARY 20, 1929

Since one of the fundamentals of group banking is the concept that the holding company should have assets of its own (other than bank stocks) to strengthen the position of the units, it was necessary that the Bancorporation acquire funds by selling stock for cash. Up to February 20, 1929, banks had been acquired only through an exchange of stock. One unavoidable difficulty, however, had arisen. There usually was an obstreperous minority which objected to the exchange of stock and demanded cash for its holdings. The Bancorporation's inability to meet this demand convinced the management that it should have money for this purpose as well as to strengthen the organization. Accordingly, it arranged to sell 100,000 shares of Bancorporation to the general public.

This stock was offered on February 20, 1929, by the Minnesota Company at $50.35 per share. Fifty dollars represented the par value, and thirty-five cents the accrued dividend. The stockholders of Bancorporation waived their preëmptive rights to the stock so that it could be offered to the public. In view of the strong demand for stocks, underwriting was not considered necessary. Instead, the Minnesota Company conducted a campaign to market the stock.

A great deal of publicity appeared in newspapers and magazines, exploiting the growth prospects of the Northwest. It pointed out that a group organization would strengthen the banking structure and that an investment in the stock would be profitable because the banks would share in the future growth. Much was made of the factor of diversification, that the territory included the manufacturing and wholesaling activities of the Twin Cities, the corn and hog belt of Iowa, the wheat areas of the Dakotas, the lumber region in Montana, and the world's iron-mining center in Minnesota, and the great copper mines of the West. These articles recognized that the territory was comparatively unsettled, that the future would bring growth to the area, and that banking organizations would realize increasing profits from this growth. The greatest emphasis was placed on the prospective development of the territory.

Window displays were quite freely used, running from sheaves of wheat and sacks of flour to iron and copper ore, and gold from the Black Hills. Figures were quoted showing the steady growth of population in the territory.[18] This publicity proved so successful that investors stood in line to subscribe to stock in the new organization; the entire issue of 100,000 shares sold readily, yielding the Bancorporation treasury something over $5,000,000 in cash. Thus fortified, Bancorporation officials resumed their activities with renewed vigor.

RAPID EXPANSION, FEBRUARY 20–AUGUST 15, 1929, MOSTLY IN THE DAKOTAS

The next banks acquired were in South Dakota — the Citizens National Bank of Watertown and the First National Bank of Watertown. The city of Watertown, located in northeastern South Dakota, at that time had a population of 11,000. It was an important railroad terminal, and a network of good roads crossed there. The soil is rich, and while the rainfall does not approach that in Minnesota, for many years it had been ample to produce substantial crops. Banks in this town looked profitable and advantageous to the Bancorporation, and Mr. Robert Macgregor began negotiations to acquire control of at least one. He first approached the Citizens National Bank, which had capital and surplus of approximately $200,000 and deposits in excess of $2,000,000. While discussions were under way, Mr. Macgregor completed a deal with the president of the First National Bank. This bank had capital and surplus of $210,000 and deposits of approximately $2,700,000.[19] Mr. Macgregor had hoped to acquire one bank; to his surprise, he obtained both.

On his way back from Watertown, Mr. Macgregor stopped at Fergus Falls to talk with the president of the Fergus Falls National Bank. This bank had a capital and surplus of approximately $215,000 and deposits in excess of $2,000,000. Fergus Falls was a thriving town of some 8,500 people located in the lake region of Minnesota. Being of glacial origin the surrounding territory is extremely spotty. Excellent farming land lies next to poor sand and gravel deposits, but the territory receives ample rainfall. The farmers are generally prosperous, and the town reflects prosperity. The Fergus Falls National Bank had been a correspondent of the Northwestern National, and a close friendship existed between the officers of the two banks. Under the circumstances, the president was quite willing to put his bank into the Bancorporation, for he was confident that he would be left in charge of activities in Fergus Falls, and the exchange looked profitable. On April 29 it was announced that the Fergus Falls National Bank had joined the Bancorporation.[20]

Mr. Macgregor got in touch with the Security National Bank of Sioux Falls, South Dakota, which had capital and surplus in excess of $560,000 and deposits of approximately $5,500,000. In the past it usually had done business with the First National Bank of Minneapolis, not with the Northwestern National. Nevertheless, Mr. Macgregor discussed the situation with the president and convinced him of the advantages of group banking so effectively that on April 18, 1929, the Security National Bank of Sioux Falls also joined the group.[21]

By this time things were moving rapidly. The board of directors of the Bancorporation empowered Messrs. Macgregor and West to talk to E. P. Wells regarding his banks around Jamestown, North Dakota. Wells' main bank was the James River National Bank of Jamestown, and he had some five other banks in surrounding communities. Since Wells was desirous of withdrawing from his exacting activities because of his age, he readily agreed to turn his banks over to the Bancorporation and take stock in exchange.[22] The Bancorporation wanted only the one large bank, but Wells insisted on exchanging all his banks. This problem was solved by merging the small banks with the James River National Bank at Jamestown. The James River National had capital and surplus of just under $200,000 and deposits of approximately $1,500,000.[23]

Until this time Mr. Edward Williams Decker had assumed full responsibility for the operations of the Bancorporation, and most of the actual negotiations had been carried on by Messrs. Decker and Macgregor. Mr. Decker, however, was entirely too busy to attend to operating both the Northwestern National Bank and the Northwest Bancorporation. The board of directors of Northwest Bancorporation decided to elect a vice-president and general manager to be in full charge of operations and acquisitions. On April 15, 1929, a committee was appointed to consider the matter and after due deliberation Mr. J. Cameron Thomson was recommended for the position.[24]

Mr. Thomson was eminently fitted for this position by his ability, energy and, above all, his friendly, magnetic personality. He was born on September 20, 1890, at Emerson, Manitoba, and moved to Minneapolis with his parents in 1903. Upon completing his education in the public schools in Minneapolis in 1905, he entered the employ of the Minnesota National Bank. In 1907 he joined the staff of the Northwestern National, where he became assistant cashier in 1918. He was extremely active in American Institute of Banking work, having passed through the various offices of the local chapter and eventually achieved the presidency of the national organization. In 1926 he was promoted by the Northwestern National to be vice-president in charge of new business, a position which he filled successfully.

The directors of the Bancorporation regarded him as an ideal head for the new company. Since he was not well known to the officers of member banks, Mr. Decker sent him on a tour of inspection to all the group banks. He left Minneapolis on May 16, 1929, and, since time was at a premium, he made part of the trip by airplane. Mr. Thomson stayed in each town long enough to become acquainted with both the local directors and the bank employees of the banks at Fargo, Moorhead, La Crosse, Mason City, Watertown, and Sioux Falls and ended his trip in the Black Hills; he made a very favorable impression. On June 20, 1929, he was elected vice-president and general manager of the Northwest Bancorporation.[25] Thenceforth he was intimately connected with all its activities.

So far, many member banks had been in excellent shape, and the Bancorporation had acquired them through a simple exchange of shares. Since some difference of opinion usually developed regarding the valuation of certain assets of a bank, a plan of acquisition was worked out to avoid this difficulty. The officers of local banks were permitted to make their own appraisal of the assets, and on the basis of book value the exchange of stock was agreed upon. The officers of the Bancorporation, however, retained the privilege of refusing any assets which they regarded as questionable. These assets were purchased by the old stockholders from the unit bank for cash.

Since this procedure cleaned up the assets of the local bank and left the local bank's former stockholders owning the criticized assets, and usually they had difficulty in raising the money necessary to purchase these assets, they sometimes borrowed from the Bancorporation on their notes secured by the take-outs, by some Bancorporation stock, and by other collateral.[26]

Aberdeen, South Dakota, in 1929, had a population of some 16,500. It was the local financial center and was served by numerous banks.[27] Despite the economic strength of the territory, conditions were not thriving during 1928 and 1929. Local drought in 1928 had cut down the yields and reduced farmers' income. Consequently, general business in Aberdeen felt the pinch. Banks in this territory which had survived the agricultural depression of the 'twenties were not inclined to be liberal, but the recurrence of pressure commenced to burden the Aberdeen banks. Collections became progressively more difficult, renewals on a wholesale scale became necessary, and it became increasingly difficult to collect even the interest on many notes.

With the progress of renewed deflation it became painfully evident that bank failures might ensue. The officers of the Northwest Bancorporation sent Mr. Robert Macgregor to Aberdeen to investigate the situation. Upon examination, he decided that, while the situation was not hopeless, immediate action was imperative. He held long conferences with the officers of the First National Bank, the Citizens Trust and Savings Bank, and the Dakota National Bank, all of Aberdeen. It was decided to merge the three banks by having the First National purchase the other two, after which the Bancorporation would acquire the First National by exchange of stock.

On June 12, 1929, the First National Bank of Aberdeen agreed to buy the Dakota National Bank.[28] The details of this purchase are interesting. The First National agreed to pay $20,000 for the good-will and the business and agreed to assume all deposit liabilities. The Dakota National Bank agreed to pay the First National for assuming its liabilities an amount equal to the liabilities assumed. It applied on this amount all its cash, including the $20,000 and all cash in the bank, bonds, securities, and high-grade assets, its bank building, and certain other assets. The unpaid balance was represented by a note secured by the residual assets. All liquidation from the residual assets was to be applied on the note and when it was paid, both principal and interest, the remaining residual assets were to be released to the stockholders of the Dakota National Bank.

The acquisition of the Citizens Trust and Savings Bank was slightly more complicated. On June 14, 1929, the First National bought the good-will and business for $10,000 and assumed the deposit liabilities.[29] In return for this, the Citizens Trust and Savings Bank agreed to pay an amount equal to the deposits assumed, applying on this the cash, bonds at market, and other good assets. The deficiency was represented by a note secured by the residual assets. As part of the deal the former stockholders contributed $60,000 to the bank. This was included in the cash which was turned over to the First National. It was agreed that, when the First National was fully paid, the residual assets would be released to the vendor.

The Northwest Bancorporation and the stockholders of the First National Bank of Aberdeen entered into a contract on June 5, 1929, by which the First National became a member of the group.[30] The contract was to become effective only if 51 per cent or more of the stockholders of the First National agreed to it. Each share of stock of the First National was to be exchanged for 6 7/10 shares of "Banco," as the company and its stock are usually called. The

Bancorporation rejected assets in the portfolio of the First National which were carried on the books of the First at $99,438.69; these the old shareholders agreed to buy for cash. The shareholders obtained the cash by borrowing it from the Bancorporation on a note secured by the assets purchased and 2,000 shares of Banco stock. All liquidation on the collateral was to be applied on the note, and if the note was not paid in full at maturity, the Banco stock could be levied upon. In addition to this purchase of poor assets, the old stockholders were required to guarantee prompt payment of all assets of mediocre quality. In order to substantiate this guarantee, the stockholders pledged an additional 2,000 shares of Northwest Bancorporation stock.

Since everyone concerned was anxious that the deal go through, events moved rapidly. As soon as all contracts had been signed, the Dakota National Bank and the Citizens Trust and Savings Bank sold their businesses to the First National. The stockholders of the First National Bank exchanged their stock for Banco, borrowed the necessary money, purchased the poor assets and guaranteed the prompt payment of the remainder. The augmented First National Bank of Aberdeen on June 11, 1929, became a member of the Bancorporation.

In Duluth the First National Bank and the American Exchange National Bank had merged early in 1929 as the First and American National Bank of Duluth.[31] This bank had capital and surplus of $7,000,000 and deposits of approximately $35,000,000. It had a strong board of directors, several members of which were reputed to be personally worth over a million dollars. Since this bank had long maintained close contacts with the Northwestern National Bank, negotiations relative to its joining the group were not unexpected. After some discussion, the board of directors concluded that the bank would be better off as a group member than as an independent, and a basis of exchange was agreed upon. Though considerable effort was made to keep these negotiations secret, in view of the number of people involved, success was impossible. Local papers soon were carrying items of gossip on their financial pages concerning big doings in certain banks and the quick trips which officers of a certain bank holding company were making to a neighboring town. Other commentators whispered that speculators had better watch the action of Bancorporation stock. On July 3, 1929, the exchange of stock was publicly announced.[32]

Another important development was the acquisition on July 10, 1929, of the United States National Bank in Omaha and its affiliated institution, the United States Trust Company. Since the United States National Bank had capital funds of approximately $2,423,000 and deposits of $20,261,000, and the trust company had capital funds of $368,000 and trust assets of $11,657,000, they were influential units in their territory.

The acquisition of banks was much easier than the officers of the Bancorporation had anticipated. In fact, group banking offered such obvious advantages to all concerned that Banco experienced little opposition. The major problems were auditing the books and negotiating an equitable exchange of stock.

EFFECT OF A RISING STOCK MARKET

The steady rise in the price of Banco stock in the open market aided in the acquisition of unit banks; in fact, it does not seem far-fetched to say that the rising stock market acted as an irresistible force which catapulted banks into the group. For instance, if the groups offered 1,000 shares of Banco for a unit bank conservatively worth $50,000, its stockholders occasionally refused the offer. When Banco reached a market price of $60 a share they commenced to wonder if they had made a mistake, and when it reached $75 a share they knew they had. Within a few days they appeared in Banco's office to see whether or not the offer was still open. While usually it was not, the Bancorporation officers were always willing to make a new offer which the country bankers found attractive.

While the Bancorporation made no effort to make a market for its stock, its officers were very proud of it, they talked about it, advertised it, proudly reported favorable developments, and kept readily available all facts and figures concerning the balance sheet, earnings statement, dividend policy, and future prospects. Those country bankers who were stockholders constantly talked to their customers about it.

Since the stock was freely bought and sold in the Twin Cities and, likewise, since various security dealers specialized in it and stood ready to buy or sell all that was offered, a strong market developed. If dealers accumulated any excess stock, their salesmen took it and distributed it to investors who would not readily resell it. Since the entire country was optimistically stock-minded in the summer of 1929, the salesmen experienced no difficulty in selling Banco to the investing public. In fact, the stock was favorably regarded by so many investors that the floating supply had a tendency to seep away into the safe-deposit boxes of permanent investors.

Since the Bancorporation officials regarded this rising market with pride and realized that because of it so many banks voluntarily joined the group, they were anxious to aid and preserve it. Both Mr. Thrall and Mr. West realized that the price was advancing because of a limited floating supply and a large and growing demand, and they worried lest some country bankers dump stock on the market and thus slow the advance. Since a contract had been drawn up and used in the acquisition of banks, whereby the new stockholders usually agreed not to sell their stock for varying periods of time, this potential difficulty was avoided. Thus the potential supply of stock was limited, while the investing public continued to clear the floating supply off the market. Because of this combination of factors, together with the stock-mindedness of the general public, the stock continued to advance in price and its owners were triumphant. Every advance in the general market persuaded additional banks to join the Bancorporation, and the movement toward the acquisition of banks moved irresistibly along.

The Second Sale of Stock, August 15, 1929

By August, 1929, the Bancorporation had practically exhausted its funds, and Mr. Decker and Mr. Thomson felt that it was necessary to raise more money by offering new stock. Accordingly, on August 15, 1929, the Northwest Bancorporation issued rights to its stockholders entitling them to buy at $62 a share, one additional for each 10 shares held.[33] The offering was underwritten by the Minnesota Company and A. G. Becker and Company, of Chicago. These two companies headed a syndicate which agreed to buy all the stock not taken by the stockholders. Inasmuch as the market for the stock was $72 when the new shares were being offered at $62, the rights commanded a substantial price. Through them some 95,000 shares were offered and taken by the stockholders. The underwriters were not obliged to take a single share; they merely received a commission. The sale of this stock gave the holding company $5,700,000 in cash, and the drive to acquire additional banks went merrily on.

Interests affiliated with the national packing companies owned several banks in packing centers, among them the Stock Yards National Bank of South Omaha, the South Omaha Savings Bank, the Stock Yards National Bank of South St. Paul, and the Live Stock National Bank of Sioux City, Iowa. All were large, did a thriving business with cattle-raisers throughout the territory, and financed livestock operations at the stockyards as well. It was not difficult to acquire these banks. On August 23, 1929, the Stock Yards National Bank of South Omaha and the South Omaha Savings Bank joined the Bancorporation.[34] The other two followed suit, the Stock Yards National Bank of South St. Paul on September 7, and the Live Stock National Bank of Sioux City, Iowa, on September 12.[35]

The next point of development was Des Moines, Iowa. On August 19, 1929, the magazine *Time* contained the following: [36]

When half the banking resources of the commercial filter of the country's richest, most literate agricultural State become concentrated in one bank, that situation is significant. The State is Iowa — farm products $750,000,000 yearly, industrial products $800,000,000. The filter is Des Moines, population 151,900. The bank will be the Iowa–Des Moines National Bank & Trust Co., resources $40,000,000, result of a merger (to be formally voted next week) which has more relative importance to the corn belt than the recent stupendous bank mergers in Manhattan, Chicago, or San Francisco have to their districts. It means that small metropoles — and Des Moines is typical of several — are moving against dependence upon the great financial centres. It means too that the half-billion and billion dollar banks must look increasingly to the country's greater corporations and to foreign commerce for their business. The banks of smaller cities are tending to look after their regional affairs. . . . Des Moines is a city of a few dozen men. They operate its dozen banks (total resources $80,000,000), its 43 life, fire, and casualty insurance companies (total assets $209,684,400), its 400 manufacturing establishments, its newspapers, national magazines (Meredith *Better Homes and Gardens* circulation 1,000,000 and *Successful Farming* circulation 1,000,000), its five department stores (Younkers, notable) — all the means which the Des Moines trade area of 1,000,000 people need for their business. Most of the men who control all this business are on the directorate of the new bank. Directors will include the Hubbells, richest Iowa family after the Maytags (washing machines) of nearby Newton. The Hubbells own the $100,000,000 Equitable Life Insurance Company of Iowa, and $15,000,000 to $20,000,000 of Des Moines real estate. Connecticut-born, lawyer-trained Frederick Marion Hubbells, 90, is head of the family. He acts as chairman of the insurance company. Two much younger Hubbells, Fred and Jim, financed and starred on the Des Moines polo team for several years.

Chairman of the new bank is to be Louis Charles Kurtz, 62, jocularly called a tinner because he learned that trade in his father's wholesale hardware, plumbing and heating supplies company. To him was left the responsibility for a bank when its president went off to work for the famed Chicago Banker — Brothers Reynolds, who were also one time Des Moines bankers. Active head of the new bank will be Clyde Edward Brenton, 61. The Brentons are an old Iowa banking family, with homestead at Dallas Center, 24 miles west of Des Moines. The late William Henry Brenton founded a private bank at Dallas Center, and extended it into a chain. He also acquired Iowa farm land. When he died his sons inherited the banks and 10,000 acres of land. Clyde Brenton has no children of his own, so he adopted Harold, his nephew, who, now 30, married and father of two children, is the sole heir to the Brenton fortune. He is to be vice-president of the new bank, his father the president.

So wrote the magazine describing the situation. Actually there was more to the situation than a casual glance revealed. The State of Iowa had undergone drastic deflation in the farming industry during the 'twenties, which had resulted in falling land values and mortgage foreclosures. Country banks had closed in droves. The banks in Des Moines formed the hub of the local financial organization and the country troubles affected them seriously. This creeping financial paralysis in the face of apparent prosperity gradually engulfed the Des Moines banks. Both the Des Moines National, with its affiliated institution the Des Moines Savings Bank and Trust

Company, and the Iowa National (the Brenton bank) were affected by this development. Despite the fact that bread and butter earnings were substantial, the banks accumulated "other real estate" steadily and it became apparent that losses must be faced in many commercial loans. Add to this the fact that losses were appearing in the bond accounts and it becomes obvious that heavy charge-offs were inevitable. The banks were not insolvent, but it would take a considerable volume of new money to restore their capital structures to a condition of sound health. Since drastic action was necessary to restore the situation, consideration was given to merging the three banks under Brenton management. Since the managements of the banks were willing and even anxious to accomplish this merger, the details were easily arranged. An agreement was drawn up to merge the three banks as the Iowa–Des Moines National Bank and Trust Company.

Since the motivating force behind their merger was the necessity of obtaining new capital, the Brentons made a rapid survey of the local situation. Realizing that they could not obtain sufficient funds in Des Moines, young Mr. W. H. Brenton jumped onto the train for Chicago.[37] He had hardly commenced contacting possibilities when a wire from his Uncle Clyde recalled him to Des Moines. Here he found his uncle closeted with Mr. E. W. Decker, discussing the details of a union of the merged bank with the Bancorporation. The contact had been effected through the head of the local telephone company, who knew both the principals. Mr. Brenton was not only willing but also anxious that his bank join the Bancorporation, while Mr. Decker was delighted at the opportunity of acquiring an important, profitable bank on advantageous terms.

All parties being willing, matters progressed favorably; a contract was drawn up between the stockholders of the three banks, who had already consented to the merger, and the Bancorporation.[38] Each shareholder agreed that, when he received the stock in the new bank, he would transfer it to the Bancorporation and receive at his option either 4½ shares of Bancorporation stock or $315 in cash. The shareholders agreed that they would organize a holding company having 20,000 shares of stock which would be distributed pro rata among the stockholders of the new bank. All assets of the banks which had been charged off would become the property of the holding company, and the Bancorporation would issue 20,000 shares of its stock to the holding company. It was agreed that the Bancorporation should examine the assets of the new bank, and if it discovered more than $2,000,000 of poor assets, it could at its option cancel the agreement. If, however, poor assets were less than that amount, the Bancorporation should loan the holding company an amount equal to the book value of the poor assets, and the holding company should buy the poor assets from the bank. The loan was to be evidenced by a promissory note of the holding company and secured by pledge of all the stock of the holding company.

When the Bancorporation examined the assets of the new bank closely, it rejected $3,250,000 of them. Despite this large amount, it shortly discovered additional questionable assets. Since the Bancorporation was very anxious to obtain this bank, it advanced the money necessary to cover the rejected assets and closed the deal.[39] With these arrangements completed, the Iowa–Des Moines National Bank and Trust Company joined the Northwest Bancorporation on September 13, 1929.[40] This date is also memorable as that on which the Bancorporation stock was listed on the Chicago Stock Exchange.[41]

Rapid Expansion, September, 1929

Since its organization in January, 1929, the Bancorporation had made progress inconceivable to even the most optimistic at the beginning. Several great banks, as well as a large number of medium-sized organizations, had been acquired. It seemed as though most of the desirable banks in the trade territory were already members and the Bancorporation would have to commence acquiring smaller banks, go farther afield, or cease expanding.

It was at this time that Mr. Decker made a proposal, the sheer audacity of which stunned even his own officers. It was nothing less than the acquisition of the First National Bank of Minneapolis by the Bancorporation through a merger of the First National and the Northwestern National Banks. When this scheme was broached to Mr. Lyman E. Wakefield his reaction was not favorable. There was no doubt of the increased earning power that such a merged bank would possess; the reduction in overhead alone would swell profits. Nevertheless, the combined organization would be awkwardly large, difficult to administer, and subject to the criticism of too great concentration of banking power in the community. The disadvantages appeared to more than offset the potential advantages, and Mr. Wakefield remained opposed to the idea. The Bancorporation stock, first issued at $50.35 a share, had gone to $72.00, and then every new acquisition of a bank had caused the stock to advance. While the idea of a merger between the Bancorporation and the First National Bank of Minneapolis never reached a definite form, it is possible that it helped to advance the stock, which sold at $100 a share on September 16, 1929.[42] The speculators slated Banco for 150 within three months. Since Mr. Jaffray was no more enthusiastic over the merger idea than was Mr. Wakefield, the idea never developed into definite form. Northwest Bancorporation stock fell from 100 to 80.

Speculators were not long disappointed, however, for on September 24, 1929, a deal was announced which would bring the Midland National into the Northwest Bancorporation.[43] The Midland was the third largest commercial bank in Minneapolis, having capital and surplus of $1,600,000 and deposits of some $24,000,000. It was rumored that the Midland would be merged with the Northwestern, a move which would yield important operating economies, but the Midland continued to operate as an independent bank. Probably its physical location was the main reason for retaining its corporate structure. It was situated near the Minneapolis Chamber of Commerce and drew a very important volume of business from that source. Its merger with the Northwestern National would have given the First National Bank the advantage of propinquity in the competition for Chamber of Commerce business.

The next campaign planned in the Bancorporation offices was the invasion of Montana. Mr. Decker instructed Mr. Macgregor to open negotiations with the controlling stockholders of desirable banks. Mr. Macgregor's first attempt took him to Great Falls. The largest bank in this thriving town was the First National; the second largest was the Great Falls National Bank, with capital and surplus of $350,000 and deposits of $2,500,000. The controlling stock in the latter was owned by Messrs. Lee M. and Shirley Ford, who had inherited it from their father.[44] Since the Fords believed in the advantages of group banking, not to mention the possibilities of profit in this development, they were persuaded to exchange their stock for that of the Bancorporation on September 9, 1929. Shortly after this, Banco acquired several other banks in the State of Montana.

Substantially all the banks which had entered the Bancorporation were large, important, profitable institutions in key centers. (The only bank having deposits under $1,000,000 was the one at Sturgis, South Dakota.) By October, 1929, the important banks that were available in the territory naturally tributary to Minneapolis and St. Paul had become affiliated with the Bancorporation or with rival organizations. Some of the city bankers opposed the acquisition of small banks on the ground that the potential profits would not be worth the greater effort required to manage them.

The Northwestern had always been well acquainted with the management of the Union Investment Company of Minneapolis and its chain of small banks, and particularly with Mr. Theodore Albrecht. Mr. Albrecht had demonstrated beyond a doubt that under proper management the operation of small banks could be both profitable and safe. With this example in view, a considerable faction developed at the Northwest Bancorporation desirous of acquiring small banks; another faction, equally opposed to the undertaking, claimed that city bankers had not the proper experience to manage small banks successfully. Eventually a compromise was worked out to satisfy both factions. Northwest Bancorporation would take on small banks if it could acquire Mr. Albrecht and his organization to do the work. At this time control of the Union Investment Company was for sale. Accordingly on October 6, 1929, an exchange of stock took place which brought the Union Investment Company and its 31 small banks into the Northwest Bancorporation.[45] At first the Union Investment Company retained the ownership of its banks and carried on its operations as an independent unit; as additional small banks were acquired, title was placed in the Union Investment Company, and the banks were placed under Mr. Albrecht's capable supervision.

The Metropolitan National Bank of Minneapolis, with its capital

Chart XI. Northwest Bancorporation Group in 1929

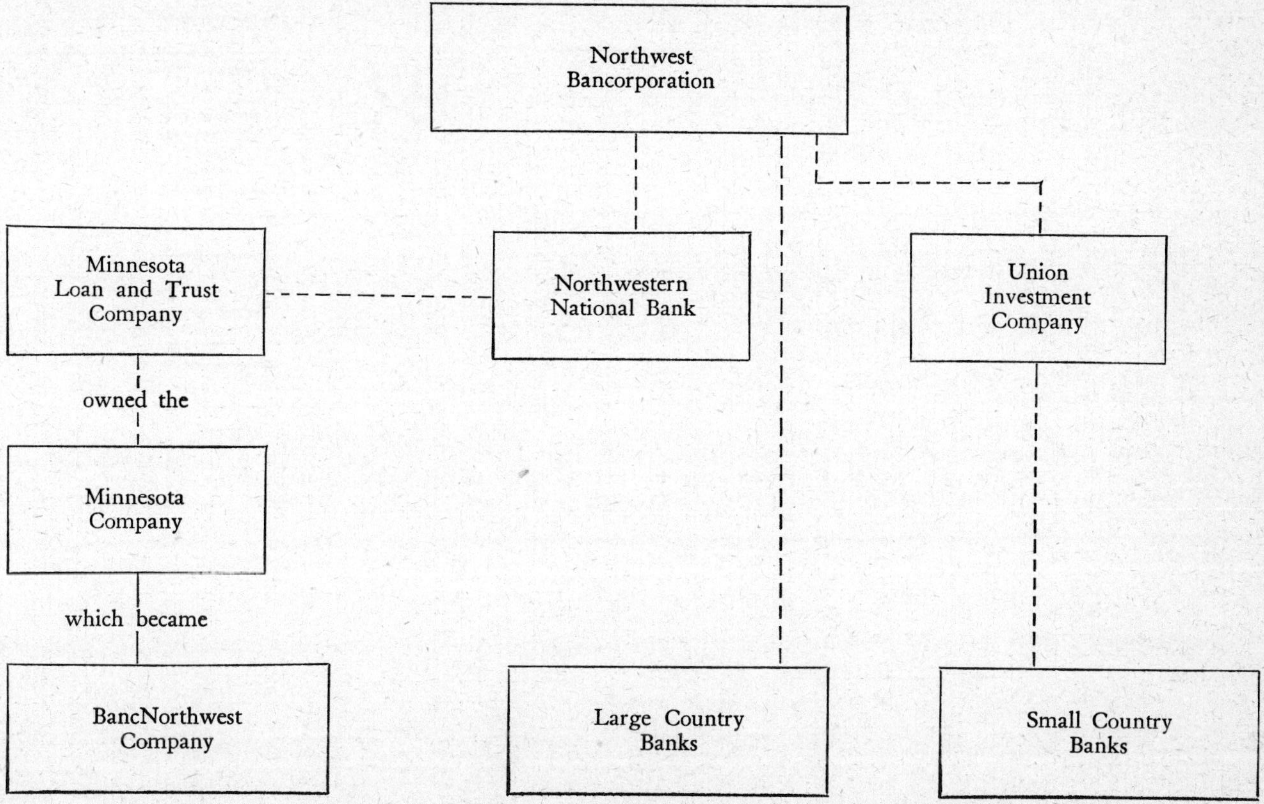

and surplus of $1,354,000 and its deposits of $11,159,500, had long been an alluring prize. The Bancorporation became anxious to acquire this bank and made its stockholders a very attractive exchange offer. Bancorporation officers were afraid that First Bank Stock would outbid them but their premonitions proved false. On October 6, 1929, the Metropolitan National stock was exchanged for that of the Bancorporation.[46]

Because the Minnesota Company, Banco's investment affiliate, had many joint underwritings with investment houses in Spokane, its officers had intimate financial connections in that city. Always mindful of potential members for Banco, Messrs. Thrall and West, while exploring the possibilities of obtaining an affiliate in Spokane, discovered that the owners of the Spokane and Eastern Trust Company were open to an offer. This bank had capital and surplus of $1,318,000 and deposits of $12,318,000. Negotiations progressed smoothly; the terms of exchange were quickly settled; and on September 14, 1929, the Spokane and Eastern Trust Company became the Bancorporation's westernmost outpost.[47]

The Third Sale of Stock, November 15, 1929

By September, 1929, the Bancorporation had again expended most of its cash. Its increasing bulk necessitated the possession of more liquid assets than the original plans had provided for. Moreover, the management was perturbed over the future of general business. It was becoming necessary to issue more stock. Banco voted to offer its stockholders the right to subscribe to new stock in the ratio of 1 share for each 10 shares held.[48] Because at that time the stock was selling above $85.00 per share in the general market, $82.50 per share was tentatively set as the offering price. The Minnesota Company, the security affiliate of the Minnesota Loan and Trust Company, approached A. G. Becker and Company regarding the organization of a syndicate to underwrite the new issue. A group was formed, but before the final papers were signed the market price of the stock slipped below the $82.50 per share agreed upon, and the underwriters withdrew. Negotiations were hastily renewed, and the price was revised to $72.50 a share. The underwriter's commission was to be $2.50 for each share.[49] The issue would total about 145,000 shares, and at $70 per share it would net Banco approximately $10,000,000 in cash. Since the deal was too large for A. G. Becker, that company proceeded to organize an underwriting syndicate composed of some 75 nationally known houses.[50] Each underwriter took only a small part of the issue. Rights were offered but they were not placed in the mail until October 30; they were to become effective November 15.[51]

Scarcely had the underwriting agreement been signed than a cataclysm engulfed the general market. All stocks plummeted downward. Bancorporation was no exception, and by the time the rights became effective at $72.50, the stock could be bought in the open market at $50 per share. The rights were extended several times in the hope that the market would right itself, but only a negligible amount of stock was taken.

When it became evident that the stockholders were not in a buying mood, the Bancorporation called upon the underwriters to pay for the issue. The syndicate was so strong and well organized that it succeeded in meeting this demand, and the Bancorporation entered the depression which followed the stock-market crash with the proceeds of the sale in its portfolio. Efforts were made from time to time by the underwriters to dispose of the stock, but the market was sick, and any effort to sell only drove prices downward. Fifty was a nominal quotation, good for only a few hundred shares. Since to dispose of the entire underwriting would completely destroy the market, the underwriters made every effort to hold the stock. Jubilation reigned in the Bancorporation offices, for the management felt that it had done a master stroke of business in selling the stock at such a favorable price, and the large volume of cash on hand gave the officers confidence in their ability to meet the future.

Despite the collapse of the stock market and the slackening of economic conditions, Banco's officers were optimistic. They regarded the situation as another temporary depression and fully expected that after a few months conditions would turn upward. Under the circumstances they could see no reason for alarm. Accordingly there was business as usual, and full advantage was taken of depressed conditions to add member banks.

In Montana things were not going smoothly; Mr. Macgregor was instructed by Mr. Decker to redouble his efforts to acquire Montana banks. Negotiations with the Marcus Daly heirs resulted in the acquisition of the Daly Bank and Trust Company of Anaconda, Montana, and the First National Bank of Dillon, Montana.[52] The Daly bank had capital and surplus of some $214,000 and deposits of $4,161,000; the First National of Dillon had capital and surplus of $421,000 and deposits of $3,714,000.

The Central National Bank of Minneapolis was acquired by the Bancorporation on November 20, 1929. Since this was located on the outskirts of Minneapolis, the management problem would be relatively simple.

During 1929 the Bancorporation had grown with amazing rapidity, having acquired a total of 90 key banks of which 9, including the Northwestern National, were in Minneapolis; 81 were scattered through the Northwest territory. Located in 75 towns, these banks were serving 500,000 customers, or 1/20th of the total population of the area. Total resources as of December 31, 1929, amounted to $468,778,262.[53] Mr. E. W. Decker wrote as follows in his letter to stockholders dated December 31, 1929:[54]

During the short period of one year since the Northwest Bancorporation was organized the people of this territory have become manifestly conscious of a new and brighter outlook for business growth and development.

They have begun to experience a new feeling of security as they have come to realize that this large group banking organization is operating here to build up confidence and to make the midland Northwest financially independent.

The growth of group banking organizations during the past year is evidence that the plan which we adopted is steadily gaining favor. In my own opinion group banking is exceptionally well suited to the needs and conditions of the Northwest as they have existed during the last ten years.

During the year the Northwest Bancorporation paid dividends at the rate of $1.80 and reported pro forma operating earnings of $4.50 a share. The balance sheet of the holding company itself, apart from that of the banks, showed assets other than bank stock of about

$11,627,391.[55] The difference between this figure and the approximately $20,000,000 raised by the sale of new stock was accounted for primarily by the purchase of member-bank stocks for cash and loans made in connection with the acquisition of the stock of affiliates.

The Bancorporation had outstanding some 1,606,993 shares of stock with a tangible asset value of about $37.00 a share, compared with a book value of $57.40.[56] The stock was widely held, generally in small blocks; the largest holding amounted to less than 2 per cent of the total. The officers and directors of the Northwestern National and affiliates held the largest unified group of blocks, a total of 213,920 shares; the Iowa–Des Moines National Bank and Trust Company held 27,441 shares; the First and American National of Duluth, 107,973 shares; the United States National Bank and Stock Yards National Bank group of Omaha, 25,704 shares; and the Spokane and Eastern Trust Company, 11,581 shares.[57] Thus, 386,519 of the 1,606,993 shares outstanding were held by the officers and directors of the five largest member banks. During the year 342,860 shares had been sold for approximately $20,000,000 in cash, and 1,264,124 shares had been issued in exchange for the stock of member banks.

During 1929 the Northwest Bancorporation expanded with amazing rapidity; in fact, its expansion amazed its own officers. The original plans had called for the acquisition of a small group of carefully selected banks which should be large, important, profitable, and well diversified both economically and territorially. Since the plan answered a definite need and offered advantages to all concerned, including great possibilities of profit, country bankers clamored for admission; and the Bancorporation officers, highly pleased with developments, warmly welcomed the applicants. The dangers inherent in the banking situation in the Ninth Federal Reserve District were well known to every active banker; and inasmuch as the pooling of resources, the creation of a central treasury with adequate resources to aid during times of trouble, economic and territorial diversification, continuity of able management, and the supplying of desirable but expensive auxiliary services greatly minimized the dangers, the country bankers were eager to join the Bancorporation in order to strengthen their position.

Unable to dispose of the last issue of stock on the general market, the underwriters approached Mr. Decker and the other Bancorporation officers and directors relative to finding a local market. Mr. Decker, knowing the situation thoroughly and being optimistic, believed that the stock was worth far more than its nominal market of 50. He thought that a local syndicate could be formed to take over at least a portion of the underwriters' stock at $50 a share. He experienced little difficulty in organizing such a group; it purchased 72,000 shares.[58] It is rumored that despite the fact that he was not a wealthy man, Mr. Decker took a substantial participation.

EXPANSION IN 1930 AND 1931

When the Minnesota Loan and Trust Company had organized an investment affiliate, it had been logical to call it the Minnesota Company. After the Northwest Bancorporation had been organized, the Minnesota Company had broadened its scope and had served the entire organization. Since the management of the Minnesota Company felt that its name was too limited in scope, it was changed in January, 1930, to the BancNorthwest Company, and ownership was transferred from the Minnesota Loan and Trust Company to the Northwest Bancorporation.[59]

During the same month Mr. Decker made arrangements to acquire a bank in St. Paul, the Empire National Bank. Although this bank was small, it seemed to have excellent prospects.[60]

In May, 1930, the Northwestern National Bank moved into its new building located in Minneapolis between Sixth and Seventh Streets, fronting on Marquette Avenue.[61] This building, a combination bank and office building, erected at a cost of $6,000,000, provided quarters for the Northwestern National Bank, the Minnesota Loan and Trust Company, the BancNorthwest Company, and the Northwest Bancorporation.

Bancorporation officers had always considered the idea of merging the Metropolitan National with the Northwestern National. After the Northwestern was settled in its new quarters, there seemed to be plenty of space to care for additional business. Accordingly, on November 10, 1930, the Metropolitan National transferred its assets and liabilities to the Northwestern National and

NORTHWESTERN NATIONAL BANK BUILDING
Minneapolis, 1930

proceeded to liquidate its miscellaneous assets. The staff of the Metropolitan, as well as many of its officers, was taken over by the Northwestern.[62]

During 1930 the Bancorporation acquired 31 banks. Of these, 12 were definitely solvent and were taken over voluntarily. Nineteen, however, were in straitened circumstances and probably would have been forced to close, had Banco not come to their rescue.[63] The Northwest Bancorporation considered it worth while to take over these distressed banks, for this action strengthened the general banking structure at a very small cost. Every bank taken over was audited by Bancorporation officials, and the old stockholders were forced, in so far as possible, to take the losses. Those assets which were in dispute were replaced with cash in the portfolio of the local bank. When a bank was obviously insolvent, the old stockholders were forced to pay an assessment. When banks were merely frozen, Banco took over their stock and purchased the frozen assets for cash, usually holding them under a liquidating agreement.

At the close of 1930 the Northwest Bancorporation owned stock in 117 banks;[64] it had acquired 121, but 4 had been merged with other institutions. During the year it had sold no stock for cash, but it had issued some 56,919 shares in exchange for banks acquired, making a total of 1,663,912 shares outstanding. It had paid dividends of $1.80 per share, and its pro forma operating earnings amounted to $3.87.

During Banco's first two years, 98 banks came into the corporation with no change in their capital structure; 2 of these had just been recapitalized before joining the group. Fifteen members assumed another bank as part of the acquisition drive, and 5 Northwest Bancorporation affiliates assumed the deposits of insolvent banks. The Bancorporation supplied capital and acquired new charters for 5 banks in localities where independents had failed and there was a shortage of banking facilities.[65] At the year-end Bancorporation had assets other than bank stocks of $9,843,993. By the end of 1930, Bancorporation had as many banks as it wanted. It decided to make no further additions, except under extraordinary circumstances or where acquisitions would forestall disaster.[66]

In September, 1930, it launched a campaign to sell Banco stock to employees and officers. Arrangements were made to purchase the stock on the open market and resell it for a 20 per cent cash payment and salary deductions of $2.00 per share per month. No employee, however, could pledge more than one-quarter of his salary.[67] Since the employees and officers of all member banks were enthusiastic over the future of the Bancorporation and convinced that the stock was worth far more than its market price, they bought liberally and pledged their future incomes freely. During the ensuing months, Banco's market sank relentlessly. In a short time employees found their notes often greater than the market value of their stock, but their monthly payments dragged on to the bitter end.

Since it had been felt for some time that the maintenance of the Union Investment Company as an independent subsidiary was awkward, and that operations would be facilitated by its merger with the Bancorporation, the Union Investment Company transferred its bank stocks to the Bancorporation, and its staff, continuing almost the same functions, became employees of the Bancorporation on May 6, 1931. In the course of time the operation of the small banks and the Union Investment Company employees were knit into the Bancorporation structure. The charter of the Union Investment Company was kept alive and it was used as a liquidating company. Miscellaneous, poor, and charged-off items from the Bancorporation were transferred to it and held for eventual disposal.

During 1931 the Bancorporation had acquired 11 banks. August 5, however, was an important day in Banco's history. On that date it acquired the First National Bank of Denison, Iowa.[68] Not that this bank was important in itself, but it represented the last acquisition. Since that time Banco has rejected all overtures.

On December 31, 1931, the Northwest Bancorporation owned stock in 127 banks, 9 investment companies, and 3 livestock loan companies.[69] This figure was considerably smaller than the number of banks acquired, but the assets and deposits of some had been merged with others. In final settlement for banks acquired during 1931, Banco issued 8,419 shares of stock, bringing the total number of shares outstanding to 1,672,331.[70] Pro forma operating earnings for the year were $3.43 and dividends amounted to $1.80 per share. The Bancorporation itself had assets other than bank stocks of slightly less than $6,000,000.[71] A considerable percentage represented take-out loans made to acquire member banks, which were secured by assets not susceptible to ready liquidation. The combined resources of the member banks and the Bancorporation aggregated $418,720,511 on December 31, 1931.[72] The Minneapolis members possessed $149,228,193, or approximately one-third of the assets, while two-thirds were located out of town. Although Banco's country banks were strong, they were none the less susceptible to country-bank ills. Such a large percentage of country assets placed the Bancorporation in a vulnerable position, for it increased its possibilities for troubles.

Northwest Bancorporation had experienced a period of growth. It was amazingly successful in its acquisition of important banks, and a substantial portion of the cash which it received from the sale of stock to the public was employed in strengthening the capital structure of member banks as they were acquired. At the end of 1931 the organization had successfully ridden the primary depression. Its banks had all stayed open, and not a depositor had experienced a loss. Unfortunately, however, the strain was beginning to tell. The Bancorporation no longer possessed a large volume of readily marketable assets.

CHAPTER X

ORGANIZATION OF THE FIRST BANK STOCK CORPORATION 1929–1931

The First National Bank of Minneapolis, 1929

Since city banking was profitable, losses were moderate, and volume tended steadily higher,[1] many officers of the First National Bank of Minneapolis were well content. It was a gentleman's business, and one they knew well. The transactions were bona fide commercial ones, loans made to finance the flour mills and wheat elevators, the wholesalers, merchants, manufacturers, and security dealers — large loans devoid of harassing detail.

While this city division was of primary importance to the First National Bank, its business with country banks had been increasing over a period of many years,[2] and by 1929 was promising to pass the city business in volume and profits. Many country bankers all over the region cleared their checks through the First National, maintained large balances, deposited their seasonal excess funds, and borrowed whenever their territories needed extra money. Since various areas in the region had different periods of demand for and excess of money, the First National as a regional bankers' bank was in an advantageous position. It channeled the seasonal excess funds from some into other areas with seasonal deficiencies, and over the region as a whole the excesses approximately canceled the deficiencies. This business was done in wholesale amounts and proved to be very profitable. Under these circumstances the officers of the First National Bank who supervised this country-banking business were very anxious both to enlarge the territory and to increase the number of regional country banks they served.

While both divisions were recognized by the senior officers as vital to the First National, each officer had his preference. One group championed city business and the other country business, but the most extreme partisan would never have advocated the abandonment of either.

The head of the country-bank department during the 'twenties was Paul J. Leeman.[3] Born February 9, 1883, in Greene, Iowa, he was educated in the public schools at Kenosha, Wisconsin, where he commenced work in 1899 as a bank messenger. In 1902 he left Kenosha for the First National Bank of Minneapolis; in 1912 he became a vice-president.[4] For years he served as field man, maintaining constant contact with country bankers. His was an arduous job involving long miles in smoky, dirty trains, freezing drives behind horses from local livery stables, nights in poor hotels, and meals in even poorer restaurants. With the partial perfection of the automobile, these trips combined banking with automobile repairing.

Leeman was short, heavy-set, powerful, his manner gruff and abrupt, often to the point of rudeness, but he was hail-fellow-well-met with the country bankers. Whether in church, on the golf course, or in more frivolous surroundings, he fitted into any group and was all things to all men. Since he could see nothing wrong with his friends and nothing right with his enemies, there was no golden mean to his popularity. Because his country bankers were his friends, he fought for them when other officers would have called their loans and refused them accommodations. Leeman was aggressive, domineering, and tenacious in building up the country-banking business of the First National Bank of Minneapolis. The First of Minneapolis competed for country business not only with the Northwestern of Minneapolis and the First National and the Merchants National in St. Paul, but also with banks in Omaha, Kansas City, Des Moines, Chicago, and even New York.[5]

Because country-banking business was important, the chaotic banking conditions of the 'twenties were a matter of great concern to the officers of the First National Bank of Minneapolis.[6] They discussed methods of avoiding future banking collapses, but their thoughts always traced standard patterns. The officers of the First National wanted to be left alone to run their own profitable business; they preferred to leave other bankers to their own problems.

From a practical standpoint, where the business of the First National left off and that of others began was usually a matter of expediency. The First did not hesitate to take a stand in any situation which either directly or indirectly involved its own interests. An outstanding example of this policy was, as we have seen, its successful attempt during the early 'twenties to forestall a disastrous banking collapse in Minneapolis. Its success in this venture, the regrettable situation of country banking, and the realization that the First's prosperity was inextricably entwined with that of the entire Ninth Federal Reserve District prompted the officers to consider methods of strengthening country banking, but with no definite result. The First National of Minneapolis was not yet ready to assume additional responsibility.

During the first week of January, 1929, with the holidays over and the rush incidental to the year-end and the issuance of monthly statements subsiding, it was business as usual around the First National Bank of Minneapolis.[7] The first alarming news that its officers had of the Bancorporation was that Fargo was joining the Northwestern — incredible news, indeed. Fargo was the First National's oldest customer, and it carried a large average balance. Mr. Weiser of Fargo denied that there was anything personal in the matter. He was just coöperating with the Northwestern National Bank of Minneapolis in organizing the Northwest Bancorporation.

Leeman was furious, because this account was an important one and he was afraid that this development meant that the First would lose it; finally he concluded that, since an occasional loss was inevitable, there was no reason for being perturbed. He subsided into a state of pleasant relaxation which lasted until he made a tour of the country banks. In nearly every bank he visited he discovered traces of some Northwestern officer, or he was confidentially advised that the bank had turned down an offer to affiliate with the Bancorporation.[8] During February and March, 1929, almost every day saw another bank added to the Bancorporation; many were banks which previously had stated that they had refused offers. It was this aspect of the situation which drove Paul Leeman into a frenzy of excitement and perturbation. He stormed about, insisting that the end of unit banking was at hand, and that if the officers did not bow to the trend of the times they deserved to lose. Each time the Bancorporation acquired a new member, he repeated his arguments with increasing conviction and fervency. Eventually he prevailed, and action followed.

FIRST BANK STOCK INVESTMENT COMPANY, APRIL 1, 1929

Since country-bank officers, upon receiving an offer from the Bancorporation, often approached either the First National Bank of Minneapolis or the First National Bank of St. Paul and asked to affiliate, the two banks decided to make arrangements to purchase stock of these banks. And so, in March, 1929, they announced the organization of a jointly owned subsidiary, the First Bank Stock Investment Company, to begin business on April 1, 1929. George H. Prince of the First National Bank of St. Paul was elected chairman of the board; Paul J. Leeman became president; and Messrs. Lyman E. Wakefield and R. C. Lilly were made vice-presidents.[9] Capital funds for the new company in the amount of $1,000,000 were supplied half by the First St. Paul Company and half by the First Minneapolis Company. Thus prepared, the two banks were ready to compete with the Bancorporation in the field of acquisition. Leeman asked country bankers to see him before they disposed of their banks. He wrote innumerable letters and visited banks whose owners he suspected were seriously considering an offer from the Bancorporation.

The first action of the Investment Company was the incorporation of the National Bank of Valley City, North Dakota, to succeed the First and Security National Bank.[10] Next, Leeman learned that the Merchants National Bank of Fargo was available. Negotiations were hastened when it was discovered that the Bancorporation was also interested. The stockholders of the old bank and the Investment Company soon worked out a plan whereby the Merchants National Bank and Trust Company succeeded the Merchants National Bank of Fargo, the stock of the new bank going to the Investment Company.[11]

During the spring and summer of 1929, the acquisitions of the First Bank Stock Investment Company were as follows:[12]

Chart XII. First Bank Stock Investment Company in 1929

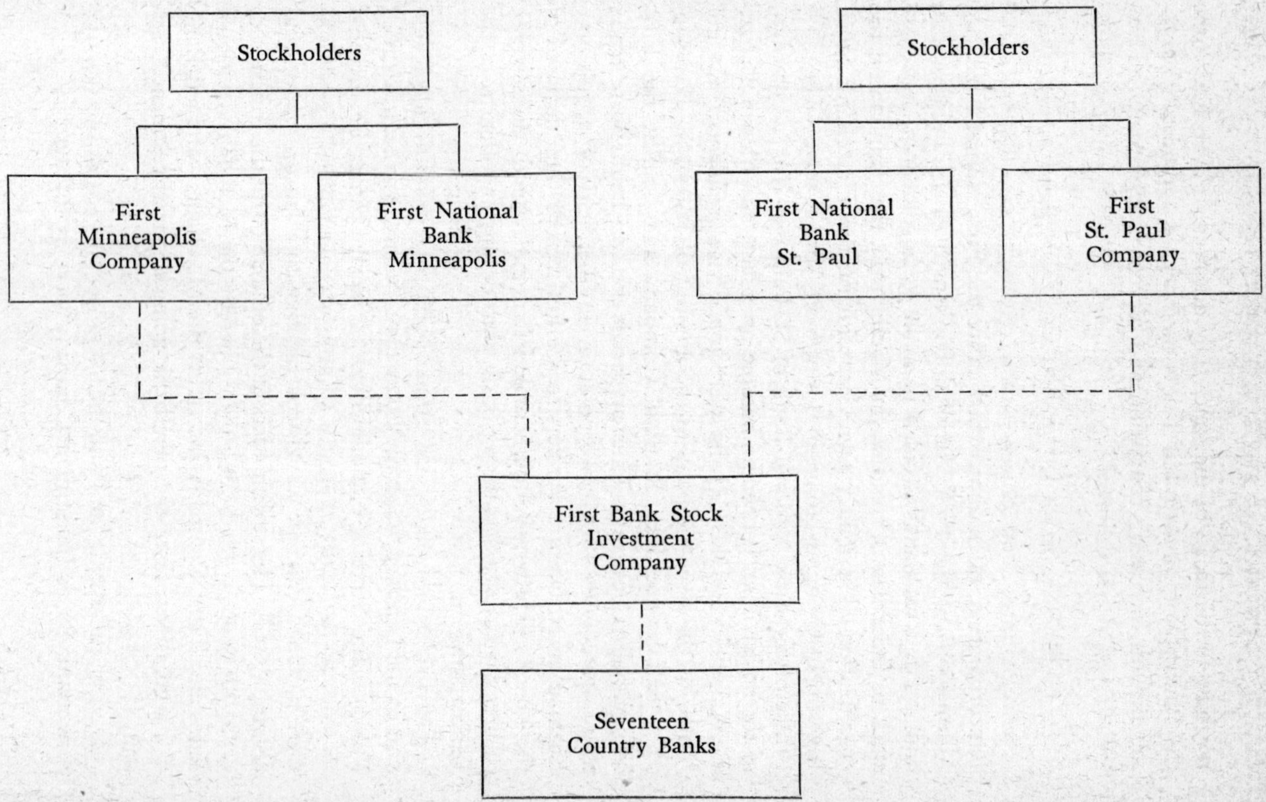

Date	
5–14–29	National Bank of Valley City, Valley City, North Dakota (succeeding First and Security National Bank)
5–15–29	Merchants National Bank and Trust Company, Fargo, North Dakota (succeeding Merchants National Bank)
5–18–29	Aberdeen National Bank and Trust Company, Aberdeen, South Dakota
5–18–29	First State Savings Bank, Aberdeen, South Dakota
6– 5–29	First National Bank, Owatonna, Minnesota
6– 6–29	First National Bank, Graceville, Minnesota (assumed Barry State Bank, Barry, Minnesota, and Johnson State Bank, Johnson, Minnesota)
6– 8–29	First National Bank, Hebron, North Dakota
6–12–29	First National Bank, Rochester, Minnesota
6–25–29	First National Bank, Brainerd, Minnesota
7– 1–29	National Bank and Trust Company of Jamestown, Jamestown, North Dakota (succeeding Citizens National Bank, Farmers and Merchants National Bank, and Security Savings Bank)
7– 1–29	First National Bank and Trust Company, Vermillion, South Dakota (succeeding First National Bank and Vermillion National Bank)
7–13–29	Northfield National Bank and Trust Company, Northfield, Minnesota (succeeding Northfield National Bank)
7–19–29	First National Bank, New Rockford, North Dakota
7–27–29	American National Bank in Little Falls, Little Falls, Minnesota (succeeding American National Bank of Little Falls)
7–30–29	First National Bank, Cando, North Dakota
8– 1–29	Red River National Bank and Trust Company, Grand Forks, North Dakota (succeeding Northern State Bank)
8– 9–29	First National Bank in Cooperstown, North Dakota (succeeding First National Bank of Cooperstown)

Although known as country banks, these institutions were far removed from the tiny banks of rural hamlets. On December 31, 1929, the National Bank of Valley City had capital funds of $138,000; Fargo had $335,000; Brainerd, $218,000; Rochester, $384,000; Little

Falls, $151,000; and Grand Forks, $268,000. The average was $164,-400; the total, $2,794,000.[13]

Despite the First Bank Stock Investment Company's rapid acquisition at favorable prices of seventeen medium-sized banks with a promising future, Leeman was dissatisfied, for he had encountered unexpected difficulties.[14] The major obstacle had been the reluctance of stockholders to sell their banks for cash. Usually the controlling stockholder had a sentimental interest in his bank; he was hesitant even when assured that he would be left to run it. Another obstacle in the way of a cash sale was the taxes involved. Many bankers had plowed back their earnings for years until the book value of their stock showed an extremely large increase. A cash sale required that this be reported as income in one year, incurring heavy taxes; an exchange of stock removed the difficulty. The Northwest Bancorporation was offering either cash or stock and found that country bankers usually preferred stock. They felt that if city bankers were willing to invest money and take stock, they should be given the same privilege. Moreover, in 1929 the whole country was stock-minded and convinced that equities would advance. If some of the holders wanted cash, Bancorporation was always willing to make a cash payment and throw in a sizable block of stock as well. Leeman was unable to meet this competition and time and again he lost to Banco, despite the groups' general policy of not bidding directly against each other.

Another plague to the Investment Company was the fact that it cost a lot to buy banks and that even slow expansion would exhaust its cash. The company had long since spent its first million.[15] Now other plans had to be made.

Since experience demonstrated the difficulty of buying banks for cash when the competitor was offering stock, the senior officers of the two First National Banks decided to pursue the same policy as the Northwestern by organizing a holding company to acquire the stocks not only of country banks, but also of the First National Bank of Minneapolis and the First National Bank of St. Paul.

FIRST NATIONAL BANK OF ST. PAUL, 1930

THE FIRST BANK STOCK CORPORATION, AUGUST, 1929

In August, 1929, the First Bank Stock Investment Company changed its name to the First Bank Stock Corporation and elected new officers. Mr. C. T. Jaffray became chairman of the board, George H. Prince, president, Messrs. Lyman E. Wakefield and R. C. Lilly, vice-presidents, and Paul J. Leeman, vice-president and general manager.[16]

For some time officers of the First Bank Stock Investment Company had been negotiating to acquire certain Montana banks owned by interests affiliated with the Anaconda Copper Company. The three banks which it wanted particularly were the Metals Bank and Trust Company, Butte (capital funds $1,328,185 and deposits $21,-193,525); the First National Bank of Great Falls (capital funds $789,937 and deposits $12,360,039); and the Western Montana National Bank of Missoula (capital funds $407,037 and deposits $4,-435,804).[17] These had been too large to handle under the investment company setup, and anyway the owners preferred stock. With these two obstacles out of the way, a deal was made to acquire these banks together with the First National Banks of St. Paul and Minneapolis. On August 27, 1929, the stockholders of the banks concerned were asked to deposit their stock for exchange into that of the First Bank Stock Corporation.[18] The plan was to become operative as to each of the banks when 51 per cent of its stock had been deposited. Each share of the First National Bank of Minneapolis was to be exchanged for 4 shares of First Bank Stock; each share of the First National Bank of St. Paul for 18 shares of First Bank Stock; each share of the Metals Bank and Trust Company of Butte for 26.6 shares of First Bank Stock; each share of the First National Bank of Great Falls for 40 shares of First Bank Stock; and each share of the Western Montana National Bank of Missoula for 16 shares of First Bank Stock.[19]

Since it was necessary that the First Bank Stock Corporation raise cash by selling stock, an issue of 200,000 shares was offered to the general public on September 6, 1929, at $47.50 a share.[20] The issue was not underwritten by outside dealers but was offered for sale through the two security affiliates of the First Bank Stock Corporation, the First St. Paul Company and the First Minneapolis Company.[21] This issue was ten times oversubscribed. People patiently stood in line to enter their subscriptions, and bank officers were besieged by influential customers who wanted their allotments increased. The issue was swept from the dealers' shelves, and the First Bank Stock Corporation acquired approximately $9,500,000 in cash.

The two security affiliates of the First National Bank of Minneapolis and the First National Bank of St. Paul had supplied the funds for the First Bank Stock Investment Company by purchasing all of its stock for cash. Thought was given to its disposal, and finally it was offered for sale to officers and employees of all banks in the group.[22] The entire block was quickly absorbed.

The groundwork had been well laid and the stockholders of the various banks readily deposited their stock for exchange. In fact, substantially all the outstanding stock came in. On October 31, 1929, all the banks under the deposit agreement became affiliated with the First Bank Stock Corporation.[23]

Since many banks previously refusing cash offers had stated that they would welcome an exchange of stock, Paul Leeman was soon busy reopening negotiations. He was warmly received in most instances, and terms of exchange were easily reached. On October 31, 1929, the following banks, in addition to those previously mentioned, joined the group: [24]

National Park Bank in Livingston, Livingston, Montana
Farmers National Bank, Alexandria, Minnesota
Austin National Bank, Austin, Minnesota
Midland National Bank, Billings, Montana
Farmers National Bank, Blue Earth, Minnesota
First National Bank, Blue Earth, Minnesota
First National Bank, Calumet, Michigan
First National Bank, Fairmont, Minnesota
First National Bank, Hancock, Michigan
Montana National Bank, Havre, Montana
American National Bank, Helena, Montana
Montana Trust and Savings Bank, Helena, Montana
National Bank of Montana, Helena, Montana

First National Bank, Heron Lake, Minnesota
First National Bank, Highmore, South Dakota
First National Bank, Laurium, Michigan
First National Bank, Lidgerwood, North Dakota
First National Bank, Mankato, Minnesota
Mankato Loan and Trust Company, Mankato, Minnesota
First National Bank, Miles City, Montana
First National Bank, Miller, South Dakota
First National Bank, Ree Heights, South Dakota
First National Bank, St. Lawrence, South Dakota
First State Bank, Shelby, Montana

During the remainder of 1929, progress in acquiring banks continued. Paul Leeman and the other officers of First Bank Stock Corporation, as well, were constantly on the road preaching the gospel of group banking. So successful was this campaign that the offices of the First Bank Stock Corporation usually were crowded with interested country bankers.

Despite the fact that the Bancorporation had started first and had had first choice of the country banks, there were many desirable ones which because of ancient enmities would not join the Bancorporation. By force of circumstances, these banks had become ardent friends of either the First National Bank of Minneapolis or the First National Bank of St. Paul, and now they flocked in, demanding admission to the First Bank Stock Corporation.

Since the stock market had broken before the First Bank Stock Corporation had made much progress, its stock did not receive the full benefit of a rising market. Perhaps this was just as well, for, inasmuch as the stock had not skyrocketed, it had not so far to drop.[25] The general public, notwithstanding its experience, was still stock-minded and regarded low prices as a heaven-sent opportunity to buy.

Acquisition Policy of the First Bank Stock Corporation, 1929

The First Bank Stock Corporation wanted only banks obviously able to earn their bread and butter. If a bank could not produce operating earnings under conservative management, there was no point in acquiring it.

In many cases, country banks had allowed losses to accumulate while they paid dividends out of operating earnings. Most desirable were the banks with substantial earning power and sufficient good assets to cover all their liabilities which could be taken over by a simple exchange of stock. When the stock had an equity, First Bank Stock was willing to pay for it with its own shares. When there was earning power but no equity, First Bank was willing to supply new capital and pay for good-will with a block of stock. Paul Leeman was conservative enough to insist that the banks have sufficient clean assets to cover liabilities. Only occasionally did he let enthusiasm run away with judgment and, fearing that the Bancorporation might get there first, allow questionable assets to remain.

During the latter part of 1929 the following banks were acquired:[26]

Date	
11– 1–29	Hennepin State Bank, Minneapolis, Minnesota
11– 2–29	Commercial National Bank, Bozeman, Montana
11– 6–29	Merchants National Bank, Cavalier, North Dakota
11–27–29	First National Bank, Bismarck, North Dakota
12– 1–29	Red Wing National Bank and Trust Company, Red Wing, Minnesota
12– 2–29	Peoples State Bank, Little Falls, Minnesota
12– 3–29	First National Bank, Rolla, North Dakota
12– 4–29	First National Bank, Austin, Minnesota
12– 4–29	National Bank of Benson, Benson, Minnesota
12– 9–29	Security State Bank, St. Paul, Minnesota
12–13–29	Merchants National Bank, Sauk Centre, Minnesota
12–16–29	First National Bank, Gettysburg, South Dakota
12–17–29	Clark County National Bank, Clark, South Dakota
12–18–29	Potter County Bank, Gettysburg, South Dakota
12–19–29	State Bank of Litchfield, Litchfield, Minnesota
12–20–29	Pipestone National Bank, Pipestone, Minnesota
12–21–29	Security National Bank, Willmar, Minnesota
12–28–29	First National Bank, Harvey, North Dakota
12–28–29	First National Bank, Lemmon, South Dakota
12–28–29	National Bank of Lewistown, Lewistown, Montana
12–28–29	First National Bank, New England, North Dakota
12–28–29	First National Bank, Spring Valley, Minnesota
12–30–29	First National Bank, Glen Ullin, North Dakota

The annual report of the First Bank Stock Corporation for the year ending December 31, 1929, stated as follows:[27]

Since the last report to stockholders covering the operations of your corporation, the First Bank Stock Corporation's system of banks has been progressively expanded and at the close of the fiscal year, December 31, 1929, it included 85 affiliated institutions all situated within the boundaries of the Ninth Federal Reserve District. All units of the group are being maintained at a high point of operating efficiency, providing their communities with the most adequate banking and credit facilities, and affording their depositors a maximum degree of security.

The operations of the group are also being reflected in restored confidence throughout the territory and a consequent firmer foundation for stabilized conduct of general business.

We are now concentrating our attention upon the development of the coördinated activities of the group making available to the trade areas and customers of each unit the greater facilities of the system as a whole.

In expanding the First Bank Stock Corporation system we are maintaining the position of affording opportunity to the independent bank upon its own volition to affiliate with the Corporation and new affiliations are being accomplished only upon this basis. The growth of the group is evidence that the independent banker recognizes the benefits to be derived by association with your corporation. Negotiations for the affiliation of a number of additional banks are now pending and will be announced from time to time.

The president's report to directors at a meeting, held February 18, 1930, contained the following:[28]

A comparison of deposits in our banks at their respective dates of acquisition and December 31, 1929, is as follows:

Total deposits at acquisition date,	\$365,939,180.46
Total deposits December 31, 1929,	\$359,594,273.24
Showing a decrease of	\$ 6,344,907.22

This seems to us a very satisfactory showing in view of the fact that most of our banks were acquired after September 1st, which is the time of year when deposits are at their highest peak, and the seasonal decrease in deposits in the Minneapolis and St. Paul banks alone amounted to \$7,679,893.79, so there was really a gain in deposits of banks in the country districts amounting to $1,334,986.57. In addition to the above figures, banks acquired since the first of the year have deposits of $4,843,299.05. The gain in deposits of banks in the smaller towns is due, we believe, to reestablished confidence in the banks in which the corporation has purchased control. This is especially true in one or two instances. For example, at Benson, Minnesota, a town of 2500 population, where there have been three bank failures in the past three years, we opened a bank the second day following the closing of the last bank, and the deposits in sixty days have been built up to $240,000 — this in spite of the fact that practically all of the available funds of the community were tied up in the closed banks, which shows that the establishment of banks by us in some places has brought back into circulation money which has heretofore not been deposited in banks. At Grand Forks, North Dakota, we reorganized a bank that had had a very severe shrinkage of deposits the six months preceding the time we took the institution over. Deposits increased from $500,000 at the time we took the bank over to $860,500 on December 31, 1929. At Litchfield, Minnesota, where we took over a bank that was experiencing a run, the run was not only checked, but as soon as the announcement was made of the affiliation of the institution with the First Bank Stock Corporation, deposits increased in spite of the fact that we consistently refused to accept deposits taken out of the two remaining banks there.

We intend to continue our conservative policy of writing down the book value of buildings, furniture, fixtures, etc., and believe we can materially increase our earnings by loaning out the bank's funds much more closely than has heretofore been possible in high-grade bonds and commercial paper. The tendency of the unit bank in this territory since 1920 has been to operate with exceedingly high reserves because of the uneasiness in the minds of the public as to banks in general, and, as a result, the earnings of the different banks have been materially decreased. We believe that, with confidence restored in most of these towns, the different institutions can safely loan out a much larger percentage of their funds, which naturally will result in increased earnings. We also believe we can effect a large saving by group coverage of insurance and by the use of standardized forms and statements with the resulting ability to purchase in larger quantities at a lower cost.

We are finding some opposition from independent banks and also from individuals to the group banking system. This, however, has not reached a point where it is, in our opinion, at all serious. In fact, the

Chart XIII. First Bank Stock Group of Banks in 1930

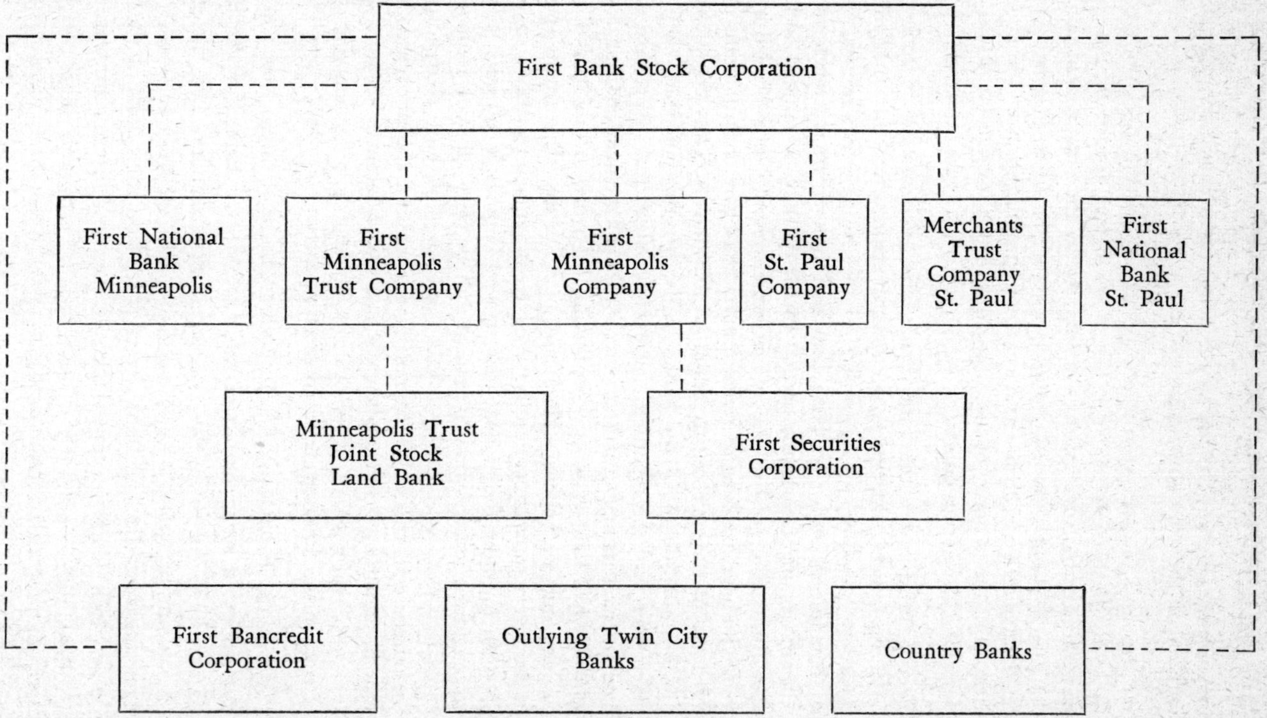

majority of the unit banks are apparently interested in becoming affiliated with one of the group organizations.

We are also pleased to announce that, so far, the operations of the banks in the First Bank Stock Corporation have apparently not in any way affected the bank balances maintained by the independent banks in the First National Bank of Minneapolis and the First National Bank of St. Paul, which we believe is a very definite indication of the favorable attitude of the majority of the unit banks in this district toward the First Bank Stock Corporation.

The organization of the First Bank Stock Corporation in some ways has been rather a difficult problem as, of course, we had no established precedent to follow, owing to the fact the company has been a pioneer in their line of work. We have, however, built up what we believe is an efficient organization at the present time. We have organized and have operating at the present time an efficient examining force headed by two men who have had long experience in national bank examinations in this territory. We are pleased to announce they have recently completed the first examination of all the banks in the organization since they were taken over, and the reports are uniformly satisfactory. We have organized an Investment Department under the management of Chan Kibbee, who has had long experience in this line of work in this section of the country, and we believe without any question this department is going to show very satisfactory results. We have organized recently a collection department under the management of Mr. Thomas, a collection attorney of long experience, who we believe will be very efficient in handling paper that may be classified as slow, and assets we have charged out in the purchase of banks. We are putting in each unit a uniform accounting system, which we believe, when we have the different units functioning smoothly, will not only prove efficient, but will be a considerable saving of time to the different banks in the Corporation.

While the First Bank Stock Corporation had pursued a conservative policy, it often had paid more than book value for the banks acquired. To be sure, this practice was customary, and the stocks of solvent, profitable banks normally sold well above book value. The stocks of the unit banks were placed on the books of the First Bank Stock Corporation at their acquisition price. On December 31, 1929, they were carried at $114,949,863.92, and other assets of First Bank Stock totaled $7,926,031.85. Since there were 3,016,870 shares of First Bank Stock Corporation outstanding, book value per share was $40.48, while the net tangible asset value amounted to $18.45 a share.[29] A dividend rate of $1.00 per year had been established, and this was more than covered by the earnings of the First National Bank of Minneapolis and the First National Bank of St. Paul. Pro forma earnings for 1929 amounted to $2.41 a share.

The stock which had been issued early in September at $47.50 a share had gone to $64.75 by September 18, 1929, but six days later had declined to $55. After the general market crash it sagged, in unison with other stocks, until on the last day of 1929 it reached $35.[30]

First Securities Corporation, December, 1929

The Twin Cities had never had an underwriting organization, although they represented an important financial market, and local companies often floated security issues in the eastern markets. To be sure, the First National Bank of St. Paul and the First National Bank of Minneapolis had security affiliates which distributed bonds, and several member banks had bond departments.

Since a participation in national deals was most possible for large companies with substantial resources, such a company was formed. It was called the First Securities Corporation. It had a capital of $6,000,000 and a surplus of $1,500,000 and it dated from December, 1929. The capital was supplied by the First Minneapolis Company and the First St. Paul Company.[31] The new First Securities Corporation took over their organizations, employees, and business. Mr. R. W. Webb of the First Minneapolis Trust Company became chairman of the board, and Mr. Julian B. Baird was made president.[32]

This organization was to participate with the national houses in underwriting new issues of stocks and bonds, and to join the selling syndicates in retailing securities in the Twin Cities and in Butte, Montana. In addition, the company would underwrite issues of local securities, making it unnecessary for local business firms to float their issues in New York City.[33] It would also supply the bonds for sale by member banks and supervise their activities in this connection.

Since each member bank represented in effect a branch office having close, confidential contact with investors and full, accurate knowledge of sales prospects, the management realized that group banking offered an unparalleled opportunity for the development of the retail security business; since each local banker knew not only his own customers but also the financial status of everybody in the community, he could supply security salesmen with live prospects and secure for them a friendly reception. Many country bankers, however, were wary of security dealers, partly from antagonism toward and suspicion of the Twin Cities and partly from fear that savings deposits would leave local banks. It was necessary, therefore, to win their approval for this business.

Accordingly, in March, 1930, an executive conference was held in Minneapolis at which was present a cross section of the First Bank Stock Corporation's officers of unit banks. These men were addressed by various speakers, who explained the activities of the central office. Mr. Baird, the president of First Securities Corporation, spoke as follows:[34]

When the First Bank Stock Corporation was organized, we found ourselves with two major securities affiliates, the First St. Paul Company and the First Minneapolis Company, doing a business of approximately the same size and scope, in addition to which there were a number of points, such as Butte, Mankato, Austin, Owatonna, and others, where a well defined investment business had been developed. A committee was appointed by Mr. Jaffray to study the whole matter of the investment business, including the matter of outside investments for member banks' own portfolios, with a view to developing a coördinated policy throughout the group. This committee approached the matter with no thought in mind of a single securities company, but as problem after problem came up demanding a solution, it became more and more evident that to reach the maximum of effectiveness and service, it would be necessary to weld the whole into a single organization. For instance, it became evident that there was much overlapping of sales effort, which already has been entirely eliminated. Further, by combining our resources, buying and distributing power, we would be the largest single factor in the securities business in the Ninth District, and it became evident that, if we took advantage of our position, we could exert an influence in the organization of issues locally and attain a position in eastern syndicates never before possible. By pooling our resources we also could more highly develop specialized departments such as buying, municipal, research, and trading. We felt we would be in a position to bring to bear a more searching analysis of new issues, and facilities for keeping closely in touch with the affairs of corporations whose securities we have handled in a manner not heretofore possible. As the First Bank Stock Corporation becomes more and more cohesive, the effect of the sale to customers of undesirable securities by any member of the group is certain to be a reflection and a detriment upon the whole group. I believe it is self-evident that none of the banks outside of the Twin Cities could possibly afford to maintain a technical staff necessary to conduct an all-round investment business as effectively as a central organization.

In the course of our discussions, it was decided that the function in advising and coöperating with member banks in the matter of investments for their own portfolios should be entirely divorced from the general securities business conducted with customers, in order to remove any suspicion that the character of investments of the member banks might be unduly influenced by the desire of the management of the securities company to make a profit for that company. Mr. Kibbee's department in the First Bank Stock Corporation is, therefore, entirely independent and apart from the Securities Corporation.

As the preeminent securities organization in the Ninth District, and with our far-flung affiliations, we have, I believe, a marvelous opportunity. Look back to the end of the war and see the enormous development that has taken place in the investment banking business, not only in this territory but in the nation as a whole. There is nothing to indicate that this growth will not continue in the next decade, and we are in a peculiarly strategic position to reap our full share of the growth that may take place in the investment business in this territory, if, as an organization, we measure up to the opportunities before us. There is not a bank represented here whose business is not being affected every day by the inroads being made on deposits through their customers' growing interest in the purchase of investment securities, good, bad, and indifferent. I think we all must recognize that our bank customers, particularly our savings depositors and certificate holders, are going to succumb to the importunities of the securities salesmen, financial literature, and the lure of the financial pages of our newspapers and magazines.

The day has largely gone by when the more intelligent depositors will be willing to keep large time deposits in our banks permanently. This may seem like heresy to some of you, but I think it is, nevertheless, coming to be recognized. You are all aware of the fact that savings accounts in the Ninth Federal Reserve District, as well as in the United States as a whole, showed a substantial decline during the past year for the first time in many years. In Minnesota alone in the year ended June 30, 1929, a bulletin of the American Bankers Association shows a decline in the number of savings depositors of 124,000.

To stay out of the investment business because to push it may affect some of our time deposits is futile. It is just a question over a period of time as to who gets the business and whether the interests of our clients are protected through seeing that their funds are directed into appropriate channels.

It came up in discussion in committee meeting that some of them thought I meant possibly a direct solicitation of savings deposits. I did not have that in mind, and perhaps that is not clear. In our institutions here in the Twin Cities we have never gone out and actively solicited savings depositors. We have, however, never been disturbed if a savings depositor wanted to draw out his funds, or if we thought he was considering investments we always made every effort to attract that business in rather than wait until it had all gone to other channels.

We believe that as a representative Northwest institution we should play a very important part in the upbuilding of this territory through the origination of the right kind of local issues, the effect of which will be to keep our investors' money in this territory and to build up our own industries. The management of the Securities Company is heart and soul in favor of aggressively developing this phase of our business because we believe that we can serve at the same time the best interests of a great many of our investors and of this territory. Last but, nevertheless, not to be ignored, this end of our business is not only the most constructive but is the most profitable. We naturally would like to be able to count on your coöperation in the matter of marketing our own originations, but we have no right to ask for it except as we make good on what we say we can do. We hope you will approach this matter sympathetically, and those who are skeptical will give it a trial.

At the same meeting the following remarks were made by another officer concerning sales methods: [35]

The aim of the First Securities Corporation is to give our affiliated banks an opportunity to increase their earnings through the sale to their customers of high grade investment bonds and stocks. Some of you have, in the past, done a securities business, but to a majority this is an entirely new idea and one which at first may seem to be opposed to your best interests. Why, you ask, should we encourage our depositors to withdraw money from our institution with which to buy bonds? As Mr. Baird has said, it is in no sense our intention that you do so, except where your own experience has taught you that if you do not offer an investment to your customer, he is going elsewhere to seek investment advice, so readily available on all sides, and the money will leave your bank with no compensating profit to you. Naturally, we must leave to your good judgment the extent to which the sale of securities in your community should be pushed, but we can assure you that it is the experience of most banks that have opened bond departments that there is more to be gained than lost by being able to take care of the investment demands of your clients.

As you already know from our letters, a check is mailed about the 10th of each month for your share of the profit on the sales made by you, or by our representative in your community due to the influence and prestige of your bank. The checks which we mailed February 10 were, in many cases, substantial ones and we have reason to believe that those of you who received them feel that you were well paid for the time spent. Naturally, we hope that as our system begins to function better the checks will be larger, and more and more of the group will be participating in these profits.

I think you are all familiar with the confidential code letters used on our stock sheet to indicate the amount of commission on each issue. Extra copies of this code are available here today.

The question has been raised as to why, if a bank purchases through the First Bank Stock Corporation securities on our list, the same commission should not be paid them as it would if the bond were sold to a customer. I think what I just said explains this, in part at least. The commission is paid for actual effort on your part in selling a security. On purchases for your investment account, which involve very little of your time and effort, we feel that no commission is due. We do want, however, all the banks in our group to be able to get a better price on bonds bought from us than they could receive otherwise, and we have, therefore, recently decided that on all purchases made from the First Securities Corporation by the First Bank Stock Corporation, we will allow the same discount that we do to dealers. This discount will, of course, be passed on to you by them, so the effect will be that your bonds will cost you less than before. This discount will not be as large as the commissions you will receive in cash on securities sold to your customers but in most cases will be more than the usual one-quarter.

As soon as you are ready, our advertising department will be glad to prepare advertisements for publication in your local papers, to be followed later by others announcing the investment service you now can offer. I have here a good illustration of active coöperation on the part of one of our number, the First National Bank of Rochester, along the line of publicity. On the same day that an announcement appeared over the name of the First Securities Corporation in the Rochester paper, Mr. Chapman himself wrote and published the following:

> The First National Bank of Rochester, Minnesota, takes great pleasure in announcing the initiation in Rochester of a modern investment service as one of its departments, available to Rochester and vicinity through its affiliate, the First Securities Corporation of St. Paul and Minneapolis.
>
> The department will be assigned Desk "H" in the main banking room and be in charge of Mr. Fred Luezinger of the First Securities Corporation, assisted by officers of this bank. Mr. Luezinger will be at his desk in Rochester on Tuesday and Wednesday of each week, but service will be available continuously.

Our affiliates, the First National Banks of Spring Valley, Austin, and Owatonna, and the Austin National Bank and Security National Bank and Trust Company of Red Wing, are initiating a similar service through the First Securities Corporation.

Our officers are hard at work preparing for your checking and revising the list of people in your community now receiving our monthly list of investment offerings. Each of these monthly lists will refer to our affiliated banks and will urge that investors in communities where these banks are located place their orders or make inquiries as to investments through an officer of that bank. A live mailing list is very desirable, and we ask in advance your coöperation in correcting the lists when you receive them, adding, of course, as many names as you can of potential bond buyers.

It is our intention, of course, to tie in to your bank all customers in your territory, not only for the purpose of selling bonds, but also to obtain other new business for you. All correspondence from our offices to such investors will refer them to you in connection with payment of bonds at maturity, redemption of bonds by call before maturity, collection of coupons, etc. Copies of such letters will be sent to you for your information, and there will be no attempt made to divert any such transactions direct to the Twin Cities. We are fully aware of the value of the local contact and most anxious to preserve it.

To sum up the assistance that the member banks can give to the First Securities Corporation, and the ways in which they can coöperate with the First Securities Corporation, I mention the following:

(1) Gradually through your assistance we can build up a mailing list of very live prospects and security buyers — people who are today investing in securities or stocks of a general character offered by a multitude of security salesmen or through the mail or by advertisement.

(2) You can assist us through coöperating with our salesmen, who in turn will coöperate with you, by giving them names of good prospects who are actually security buyers, by introduction in many instances to the above-mentioned people, and by discussing with our salesmen their financial condition and the probable class of securities that would best be fitted to their needs.

(3) You can assist us by talking to the customers of your bank as they come in to discuss with you their problems and suggest to them investments rather than wait for them to discuss the matter with you, as in many instances the investment will have been made before the matter is taken up with you.

(4) When you return to your respective banks, we suggest that the officers and employees of your institution be gathered together for the purpose of explaining to them the activities of the First Securities Corporation, pointing out to them where in their daily contacts with customers of your bank they can be of assistance in either suggesting securities to them or directing them to the officer in your institution designated to handle such matters.

When and as the time seems proper, it is our intention to subscribe to some sales course and gradually have various designated individuals in member banks take such course at our expense with the hope that this will materially increase their value, not only to the local institution but to the First Securities Corporation and the First Bank Stock Corporation as a whole.

Since this plan of organization was practical and well worked out in every detail, it was immediately successful. Local bankers supplied the prospects; the First Securities Corporation supplied the securities; and the Corporation's salesmen, aided and assisted by the local bankers, made the sales. Had times been prosperous, the Corporation ought to have made huge profits.

The creation of this company represented an attempt by local financial interests to obtain independence from the East and to round out their financial organization. Twin City commercial banks now were affiliated with regional country banks. Trust companies afforded adequate services. There were local savings banks, insurance companies, and a strong retail investment organization. The First Securities Corporation filled the last gap.

First Bancredit Corporation, December, 1929

During the late 'twenties the management of the First National Bank of St. Paul had given some thought to installment finance, a business then prospering in the hands of specialized credit companies which borrowed money wholesale from the commercial banks and loaned it retail to the public. The interest rate paid the bank was low, the rate charged by the credit companies was high, the risk was nominal, the volume expanding, and the profits multiplying.

Mr. Lilly, the astute president of the First National Bank of St. Paul, toyed with the idea of eliminating the middleman and obtaining the profit for his bank. He convinced other members of First Bank Stock's managing group of the possibilities, and plans were made to enter this field.

In December, 1929, the Lumberman's Acceptance Corporation of Chicago was purchased and its office moved to St. Paul.[36] Its original capital of $580,000 was increased by First Bank Stock in January, 1930, by an additional $500,000.[37] The company was to be renamed the First Acceptance Corporation, but when it was discovered that another company already had this name, it was called the First Bancredit Corporation.[38] Mr. L. M. Lilly became president of this company; Mr. R. C. Lilly, vice-president; and Mr. Julian B. Baird, treasurer.[39] Mr. L. M. Lilly, the executive head, had had a number of years of experience in the finance business before organizing this company and was well qualified to lead it.

The company's business comprised three major divisions: the Lumberman's Finance Plan, the Crane Budget Plan, and eventually the Insurance Finance Plan.[40] The Lumberman's Finance Plan was the first instituted by the company and involved the purchase from certain qualified, financially sound lumber dealers in the United States of junior financing on homes occupied by owners who had an equity of at least 20 per cent and had the ability to pay. Under this plan loans were made to finance the lumber and materials for the construction of homes or for additions or repairs to them; they were secured by a second mortgage and repayable monthly.

The Crane Budget Plan was very similar, with the exception that loans made under it were to finance the installation of Crane Plumbing fixtures, and their payment was guaranteed by the Crane Company. This type of loan was handled through Crane dealers, who, when they sold fixtures to a customer, offered to have them installed and to finance them for as long as three years. Since the Crane Company sold its products nationally, this meant acquiring loans on a national scale, and the officers of First Bancredit anticipated a large and growing volume of business. The Crane Plan was the forerunner of Title II, Federal Housing Administration, which was modeled after it.

The Insurance Finance Plan was a scheme which made possible the payment of insurance premiums (except life insurance premiums) on the installment plan. It was based on the principle that certain insurance coverage carried with it, on either a pro rata or short-rate basis, a returnable premium in the event of cancellation. The agent writing the insurance secured a down payment of 25 per cent or 30 per cent as the case required, added the finance premium which was 1 per cent a month, and arranged for his client to pay the total amount in equal monthly installments. At the same time, the client signed an agreement with the finance company and a power of attorney permitting the cancellation of the policy if he should fail to meet a payment within thirty days after it was due.

The return premium was sufficient to cover the entire loan. This plan was tried on an experimental basis until 1936 when a simplified plan was aggressively promoted.

PROGRESS IN 1930–1931

During the early part of 1930 the First Bank Stock Corporation was still willing to acquire banks. Acquisitions were as follows:[41]

Date	
1– 2–30	Minnesota National Bank, East Grand Forks, Minnesota
1–15–30	First National Bank, Windom, Minnesota
1–16–30	North Side State Bank, Albert Lea, Minnesota
2– 1–30	Freeborn County National Bank and Trust Company, Albert Lea, Minnesota
2– 4–30	American National Bank, Forsyth, Montana
2–25–30	First State Bank, South Heart, North Dakota

By March, general conditions were becoming worse. The management of the Corporation felt that it had acquired a good cross section of the banks in the territory and needed time to organize operations. Accordingly, it decided not to take in any more banks.[42] However, since certain negotiations already undertaken had not yet terminated and certain other banks requested admission, quite a number were actually acquired during the remainder of the year. They were the following:[43]

Date	
3– 6–30	First National Bank, Park River, North Dakota
3–10–30	Chouteau County Bank, Fort Benton, Montana
3–17–30	Security State Bank, Robbinsdale, Minnesota
3–20–30	First National Bank, Neche, North Dakota
3–25–30	State Bank of Lake Elmo, Lake Elmo, Minnesota
4– 5–30	Farmers State Bank, Rothsay, Minnesota
4– 7–30	Northwestern Trust Company, St. Paul, Minnesota
4–17–30	First National Bank, Jordan, Montana
4–17–30	Union National Bank and Trust Company in Minot, Minot, North Dakota
4–25–30	Farmers State Bank, Lakefield, Minnesota
4–26–30	First National Bank, Leola, South Dakota
5–19–30	Security National Bank in Huron, Huron, South Dakota

5–20–30	Farmers and Merchants National Bank, Minneota, Minnesota
5–22–30	Farmers and Merchants National Bank, Ivanhoe, Minnesota
5–22–30	Northwestern Bank, Langdon, North Dakota
6– 3–30	First National Bank, Bowbells, North Dakota
6–20–30	First National Bank, Blooming Prairie, Minnesota
6–22–30	First National Bank, Bison, South Dakota
7– 9–30	State Savings Bank, St. Paul, Minnesota
7–14–30	First State Bank, St. Paul, Minnesota
8– 6–30	Forsyth State Bank, Forsyth, Montana
12– 1–30	Benson County State Bank, Minnewaukan, North Dakota
12–15–30	Montana State Bank, Philipsburg, Montana
12–22–30	Powder River County Bank, Broadus, Montana

In some cases the owners received shares of First Bank Stock Corporation in exchange for their stock, in some they received nothing, and in a few situations they were obliged to contribute cash to cover existing losses. In every instance, however, the depositors were fully protected.[44]

Since First Bank Stock had the Northwestern Trust Company and the Merchants Trust Company of St. Paul, a merger seemed to be the best solution; on November 15, 1930, the two units became the First Trust Company of St. Paul with Mr. Philip L. Ray as president.[45] Mr. Ray, born in 1890, was the son of a banker in Mankato, Minnesota. After his graduation from the University of Minnesota, he worked in Duluth for Mr. J. L. Washburn. In 1917 he organized an investment firm known as Philip L. Ray and Company. By 1926 he had become assistant to the president of the First National Bank of Duluth, and in 1928 he was made an executive vice-president. The following year he joined J. and W. Seligman, leaving there in 1930 to head the First Trust Company of St. Paul.[46] The merger of the two units left St. Paul with one outstanding trust company.

During 1931 the following banks were acquired:[47]

Date	
1– 5–31	First National Bank in Paynesville, Paynesville, Minnesota
2–16–31	Merchants and Miners National Bank, Ironwood, Michigan
3– 2–31	First National Bank, Princeton, Minnesota
3–30–31	Farmers National Bank, Waseca, Minnesota

4–25–31 Luverne National Bank, Luverne, Minnesota
5–16–31 Citizens National Bank and Trust Company, Sioux Falls, South Dakota
6–30–31 First National Bank in Wheaton, Wheaton, Minnesota

With the acquisition of the First National Bank in Wheaton, the First Bank Stock Corporation brought to a close, with one minor exception, its acquisition of banks. Since that time, it has resolutely refused to add to its responsibilities.

Since the First Bank Stock Corporation had required the former stockholders of acquired banks to take existing losses by the contribution of cash, the removal of poor assets, the guarantee of assets, or a reduction in the amount of First Bank Stock issued, considerable progress had been made in strengthening the banking structure. The contributions of former stockholders were as follows:[48]

Assets Removed by use of Capital Structure of Old Banks Placed in Liquidation	$4,994,465.70
Assets Rejected and Removed by Cash Payment	2,575,390.61
Potential Losses Left on Bank's Books (considered of questionable value and allowance made therefor in purchase proposal)	2,245,056.32
Assets Removed under Guarantee	1,350,946.47
Total Amount Eliminated	$11,165,859.10

Whenever the contributions of former stockholders were not sufficient to restore a clean capital structure to the unit bank, the First Bank Stock Corporation corrected the situation by organizing a new bank and buying its stock for cash. The First Bank Stock Corporation had acquired on an average 98.65 per cent of the shares of its subsidiaries. Its own shares were scattered, although 88 per cent was held in the Ninth Federal Reserve District. There were 18,277 stockholders having an average holding of 171 shares, and the largest single holding amounted to less than 4 per cent of the total. The organization was regional in both business and ownership.[49]

From its organization in 1929 the First Bank Stock Corporation expanded rapidly in number of banks, and more gradually in total assets. Some two-thirds of its assets were represented by Twin City banks (approximately one-third by the First National Bank of Minneapolis and one-third by the First National Bank of St. Paul). All the other banks combined had only one-third of total assets.[50]

By the end of 1931 the period of organization was over, and the First Bank Stock Corporation was an important factor in the Ninth Federal Reserve District.

CHAPTER XI

THE LIQUIDATION OF THE NEW ERA 1929–1935

The Gathering Clouds, 1928–1929

The cities in the Ninth Federal Reserve District experienced mounting prosperity from the early 'twenties to 1927. By that year business had approached boom proportions; manufacturing and building were close to their physical maximum; unemployment was practically unknown. The whole system was being pushed by an excessive amount of spending for such capital goods as homes, apartment houses, hotels, office and factory buildings, highways and transportation facilities. An apparently insatiable demand for automobiles was prodding the industrial system.

Since by 1927 production in many lines was at its physical maximum, it became increasingly evident that further expansion would be difficult. Unfortunately, however, costs continued to mount, and profit margins started to narrow. As the physical limitation of production loomed large, a limit to demand also appeared on the horizon. After all, there was use for only a certain number of houses, hotels, and apartment buildings; these structures had been multiplying rapidly for several years; and by 1927 it seemed likely, at least to a few people, that if the limit was not already in sight, it soon would be.

As we have discussed in previous chapters, the farm industry in the Ninth Federal Reserve District had never fully recovered from the collapse of the World War boom. True, prices had risen from the lows of the early 'twenties; farming costs had been slashed; diversified farming had been developed; and the worst of the debt structures had been liquidated through foreclosures, bankruptcies, and voluntary compromises. Most farmers, however, were still not prosperous: they eked out a meager living in the shadow of debts and taxes.

The year 1929 proved unsatisfactory to local agriculture, for certain areas experienced a partial crop failure. What injured farming was diminished production, for prices were comparatively high. No. 1 dark northern wheat sold in December, 1929, at \$1.3075 a bushel compared with \$1.2175 the previous year; butcher steers sold at \$10.50 a hundred pounds, a price identical with that of the previous year.[1] The one weak price was that of butter, which sold at 37½ cents compared with 47 cents the previous year.[2] Since this price weakness resulted from increasing stocks of butter in storage, it seems reasonable to place the responsibility on the popular policy of persuading farmers to abandon wheat for mixed farming, especially dairy farming. This had been successful, but it had produced increasing stocks of meat and dairy products. Although the price level of dairy products was lower, the increase in production had been sufficient to raise farm income in the diversified areas in 1929 above that in 1928.

The stock market in 1929 paid little heed to the condition of general business and of farming. It was thronged with enthusiastic speculators. A few capitalized next year's prospects, but apparently the rank and file bought only to sell at a higher price. Perhaps it was the stock-market gains which fostered such open-handed spending and made possible the feverish urban prosperity of the late 'twenties. The surging upswing of the market drove prices far beyond all reasonable expectation of future prosperity and eventually divorced stock prices from values.[3] But this did not matter, for stocks apparently were not bought for value; they were merely numbers in the national game of roulette. The discrepancy between stock prices and real values and the faltering advance of business from precarious levels made many a realist pause and shake his head. While it is a popular myth that everybody was enthusiastic in 1929 and that the stock market collapsed of its own volition, this belief ignores the fact that the market has no mind of its own but merely reflects the opinions of the trading public. Actually the stock-market crash came about because an important segment of the market considered prices too high and began to sell.[4]

THE COLLAPSE IN NEW YORK, OCTOBER 3–29, 1929

On that fateful morning of October 3, 1929, the selling on the New York Stock Exchange and on the Curb was persistent. Every "buy" order was filled and still more stocks came out. As prices declined, pessimistic traders who had been afraid to sell grew bolder; and as they offered stocks for sale, former bull traders rushed in to sell and insure their profits. By October 19 the early trickle of "sell" orders became a flood which swept prices before it.

On October 24, 1929, hysteria descended upon both the Curb and the New York Stock Exchange.[5] All efforts to check it proved to be but puny thrusts. Within a few hours on October 24, 1929, shares to the number of 19,232,000 changed hands, and the advances of many months were swept away. Once prices started downward, efforts to avert the crash were hopeless. Falling prices exposed "stop loss" orders and wiped out thin margin accounts. As margins were wiped out and owners failed to protect them, the stocks in these accounts were thrown upon the market. Because buyers were few, this forced liquidation drove prices down still lower. The movement formed a crushing spiral. The liquidation of a few accounts forced other accounts to liquidate, depressed prices still further, and increased selling. Not all the decline, however, was forced. The initial impetus was voluntary, and the collapse was aided by the persistent pounding of the bear traders; but the greatest contributory factors were the ridiculous height of the market and the realization of that height by a substantial percentage of traders. It was steady liquidation by this group which constituted the driving force behind the collapse.

On Friday, October 27, it seemed that the break had been checked, but this was only a momentary development. On October 28 the break continued and 13,365,700 shares were traded. On October 29 a stampede engulfed the markets and on that one day 23,506,330 shares changed owners. On the two days, Saturday, October 27, and Monday, October 29, combined, some $18,000,000,000 was lopped off security values.

During the early period the break involved only the speculators; soon, however, the whole banking and financial fraternity became concerned. Since the stock-market advance had been financed largely by call money loaned by the nation's great banks and other corporations, the panic had wide repercussions.[6] A decline was permissible, of course, but orderly marketing had to be maintained.

The Wall Street banks coöperated in lenient policies, making available ample call money for optimistic purchasers. While the Wall Street banks labored to save the situation, the market plunged on downward. Their efforts looked feeble in the face of the decline, but in one respect they were outstandingly successful: they kept the market open.[7] Speculators suffered crushing losses, but the market continued to function. As 1929 lengthened into 1930, prices continued to sag. Day after day they crept downward until the early summer of 1930, when at last the prices leveled off and for a time gave promise of turning.[8]

In the October (1929) crash most of the professional speculation had been on the bear side of the market. By mid-1930, however, prices had gone so low that the bull side took on a new glamor for the professionals. In consideration of 1928 and 1929 earnings, stocks were on the bargain counter, and shrewd analysts rushed in to buy. The result was a temporary upswing of prices and a secondary wave of optimism. But, because the general business picture for 1930 was drab and earnings were low, even the stock prices of 1930 began to appear unduly high. Confidence seemed to evaporate, and once again stock prices turned downward.[9] Whereas the 1929 crash had caught the optimistic general public, the 1930 crash caught the professional speculators and investors.

Aftermath

It is impossible to estimate accurately the total effect of the stock-market collapse on general business. From one standpoint the market seems to be just a barometer forecasting general business conditions; actually it influences general business, at least to some extent. When the market surges upward, profits are large, spending becomes easy, and business improves. A decline brings losses and tightens spending. Moreover, the market is an important psychological factor: a rising market radiates enthusiasm and optimism, while a declining market spreads pessimism and gloom.

There is little point here in tracing the course of the security market month by month. Its general trend was downward from September 3, 1929, when the industrial averages closed at 381.17, to its low point on July 8, 1932, when the industrial averages closed at 41.22. Its pattern was the usual one, a decline followed by a recovery of from a third to a half, then another break to new lows.[10]

Its course mirrored national business conditions. Business volume started to decline in 1928; each year thereafter to 1932 it fell steadily.[11] Building volume, both residential and industrial, declined until it almost reached nothing. Houses and apartments were vacated; rents declined, and increasing vacancies and poor rent schedules effectively stopped new building. When factories found no outlet for their products, they reduced output or even closed until the market should have absorbed the goods already in stock. Their curtailment threw thousands out of work. The numbers of unemployed mounted daily. Declining profits and increasing unemployment started a spiral of deflation. The unemployed cut their buying, thereby forcing more factories to close and increasing unemployment.

Although it is not directly a part of our story, we have discussed at some length the national collapse. The Central Northwest was involved in this crash, since it was one part of the whole, and naturally the national collapse affected local developments. Declining security markets wiped out local investors, and poor business in the nation brought adverse pressure upon the market for local products. The iron mines in northern Minnesota felt the pinch as the volume of steel sold declined. Mining operations in 1930 shrank almost to nothing. The mining towns twiddled their thumbs, and the lake ports threw pebbles into the water.

In the Twin Cities conditions first duplicated those of 1920 and 1921; then gradually they grew worse. Recovery was still-born. The year 1931 was worse than 1930, and 1932 was still worse.[12]

Farming conditions in the Ninth Federal Reserve District were incredibly poor. The year 1928 was only mediocre, and farm income in 1929 was but 90 per cent of that in 1928.[13] The year 1930 was marked by poor crops and low prices. In December, butter sold at 27 cents a pound as compared with 37½ cents a year earlier; milk sold at $1.75 a hundred pounds as compared with $2.30; eggs were 26½ cents a dozen as compared with 39½ cents; and potatoes were only 77 cents a bushel as compared with $1.28.[14] Total farm cash income in the Ninth Federal Reserve District was 21 per cent less than in 1929.[15] In 1931, farm income was only 63 per cent of that in 1930.[16] Crops in 1932 were fair, but prices remained low, and the total farm cash income was only 66 per cent of that in 1931.[17] Gross income was the lowest since 1912, and net income was the lowest on record.

Defaults and Reorganizations in the Northwest

The failure of Foshay in 1929 might be said to mark the start of the depression; it seems more accurate, however, to label this event the end of the 'twenties because Foshay's failure resulted not from any general collapse, but from an advanced case of optimism which produced too rapid an increase in fixed charges. His three banks closed: the two in Minneapolis were assumed without loss to depositors by the local banks; the one in St. Paul failed. The Foshay Holding Company collapsed, wiping out the stockholders completely. The Foshay Tower fell into the hands of the bondholders, who ever since have been worrying about high taxes and the high operating costs of such an odd structure.[18] It has presented a problem of many facets and scant remuneration.

The Foshay operating company, known as the Public Utilities Consolidated Corporation, operated a diverse group of small properties scattered from Latin America to Alaska. This company had outstanding some first-mortgage bonds, a debenture issue, a preferred stock, and a common stock. It defaulted at the time of the general collapse, and Mr. Joseph Chapman, formerly of the Northwestern National Bank and the L. S. Donaldson Company, was appointed receiver.[19] Somewhat to the amazement of all concerned, an analysis brought out the fact that the operating companies possessed substantial earning power. Accordingly, the receiver obtained court permission to continue interest payments on the first mortgage bonds.[20] Despite this one bright aspect, the situation as a whole was extremely drab: investors in Foshay equities were wiped out; many saw their life savings go down in the crash.

The next outstanding financial casualty in the Ninth Federal Reserve District was the Minnesota and Ontario Paper Company, in which promoter-control was combined with investment-banker sale of securities. The company dated back to 1884, when E. W. Backus acquired the lumber firm of Lee and McColloch with its capital of \$6,000 and changed its name to E. W. Backus and Company.[21] By 1892, even without the addition of outside capital, the equity of the company had increased to \$600,000.[22] In the next few years, expansion was rapid as the company organized timber and railroad subsidiaries.[23] In 1899 William F. Brooks became a member of the firm, and again its name was changed, this time to Backus-Brooks Company.[24] Expansion did not slacken, and through subsidiaries the company acquired timber, water power, railroads, banks, lumber mills, pole and tie companies, town-sites, box factories, and paper mills. In 1908 Backus-Brooks worked out a financial agency agreement with Peabody, Houghteling and Company of Chicago whereby the bankers agreed to advance funds to the company and to sell its securities to the public.[25] On October 8, 1908, the Minnesota and Ontario Power (later "Paper") Company was organized to take over the Backus properties.[26] Its common stock went to Backus-Brooks Company. The bankers sold various bond issues to the public.

In 1925 the Minnesota and Ontario Paper Company issued a trust deed and mortgage to the Minnesota Loan and Trust Company, as trustee, and Peabody, Houghteling organized a syndicate to sell \$16,000,000 worth of bonds to the general public.[27] Substantially all the Twin City houses handling bonds participated in their offering and the investors of the Ninth Federal Reserve District bought freely. Other issues were offered in the course of time.

The onslaught of the depression nearly extinguished the market for lumber, and that for newsprint dwindled. As a result of the long expansion in the pulp industry, which finally caused capacity to pass even potential demand, prices fell to or below the cash costs of production; earnings disappeared. Losses and interest payments reduced the Minnesota and Ontario Paper Company's current assets to less than its current liabilities. As a result, it could not meet a maturity of \$3,500,000 of notes coming due on March 1, 1931. On February 28, 1931, therefore, E. W. Backus was appointed receiver of his former company only to be replaced on November 30 by Messrs. C. T. Jaffray and R. H. M. Robinson.[28]

An examination of the Minnesota and Ontario Paper Company brought to light a regrettable situation. It constituted, indeed, a "paper" empire, thrown together in a feverish drive for size and with little regard for operating economies. In some cases the available timber supply was depleted. Many of the timber reserves were of little immediate use; from a near-term point of view they served merely to increase fixed costs. Some of the manufacturing units were efficient, others were obsolete. The company, as a whole, could not operate profitably except during periods of high prices and substantial activity. A physical reorganization had to be effected before a financial one would be possible.[29]

The Baker companies by the end of 1930 had built up a tortuous financial structure involving some $5,036,200 worth of bonds and mortgages, $1,953,253 in collateral notes and bonds, and $1,035,000 in preferred stock.[30] Most of the properties stood on leased ground. To further complicate the setup, most of the debt had crossed liens; in other words, a bond issue constituted a first leasehold mortgage on one building, a second mortgage on another, and a third mortgage on still another. Although 1930 was not a prosperous year and trouble was brewing, many of the Baker tenants were under long-term lease, and the deficit of the consolidated company decreased from $139,170 in 1929 to $98,413 in 1930.[31] Meanwhile, the real-estate depression was becoming more serious. The Baker deficit grew larger and larger: it was $202,271 in 1931, $349,768 in 1932, and $344,095 in 1933.[32] In 1932 it defaulted on one issue after another.[33] Some payments were made late; various compromise settlements were worked out; but to the utter dismay of local security-holders, the whole pyramid of debt collapsed.[34] This calamity was a reverberation of crashing Twin City real-estate values.

Another disastrous failure was that of the widely advertised Nicollet Hotel. Its business declined as the depression advanced, and its meager earnings were replaced by a growing deficit.[35] Net current assets were swallowed up by the operating deficit, the ground rent, and interest on the leasehold bonds. On July 1, 1932, the company defaulted interest.[36] Public-spirited citizens, who had bought these bonds in their own interest and for the glory of Minneapolis, soon began to wish that they had had more insight and less zeal. Eventually a plan of reorganization was worked out whereby the ground-owner transferred the ground to a new company, accepting in return a first mortgage with interest payable only out of earnings. The former bondholders were given preferred stock.[37]

Meanwhile, the Minneapolis Theatre Company was having a stormy career. It had been reputed to be a strong company. The property was leased to a subsidiary of Paramount-Publix for an amount sufficient to pay the taxes, ground rent, and interest and principal payments on the leasehold bonds.[38] Its bondholders slept the sleep of the innocent and the just; rude was their awakening when Paramount-Publix went into the hands of a receiver. Even then many bondholders of the theater company did not realize that lease obligations are not binding on a receiver, and that claims for future rents are not allowable in a receivership or in bankruptcy proceedings. Many thought, however, that, even with the lease disaffirmed, such a beautiful building could easily be leased to some other operator. The lease was canceled as of April 30, 1933, and interest on the bonds went into default.[39] Efforts were made to lease the theater, and all sorts of experimental leases were entered into, but in each case the lessee canceled the lease within a short time. It became painfully evident that no matter how low the rent, operating costs were too high. The New Era palace did not fit into the New Deal depression.

These were but a few of the local defaults which rocked the early 'thirties. The promotional ventures went first, but sounder companies followed. As the years lengthened into the future a large segment of local financial issues fell into default. Persistent defaults, falling security prices, and passed dividends cramped the average investors and wiped out the more optimistic. They also ruined the reputation of investment banking.

NORTHWESTERN BANKING, 1929–1932

The effects of the 1929 collapse on city banks in the Ninth Federal Reserve District were comparatively mild. To be sure, they had some loans to customers secured by stock-exchange collateral, but the total amount was moderate and well protected. These loans were collected with little difficulty. The decline in general business caused a slump in loans and some repayment. The poor crops made the shrinkage painful in country banks. The liquidation was orderly, however, for country bankers had learned a bitter lesson in the 'twenties.

During 1930, 1931, and 1932, the most marked characteristic of the banking structure was a gradual but steady decline of deposits. Although city-bank deposits declined moderately, country banks felt the full force of the shrinkage. Even the most solvent rural banks saw their deposits dwindle. Business was so poor that people's expenses exceeded their incomes. Some sections of the country were hit far harder than others. Outstanding trouble spots were the wheat, cattle, and mining areas, which led the decline. Although dairy and mixed farming areas were far from prosperous, their more diversified production held up better. Checks for cream and eggs brought in a small flow of cash. While federal and State aid helped the farmers, conditions remained poor. The steady shrinkage in agricultural exports kept farming depressed and prices low. Finally "poor" prices of the 'twenties seemed high in comparison. In 1932 No. 1 dark northern wheat sold in Minneapolis at 49 cents a bushel; butcher steers brought $4.00 a hundred; and potatoes, 27 cents a bushel.[40]

The abandonment of the gold standard over large areas of the world and the depreciation of important currencies had a most unfavorable effect on the United States. First came a steady outflow of gold as foreign balances were withdrawn. More disastrous was the effect upon foreign trade. The depreciation of currencies acted as a direct subsidy to foreign manufacturers and as a penalty on United States exports. This was a harmful blow, following as it did immediately upon a severe depression. In addition, foreign nations desiring to acquire gold sold stocks and securities, thereby depressing the American securities markets.

Because of the declining exports, the falling prices of foodstuffs, and the lessening values of securities, the Northwest, remote as it seemed from Europe, suffered with the rest of the world. Farmers found little demand and poor prices for their crops, and their incomes declined almost to nothing. In its turn, urban business, which in the last analysis is dependent upon farm prosperity, also suffered. While a decline in income was merely disconcerting to farmers who were out of debt — and in 1930 about 46 per cent of the owner-operated farms in Minnesota and Montana, 40 per cent in South Dakota, and 33 per cent in North Dakota, were unmortgaged — it was downright disastrous to those burdened with obligations.[41] This was one respect in which no progress had been made during the 'twenties. In 1920 the total farm-mortgage debt in the Ninth Federal Reserve District totaled $1,157,100,000; in 1928, $1,264,600,000; and in 1930, $1,159,500,000.[42] This stability had survived all the defaults, foreclosures, repayments, and voluntary compromises. Actually a considerable portion of the debt had been removed from the portfolio of local banks only to reappear in the possession of joint stock land banks, federal land banks, and State agencies. There had been a modest reduction in interest rates, and many mortgages were on an amortization basis. More outstanding was the improvement made in the chattel-mortgage and unsecured farm-loan situation. Most banks had learned something from the 1920 crash; their farm loans were on a more conservative basis than had existed at that time. Nevertheless, farmers were in no position to stand the depression of the 1930's. Defaults soon became common. The farmers simply did not have the cash income necessary to meet their payments. Bankers, as usual, hesitated to levy on the collateral. When payment was forced, losses usually developed, and extensions and refundings were the rule.

In the Twin Cities the first effect of the depression was a general liquidation. Business concerns reduced the volume of their business, and this in turn reduced the necessity for bank loans. The sale of inventories supplied funds to pay the bank loans, making the banks increasingly liquid.

Loans and discounts and deposits in the city banks of the Ninth Federal Reserve District reacted as follows:[43]

	Loans and Discounts	*Deposits*
1929	$239,000,000	$454,000,000
1930	226,000,000	466,000,000
1931	222,000,000	431,000,000
1932	176,000,000	384,000,000
1933	177,000,000	378,000,000

Deposits declined $76,000,000, of which $62,000,000 was supplied by the repayments of commercial loans and discounts.

For country banks in the District the figures were as follows:[44]

	Loans and Discounts	*Deposits*
1929	$696,000,000	$1,180,000,000
1930	611,000,000	1,082,000,000
1931	478,000,000	879,000,000
1932	384,000,000	704,000,000
1933	288,000,000	616,000,000

Deposits declined $564,000,000, while loans and discounts fell $408,000,000. These figures do not present a true picture, for they are distorted by the elimination of numerous banks and indicate a decline greater than that which actually occurred in most country banks.

The most remarkable thing about the two sets of figures above is the contrast between the moderate decline in city-bank deposits and the substantial shrinkage in the deposits of country banks. The city banks were supplied, to a great extent, with funds to meet their declining deposits by the normal repayment of commercial loans; collections did not represent a serious problem. To be sure, the loans which were repaid were the most liquid ones in the banks' portfolios, but although the advance of the depression weakened most loans, there was no reason to force payment. The bank had only to obtain additional collateral, insist upon payment of interest in cash, and renew the notes periodically. Of course, enforced payment often would have caused the realization of heavy losses; fortunately, it was not often necessary. Because values were not fair in the trough of the depression, city banks which did not need cash were willing to carry their debtors.

In the country districts some normal repayments occurred, and loans and discounts declined modestly from the decline in business, but a large proportion of country-bank loans were frozen and collections were difficult. The steady decline in deposits precipitated the necessity of raising money in large sums. The result was an unrelenting drive on the part of country banks to obtain payment. Every possible pressure was put on borrowers; well-secured loans were collected from solvent debtors until finally many of the remaining notes were not only frozen but of questionable value.

Many of the loans of country banks were secured in the final analysis by real estate, and the collection problem was heightened by the absence of a good real-estate market. This was also true, but to a lesser extent, in city banks. The overbuilding of urban real estate during the 'twenties had harmed the city market; the depression wiped it out. With foreclosure and distress sales on every hand, prices crashed, and there were few buyers even at ridiculously low prices. Few were willing to borrow money in order to buy real estate.

Country conditions were even worse, for the decline in farm earnings destroyed both the desire and the ability of farmers to buy, while foreclosure sales forced the transfer of property.[45]

Despite their reluctance, commercial banks, farm-loan banks, insurance companies, and private investors were eventually forced to foreclose. During 1930, 1931, and 1932, both rural and urban foreclosures mounted steadily. Politicians began to espouse the debtors' cause, and the legislatures of the various States pondered over bills to protect owners against creditors. A flood of legislation attempted to discourage foreclosure and to keep the debtor in possession of his property. One common measure prohibited foreclosure during certain periods, provided that the debtor paid the taxes and a fair rent based on the appraised value of the farm. Another lengthened the period of redemption.

Not content with this legislation, farmers in various sections of the Ninth Federal Reserve District organized themselves into so-called "holiday" associations, the avowed purpose of which was to obtain a holiday from foreclosure and chattel-mortgage sales. By a policy of violence and intimidation these groups broke up forced sales and drove off prospective buyers. If they did allow a sale to proceed, they saw to it that the debtor bought in the mortgaged property for a nominal sum. The activities of these associations often brought them into conflict with the law, but public sentiment was with the local debtor as against his creditor. In some cases local law-enforcement agencies were either indifferent or helpless.

City and country banks were experiencing some similar developments. Liquid loans were repaid voluntarily, and business men were too discouraged to borrow further. The steady decline in deposits forced the banks to urge payment, and well-secured loans were repaid. On the surface the banks were strong; in general, collections approximated withdrawals. The danger lay in the fact that many of the remaining loans were of doubtful quality; the application of pressure might yield only losses. Then, too, many of these doubtful loans were the kind which would be repaid eventually; it was not good banking procedure to press aggressively for payment under the existing conditions.

In some areas where deposits underwent drastic shrinkage, bank closings were accelerated. The record of the Ninth Federal Reserve District follows:[46]

Year	*Number of Banks*	*Number of Failures*
1929	2,353	85
1930	2,118	156
1931	1,816	271
1932	1,658	136

Small country banks closed in large numbers. Since the closed banks were small, the total volume of deposits was nominal in comparison with the total. But the closing of these banks was none the less disturbing, and, although panic was not widespread, a currency-hoarding movement sprang up. During 1931 and 1932, deposits disappeared in the form of currency and were not replaced, a development which contributed to the strain on the banks.

Unfortunately there was no machinery in existence capable of effectively aiding banks until on December 6, 1931, President Hoover recommended the passage of a bill organizing the Reconstruction Finance Corporation and authorizing it to sell government-guaranteed bonds and to loan the proceeds.[47] This bill was passed on January 22, 1932.[48] The RFC, as it soon was called, moved aggressively to the aid of distressed but solvent banks.

Early in 1932, when it became more and more obvious that the banking system could not survive without further modification, the Glass-Steagall Bill was proposed. Its most important provision permitted Federal Reserve Banks to use government bonds in place of commercial paper as collateral for note issues. This act, passed February 27, 1932, removed one of the major defects in the banking system.[49] From May 5 to July 6, 1932, the Federal Reserve used $682,000,000 in government bonds as collateral for note issues, thereby freeing a like amount of gold.[50]

Even after the enactment of the Reconstruction Finance Corporation Act and the Glass-Steagall Act, it still was difficult for small banks to obtain funds. To be sure, the market for government bonds was good, and commercial paper could be discounted with the Federal Reserve, but few small banks had either commercial paper or government bonds. Loans could be obtained from the RFC, but this was usually a distressing procedure involving time, publicity, and red tape. Larger banks were reluctant to advance funds to smaller banks. The whole system was clumsy. Nevertheless, solvent banks usually succeeded in obtaining funds, even though with difficulty, and managed to stay open. What was causing the trouble was not a lack of liquidity, but the fact that the depression was forcing the collapse of values and the recognition of losses. This situation, coupled with steadily declining deposits, could yield nothing but bankruptcies.

The first seven months of 1932 had been extremely black, but the last five revealed glimmers of recovery.[51] Crops were excellent and, despite low prices, business improved. Then, too, the stock market advanced 22 per cent; the physical volume of production increased 12 per cent; factory employment advanced 10 per cent. The business of the entire world turned sluggishly upward that summer.[52] It seemed as though, barring unforeseen developments, the worst was over.

The presidential election, however, unsettled conditions in the United States. While economic conditions in the rest of the world steadily tended upward, they faltered in the United States and then declined precipitously. The stock market fell; the price of high-grade bonds cracked; general commodity sales slowed down; and general credit payments ceased. The nation again became suspicious of its banks and started local runs. The outflow of currency from the banks mounted day by day. By February the situation had assumed the aspects of a panic.

The Governor of Nevada, on November 1, 1932, proclaimed a State-wide banking moratorium for twelve days.[53] Such holidays were no innovation in the United States. They had been used freely in such emergencies as the Chicago fire of 1871, the Boston fire of 1872, the Baltimore fire of 1904, and the San Francisco earthquake of 1906. Again in 1907, there had been certain State holidays. As recently as 1931, Florida had limited withdrawals to 20 per cent for a period of 90 days, and an Oregon law passed in 1930 permitted banks to suspend business for 60 days.

The flare that was to ignite the nation was burning in Detroit on February 13, 1933. On February 14, Governor Comstock signed a proclamation closing all Michigan banks.[54] The closing of the Michigan banks threw the burden on those in Chicago, Cleveland, and New York. Local authorities imposed restrictions on withdrawals in Indianapolis, Cleveland, and Dayton. On February 21, New York and New Jersey passed laws allowing banks to restrict the percentage of a customer's balance subject to withdrawal.

On February 27, Ohio finally passed a law permitting banks to close; 500 of them did so immediately. On February 28, Arkansas, Delaware, and Pennsylvania passed similar laws. On March 1, Minnesota permitted banks to suspend for 15 days. It is useless to catalog the spread of suspensions. The grass fires of local panics rose to a national inferno, and by March the banking structure lay in ruins.

Bank Holiday, March 6 to 13, 1933, and New Banking Legislation

On Monday, March 6, 1933, President Roosevelt, taking advantage of the unrepealed powers conferred upon the President during World War I, declared a national moratorium until the night of March 9.[55] The banks of the nation were to remain closed. This move met with general popular approval, for drastic action was recognized as necessary.

Reopening the banks, however, was imperative. The Federal Reserve Board, the Secretary of the Treasury, and the Comptroller of the Currency worked ceaselessly. The result was the Emergency Bank Act (including the Bank Conservation Act) of March 9, 1933, which delegated the following powers:[56]

1. To the President of the United States, authority to close the banks;

2. To the Secretary of the Treasury, authority to regulate the business of the banks during such an emergency period as might be declared by the President;

3. To the Comptroller of the Currency, authority to appoint a conservator for a national bank whenever he deemed it necessary in order to conserve its assets for the benefit of the depositors and creditors, and to effect the reorganization of such national banks as the conditions and circumstances warranted;

4. To national banks, the privilege of issuing preferred stock, to be purchased by the RFC, in order to strengthen their capital structure;

5. To bank depositors and stockholders, authority to reorganize banks with the consent of 75 per cent of the deposits and 66⅔ per cent of the stock;

6. To the Federal Reserve Banks, authority to issue Federal Reserve Bank notes to the extent of 100 per cent of the value of government obligations or 90 per cent of commercial obligations;

7. To the Federal Reserve Banks, authority to discount the notes of member banks secured by collateral previously not eligible for that purpose;

8. To conservators, authority to carry on a general banking business and to handle new deposits on a segregated trust basis.

Reopening of Banks, March 13, 1933

A presidential proclamation, dated March 9, 1933, extended the bank holiday.[57] The following day the President issued a proclamation authorizing the Secretary of the Treasury to prescribe regulations under which any member bank of the Federal Reserve System and any other banking institution organized under the laws of the United States might perform any or all of its usual banking functions, except as otherwise prohibited.[58] This order also permitted State banking authorities to allow their banks to reopen.

The order required all Federal Reserve members to obtain a permit to reopen. Applications were to be handled through local Federal Reserve Banks designated as agents of the Secretary of the

Treasury. Banks were ordered to refrain from paying out gold or gold certificates. The order provided that, upon obtaining a permit, banks in reserve cities could open on or after March 13; banks in clearing-house cities could open on or after March 14; and country banks could open on or after March 15.[59]

The necessity of obtaining permits caused a great deal of confusion, for each bank had to be examined before it was licensed to reopen. The physical task of examining banks was onerous. National bank examiners and employees of the Federal Reserve Banks worked day and night to reopen banks as fast as possible. Only those obviously solvent were licensed on the first examination. In all cases of doubt conservators were appointed. Since scarcity of experienced conservators soon developed, a practice was made of appointing one of the bank's former officers. This method worked very successfully.

In the Ninth Federal Reserve District in March, 1933, there were 1,460 banks, 540 of them member banks.[60] By March 15, 1933, some 388 banks were licensed for unrestricted operation.[61] The first examination was completed on April 12, and some 969 banks were allowed to open without restriction; by December 27 there were 1,225 banks open.[62] On June 27, 1934, some 531 member banks out of a possible 540 were open, and some 887 non-member banks out of a total of 920 were open.[63] Thus, only 9 member banks and 33 non-member banks did not reopen. To be sure, many of the banks which reopened did so only after a scaling of deposits and a complete reorganization. Nevertheless, by the end of 1933 some 1,448 banks, and by the end of 1934 some 1,432 banks, were open in the Ninth Federal Reserve District.

Some of the reorganizations were mild affairs consisting merely of the strengthening of capital funds by further contributions from stockholders or sale of preferred stock to the RFC. Some of the later reorganizations, however, were drastic and involved the waiving of a portion of deposits. There were three major methods used in reorganizing banks: the "capital correction plan," the "creditor waiver plan," and the "Spokane sale plan."[64]

The "capital correction plan" was utilized only in instances where losses and unacceptable assets did not exceed capital funds. Losses were all charged off, and capital funds were restored either by the stockholders or through the sale of preferred stock to the Reconstruction Finance Corporation. The charged-off assets remained the property of the bank and as they were changed into cash from time to time, they would be credited to the surplus account.

The "creditor waiver" type of reorganization, though it had been in use for many years prior to the bank holiday, had been very awkward. Since there was no way of forcing dissenting creditors (depositors) to abide by the plan, it became necessary to pay dissenters in full, putting a premium on non-conformance. The Bank Conservation Act made it possible for 75 per cent of the creditors and 66⅔ per cent of the stock to bind all concerned.[65] This plan of reorganization was used whenever losses were greater than the capital funds and when deposits were impaired. The depositors agreed to waive a percentage of their deposits, and the equivalent in poor assets was transferred to trustees for the benefit of the depositors. The capital funds were restored by the old stockholders, the sale of new stock, or the sale of preferred stock to the Reconstruction Finance Corporation.

The "Spokane sale" type of reorganization was frequently used, particularly when the volume of acceptable assets would yield immediately less than 50 per cent to the depositors. It provided for the formation of a new bank which bought a portion of the assets of the old bank at an appraised value and paid for them with an equivalent payment on the certificates of the receiver of the closed bank.[66] Usually this payment consisted of a deposit credit on the books of the new bank. In most cases arrangements were made to borrow funds from the RFC. In this type of reorganization the right of substitution was given to the new bank. The receiver of the old bank continued with the liquidation of its assets and the enforcement of its rights.

The Bank Conservation Act was definitely an emergency measure. More permanent provisions were made by the Banking Act of 1933, signed on June 16 of that year. This act provided as follows:[67]

1. No bank stock certificate shall represent stock of any other corporation except that owning the bank's premises;

2. No bank shall have any investment affiliate, nor shall it deal in any securities except State, municipal, and government bonds;

3. No bank shall act as agent to make stock-exchange loans;

4. No bank shall pay interest on demand deposits;

5. The Federal Reserve Board shall fix maximum rates of interest on time and savings deposits;

6. No bank shall either directly or indirectly make loans to its own officers (all officer loans in existence could be renewed for not over two years);

7. Bank officers must report all personal loans to their board of directors;

8. Banking authorities may examine bank holding companies simultaneously with banks;

9. After 1938, holding companies must possess free assets other than bank stocks equal to 12 per cent of the par value of stocks owned (this was to be increased 2 per cent a year until free assets equaled 25 per cent of the par value of bank stocks. All earnings in excess of 6 per cent of book value were to be retained until free assets equaled 25 per cent of par);

10. National banks shall have the same right to establish and operate branches as State banks;

11. Holding companies must obtain a permit to vote bank stocks (unless permits are granted, banks cannot receive U. S. deposits nor pay dividends, and charter may be revoked);

12. There shall be no double liability in the case of any national bank stock;

13. Commencing January 1, 1934, deposits shall be insured up to $2,500 per depositor. After July 1, 1934, the first $10,000 was to be 100 per cent insured; the next $40,000 to be 75 per cent insured; and the excess, 50 per cent insured.

One result of this law, besides many others, was the forced liquidation of banks' security affiliates and their restriction to bona fide commercial banking and trust administration. It also broadened the powers of governmental authorities, giving them full control of bank holding companies. Forbidding the payment of interest on commercial balances and regulating the maximum rate on time deposits was likewise constructive. The temporary insurance of deposits became effective on January 1, 1934, but the increase specified in the original act was superseded when on July 1, 1934, the coverage was placed at a maximum of $5,000 per depositor.[68]

In 1935 a new act (known as the Banking Act of 1935) again modified the banking laws. It contained the following provisions:[69]

1. An open market committee was to be organized, consisting of 7 Federal Reserve Board members and 5 representatives of the 12 regional Federal Reserve Banks, with authority to control credit by open market operations.

2. The statutory 7, 10, and 13 per cent reserves were to be retained; the Board was to be permitted to double but not to reduce them.

3. The Federal Deposit Insurance Corporation was to be permanent; the coverage was to be fixed at $5,000. The annual assessments for this purpose were to be one-twelfth of one per cent of average deposits.

4. Bankers were forbidden to serve on the boards of more than two banks.

5. Banks could make five-year real-estate loans for not over 50 per cent of the value of property and not in excess of either capital and surplus or 60 per cent of time deposits, whichever was the greater. Ten-year amortization loans could be made up to 60 per cent of the value of property, provided that the loan would be amortized 50 per cent by its maturity.

The Banking Act of 1935 serves as a milestone marking the end of the financial collapse. By then, the entire banking structure had been changed. Actually, the United States was off a gold standard; in effect, our currency was based on government bonds and commercial paper and gold, and supposedly it was subject to regulation. The rediscount provision of Federal Reserve regulations had been broadened until they allowed banks to rediscount a large part of their assets. The Reconstruction Finance Corporation stood ready to loan funds on any type of collateral, as well as to buy preferred stock in solvent banks. The Federal Deposit Insurance Corporation was prepared, in case an insured bank was insolvent, to take up the loss, promptly paying in full all deposits of $5,000 or less. There were an elastic, managed currency, 100 per cent liquidity, and presumably no possibility of loss. This system, so perfect in theory, is now being tried by the test of time.

CHAPTER XII

THE BANCORPORATION RIDES THE STORM 1929–1934

Business as Usual, 1929–1931

In chapter xi we have discussed the impact of the depression on the national and regional economic and banking structures, and the resulting changes in the banking laws of the nation. Let us now consider the experiences of the Northwest Bancorporation during this period of change.

In general the year 1929 was one of enthusiasm and prosperity for the Northwest Bancorporation, and little thought was given to the fact that business turned downward during the last quarter of the year. The officers were interested primarily in expansion, and to a lesser extent in internal organization. We have already discussed the movement toward expansion and shall not mention it further, but the attempt at internal organization deserves consideration.

Since the Northwest Bancorporation was new, it needed to perfect an operating routine and educate its staff in procedure. Legally the Bancorporation was only the controlling stockholder in its group and, as such, had no authority beyond electing the boards of directors. Actually it planned to exercise considerable supervisory authority.[1] Its powers were determined only after much discussion between its officers and those of the member banks. It was decided that the Bancorporation deserved complete and accurate information. Its officers could make recommendations and lay down general policies, but they could not enforce obedience. Member-bank directors and officers were to be supreme in local affairs, subject only to general supervision. While they were to make loans on their own responsibility, they were to report individual loans above a certain amount to the Bancorporation.[2] Since large loans were rare, local officers reported only a fraction of their new loans. Even if the Bancorporation criticized it, a loan stood until collected or made acceptable.

While local managements had control of their investments as well as their loan policy, they relied on the investment department of the corporation (after it was established) for recommendations as to policy as well as particular issues. Many of the smaller banks authorized the corporation to make investments for them subject to their approval; while the larger banks, equipped with their own investment departments, exercised their own initiative, consulting with the corporation as to policy.[3]

Only a few functions, such as purchasing supplies, advertising, and legal activities, were centralized, and these only to a limited extent. The Bancorporation went to great lengths to standardize and install a uniform accounting system and to provide for a central auditing and examination department. This central bookkeeping division required frequent reports in order to prepare consolidated figures; the auditing division determined and maintained accuracy, while the examination department inspected the quality of assets.

A budget, worked out jointly by the officers of the unit banks and of the Bancorporation, estimating the income and expenses of each independent bank provided an important means of control.[4] The Bancorporation officers, by comparing banks by size, character of territory, character of assets, and other tests, classified similar units. Local officers were called upon to explain why their income was lower or their expenses were higher than those of comparable banks. Unusual circumstances could justify a variation, but it had to be explained to the officers of the Bancorporation.

Despite the procedure of the Bancorporation, unit officers were left with a great deal of local prestige and authority. The suggested procedure was not instituted all at once, but 1929 and 1930 were marked by its gradual initiation. A policy of education brought officers of member banks to the Bancorporation for instruction and training.[5] In some cases employees were transferred from one bank to another with the approval of the banks affected. But in so far as possible, the Bancorporation did not interfere with local management. By the end of 1930 great strides had been made toward perfecting an operating organization. During 1930, general business continued to decline both in volume and in profits, but there was no tendency toward panic. The credit structure in the Ninth Federal Reserve District appeared strong, and orderly liquidation was maintained.

The year 1931 saw an intensification of 1930. Although no runs developed on the Bancorporation banks, business concerns paid off their loans and declining business and agricultural depression made deposits shrink steadily.[6] Business organizations operating at a loss fell back on their reserves, while the unemployed drew down their balances. For instance, the First National Bank of Grantsburg, Wisconsin, on December 31, 1930, had deposits of $522,517; on December 31, 1931, deposits had dropped to $450,928.[7] In the Iowa–Des Moines National Bank deposits declined from $33,038,811 to $26,994,707;[8] in the Stock Yards National Bank of South Omaha from $9,297,662 to $6,676,342;[9] in the Spokane and Eastern Trust Company of Spokane, Washington, from $14,063,726 to $10,796,188;[10] and in the Northwestern National Bank of Minneapolis from $101,484,911 to $92,609,818.[11]

Nevertheless, the Bancorporation banks remained in an easy position. The repayment of loans which resulted from poor business amply covered withdrawals, and pressure on loans produced liquidation. On December 31, 1930, cash and governments of affiliated banks equaled 32 per cent of its deposits.[12] It could hardly be said that the Bancorporation was embarrassed under the circumstances. As a matter of fact, it finished 1931 in the same relative condition, its percentage of cash assets being 32 per cent of affiliated banks' deposits.[13] Under these circumstances Bancorporation officers were not worried about either solvency or liquidity, but they were concerned over the decline in earnings. They urged member banks to cut expenses and to increase income. They counseled affiliated bank officers to make reasonable loans and to refuse no customer who would have received credit under normal circumstances.[14] Officers were told to appraise both collateral and prospects in the light of normal, long-time conditions and not to be unduly influenced by the near-term outlook. This policy, said Banco, would build up earnings, produce new customers, and heighten the prestige of the Bancorporation. The Bancorporation's attitude rested on the assumption that the depression was a normal, recurring one and that conditions would soon turn for the better.

In spite of basic optimism, however, the Bancorporation was conservative. Toward the end of 1931 it advised member banks to repay all borrowed money and free pledged bonds.[15] This suggestion referred primarily to the policy of securing government and State deposits by the pledge of the bank's best bonds. The next step was a campaign to clarify for country bankers the Federal Reserve Bank's rules governing the eligibility of paper.[16] Every possible credit accommodation was to be supplied to the public, and loans were to be judged in the light of normal conditions rather than those of the current depression. At the same time, the banks were to take every precaution to protect themselves. Bancorporation officials were very mindful of their responsibility to the Ninth Federal Reserve District. They pointed out to unit bank officers that, while Banco and First Bank Stock owned the controlling stock in the banks in the territory, together they had 46 per cent of the total deposits.[17] There were only 51 banks in the district, other than group members, which had deposits of a million dollars, and every one of these banks was a correspondent either of the First Nationals of St. Paul and Minneapolis or of the Northwestern National of Minneapolis.[18] Thus, any action of the groups was important. Especial care was to be exercised to avoid panic, and all banking must be maintained on a broadminded, level-headed, intelligent basis.

During the latter part of 1931 and early 1932, Banco's officers hopefully waited for conditions to improve. Under normal circumstances, the expected domestic upturn might have occurred, but the repercussions of European developments destroyed foreign trade, and what should have proved the bottom of the depression became only a springboard from which conditions dived to new lows. Had the depression lifted in 1931, there seems little doubt that Banco's policies would have been justified.

PESSIMISM, 1932

Instead of turning upward, however, business resumed its downward course in 1932, and bank deposits declined steadily. In the First National Bank of Grantsburg deposits amounted to $450,928 on December 31, 1931, but by December 31, 1932, they had declined to $392,197.[19] In the Iowa–Des Moines National they had declined from $26,994,707 to $24,390,593;[20] in the Stock Yards National of Omaha from $6,676,342 to $5,837,381;[21] and in the Northwestern National Bank of Minneapolis from $92,609,818 to $78,779,432.[22] While the decline was not rapid, it was persistent. Meanwhile, payments continued to offset withdrawals, and the Bancorporation's ratio between liquid assets and total deposits remained relatively constant. However, a stunted volume of business, fewer commercial loans, and declining earnings from interest seriously threatened the total earnings. Nothing could be done to increase interest income, for rates were competitive and the volume of loans could be raised only if the standards were lowered. By 1932 Bancorporation officials had lost their optimism, and they remained adamant in their resolve not to lower the standard of new loans.

With interest income relatively fixed, the only alternatives were to secure miscellaneous income and to reduce expenses. Fortunately, the free and easy methods of banking during the previous decade left room for reform. Throughout 1932 the Bancorporation experimented with minimum balance charges, service, float, and exchange fees, and penalties for an excessive number of checks. A few group banks had always levied these charges, but many country bankers boasted of never charging anything but interest. Although bankers had avoided these service charges because of the competitive conditions, competition did not prove to be serious; with the group banks in the lead, the independents followed. Even where they did not, the group did not lose accounts; faith in the strength of the group banks made their customers willing to accept extra charges.

The largest piece of economy was the reduction of the interest paid on demand and time deposits. While these rates were not so high as they had been during the early 'twenties, they were still substantial. Four per cent was the established country rate on time money; a few banks paid 5 per cent. Rates on demand deposits varied around 2 per cent. The Bancorporation exerted gradual pressure on its banks to increase minimum balance requirements and to reduce the interest allowed. While final authority remained with the local officers, inasmuch as local conditions varied, rates generally were reduced at least 1 per cent. The results of this policy are apparent in the fact that interest paid amounted to $7,218,773 in 1931 and to $5,505,348 in 1932.[23]

Another economy was effected by reducing salaries, and another by reducing the number of bank employees to a minimum.[24] Those remaining were reclassified and their salaries revised to the level justified by their work. This was an innovation, for Bancorporation banks long had tended to base salaries on seniority. Perhaps the officers suffered the most. At least many of them found their income sharply curtailed. A general salary cut on a percentage basis followed. Salaries amounted to $5,993,685 in 1931 and to $5,230,564 in 1932.[25] Interest earned fell from $19,486,779 to $15,509,070, while operating earnings declined only from $5,741,625 to $4,405,544.[26]

During 1932 the Banco banks contrived to improve their loans. No sound loan was refused that could be rediscounted with the Federal Reserve Bank. Other loans were whipped into shape, and by the end of 1932 assets equal to 71.54 per cent of deposits were classed as liquid.[27] While pressure was exerted on questionable loans, they were still renewed as a last resort. Giving both the bank and its customers more time to effect a recovery was considered a sensible policy, and the result was a separation of the sheep from the goats.

Developing Losses of the Bancorporation, 1931–1932

Losses inevitably made their appearance, despite Banco's reluctance to incur them. Borrowers refusing to struggle longer with their properties surrendered them to the banks. In many instances borrowers in default attempted to retain their properties, leaving the bank no choice save legal action. Wherever possible, trouble was avoided but by 1932 it had to be faced.

At first, losses were borne by the member banks and gradually certain banks displayed their weakness. One of the first was the Security State Bank of Norfolk (Nebraska). It had been experiencing losses, but Banco was not disturbed until its auditors discovered that certain officers had defaulted to the extent of $133,303.[28] While the bank was covered with a blanket fidelity bond, the insurance company disputed the claim, offering a settlement of

$112,085 and recoveries up to the difference.[29] The bank accepted this and the Bancorporation contributed the balance.[30]

Perhaps the most costly situation was the Bank of Spearfish (South Dakota), a cattlemen's bank located in a very small town in the Black Hills. It did a business with the cattle industry in long-term range loans which belied the size of the town. Before existing loans matured, the bottom fell out of the cattle market, causing severe losses on most cattle paper. The bank was unable to make good the losses on endorsed paper and called on the Bancorporation for help. Time after time the Bancorporation put in funds until finally its contributions aggregated more than the total capital, surplus, and deposits of the Spearfish unit. Legally the Northwest Bancorporation could have avoided liability by letting the bank fail, paying a $25,000 assessment, and washing its hands of the entire affair. Instead, it stood squarely behind its avowal that no depositor should ever lose a penny in a Bancorporation bank. The financial loss was severe, but Banco's reputation remained untarnished. A similar situation arose in the Stock Yards National Bank of Omaha and, in fact, in several other cattle banks.

Next in severity of losses came the Montana banks. Since there had been optimistic management of these during the late 'twenties, many of their loans were not well secured. The copper mines closed, bringing depression with startling suddenness. Since building ceased, the Montana lumber industry dwindled. Cattle and wheat prices fell to depression lows. Crops were ruined by consistent drought. Montana became one of the most depressed areas in the United States. Borrowers defaulted on their loans, and deposits shrank. Montana banks experienced paralyzing losses, and the Bancorporation repeatedly contributed funds where necessary to keep them open.

Wherever a locality was dependent on wheat, depression was severe and losses were heavy. Conditions, however, were not so straitened as during the 'twenties for two reasons: first, most agricultural communities had progressed from complete dependence on the wheat industry; and secondly, banks had learned a lesson from the past and had local loans relatively well secured. In the mixed agricultural, dairying, manufacturing, and diversified communities, losses developed, but well-managed and conservative banks kept them at a minimum. Where an industry like copper-mining collapsed, the whole community suffered materially; or when prices vanished, as in the cattle industry, losses were large. Moderate losses were experienced in every Northwest Bancorporation bank. In every instance Banco, if necessary, contributed funds and kept its member bank solvent. All told, the Bancorporation during the experience made contributions to 39 of its present affiliated banks, some of which were for the purpose of aiding them in retirement of preferred stock in advance of maturity.

RECAPITALIZATION OF THE BANCORPORATION, 1932, AND RUNS ON MEMBER BANKS, 1933

In 1929 the Bancorporation had placed the stocks of subsidiaries on its books at cost, a practice customary in the 'twenties. Since the prices paid were greatly in excess of net tangible asset value, the book value of Bancorporation stock was far above its net tangible asset value. In November, 1932, the management decided to recapitalize the Bancorporation by writing off all intangibles, adjusting the investment in stocks of subsidiaries to net tangible asset value, changing the par value of its common stock from $50 to no par, writing off all known losses, and providing a reserve of $14,000,000 for contingencies.[31] This recapitalization was really only a revision of accounting methods and did not change the position of the stock, but it proved very upsetting to the stockholders' peace of mind.

Despite the seriousness of losses, member banks remained liquid and during most of 1932 did not experience any severe runs. True, deposits declined, but withdrawals were orderly, caused by economic conditions rather than a loss of confidence. As the new year (1933) commenced, however, a growing lack of confidence in the nation's banking structure became apparent. The Ninth Federal Reserve District was singularly free from disturbance, but bank failures in other districts had their effect. Runs in New York, Chicago, Cleveland, and Detroit made front page news and hastened the departure of confidence. Rumors spread that no bank was safe. Currency hoarding set in, and the suspicious began demanding gold.

By February, 1933, bank runs had developed in various parts of the Ninth Federal Reserve District. One of the first to affect the Bancorporation was on the Security National Bank and Trust Company of Faribault, Minnesota. Farmers from all over the territory crowded into town and congregated uneasily in the streets. Timorous depositors commenced to withdraw their money, and almost immediately a full-scale run was in progress. Realizing the urgency of the situation, the president of the bank telephoned Bancorporation officials for help. They immediately obtained a large quantity of cash from the Northwestern National Bank and asked for a police escort. The cash was placed in one car, and with a police car ahead and one behind, the officers sped down to Faribault. With sirens screaming and lights on, the cars entered the town and drew up in front of the bank. Precaution was ostentatious as bundle after bundle of currency was carried into the bank and stacked up in the tellers' cages in plain sight. It was then announced to the panicky depositors that the Bancorporation stood one hundred per cent behind the bank and that there was enough cash on hand to pay all depositors in full.[32] This little drama was sufficient to restore confidence, and the run subsided.

Another sudden run was that on the First National Bank of Grantsburg, Wisconsin, a little agricultural center peopled by phlegmatic Scandinavians. There had never been a bank failure in the community, and normally the people's faith in their banks was complete. National developments, however, upset confidence and late in February, 1933, a run set in. Mr. H. A. Anderson, the president, had not expected trouble and the bank had little cash in its vault. Mr. Anderson immediately telephoned the Bancorporation for help. At once the wheels began to turn: money was obtained from the Northwestern, a car hurried it to the airport where a plane waited, and it arrived in Grantsburg barely an hour after the appeal was made. All the local citizens who demanded cash were paid in full.[33]

The most important run on a Bancorporation bank was on the Spokane and Eastern Trust Company. Some other banks in the city were reputedly insolvent; runs on these had started the last day of February. At the outset the Spokane and Eastern was not affected. The first jolt came when several banks in Spokane and surrounding territory failed to open one morning. Attention veered to the Spokane and Eastern, and depositors poured in to get their money. While the Spokane and Eastern had a generous supply of cash on hand, it was not sufficient to stem the tide. The Federal Reserve was asked for assistance. Unfortunately, since the bank's eligible paper had been rediscounted previously, no funds were obtainable from that source; its real-estate mortgages, however, were in excellent shape and not pledged. The RFC arranged to advance money with the mortgages as security. Bancorporation officers coöperated in securing this loan and a loan from an affiliated bank; thus, funds were available to meet withdrawals, and gradually the run subsided.[34]

These are but samples of the runs which developed all over the country. Many of the Bancorporation banks experienced severe runs during the latter part of February and the first few days of March, 1933. In every case, however, member banks met all withdrawals without delay.

One noticeable feature of the situation was the quiet prevailing in Minneapolis and St. Paul. Some withdrawals occurred, but the Cities were not panic-stricken and no drastic runs took place.[35] The Twin City population had developed implicit confidence in their banks. For forty years there had not been a serious banking collapse. During that period a generation had grown up which did not know the meaning of bank failure. The great banks had stood as pillars of strength which not only met their own obligations promptly and in full but also, where possible, assumed moral responsibility for smaller banks and stood behind them in time of need.

Closing and Reopening of Bancorporation Banks, 1933

When the government proclamations ordered all banks to close their doors, every unit of the Bancorporation was still meeting all withdrawals; nor was there any reason to fear that they could not continue. In a few, cash and liquid assets were depleted, but others were still liquid enough to aid the embarrassed units. The larger banks in particular were in good shape, and the system as a whole needed no immediate assistance. Nevertheless, banking was in such chaos that the presidential proclamation ordering banks to close came as a relief. The worst had happened; beyond could lie only improvement.

Immediately after the closing, permission was granted for banks to perform certain restricted transactions. The Bancorporation banks took advantage of this privilege and continued to make change, receive payments, release collateral and items in safekeeping, and permit access to safe-deposit vaults. In due course, they were permitted to release money for food and for other necessities.

The Bank Conservation Act permitted banks to reopen upon permission from the local Federal Reserve Bank. Every Bancorporation bank was permitted to reopen immediately. This fact is even more impressive when we remember that the Ninth Federal Reserve District, because of its heavy dependence upon agriculture, had formerly been one of the weakest spots in the national banking structure.

The Banking Act of 1933 made drastic changes in banking laws, and the Bancorporation had to adjust its operation to the new regulations. One provision of the law was that banks, except for certain modest dealings in State, municipal, and government bonds, must get out of the investment business. The Bancorporation decided to liquidate its investment affiliate, the BancNorthwest Company. Immediately Messrs. Thrall and West, the principal officers of the company, offered to buy the business, good-will and certain assets, but not the name.[36] They agreed to change the name and to divorce the company from any connection with the Bancorporation or its member banks. Eventually their offer was accepted.

In June, 1933, the question of merging the Minnesota Loan and Trust Company with the Northwestern National Bank under the name Northwestern National Bank and Trust Company was discussed. On June 22 the executive committee recommended the merger, and on the same date the board of directors of the Northwest Bancorporation voted that, when they received permission to vote the stocks of the two banks, they would vote in favor of the merger.[37] Under the Bank Act of 1933, holding companies were forbidden to vote the stock of member banks without a permit. If the permission was refused, the charter of the member bank could be canceled. Bancorporation officers were instructed by the board of directors to apply for a permit for each member bank.[38] After a moderate delay all were granted, and the Bancorporation received full rights.

During 1933 Banco continued to strengthen the capital funds of its member banks, contributing $2,444,972.[39] Since to all practical purposes it had exhausted its liquid assets in 1932, it was forced to borrow money. It borrowed $500,000 in Chicago on the security of the stock of the United States National Bank of Omaha.[40] Then it arranged to secure a loan of $2,500,000 from its directors.[41] Thus fortified, the Bancorporation officers returned to the task of strengthening their member banks.

The new banking act provided that bank officers might not borrow from their own banks; they must pay all old loans within two years; and they were to report to their board of directors all personal loans from any source. On July 14, 1933, officers of the Bancorporation affiliated banks were notified that they had 90 days in which to report loans and to make provision to repay loans from their own banks.[42] This did not seriously affect the great majority, but it proved embarrassing to a few. A committee was appointed to consider each case and aid in refunding loans from outside sources.[43]

At the same time consideration was given to so-called "syndicate loans." These had been made to officers and directors in 1930 to finance the purchase of Bancorporation stock. Most of the loans had been repaid, but a few had never been collected. The committee took up these defaults with the debtors, generally receiving payment. In a few cases compromise settlements were arranged and the losses charged off.

Meanwhile, changes were occurring in the official family. Mr. E. W. Decker moved from the presidency to chairmanship of the board on June 27, 1933, and Mr. J. Cameron Thomson took over the office of president.[44] On January 9, 1934, Mr. Decker retired from all connection with the Northwest Bancorporation and its affiliates.[45]

Guaranty of Bank Deposits, 1934

Since the Banking Act provided for the insurance of bank deposits, beginning in January, 1934, and for the assessment of insured banks, it became necessary to provide funds for these requirements. On August 10, 1933, the Bancorporation recommended that all member banks accrue by January 1, 1934, a reserve of one-half of one per cent of deposits.[46] Another problem also arose to plague the Bancorporation. Conferences with federal officials brought out the fact that the Federal Deposit Insurance Corporation would not insure the deposits of a bank unless its capital funds equaled or exceeded 10 per cent of its deposits.[47] By that time few Bancorporation banks could meet this requirement. Rigid charge-offs, often of potentially valuable assets, had greatly reduced capital funds. There was only one course open. On September 14, 1933, Mr. Thomson presented to the board of directors a report of the aid which the Reconstruction Finance Corporation was extending to banks through the purchase of preferred stock and capital debentures.[48] After some discussion, the board authorized Mr. Thomson, in coöperation with two directors, Mr. Crosby and Mr. Heffelfinger, to attempt to work out for the Bancorporation a plan embodying the aid of the Reconstruction Finance Corporation.[49]

On December 11 Mr. Thomson reported to the Board that an arrangement had been made with the Reconstruction Finance Corporation whereby the Union Investment Company would borrow $3,000,000 and the affiliates of the Bancorporation would sell $22,900,000 of preferred stock.[50] The Union Investment Company loan would be secured by $3,100,000 in real-estate mortgages, and the proceeds would be loaned to the Northwest Bancorporation on its note, which also would be pledged with the Reconstruction Finance Corporation.[51] The Bancorporation's funds would be used to repay previous loans.

Under the agreement the member banks were to apply 40 per cent of their net earnings to retiring preferred stock, and the Bancorporation was not to pay dividends without the consent of the Reconstruction Finance Corporation.[52]

As part of this agreement, all member banks charged assets down to bedrock values and sold preferred stock to restore their capital funds. The Bancorporation wrote down its valuation of member-bank stocks, reduced the stated value of its capital stock to $8,000,000, and set up an additional $12,000,000 reserve for contingencies.[53]

While most banks sold some preferred stock, the largest issues were the following:[54]

Northwestern National Bank, Minneapolis	$5,000,000
First National Bank, Albert Lea	200,000
First and American National Bank, Duluth	1,500,000
National Citizens Bank, Mankato	250,000
First National Bank and Trust Company, Fargo	600,000
Bank of Spearfish, Spearfish	250,000
First National Bank, Dillon	450,000
Daly Bank and Trust Company, Anaconda	500,000
Union Bank and Trust Company, Helena	400,000
National Bank of LaCrosse, LaCrosse	300,000
Continental National Bank, Lincoln	300,000
Stock Yards National Bank, Omaha	1,000,000
Iowa–Des Moines National Bank and Trust Company, Des Moines	3,500,000

These preferred stock issues were unnecessarily large in most cases, but it was felt that that was the time to write off or make provision for every asset not of outstanding quality. If the write-offs were too severe it would not matter, for in due course assets would be changed into cash and restored to the balance sheet. The preferred stock made it possible for every bank to comply with FDIC requirements and receive insurance immediately.[55]

By this time the worst seemed to be over. The trough of the depression had been reached: values were recovering, losses had been taken, capital funds restored, and every bank was open and insured. Depositors had not lost a penny. After long months of worry, Banco's officers were able to relax in peace. During 1934 they busied themselves with management problems. One was a campaign of merger and liquidation. It was decided that wherever banks were not able to earn preferred dividends, FDIC assessments, some return on capital funds, and enough to build up ample reserves against losses, they should be either merged or liquidated.[56] Only a few of the Bancorporation units could not meet these requirements, but these few, if not merged, paid their deposits in full and went out of business. The future was just beginning to look clear when Banco received another jolt.

MOORHEAD TRIAL: BANCORPORATION AT BAY, 1934

At that time Minnesota's politics were peculiarly rough and tumble. The political party in power was dominated by the Honorable Floyd B. Olson. Although politics had only a narrow red fringe, capital was the bugaboo of the populace, and any politician was sure of a sympathetic hearing in the rural hustings if he damned the vested interests and cried out that no man should have more than 160 acres, a team of horses, and two boxes of snuff. Since a large portion of the rural citizenry was convinced that the Minneapolis Chamber of Commerce, aided and abetted by the Twin City banks, manipulated grain prices so that they were always down when the farmers sold their crops, any attack on the vested interests was sweet to rural ears.

Political investigation of eastern banks had provided a field day for eastern politicians. Olson watched these developments with admiration. In November, 1933, the State Commerce Commission started to investigate the Northwest Bancorporation.[57] The charges were that the stock of Northwest Bancorporation had been sold in a fraudulent manner, that its sale had violated Minnesota statutes, and that the company had maintained a fictitious market to manipulate prices. Hearings were scheduled for December 4.[58] Among the witnesses to appear were Messrs. E. W. Decker, J. Cameron Thomson, and Theodore Albrecht.

At this time the State Department of Commerce consisted of Messrs. Elmer A. Benson, S. Paul Skahen, and Garfield W. Brown. Mr. W. E. G. Watson was special investigator. The witnesses were called to the stand and were asked innumerable questions. Ledgers and minute books were subpoenaed. The special investigator made every effort to prove that earnings statements were fraudulent.[59] He assumed that inasmuch as the holding company had not actually received the earnings of its subsidiaries in cash, these earnings did not constitute earnings of the parent company.

The investigators did their best to dramatize the proceedings. It was gossiped that it had been found necessary to maintain a military guard over the books and records to be used in the case. If these rumors had any point, it must have been far-fetched. One can hardly visualize Mr. Thomson stealing surreptitiously into the State Capital in order to abscond with his own records. Whatever the reason, the press carried some tall tales, and the boys in the country wallowed in vicarious righteousness.

The investigators became genuinely concerned when they delved into the Bancorporation's miscellaneous expense account. Among other items were listed those for the entertainment of visiting bankers and notables, including $270 for a dinner party in honor of M. J. Insull; $147 for the Minnesota Editorial Association; and a "miscellaneous" item of $850.[60] This was too good an opportunity to miss. The rural press editorialized on bribery, pernicious influence, and the wasting of stockholders' money. Lighter-minded individuals began to speculate on the type of entertainment provided, and eyebrows were raised at the suggestion that fan dancers might have performed for the visitors. The entire amount involved was insignificant and a matter of routine, but it served as the basis for much unfriendly publicity.

The testimony dragged on for weeks, and the daily papers mulled over the details. Finally, early in 1934, the investigation came to a close without the Bancorporation's having been allowed to tell its side of the story, as the result of the action by Governor Olson. In uncovering damaging evidence it failed, but it supplied the radical politicians with plenty of talking points.

In June, 1934, Governor Olson stated that the facts disclosed by the investigation necessitated the indictment of Bancorporation officials.[61] The Hennepin County Attorney, Ed Goff, was asked to present the matter to the Grand Jury and request an indictment.[62] When the Grand Jury at length convened and evidence was presented, publicity was not ignored. Mr. W. E. G. Watson announced that witnesses had disappeared and those remaining were most reluctant to talk.[63] Nevertheless, the matter was threshed out in detail. After careful consideration the Grand Jury refused to indict, denying evidence of any fraud.[64] With that the whole movement seemed to have reached a definite close.

Olson felt, however, that he still could squeeze out some publicity. Though the evidence, flimsy at best, was given no weight by the conservative element, it was enthusiastically absorbed by a majority of the people. The project made Olson the champion of the masses against the vested interests, and he was determined not to let it die so young. Damning Twin City bankers was bound to be popular and should strengthen Olson's votes at the next election.

The Hennepin County experience had demonstrated how extremely difficult it would be to get a grand-jury indictment. Other methods would have to be applied, and they were not difficult to find. Any citizen could swear out warrants for the defendants' arrest on charges of fraud without the formality of a grand jury. It was considered expedient to have this trial come up in a strong Farmer-Labor community. The town of Moorhead seemed suitable, for at that time the surrounding area was overwhelmingly Farmer-Labor.

Some investigation turned up a farmer by the name of Herman Bosshard, who possessed a speculative type of mind. He was said to have participated moderately in the securities market and to have dealt in wheat options. He had bought Northwest Bancorporation stock on December 14, 1931, apparently in the expectation that it would advance in price.[65] Instead, it had steadily declined in market value. It was the farmer-speculator who was persuaded to swear out warrants for the arrest of Mr. Thomson, Mr. Decker, and Mr. Wold, as well as seventeen other officers and directors of the Bancorporation.[66] Allegedly, he had been defrauded. His stock had been fraudulently issued and sold on the basis of fictitious earnings. The list of those indicted might easily have been a page from *Who's Who* in Minneapolis. It included prominent bankers, capitalists, grain men, flour-millers, investment bankers, and retailers. No other group could so adequately have represented the class against which Olson campaigned. It was a truck gardener, a little man, one of the people versus the mighty. The case was presented originally in the court of Judge C. A. Nye. Since Judge Nye's son, however, appeared as counsel for one of the defendants the judge withdrew, turning the case over first to Judge Anton B. Thompson and then to Judge John A. Roeser. Counsel for the defense immediately filed a charge of prejudice, and after much wrangling the case finally came to trial before Judge James E. Montague.

While these proceedings were going on in court, the case was also being fought in the newspapers. The most amusing and at the same time the most exasperating statements were those of certain publications which claimed that the defendants' vigorous opposition to the charges made it apparent that they feared an exposure of their transactions which, it was said, involved the flagrant mishandling of money, the watering of stocks, and other unsavory practices.[67]

In normal procedure the county attorney, Mr. James A. Garrity, would have handled the prosecution, but the matter was taken out of his hands by the office of the Minnesota attorney-general. Instead, the prosecution was headed by Mr. Roger Rutchick, assistant attorney-general, and Mr. W. E. G. Watson.[68]

A great deal of speculation arose in Moorhead as to who would pay the expenses of the trial. Obviously it would involve considerable money, and local citizens were not anxious to have the county pay for it in return for questionable publicity. Governor Olson quieted this murmur by announcing that, in view of the widespread interest, the State should pay the bill.[69] No one worried over the fact that the Governor had no right to authorize such an expenditure. In those days his word was law.

The defendants were not without their share of legal talent. Not only were the regular Bancorporation's attorneys consulted; the most famous trial lawyers in Minneapolis were called in, until the roster read like a Minneapolis legal hall of fame. There were fourteen lawyers in all. People came from afar just to see the famous personages involved in the trial, though the little town had scant accommodations to offer visitors.

When the defendants were arraigned in court, individual bail was set at $2,000, which was provided immediately.[70] Mr. Watson argued against such small bail, alleging that it was nominal in view of the size of Northwest Bancorporation and the wealth of the men involved. He was stopped somewhat abruptly by Judge Montague, who retorted that he had fixed the bail in consideration of the case before him and not of irrelevant matters.

The defendants all pleaded not guilty and requested individual trials. Mr. J. Cameron Thomson's was scheduled first.[71]

The next step was the selection of an impartial jury, a task which dragged on and on as both sides challenged freely. The State was determined that no one should get on the jury who had had the slightest favorable experience with a bank or any kind of financial institution. Many citizens of Moorhead had a favorable impression of the Bancorporation because it had come into the town in 1929 to organize a bank as a public service. This bank had a good reputation, and those who had dealt with it were friendly and sympathetic. As a result, the State challenged many prospective jurors. The attorneys for the defense were just as determined that the jurors should not be biased. When the first panel had been exhausted and a second panel summoned, it began to look as if even that would not be enough. Finally, however, the "twelve good men and true" were chosen. They comprised eight farmers, two wives of farmers, a creamery employee, and an unemployed schoolteacher.[72]

The trial of Mr. Thomson set in motion the publicity which had marked the entire proceedings. Papers all over the State carried day-by-day accounts. Much of the argument seemed intended more for the public than for the jury. Every paper blazoned pictures of the participants.

Mr. Bosshard on the stand testified to his purchase of stock, but the attorneys for the defense brought out the fact that, accustomed to speculative activities, he had made the purchase in the hope of a quick profit. The prosecution knew only too well that his testimony was not influencing the jury to favor conviction.

As a matter of fact, those indicted had been the heaviest losers because they had purchased large blocks of their own stock. This point, however, was not mentioned by the prosecution. It must not be forgotten, however, that this trial was being fought in the rural newspapers, and the introduction of the unfortunate purchaser, whether or not his woes had any bearing on the case, occasioned innumerable articles on the sins of group bankers. Every constructive act of the Bancorporation was carefully ignored. The case proceeded.

The real case hinged on the definition of earnings. If it could be proved that the Bancorporation had misrepresented earnings when its stock was originally sold, there would be some basis for the charge of fraud, and perhaps a conviction might be obtained.

The trial had its ludicrous moments, for obviously the prosecution had only somewhat vague notions of accounting technique, and it seems reasonable to assume that the jury was not composed of experts. The prosecution argued that the Bancorporation had no earnings at the time it reported earnings, because at that time it had not received them in cash from its member banks. It insisted that consolidated earnings could not be used. It appeared to be baffled by such terms as "operating earnings," "charge-offs," "reserves," "provision for reserves," "recoveries," and "capital losses." To be sure, the subject was properly one for specialized accountants, but it gave rise to hot words in court. Finally, after long, crackling oratory, the prosecution was brought to a close, and the defense at last had an opportunity to present its case.

The defense attorneys had decided on an amazing procedure. The Honorable Frederick H. Stinchfield arose and announced that the defense would not call any witnesses. It did not feel that any further testimony was necessary, for the State's witnesses had not brought out any case for the prosecution. He merely summarized the testimony and left the case in the hands of the jury.[73]

The court was stunned, and the prosecution furious. It had expected several more weeks of newspaper headlines. Since no further testimony was forthcoming, the case went to the jury. The jury withdrew for the night, bringing in its decision the following morning, January 24, 1935. It was a unanimous "not guilty." [74] Although not unexpected, this verdict brought relief to the banking fraternity. The defense attorneys were complacent over the success of their procedure. They had hoped to influence the jury favorably, but there again the reaction was unpredictable. Mr. Thomson was especially pleased to have the matter settled so that he could give undivided attention to his duties with the Bancorporation. Most jubilant of all were the conservatives to think that a farmer jury in a Farmer-Labor stronghold had brought in a verdict for the mighty. The conservative press summed up its triumph in the statement that the political mountain had labored and brought forth a mouse.

The Farmer-Labor press was savage in its fulminations and filled with articles on how often justice went astray in the courts. Olson registered hurt surprise at the decision, stating that the evidence obviously convicted Mr. Thomson. He promised that the matter would not be forgotten and that the other defendants would be tried in other courts. The case had proved a boomerang to the Farmer-Labor chieftains but not a total loss. The party had had every opportunity to heckle the vested interests. Instead of being annoyed with the jury's decision, with characteristic effrontery it used the case as a sounding board to damn the courts.

Olson's next effort, to have Mr. Decker tried on the same charges, proved disappointing. Inasmuch as Mr. Decker was no longer connected with the Bancorporation, the case received very little publicity. The most noteworthy outcome was that when Olson attempted to name his own judge to try the case, he met with bitter opposition.[75] It was alleged that concession of this privilege would give the Governor control over the Judiciary. The matter was finally argued in the State Supreme Court, which handed down the decision that the Governor had no authority to appoint judges to specific cases.[76] The case would have to be heard according to routine procedure.

Any other man would have given up, but not Olson. He launched a tirade against the courts, accusing them of overstepping their authority. He offered to debate publicly with any lawyer or judge on the proposition that the courts were gradually encroaching on the powers of other governmental divisions and usurping authority never intended for them. No one accepted his challenge, a fact which he claimed as proof of his contention. On this blustering note Olson's campaign against the bankers sputtered out. The Decker case never came to trial. In February, 1936, charges against the other defendants were quietly dropped in Moorhead, and the whole matter slid into history.[77]

By the close of 1935 the troubles of the Bancorporation were over. It had been in existence a scant six years, a short time in the history of human events but a period to try any institution. During these years the American financial structure had trembled in the balance; the American industrial system had collapsed; values were effaced; only the strongest banks had survived. The Bancorporation had undergone every possible kind of trouble: a steady drain of deposits, frozen loans, stunning losses, declining bond prices, and panic-stricken runs; but it had successfully weathered them all. It had been organized to add stability and strength to the banking structure of the Ninth Federal Reserve District and it had done just that. Except as they benefited by this stabilization, the corporation stockholders had paid the cost. What the situation would have been without the group banks is hard to say.

CHAPTER XIII

THE VICISSITUDES OF FIRST BANK STOCK 1929–1935

Optimism, 1929–1930

In chapter xii we have discussed the experiences of the Northwest Bancorporation during the depression. Now we shall consider the experiences of its colleague, the First Bank Stock Corporation. In general, developments in the two companies have been similar, but First Bank Stock's have been milder and have lacked the dramatic touch which has always characterized the Bancorporation.

The officers of the First Securities Corporation, steeped in optimism, had grandiose plans in 1930 for making their company one of the world's foremost security houses. Since it was strongly capitalized, closely connected with leading New York underwriting groups on the one hand and with an important network of banks on the other, and possessed an efficient retailing organization, their plans seemed promising. Since avid purchasing by the local investing public made retail sales large and easy, the only problem was to obtain participation in new issues. Because of the growing depression, however, high-grade, well-established firms were refraining from expansion. New issues were scarce, and the principal types available were foreign issues and the refunding of maturing obligations.[1] There were not enough refunding securities to supply the retail organization with merchandise, and the officers had to scour the region for local issues.

Despite the exuberance of the First Securities Corporation, the high command of commercial banking was not optimistic. The chief executives not only could see that conditions were steadily becoming worse, but pessimism was rooted in their very character. Messrs. Jaffray, G. H. Prince, Wakefield, and Lilly were not salesmen; they were hardheaded, conservative, commercial bankers. They regarded as deplorable the handling of the assets of the country banks they had acquired, and the early reports of First Bank Stock examiners confirmed their premonitions. Inspired by their attitude, the officers of the First Bank Stock instructed country bankers to refuse all but the most conservative loans and to work to improve the character of existing assets.

The Corporation was firm in requiring detailed reports on member banks. It instituted thorough examinations, insisted upon the installation of adequate credit files, and maintained master records.[2] The installation of credit files was a sore point with many country bankers. Since credit information was supposed by some to be a trade secret possessed by only the senior bankers and jealously guarded even from the junior officers, they resented being forced to expose their knowledge in carefully indexed files where it would be available to their successors.[3] They felt that this intrusion tore down their last defense against domination by the Corporation. Nevertheless, they followed the suggestions.

While most local affairs were left to the local banks, the Corporation gradually broadened and strengthened its supervisory system.[4] It carefully scrutinized commercial loans, but as to bonds its problems were different. Since the country banks had learned during the early 'twenties the weakness of too great a dependence upon local loans, the conservative ones tried to profit from experience by investing a portion of their funds in bonds. The slogan "Bonds for Secondary Reserves" had become popular with bankers as well as with investment dealers. Often a bank's bond account equaled 200 or 300 per cent of its capital funds. Many country bankers, however, were lamentably ignorant of bond investment. They bought bonds of poor quality, disregarding maturity and relying on the belief that they always could dispose of them in the market. Among the bonds owned by one country bank were the following:[5]

Abitibi Power and Paper Company 6s, 1931
Burson Knitting Company 6s, 1930
Chicago, Aurora and Elgin Railroad 6s, 1951
Chicago, Milwaukee, St. Paul and Pacific 5s, 2000
Consumers Company 6s, 1946
Dierks Lumber and Coal Company 5½s, 1930
Federal Screw Works 6½s, 1939

Minneapolis, St. Paul and Sault St. Marie 5s, 1938
Minnesota and Ontario Paper Company 6s, 1945
Western Newspaper Union 6s, 1944

In every case on this list the market price declined, and the bonds defaulted.[6] To be sure, some of them eventually worked out well, but not for several years. The record of the First Bank Stock's members did not differ from that of other country banks: all had heavy bond portfolios, some of excellent quality, most of them mediocre, and two poor.[7]

One of the first accomplishments of the central office was the preparation of a master list of the bonds owned by all banks. It disclosed, as a similar list had done for Banco, two facts — that unit banks had a multiplicity of issues, and that many of these bonds were of poor quality. Messrs. Jaffray and G. H. Prince were horrified and took remedial steps at once.

Since the 'twenties were the days of big-name specialists, they looked around for a star to deal with their problem. When they had found the man they gave him full authority.[8] The specialist's first act was to restrict new purchases to high-grade issues, a step definitely in the right direction. His next move should have been to review holdings and to weed out poor issues ruthlessly. Why he neglected to do this is not clear. Perhaps it was too staggering a task for one man, who was already busy approving new purchases. The banks had small holdings in hundreds of issues. Obviously one man could not thoroughly and rapidly investigate each one. He was confronted with the problem of selling without investigation, sacrificing good securities and taking unnecessary losses, on the one hand, or attempting to investigate each issue before he sold, on the other hand. Since unfortunately he chose the latter course, very few securities were sold during the first year. Meanwhile, prices sank lower and lower until most securities were quoted below their book value. At this point selling ceased.

FRONTENAC TRUST SHARES
A LOCAL INVESTMENT TRUST, 1931

The financial public still was not depressed. The cheapness of securities was common gossip, for 1930 prices were contrasted with

1929 highs. The common-stock theory of investment was still popular. Investment-trust distributors, even in 1931, found a ready market for their wares. Some investment trusts sold their shares by declaring that they could consistently pay dividends in excess of the dividend incomes from their portfolios without diminishing capital, because the appreciation in a common-stock portfolio was so large, so steady, and so dependable that it would more than offset the capital distribution.[9]

It was under these influences that the security houses of the Twin Cities decided to organize an investment trust of their own. The scarcity of new issues was beginning to pinch. A local investment trust would absorb the money flowing into the stocks of New York and Boston trusts and would give local security dealers something to sell.[10] The price of high-grade stocks had declined to figures so far below reasonable values that appreciation was inevitable. To the banker-security-dealers it seemed that fortune was smiling.

The officers of the First Securities Corporation discussed the matter with other local security houses, including BancNorthwest Company, Kalman and Company, Lane, Piper and Jaffray, Inc., and Wells-Dickey Company. The outcome was the establishment of an investment trust to be known as Frontenac Trust Shares. The board of directors was to consist of Messrs. C. T. Jaffray, L. E. Wakefield, and Julian Baird, representing First Securities Corporation; Messrs. Edward W. Decker, William A. Durst, and Henry D. Thrall, representing BancNorthwest Company; Messrs. C. O. Kalman and Edwin White, representing Kalman and Company; Messrs. C. T. Jaffray and Harry C. Piper, representing Lane, Piper and Jaffray, Inc.; and Messrs. Stuart W. Wells and J. L. Seybold, representing Wells-Dickey Company.[11]

The trust was to invest its funds in a diversified list of the finest common stocks.[12] It was ready for business on February 2, 1931, and immediately local security salesmen commenced to push its shares.[13] The member banks of both groups were informed of the trust so that they would explain it to their customers.

At the second annual group conference of First Bank Stock Corporation some of the principal items on the agenda were talks explaining Frontenac Trust Shares and pointing out that, inasmuch as

Frontenac intended to advertise locally, undoubtedly many potential investors would ask their bankers about it.[14] Thus, while a bank need not sell the trust, it could do much to aid its sale.[15] One speaker stated:[16]

Every one of the directors of the Frontenac has purchased some for their own account, and I believe anyone interested in common stocks for the long pull, not quick turn and speculation, will be a purchaser of Frontenac Trust Shares in whatever portion he believes he should put into common stocks — if you, yourself, are sold on Frontenac Trust Shares, you will sell the rest of the people in your bank, and if the rest of your people are sold, they will have something they will know all about that will always be available through your organization and will give the investor the best return for his money of any investment trust I know of, and I have studied them all.

During the following year the Twin City security houses were successful in distributing Frontenac's stock. Despite the steady decline in the price of securities, many investors in the Ninth Federal Reserve District had funds and were optimistic concerning the future of the stock market.

Deepening Depression, 1931–1932

In 1931 the banks experienced declining deposits as business volume declined and unemployment consumed people's savings.[17] Since the reduced volume of business lessened the demand for money, good loans were repaid. Since new loans were not needed, the banks' earning assets shrank.

Even as early as 1931, commercial loans caused difficulties in many cases, but First Bank Stock banks were singularly free from trouble. The Corporation advised the country banks to review their loans and to acquire adequate collateral for those which seemed doubtful. While every effort was made to strengthen loans, payments were enforced only in exceptional cases and money was always available for sound loans.[18] All in all, the bank loans were satisfactory.[19] The bond account was the Achilles' heel of the organization. During the latter part of 1931 the management of First Bank Stock gave the matter of bond holdings their personal attention. The situation was distressing. The survey of holdings was incomplete. Only a few holdings had been sold. Bonds had defaulted, prices had declined, and heavy losses lay dormant. The management, concluding that the task was too large for any one man, organized an investment committee and an elaborate research department.[20] Although the new setup worked very satisfactorily, the damage had already been done. The market had declined to the point where extensive sales would have been suicidal.[21]

The year 1932 brought a deepening of the depression. Issues in the First Bank Stock securities portfolio defaulted and prices settled lower and lower.[22] Even certain loans and discounts which a year before had looked sound and well secured commenced to falter. Losses piled up, yet the officers dared not press borrowers for payment, lest other losses be incurred. Add to all this the fact that deposits were constantly shrinking, and the situation seems to have been truly ominous.

THE DECLINE OF DEPOSITS, 1929–1935

Since the whole Ninth Federal Reserve District was feeling the decline in deposits, the First Bank Stock banks were not escaping the danger. Let us consider a few individual cases.

The First National Bank of Fairmont serves a town of approximately seven thousand, which is the county seat of Martin County, Minnesota. During the period 1929–1935 the area continued to produce ample crops, but low prices and heavy mortgages took the profits. A steady decline in the price of beef cattle not only destroyed the profit in fattening steers but even occasioned heavy losses. The whole area was depressed. Farmers ceased borrowing, and the better-situated paid their notes. Taxes, interest, and operating losses caused a slow but steady shrinkage in deposits. By years they were as follows: [23]

1929	$1,203,774
1930	1,133,603
1931	1,001,359
1932	866,737
1933	897,719
1934	787,362
1935	810,412

It can be seen that the decline in this area continued through 1934, and deposits at their low were approximately 65 per cent of their high. During the period the bank had to obtain and pay out $416,412 in cash and still remain liquid and solvent.

A second instance is taken from the city of Great Falls, which has a population of about 33,000 and is the county seat of Cascade County, Montana. It is the second largest city in the State. Great Falls supplies hydroelectric power, and its major activities encompass metal reduction, flour-milling, and oil-refining. It is the wholesaling center for a large area devoted to cattle- and sheep-raising and mining. During the depression the entire area was hard hit: crops failed, prices were low, and the metal industry nearly vanished. The deposits of the First National Bank of Great Falls receded as follows:[24]

1929	$12,360,038
1930	11,481,632
1931	9,232,749
1932	6,990,764
1933	6,860,045
1934	8,408,767
1935	9,725,795

The decline from a high of $12,360,038 in 1929 to a low of $6,860,045 in 1933 represents a total of 44 per cent.

A third instance comes from Butte, Montana, which has a population of about 40,000, and is the county seat of Silver Bow County, largest in population and smallest in area of the 56 counties in the State. The surrounding area is essentially a mining country. During the seventy-odd years of its existence, this district has yielded copper, zinc, silver, lead, gold, and small quantities of other metals. Developed between 1865 and 1870 as a silver-mining center, it has since been notable chiefly for copper. The depression of the 'thirties dealt ruthlessly with this area. Poor demand and low prices for copper closed the mines, throwing the whole community out of work. Drought wrecked the cattle ranges and burned the wheat crop year after year. With the foundation industries crushed, the collateral industries starved. The savings of people and corporations dwindled under necessitous demands. Local funds went to pay an unfavorable balance of trade. Poverty inherited the land. The Metals Bank and Trust Company of Butte was the dominating financial institution in Montana. Its deposits receded as the following figures show:[25]

1929	$21,193,524
1930	19,599,502
1931	15,087,333
1932	11,053,713
1933	11,158,086
1934	8,806,710
1935	10,202,357

The decline of deposits from $21,193,524 to $8,806,710 amounted to $12,386,814, or 58 per cent. This decline was the largest, in percentage, experienced by any First Bank Stock bank. It resulted from the complete collapse of local industry.

The banks in the Twin Cities experienced some decline in deposits during the depression, but they really occupied a favored position. Since the First National Bank of Minneapolis merged with the First Minneapolis Trust Company in 1933, we have combined their figures for previous years. The deposits of the merged institution were as follows:[26]

1929	$120,867,451
1930	121,619,029
1931	111,674,600
1932	104,722,587
1933	104,651,667
1934	128,080,592
1935	134,101,594

From 1929 to 1933, deposits declined only $16,215,000, or approximately 13 per cent, a great contrast to the shrinkages in country banks and telling evidence of the strength in a well-rounded, highly diversified city community not dependent upon any one activity. The experience of the First National Bank of St. Paul was very similar.

For the First Bank Stock group as a whole, deposits behaved as follows:[27]

1930	$384,814,125
1931	348,014,362
1932	289,721,268
1933	296,324,698
1934	360,720,619
1935	395,124,394

Between 1930 and 1932, deposits declined $95,092,857, or 25 per cent. This decline ranged from a moderate 13 per cent in one Twin City bank to between 35 per cent and 50 per cent in country areas, and reached a maximum of 58 per cent in Butte, Montana.

Under the banking laws in force late in 1932, it was permissible for a national bank to conduct a trust business or to merge with a trust company. The First National Bank of Minneapolis in January, 1933, took advantage of this privilege to combine its business with that of its affiliate, the First Minneapolis Trust Company.[28] The trust accounts were quite intact, as were savings and demand deposits;[29] and on January 31, 1933, the First National and the First Minneapolis Trust Company combined to form the First National Bank and Trust Company of Minneapolis.[30] The merger was a statutory consolidation, and the new organization assumed all the assets, liabilities, and business of both organizations. The only capital funds on the new balance sheet were those of the First National Bank.[31]

The Drive for Earnings, 1930–1935

Between 1930 and 1933, bank income declined steadily. The interest earned by First Bank Stock Corporation's banks was as follows:[32]

1930	$19,325,753
1931	18,483,268
1932	15,618,071
1933	13,008,410
1934	10,722,798
1935	9,810,617

The interest figure would have shrunk even more severely except for two developments. One was the aggressive expansion of the

First Bancredit Corporation in the field of installment financing. It sought to purchase new financing such as small loans, insured under Title I of the Federal Housing Act, retail consumer credit, and accounts receivable for the payment of insurance premiums. It hunted down business on a national scale. While each transaction was small the total grew amazingly.[33] The other unusual field was the securing of Veterans' loans by bonus certificates, a line pressed by the St. Paul group.[34]

Despite the success of both developments, they did little more than offset a portion of the decrease caused by the depression. Loan volume and interest income continued to contract. The fact that country banks always had paid high rates on certificates of deposit and savings accounts offered an opportunity partially to offset this decline. As economic changes occurred, interest rates were cut from 5 to 4 and from 4 to 3 per cent and lower as quickly as competition permitted. The amount paid out in interest to depositors ranged as follows:[35]

1930	$7,462,315
1931	7,375,854
1932	5,891,449
1933	4,167,300
1934	3,028,593
1935	1,961,924

From these figures we can see that though little progress was made in 1931, rate reductions were substantial thereafter. In general, First Bank Stock banks met the rates prevalent in their communities, in some cases offering rates lower than competing banks' but always agreeing to any general reduction. At first, independent bankers were afraid to lower their rates, but as the depression dragged on and interest income declined, they changed their views.

Many of the banks in the Ninth Federal Reserve District never had levied minimum balance fees and had been very lenient regarding exchange charges. Confronted with declining income, however, the First Bank Stock officers decided to eliminate many free services and to make charges cover direct costs. They urged upon affiliated bank officers ample exchange and float charges and a system of minimum balances. The country bankers argued that those charges would drive away customers, but actual experience proved their fears groundless. A few customers closed their accounts, but enough increased their balances to offset this decline.

On May 1, 1931, the Minneapolis and St. Paul banks instituted the following monthly minimum balance schedules:[36]

Average Balance	*Charge*
$300.00 or over	No charge
200.00 to $299	$0.50
100.00 to 199	0.75
99.99 or under	1.00

Customers were allowed twenty-five checks a month free, but were charged four cents for each additional check. Prompted by the central office, many country bankers installed comparable charges. Nevertheless, with diminishing business activity, miscellaneous earnings continued to decline. The First Bank Stock's "Other Earnings" were as follows:[37]

1930	$4,400,871
1931	3,771,450
1932	3,550,981
1933	3,254,592
1934	3,393,335
1935	3,309,245

During this period expenses were sternly scrutinized: a few old employees were pensioned and not replaced; inefficient employees were discharged; and salary reductions were effected. The treatment of employees, however, was so considerate that it provoked some censure from certain stockholders, who contended that First Bank Stock coddled its employees at the expense of its stockholders. Operating costs, including salaries, rent, heat, light, stationery, insurance, and other miscellaneous items, were as follows:[38]

1930	$10,097,735
1931	9,882,398
1932	9,034,234
1933	8,217,410
1934	8,472,362
1935	8,356,102

The decline in earnings may be seen below:[39]

Year	*Net Operating Earnings*	*Earned Per Share*	*Dividends Per Share*
1930	$5,975,138	$1.93	$1.00
1931	4,767,688	1.55	1.00
1932	4,142,940	1.34	0.50
1933	3,821,864	1.23	0.20
1934	2,579,408	0.83	0.20
1935	2,764,781	0.90	0.25

Runs on First Bank Stock Banks, 1932–1933

Though deposits declined steadily, First Bank Stock Corporation banks were singularly free from panicky runs. By 1933, however, a large segment of the public had lost faith in all banks and sometimes runs did develop.

In July, 1932, a whispering campaign attacked the solvency of the First National Bank of St. Paul.[40] Since the general public had faith in the bank, nothing serious came of it. While federal agents, attempting to check the sources of these rumors, could reach no definite conclusions, they believed them to be part of a well-organized campaign against banks all over the country.[41] Despite the general lack of confidence apparent early in 1933, no serious runs, as we have seen, developed in the Twin Cities. Withdrawals in February were heavy but orderly, and the banks were able to meet all demands. Runs developed on one or two First Bank Stock banks in the country but they were weathered safely.[42]

The most interesting run was on the Western Montana National Bank at Missoula, Montana.[43] The town of Missoula, county seat of Missoula County, with about 23,000 population, lies in a broad valley on the Pacific side of the Rockies. This beautiful valley, flanked by the Rockies, the Mission Range, and smaller mountain ranges, is irrigated by water from snow-fed mountain streams. Agriculture is important but cattle-raising also thrives in the semi-arid regions, and the mountains are covered with salable timber. The town of Missoula is the area's financial apex, its wholesale and retail trade center, the seat of the University of Montana, and the location of a sugar-beet factory, lumber mills, and miscellaneous other manufacturing enterprises.

One of Missoula's leading banks was a First Bank Stock unit, the Western Montana National Bank, which had conducted an aggressive local business and built up a substantial volume of local loans.[44] The implacable progress of the depression shook public confidence, and early in 1932 started a heavy withdrawal of savings. By June this movement had developed into a major run: some $600,000 left the bank in three days; the crowds threatened to become violent.[45] The bank wired the Federal Reserve branch at Helena to send it cash.[46] Since the First Bank Stock management kept in close touch with the day-to-day developments and it became more and more evident that the Western Montana National Bank could not stem the run with its own liquid assets, First Bank Stock deposited with the Federal Reserve Bank a sum equal to the remaining deposits.[47] The Federal Reserve Bank notified the Western Montana National Bank of this deposit and the wire was posted in the bank lobby.[48] The run ended abruptly.

In the Twin Cities during February and the first days of March, 1933, withdrawals increased, but the situation never approached a panic, for the public had a faith in banks resulting from years of satisfactory experience. At the same time, the banks were prepared to meet any contingencies. The First National Bank at St. Paul was 65 per cent liquid on the day before the bank holiday, and the First National Bank of Minneapolis was in a comparable condition.[49] Although the banks of the First Bank Stock group were able and anxious to remain open, the national bank holiday forced them to close.

The Bank Conservation Act provided for the reopening of banks which were solvent. Just as soon as the method had been determined, First Bank Stock requested the Minneapolis Federal Reserve Bank to recommend the necessary certificates.[50] Since there was no question concerning the fundamental solvency of the First Bank Stock affiliates, they were allowed to reopen immediately.[51] In no case was a reorganization necessary.[52]

Reorganization, 1933

During 1933 a new policy was adopted by the First Bank Stock Corporation. Previously it had continued the operation of all its banks in order to serve their communities, whether they produced a profit or not. Of course, it was felt that returning prosperity would make them all profitable. By the end of 1934, when bank earnings seemed to be on a permanently lower level, it was decided to dispose of certain banks that did not earn their keep. The standard adopted required each bank, while following a conservative policy, to cover operating costs and reasonable reserves for losses and still produce some net return on the capital funds employed.[53] An analysis of First Bank Stock units disclosed several that could not meet these requirements. Plans were made to dispose of them. One unit was merged with a Bancorporation bank; in a few cases banks were sold to their former officers and owners; and in a few instances deposits were assumed by an independent local bank.

By the close of 1933, the management of First Bank Stock believed that an internal reorganization, particularly a revision of property valuations, was advisable.[54] Up to this time bank stocks had been carried on the holding-company balance sheet at the acquisition cost.[55] Because most banks had been acquired at 1929 highs, this resulted in a book value for First Bank Stock greatly in excess of its net tangible asset value. The book value on December 31, 1933, was $40.27 a share, while the net tangible asset value was $11.21.[56] The board of directors voted to revalue all bank stocks at their book value, to establish a contingent reserve of $5,050,763, and to supply free surplus for these changes by reducing the par value of First Bank Stock shares from $25 to $10; thereby providing in excess of $45,000,000 for these purposes.[57]

The Banking Act of 1933 made deposit insurance a fact. In general, the Comptroller's office, the FDIC, and Federal Reserve Bank officials held to the opinion that a bank's capital funds should equal at least 10 per cent of its deposits, and that if a bank could not meet this requirement, it should sell the Reconstruction Finance Corporation enough preferred stock to raise the necessary funds. In 1933 all the First Bank Stock's banks reopened without delay. In some instances additional charge-offs and the 1934 increase in deposits reduced the ratio of capital funds to deposits. Authorities in Washington had expressed the desire that for the sake of uniformity all banks should sell some preferred stock to the RFC. The management of the First Bank Stock Corporation was confident of its ability to maintain the integrity and soundness of all its affiliates; nevertheless, in August, 1934, it was decided to sell preferred stock to the RFC. The total amount sold by nine unit banks was $1,490,000.[58] The Twin City banks did not sell any, for they had ample capital funds. Minnesota country banks sold a total of $140,000; Michigan banks, $350,000; Montana banks, $800,000; and North Dakota banks, $200,000.[59] Since the management of First Bank Stock disliked having this stock outstanding, the banks retired all but $250,000 in 1935. The remainder was retired the following year.[60]

Liquidation of Affiliates, 1933–1934

Frontenac Trust Shares had a sad career. While it was only too easy to sell its shares during 1931, the course of the stock market was downward, and the liquidating value and the offering price of the shares declined month after month. There seemed to be no bottom to the abyss. By 1933, with the market finally scraping bottom, sales were almost non-existent. This meant little to First Bank Stock, however, for the new banking laws closed the field of corporate investment securities to commercial banks, forcing the disposal of their affiliates dealing in securities. This sounded the death-knell of Frontenac. If the banks could not sell its shares, there was no use in struggling to keep it alive. Accordingly, on November 18, shareholders were advised that the trust would be liquidated,[61] and on December 12 they were notified that the liquidation would be at the rate of $10.27 a share.[62] Thus ended the Twin Cities' investment trust.

The same legislation forced First Bank Stock to liquidate the First Securities Corporation.[63] The employees of this investment company were placed in the government and municipal bond departments of the banks or absorbed into trust or commercial banking departments.

Another situation which caused many a headache in its day was the Minneapolis Trust–Joint Stock Land Bank. This company had been organized in the early 'twenties by the Minneapolis Trust Company to sell tax-exempt bonds to investors and loan the proceeds on farm mortgages.[64] All during the 'twenties its bonds had been popular with investors and had easily found their way into the most conservative accounts. The Land Bank had a stated capital of $450,000 and all of its stock was owned by the First Minneapolis Trust Company.[65] During the early 'thirties the Land Bank became progressively involved. Mortgages defaulted both principal and interest. Income fell below expenses, and the company used up its free assets to meet interest and principal payments.[66] It had to borrow money from federal agencies in order to make its own payments.[67] Gradually, the company was forced to foreclose, acquiring a heavy volume of real estate. On November 1, 1933, its outstanding bonds amounted to $3,980,000, and secured notes payable to $329,850. Its major assets consisted of first mortgages, $2,617,661; sheriff's certificates, $155,053; and real estate, $1,504,426. The mortgages were divided as follows:[68]

140 current loans	$ 501,617
24 loans delinquent less than 90 days	92,664
430 loans delinquent over 90 days	2,023,379
594 loans	$2,617,660

To make matters worse, taxes on most properties having delinquent mortgages were badly in default. In November, 1933, the company reported to bondholders that its real estate could not do better than break even on an operating basis, and consequently there would be no income available for bond interest.[69] It had, however, borrowed enough to pay the interest due on November 1, 1933. The officers were working on a plan for orderly liquidation.

On April 23, 1934, the joint stock land bank proposed a partial liquidation under the terms of which each bondholder would sell one-third of his holdings to the bank at 50 cents on the dollar.[70] Bonds were thus reduced from $3,778,000 to $2,714,000. Obviously, however, this plan was not drastic enough. More severe methods would have to be used. Accordingly, on September 14, 1934, the Land Bank suggested total liquidation.[71] The plan proposed provided as follows:

1. The stockholders would contribute an assessment of 100 per cent totaling $450,000;

2. Each bondholder must surrender his bonds under the plan;
3. Each $1,000 bond would receive, at its option, either
   A. $700 as full settlement, or
   B. $600 in cash and a certificate of participation in residual assets.

The bondholders agreed to this plan, a substantial majority choosing Option B. Most of the necessary cash was obtained by exchanging mortgages for Federal Farm Mortgage Corporation bonds and then selling the bonds for cash.

LOSSES AND EARNINGS OF FIRST BANK STOCK

The First Bank Stock Corporation had boasted proudly in 1929 and 1930 that the earnings of the Twin City banks alone would supply more than sufficient funds to pay the one dollar annual dividend on its stock.[72] Perhaps there was something prophetic about its boast. By 1930 it became evident that the country banks lay open to heavy losses; by 1931 losses were coming thick and fast. It seemed sensible for country banks to retain their earnings in order to write off losses. Accordingly, for a short period they contributed only nominally to dividends. In certain country banks, earnings were applied to losses; reserves and earned surplus were absorbed and even capital funds were impaired.[73] In order to restore capital funds, the First Bank Stock Corporation between 1932 and 1934 was forced to contribute to its members. To banks in Minnesota by December 30, 1933, it had given $1,720,977; to Montana banks, $1,391,000; to North Dakota banks, $845,000; to South Dakota banks, $271,163; and to Michigan banks, $795,264 — a total of $5,023,404.[74] In addition, it had deposited $3,125,500 with country banks to provide for anticipated losses.[75] This is a large sum, but the country banks do not account for all First Bank Stock's heavy losses. The largest single item to disappear from the balance sheet was the capital and surplus of the First Securities Corporation, which totaled some $7,500,000.[76] Some heavy losses were incurred in liquidating this affiliate, but a substantial portion of its assets was realized in cash. These were transferred to the First Bank Stock Corporation and used wherever necessary to strengthen the capital funds of banks, take out defaulted loans and discounts, make up depreciation in bond accounts, and provide reserves.

The First Bank Stock Corporation had been formed at the height of the booming 'twenties, in part to meet competitive developments, in part to strengthen the banking structure and provide stability in the Ninth Federal Reserve District, and also to increase the profits of stockholders. It made every effort to build up a well-rounded regional financial organization, comprising commercial banks, savings banks, trust companies, farm-mortgage banks, an investment company, and even an investment trust. Scarcely had the new organization swung into operation than it met the depression. Business declined, unemployment mounted, deposits shrank; the structure of investment values collapsed, loans defaulted, and bond prices sank to new lows. Banks all over the nation closed their doors. First Bank Stock had its full share of troubles, and banking seemed like a grim business. Despite vicissitudes all First Bank Stock banks remained open continuously, and every depositor was fully protected.

By 1935 the depression was over. While the glamorous dreams of the boom period had vanished beyond recall, there remained hope that normal conditions would revive earning power and justify larger dividends. The depression had confirmed with a vengeance the strengthening influence of group banking upon the general banking structure, as well as its support of conservative banking conditions.

CHAPTER XIV

CONVALESCENCE OF NORTHWEST BANKS 1935–1940

The Period of Quiet

By 1935 the trough of the depression had been passed. The natural forces of recovery, aided by the artificial stimuli of the New Deal, were bolstering up business. The benevolent government in Washington was handing out aid to the poor, the unfortunate, the unemployed, the permanent unemployables, the farmers, industrial labor, the labor unions, bankrupt industrialists, embarrassed bankers, and to all the riffraff and every rag-tag of modern society that could muster, or threaten to muster, a few votes. Under these ministrations, employment picked up, business volume improved, and the earnings statements of most industrial corporations producing consumers' goods showed substantial gains.[1] In short, from a temporary viewpoint the depression was over.

Because improvement came only to lines producing consumers' goods for immediate use and because little pickup was evident in producers' goods lines, the recovery was unbalanced. The heavy contributions of the government for charity, relief, and aid to the farmers put the purchasing power into hands which spent it immediately for consumers' goods. It created business, but only in certain lines.

The net result of the government policy in the Ninth Federal Reserve District during 1935 and 1936 was the rise of a partial prosperity. The consumer trades prospered, the prices of farm produce showed considerable improvement, the volume of freight on railroads and truck lines increased, and the factories producing consumers' goods were jammed with orders. A goodly portion of the population found abundant employment at fair wages. The building lines and the heavy industries, however, continued to be depressed and the number of their unemployed remained large. Out of the replenished incomes of those in the lower brackets came a new demand for more expensive foodstuffs, especially meat, which brought cattle and hog prices back sharply from their depression lows. While farming did not flourish, rising cattle and hog prices and government aid tended to restore farm income.[2]

The general upswing in 1934, 1935, and 1936 was so strong in many lines, and prices advanced so rapidly, that many New Dealers suspected business of profiteering. The government took steps to slow down the movement throughout the nation. Whether it was entirely the result of government action or whether business was due for a decline is immaterial; the important thing is that business fell back in the latter part of 1937, making 1938 a depression year.[3] Prices sank and sales diminished, production dragged, freight-car loadings fell off, and general unemployment reappeared.

The depression of 1938, while severe, was relatively short-lived. Since the government relief system was in full swing, there was little serious suffering from the widespread unemployment. Government aid to agriculture tended to maintain purchasing power in the country, and the flow of relief and WPA money in the cities created a steady demand for consumers' goods which tended to check the descent and to create an upswing. To companies that had survived the long depression, the one in 1938 was annoying but not burdensome.

By 1939 the effects of the secondary depression had been partially overcome. Business in the consumer industries returned to normal, manufacturing in affiliated lines picked up, employment improved, and conditions in general were better than those existing in 1938.[4] The year 1940 projected the conditions of 1939. Thus, the economic pattern of the Ninth Federal Reserve District for the five years showed 1935, 1936, and part of 1937 marked by increasing prosperity, 1938 shaken by an acute depression, and 1939 and 1940 devoted to convalescence. Conditions were better but scarcely prosperous, for a large group of men remained permanently unemployed, heavy industry was depressed, and the surface prosperity depended upon government subsidy. Probably the most upsetting factor was the government's unbalanced budget. There seemed little likelihood of its ever being balanced under the New Deal administration, and no apparent possibility of replacing the New Deal in the near future. Business men worried over what would happen when the government overtaxed its credit. Would bankruptcy, economy, or inflation result? Moreover, many business men believed that within the inner circle of government was a group basically hostile to business and determined to replace the capitalistic system with some form of socialism, and democracy with an authoritarian government. Haunted by constant foreboding, they refused to plan beyond the day at hand and avoided as far as possible any major capital expenditure.

These years (1935–1940) came the nearest to normality of any period in the history of the group banks. The latter had been formed in the hysteria of the booming 'twenties; and, before internal organization could be perfected, they had been assailed by a major depression. Just as the depression lifted domestically, European developments descended upon the country with such drastic results that in 1933 the people looked back upon the hardships of 1931 as a time of relative prosperity. The bank holiday of 1933 was the nadir. From that point conditions tended upward, but the remainder of 1933 and all of 1934 and 1935 were required to mop up the collapse of the 'thirties. Not until 1936 could conditions be called normal.

Weak, inefficient bank units had already collapsed, prices had reached their low and started upward, and modest profits reappeared. Under ordinary circumstances this period might have been called eventful, but in contrast with the previous débâcle it was almost dull. Despite a lack of drama, however, it was marked by gradual developments of the greatest importance.

The First Bank Stock Corporation Strengthens Its Capital Funds, 1935–1940

By 1935 the dangers of the depression were over for the First Bank Stock Corporation. From the high in 1930 to the low in 1934, the total shrinkage in book value approximated $18,000,000, about 33 per cent of capital funds or 4 per cent of total assets.[5]

The Corporation instituted one policy after 1933 which was of major importance. That, as we have seen, was the merger, liquidation, or sale of units unable to show operating earnings. The management did an outstanding job. The Corporation appraised the probable future of each community. Then it examined the local bank for operating-income possibilities. If the unit could not earn enough to pay actual operating expenses, there was no question; it was marked for disposal. If it could earn more than operating expenses, it was retained. For banks about to be disposed of, the first choice was merger with some other local bank. In Red Wing, Minnesota, for instance, there were three banks which created a surplus of banking facilities, and the First Bank Stock unit was liquidated and its business was sold to the Northwest Bancorporation unit.[6] The Princeton, Minnesota, unit paid off its deposits and sold its banking house and furniture and fixtures to the other (local) bank.[7] Several banks were sold to groups of local people. Only as a last resort was a bank liquidated, in which case all deposits were paid in full. The object of this campaign was to make each unit stand on its own feet. Making each unit productive would mean substantial operating earnings for the group as a whole.

The independent bankers found First Bank Stock a very fair competitor. Each unit maintained high standards of competitive practice. There were a minimum of stolen customers, no questionable loans, no cut rates, and no special favors. In fact, the code of ethics was so carefully observed that many a banker of the old school might have complained bitterly of being so tied down that competitors would run away with his business while he upheld impossible standards. At the same time, the independents were reputedly several degrees more liberal in their loan policy than First Bank Stock, a tendency which brought them a considerable volume of business. There was no attempt at retaliation. Though the independent took advantage, the standard was maintained. The Corporation, entirely aware of the situation, was well content. First Bank Stock management realized its duty of holding an umbrella over its country banks. Any attempt to meet such competition would have provoked new resistance. It was far more sensible to lose a little business than to participate in cut-throat competition.

In one direction the First Bank Stock Corporation definitely outdistanced its competitors, and that was in the First Bancredit Corporation. This affiliate went into installment financing on a broad

CHART XIV. FIRST BANK STOCK CORPORATION GROUP IN 1940

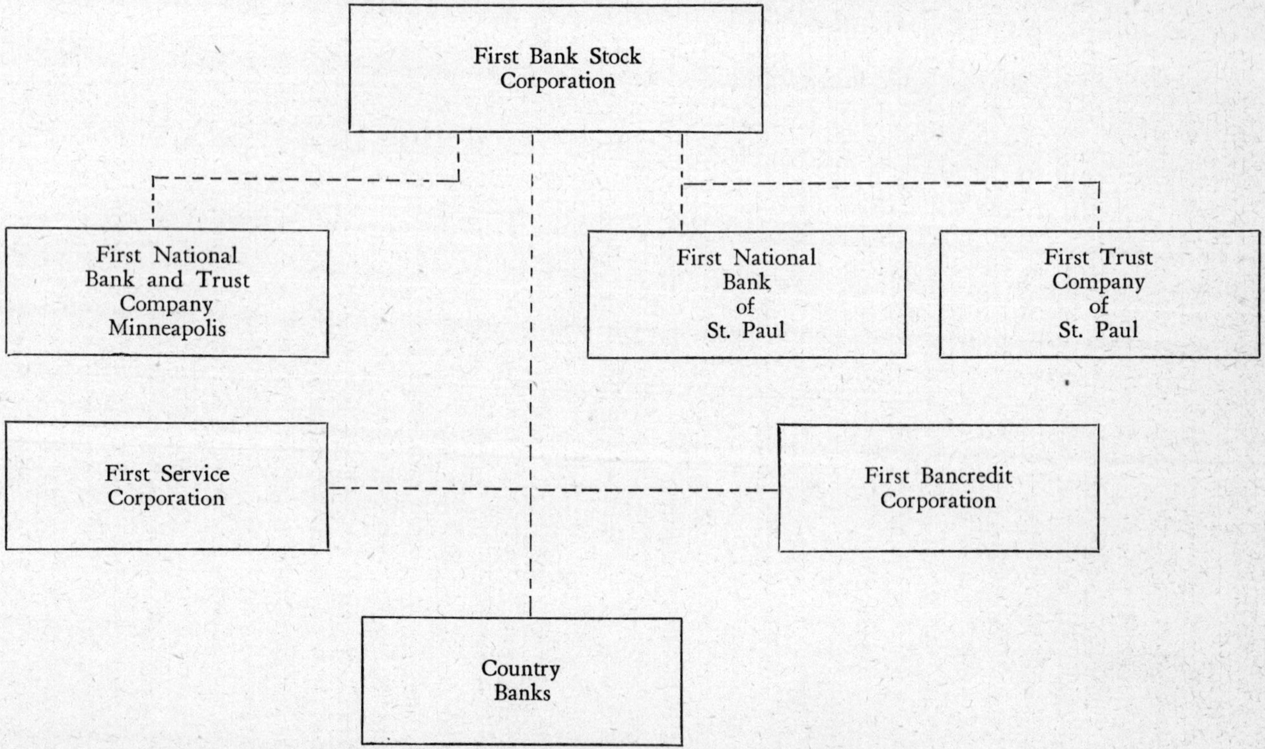

basis, aggressively soliciting business on a national scale and opening branch offices all over the United States. Its business was to buy paper, service it, and immediately sell it to one of the group banks.

The National Housing Act provided a government guarantee for certain types of loans for the rehabilitation of houses. While the law was in effect, First Bancredit was very aggressive in purchasing loans. After the expiration of the Act, the First Bancredit Corporation made arrangements with the manufacturers of building material and equipment whereby it financed their time sales, and the manufacturers guaranteed the Bancredit Corporation against loss in the transaction.[8] First Bancredit kept employed an average of some $30,000,000 in its business.

During this period First Bank Stock worked to build up reserves. Normally the group charged large sums to current operations to provide reserves for future losses. During the depression the various banks had voluntarily written off potential losses and the book value of second-grade bonds. A portion of these losses had not materialized, and many charged-off securities either had been paid in full or had staged a comeback in the market. Though many such charged-off assets were converted into cash, they were not always immediately replaced on the balance sheet. The First Bank Stock management, impressed by the disasters of the depression, attempted to operate so as to avoid unnecessary losses, but recognizing perfection as unattainable, it made substantial provisions for reserves.

The management of First Bank Stock was conservative by nature and thoroughly conversant with the risks of Northwest banking. Realizing that high earnings meant taking undue risks, it worked for steady earnings and security. A portion of earnings was diverted to provide a reserve for poor years. The management wanted to be sure that it could ride through another period of depression without serious damage. With these objectives in view, it devoted the period from 1935 to 1940 to operating conservatively, rebuilding capital funds, writing down real estate and bank buildings, providing reserves for normal losses, and accumulating emergency funds, and also maintained an unbroken record of semi-annual dividends to its stockholders.

THE NORTHWEST BANCORPORATION REBUILDS ITS CAPITAL FUNDS, 1935–1940

The Northwest Bancorporation had many reasons also to be satisfied with its record during the depression. It had paid every depositor in full on demand, and no depositor had lost a penny in dealing with its banks. The ravages of the depression had struck it severely, however, partly because of an optimistic policy during the hectic acquisition period and partly because of a preponderance of country (especially livestock) banks, but principally because the management had been confident that the depression would be short-lived and that its duty was to continue lenient credit policies.[9] Nevertheless, the Bancorporation had protected its deposits, no mean feat when we remember that deposits were approximately ten times capital funds and they had not come through unscathed. The overall record was excellent. A conservative policy of charge-offs and reserves resulted in reducing capital funds. By the end of 1933 a substantial portion of capital had vanished from the balance sheet, but the member banks restored the ratio of 10 to 1 of capital funds to deposits by selling preferred stock.[10]

The Northwest Bancorporation pursued much the same policy as that of the First Bank Stock Corporation regarding the disposal of banks. Each bank had to stand on its own feet and produce operating earnings sufficient to provide for losses, reserves for losses, and potential profits. When a unit could not do this, action was taken to merge, sell, or liquidate it. The management was firm in its conviction that if a bank could not earn under normal conditions, while pursuing conservative banking practices, it was basically unsound.[11] It believed that, while losses were inevitable in any well-managed bank, the earnings must offset them.[12] Thus, under efficient management the Bancorporation disposed of all units which did not meet its rigid requirements. A surprisingly large number of units met the Corporation's tests satisfactorily. The Bancorporation had acquired 131 banks, some of which had been merged with others upon acquisition. This number had been reduced to 94 by December 31, 1935, and mergers, sales, etc., brought the number down to 82 on December 31, 1940.[13] The remaining

Chart XV. Northwest Bancorporation Group in 1940

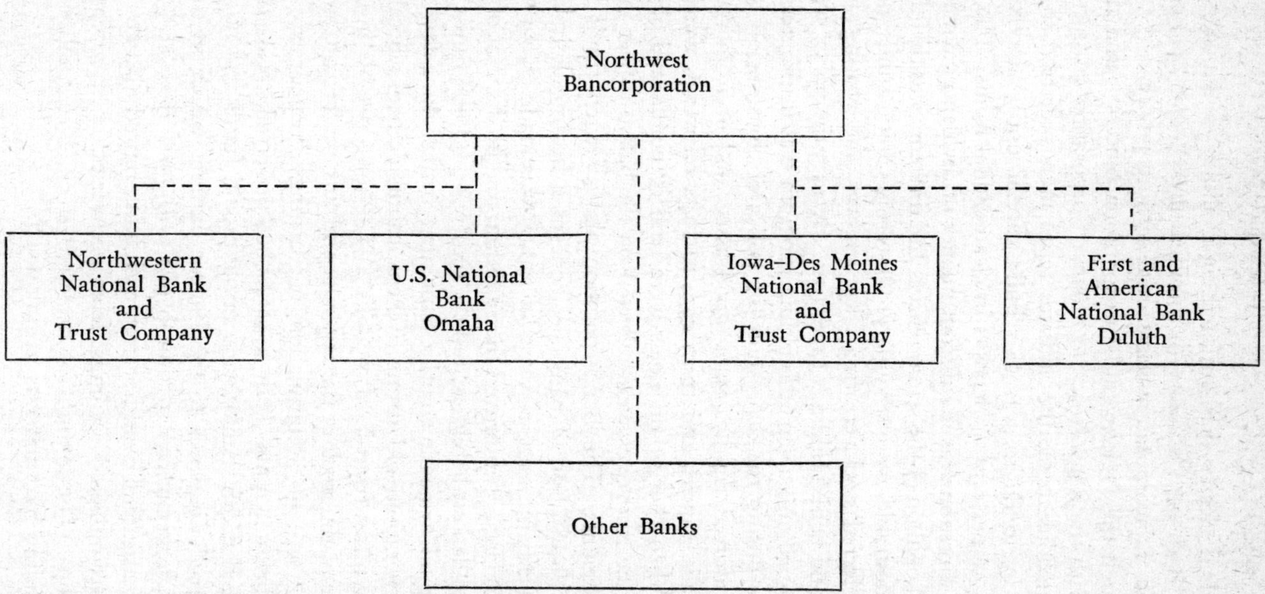

banks had clearly demonstrated their ability to withstand vicissitudes. Each bank's ability to show earnings on an operating basis gave the Bancorporation substantial earning power.

Though the Northwest Bancorporation officers found their relations with the Reconstruction Finance Corporation satisfactory, they were anxious to see the affiliates retire their preferred stock. The only way to do so was to rebuild capital until their banks had at least 10 per cent of deposits in clean capital funds. The first step in this direction was the discontinuance of dividend payments. The general opinion of the senior officers and directors was that dividends, while desirable, were secondary. Restoring capital funds, paying off the preferred stock, creating large reserves, and writing down real estate and bank buildings came first. By 1935 the policy was clearly determined and a capital-building program was in progress.[14]

Since during the depression the policy of charging off items had been enforced rigidly, many good assets had been charged off or nominally valued, and from 1934 to 1940, recoveries were substantial. When charged-off notes were paid or bonds sold above book value, the recoveries were reflected on the balance sheet in the surplus accounts. The Bancorporation also salvaged funds from the sale or liquidation of banks. Whenever it became desirable to dispose of a bank, some recovery of capital was made. Even when this was not large, it improved the situation, for the disposal of the bank reduced deposit liabilities, and the recovery of capital funds increased the capital available for the remaining banks. In a few cases the Bancorporation sold strong, solvent, profitable banks because of attractive offers from local capitalists. The most notable instance was the sale of the stock of the Spokane and Eastern Trust Company.

The constant accumulation of earnings created excess capital funds in some units. If these banks had preferred stock outstanding, they paid it off. Banks with ample capital funds and no preferred stock paid dividends to the Bancorporation, which in turn made capital contributions to unit banks with preferred stock. Just as rapidly as capital would permit, each bank retired its preferred stock from accumulated earnings, from recoveries, or from capital contributions. The amount of preferred stock, loans, and debentures outstanding by years was as follows:[15]

1933	$25,534,463
1934	24,978,933
1935	18,505,000
1936	11,538,000
1937	8,713,000
1938	6,084,500
1939	5,462,475
1940	—None—

Thus, by the end of 1940 the worst effects of the depression had been overcome: preferred stock had been retired, and capital funds had been restored. Liberal dividends in the near future were not a certainty, however, for the officers and the directors were not through strengthening capital funds and writing down real estate and bank buildings. Moreover, the directors were anxious to build up adequate reserves for future losses. The Bancorporation affiliates set aside 12 per cent of interest income as a reserve for losses. During the period 1935 through 1940, recoveries were in excess of realized losses, making net contributions to reserves substantial.[16]

The Bancorporation during those five years adjusted itself to changing conditions. Though its bona fide commercial loans continued to shrink, it did not increase its government-bond portfolio but developed new lines of business. It became noted for its aggressive pursuit of new loans and its genial cultivation of new customers. It was liberal in its relations with its country units, striving to make the officers of each country bank feel that they were running their own business. In general, this policy was successful. During this period, loans in country banks in the Ninth Federal Reserve District showed a considerably greater increase than those of city banks, a fact which tended to benefit the Bancorporation, two-thirds of whose banks were located outside the Twin Cities. Of course, it requires a considerable stretch of the imagination to classify Duluth, Des Moines, and Omaha as country points. Nevertheless, this pickup in the country did tend to benefit the Bancorporation. Despite shrinking commercial business, diminishing interest rates, and reluctance to see additions to the long-term government portfolio of its affiliates, Banco realized such a pickup in loans that interest income paused on its downward course and gave a very moderate promise of at least holding its own and perhaps turning upward.[17]

The Changing Character of Bank Assets, 1935–1940

In 1935, 1936, and 1937, deposits mounted steadily in most banks in the Ninth Federal Reserve District; in 1938 they decreased, but not enough to restore the levels of 1935; in 1939 they resumed an upward trend, reaching an all-time high in 1940. This increase was embarrassing to banks struggling to restore their capital funds to the ten-to-one ratio. No sooner would they reach it than deposits would rise again, upsetting the ratio. Apparently the increase was rooted in the persistent government deficit and the heavy expenditures for relief and agricultural benefit, but a part came from the mild improvement in business and the reduced number of banks and a part from the savings of the people and the return of money from hoarding. Whatever the source, the trend gave no indication of reversing itself. Thus, the problem of the banks became not how to meet withdrawals, but what to do with such a volume of loanable funds. Some safe outlet was needed which would bring in a fair return. The problem was accentuated by the FDIC assessments on deposits. Money had to earn insurance in addition to other expenses.

The problem of bank investments was complicated by the declining volume of commercial loans. This trend was not of recent origin but had been well in evidence as far back as the early 'twenties. Banks in the nineteenth century loaned money for 30, 60, or 90 days to aid constructive transactions, completion of which produced funds to repay the loan. This type of transaction, however, had become scarce. As concerns continued in business, they tended to retain a portion of their earnings and to supply a greater percentage of their own working capital. Finally, they were able to supply all their own normal requirements, borrowing only for unusual transactions or for seasonal or cyclical variations. Moreover, during the good security markets of the 'twenties, companies tended to sell bond or stock issues to raise working capital. By the late 'twenties successful corporations not only had made themselves independent of the banks for ordinary commercial loans but also had accumulated enough money to invest in government bonds, to loan on call in Wall Street, or to compete directly with the banks by carrying their own credit lines.

As long as the volume of business continued to expand, this trend was not noticeable, for new companies continued to borrow and older companies had to borrow to meet increasing business activity. Once the volume leveled off, the situation became most evident. Companies paid off what bank loans they had. As the depression deepened, fewer and fewer new companies came into existence. The banks thought that depression losses would so weaken companies that they would be forced to borrow when business activity picked up. This, however, did not prove to be the case. Good companies had been so frightened by the depression that they industriously saved their earnings and improved their working capital. The result was that loans and discounts increased sluggishly from their depression lows. Both the Bancorporation banks and those of the First Bank Stock Corporation felt the effects.[18] The management of both groups hoped that a revival in business would restore the volume of loans, but a strong revival seemed distant and any improvement might be only temporary. They decided that banks might just as well resign themselves to the situation.

It is generally believed that banks offset declining commercial loans by buying increasing amounts of government bonds, but this was only partially true of the banks in either group. While deposits increased steadily and the banks purchased increasing amounts of government bonds, this action did not fully offset the effect of a lessened volume of loans and discounts. It took at least five dollars invested in governments to produce as much interest income as one dollar invested in loans and discounts.

The Twin City Banks Make a Drive for New Business

This situation left only one course open to the banks: they had to develop new lines of business. One of the most important was the term loan. Formerly they had been reluctant to loan money for any length of time; now they were willing to loan it for 5 years when the security was excellent, the interest rate fair, and a portion of the loan payable annually. In some instances the group banks loaned for as long as 10 years. This change of policy was a direct result of necessity and a reflection of the very slight trouble with withdrawals experienced during the depression.[19] The major difficulty had been with the quality of loans and not their maturity. Thus, it seemed reasonable to increase the length of good loans. Bank officers concentrated on acquiring this type of business, and the results were gratifying.

With the popularization of the automobile, the large Twin City banks had taken up wholesale automobile financing. They loaned money both to dealers and to finance companies, which in turn loaned it to the retail buyers of automobiles. Though banks received a low interest rate on their wholesale loans, while the retailers of credit received a high rate, the banks had avoided retail lending because they considered it undignified. Retail lending involved much grief, and besides it was not good policy for a bank to compete with its own customers. The function of commercial banking was to loan money wholesale at low rates, keeping investments trouble-free and riskless. For years the more aggressive officers had gazed longingly at the retail field, but the older, more conservative men had made firm refusals. The only direct automobile loans made by the big banks had been made as a service to their regular customers.[20] During the late 'thirties, the Northwestern in Minneapolis commenced to push retail automobile loans. The First of Minneapolis was more reluctant, but unable to deny the success of other banks, it, too, entered the field.

Another tradition-shattering development was that of the small personal loan. The State of Minnesota had never had effective small-loan legislation, and the field had been monopolized by loan sharks. During these years a law was passed regulating this business. It legalized a rate of 3 per cent a month on amounts up to $300. The banks in their search for new business studied this situation and, concluding that a considerable portion of the borrowers who paid these rates were sound, they decided to enter the small-loan field. Of course, they loaned in so far as possible only to those entitled to credit accommodations, but they charged much lower rates than those charged by the small-loan companies.

The greatest obstacle to these developments was the mental attitude of both the general public and the bank officers and employees.

Officers and employees alike had to learn that a bank is a competitive organization and that, in order to survive, it has to compete for every scrap of business it can find. Changing economic conditions reduced its wholesale business. The retail field lay open.

The banks also had to convince the general public of their change in attitude. Formerly the man in the street had felt little direct connection with the great banks other than as a depositor. When he wanted to borrow, he turned to the automobile finance company, the mortgage lender, the chattel lender, and the personal finance company. He thought that the big banks had no interest in his problems and would scorn to make a loan of a few dollars. Now that the great banks were taking interest in this type of loan, they had to persuade the small borrower to come in and ask for it.

The three Twin City banks (the two Firsts and the Northwestern) used the same methods. They established personal loan departments and, to advertise them more widely, overcame their antipathy to the use of billboard advertising.[21] Such billboards located all around the Twin Cities invited the small man to come to the banks for personal and automobile loans. Newspapers carried series of advertisements, posters were placed in bank lobbies, and pamphlets were inserted in bank statements. The banks stressed their low rates on personal loans.

Despite the activities of both groups in developing new types of business, they did not begin to absorb all new loans. Automobiles were sold in huge numbers in the territory, mostly on credit, and the banks financed only a small percentage of them. A brief glance at the results of nationally known automobile finance companies indicates that each year they took many dollars out of the Ninth Federal Reserve District as interest on conservative automobile financing. Small loan companies also did a substantial business.[22] Not only did the automobile finance companies thrive in the Ninth District during this period; the chattel-mortgage finance companies, which financed the time sales of household articles, also flourished. A growing volume of business at high rates and a low loss ratio made the business very profitable.

The banks, however, developed a very substantial volume of loans guaranteed by the United States Government. In its anxiety to obtain easy credit for various classes of borrowers, the government, either directly or indirectly and either partially or fully, guaranteed the repayment of certain types of loans. The most prominent illustrations are the Federal Housing Administration loans for new building and the various commodity credit loans. Wherever the government assumed the risk, the banks rushed in competing aggressively for their share. From 1935 to 1940, these loans steadily increased in volume and supplied the banks with an increasing percentage of their income.

Government Competition in Selling and Buying Credit, 1935–1940

From 1935 to 1940, inclusive, the banks were constantly confronted with government competition. The Reconstruction Finance Corporation was making term loans. Originally it was to make loans that banks would refuse because of the risk involved but, as it worked out, the RFC made many loans which normally would have gone to the banks. Its rates were low. It would loan for a number of years and while actually it was conservative, it acquired the reputation of being more ready to loan than were the banks. Thus, many borrowers, just because of its reputation, took loans to the RFC which local banks would have been delighted to make. While it was impossible to appraise this competition accurately, because of the impossibility of determining which loans the banks would have accepted, there is no doubt that it amounted to a sizable sum, one that would have been very welcome to commercial banks.

The federal land bank continued to make farm loans and to that extent competed with the banks. This, however, does not appear to have been harmful. There is even considerable evidence to support the view that the federal land banks, by supplying a market for farm mortgages, helped the banks work out frozen portfolios.

The Home Owners Loan Corporation was extremely liberal in its policy, loaning at very low interest rates and tending to upset the home-loan situation. This competition was too much for the commercial banks. Since the banks used these agencies to dispose of a portion of their poor loans, they were not an unmitigated evil.

A third type of government-subsidized competition came from the Federal Savings and Loan Associations, which operated aggressively in the Ninth Federal Reserve District under charter from Washington. They advertised extensively that their deposits up to $5,000 were insured by a federal agency.

A fourth adverse development, so far as the savings deposits of banks were concerned, was the widespread popularization of United States savings bonds. They took up the greatest portion of annual savings not absorbed by the Federal Savings and Loan Associations.[23]

The period was also marked by a steady increase in the scope and severity of government regulation. National banks had always been subject to strict supervision and inspection to discover whether or not they were complying with rules. The development of the Federal Reserve System had intensified the requirements. The Federal Deposit Insurance Corporation, further, greatly broadened the government's control of commercial banks. While the corporation did not have any direct authority over banks, it did have the right to grant or refuse insurance, and this power enabled it to exercise considerable supervisory authority.[24]

The temporary-insurance plan granted immediate insurance to banks which were found by examiners to have assets equal in value to their deposits and other liabilities. The permanent-insurance plan, however, required the corporation to take the following factors into consideration:[25]

1. The financial history and condition of the bank;
2. The adequacy of its capital structure;
3. Its future earnings prospects;
4. The character of its management;
5. The convenience and needs of the community served;
6. The consistency of its corporate powers with the purposes of deposit insurance.

It is obvious that funds available to the Federal Deposit Insurance Corporation are nominal in relation to its contingent liabilities. The Corporation itself recognizes this fact. In its 1939 report it stated:[26]

> The experience of the Corporation to date does not constitute a basis for estimating either its future disbursements or its future losses. Like the past six years, the years immediately following earlier banking crises

were marked by relatively few bank failures, and relatively small losses to bank creditors, and gave no indication of either the timing or the magnitude of the losses to be experienced in the years to follow. The losses which ultimately followed were sufficient to have wiped out a reserve accumulated from an assessment of one-twelfth of one per cent per annum on total deposits of the banking system.

The present rate of assessment assumes that improvements in the structure and operation of the banking system and in standards of supervision will be successful in keeping losses substantially lower in the future than they have been in the past.

Supervisory authorities, both State and national, the Federal Reserve System, and the Federal Deposit Insurance Corporation opposed the creation of unnecessary, weakly financed, or poorly managed banks (and they placed the burden of proof on those who applied for a charter); this restriction resulted in few new banks in the Ninth Federal Reserve District between 1935 and 1940. A few failures occurred, and a series of mergers took place. The number of banks in existence in the district declined as follows:[27]

1935	1,407
1936	1,387
1937	1,360
1938	1,327
1939	1,305
1940	1,288

Declining Trend of Bank Earnings

From 1929 to 1940 the gross-interest income of First Bank Stock declined steadily. The Bancorporation showed a similar tendency, but it leveled off during the last two years.[28] Though every effort was made to increase other income, it also tended to decline. Nevertheless, net earnings were not so severely injured as might be imagined. Every effort was made to reduce expenses, and with surprising success.

Though salaries were reduced temporarily, this saving was not permanent, for, as soon as the bottom of the depression had been passed, both groups tended to restore salary cuts. In fact, salaries had to be increased in order to hold men, and the seniority policy continued. At the same time, beginning clerical salaries were increased from the low levels of the 'twenties. Other salaries in the lower brackets were increased proportionately. Despite the rising scale, total clerical salaries remained almost stationary, for efforts were made to improve efficiency.

From 1935 to 1940, inclusive, the banks in the Ninth Federal Reserve District, and especially those in the two groups, performed remarkably in maintaining their earning power in the face of a declining volume of loans and diminishing rates of interest. Most of their expenses either remained stationary or actually increased, but by eliminating cut-throat competition, unprofitable banks, and the duplication of overhead, and by merging banks, increasing the volume of deposits, installing minimum balance requirements, and particularly by eliminating interest on demand deposits and reducing the rate on time deposits, expenses were sharply curtailed thereby allowing a substantial portion of gross earnings to filter through to net.

Proposed Group-Banking Legislation

When group banking was developed in 1929 and 1930 it was greeted by a portion of the population with messianic fervor and hailed as the answer to all banking problems. Another group was equally opposed and alleged that it would mark the end of liberty for the American people. The farmer leaders of the group in the Ninth Federal Reserve District had always been bitterly hostile to the Twin Cities. They had opposed the railroads, the grain elevators, the flour mills, the Chamber of Commerce, and the great metropolitan banks. Part of the agrarian population firmly believed that Twin City business men manipulated economic conditions so that prices were low when the farmers had grain or cattle to sell, high when the farmers were buying; that the railroads kept freight rates unjustifiably high; that the money-lenders drained the country of money; and that depressions were kindled every few years to bankrupt the farming areas so that the Twin Cities could buy rural property at low prices.

This same group, headed by its political leaders, openly sneered at the development of group banking, branding it as another scheme to subordinate the rural regions and drain their wealth to the Twin Cities. The opposition amounted to almost a blind frenzy. These people feared that group banking would give the Twin City bankers complete control of the finances and credit of the entire region, as well as control of the Federal Reserve Bank, and that this financial power would be used to enslave free people. Regardless of whether the development would strengthen and improve the banking structure, they demanded its destruction.

There was another element which opposed group banking, but from a more sensible point of view. This was the small-town independent banker. He felt that customers would go to a group bank in preference to an independent, placing him at a competitive disadvantage. What he feared most, though, was that group banks would be unfair in competition, that they would aggressively operate banks at competitive points, pay high rates of interest on deposits, offer free services, be too liberal in their loan policy, and loan money at low rates of interest in order to take customers away from him, force him to operate at a loss, cut off his credit in the Twin Cities, and push him out of business. The independent banker was no laggard in promoting legislation to stop the spread of the groups.

The reforms offered by the representatives of these hostile groups centered in three main propositions. The most violent was to force group banks to disband and return their banks to local ownership; the second was to map out certain regional areas within which group banks could expand; and the third was to freeze group banks in their existing form, forbidding them to acquire any more units. Testimony on these propositions was taken by the banking committees of both the U. S. Senate and the House of Representatives. Many witnesses were heard.[29]

The depression, however, brought more serious problems to the fore, and consequently no legislation was passed until the Banking Act of 1933. Although this act was not designed primarily to regulate group banking, it did provide for the regulation and inspection of holding companies, requiring them to have assets other than bank stock and to obtain voting permits from proper authorities before voting the stock of affiliated banks.[30] The Banking Act of 1935 further strengthened and clarified this act but did not change any fundamental provisions affecting the group banks.[31]

The most remarkable thing in connection with the opposition to bank holding companies in the period 1935–1940 was the way it died down, leaving hostile legislation with little popular appeal. The astute politician found himself pounding upon a dead issue when he tried to stir up violent antagonism against the groups. The reasons seem obvious. The first was that people had made friends with the groups, and in doing so discovered that they had nothing to fear. It was the old story of closer acquaintance developing tolerance and friendship and bringing the realization that there was nothing sinister; in fact, group banking was a benefit to the country and its people rather than a detriment.

The second reason was that most people had seen what strength group banking had imparted to the Ninth Federal Reserve District during the 'thirties. Both groups had kept every bank open, and no depositor had lost a dollar or even had to wait for his money. When almost everything else crashed during the depression, money in a group bank was safe, for the groups themselves took the loss while the depositors and the community escaped unscathed. The realization that this service was general in the Ninth Federal Reserve District finally dawned, and, while some people still talked against them, a large portion placed their money in group banks.

A third factor that quieted antagonism was that the groups ceased to expand and in the six years under discussion actually contracted in number of banks. This development allayed the blind fear that groups would gradually swallow all the banks, a fear which was very real and caused much of the hostility.

A fourth, and probably the most valid explanation of the abatement, was a change in the attitude of independent bankers. The independent soon found that the groups offered fair, high-class competition. They were very conservative. They made each unit stand on its own feet. They did not give free service to excess. They paid lower rates on savings in many cases than did the independents and they refused to allow an affiliated bank to operate at a loss. The groups had many small banks. No one was of great importance, so rather than operate it at a loss over a period of time, they were willing to dispose of it. Thus, if there were too many banks in a town, it was usually the group bank which got out.

The results of the depression, the outstanding service of the groups, the softening effect of time, a growing familiarity on the part of the public, the end of expansion, and the independent bankers' realization that the groups supply fair competition, all combined to develop a more friendly feeling for Banco and First Bank Stock. By December, 1940, the threat of hostile legislation seemed to have become a part of history.

CHAPTER XV

PAST, PRESENT, AND FUTURE OF BANKING IN THE NORTHWEST

A SUMMARY

The Period of Pioneer Settlement, 1849–1915

The period of settlement in the Central Northwest contributed little to the oft-repeated tale of pioneering. Most of its history was but repetition of that which had recurred many times as the frontier crept from the Atlantic Seaboard west to the Mississippi and on toward the far Pacific. What made it distinctive was its relatively late date, the growing momentum of colonization, and the impact of revolutionary developments in transportation and manufacture. The spread of the railroad, which for the first time made available on land the long-distance transportation of goods at low cost, permitted the rise of farming on a specialized monetary basis long before the development of cities in the region. The growing industrial organization supplied not only cheap goods for sale, but also a market for raw materials and agricultural produce.

At the beginning (approximately 1849) of the period of colonization, the region had ample land and raw materials but neither population nor capital. The landless and dispossessed from the settled regions of the United States and Europe poured into the Northwest. Most of these settlers had little money. While a few had substantial amounts, this fact made little difference, for the region was still short of capital for long-time investment. Innumerable opportunities existed for the profitable use of money: lands had to be cleared and broken; roads and railroads awaited construction; houses, factories, and offices needed building. The undeveloped land and growing population created an insatiable demand for capital. Any sum was instantly absorbed, and, when applied to physical construction, it reappeared only over a period of years. Because the area constantly required physical improvement, an unfavorable balance of trade persisted, for money and liquid capital of all sorts were drained out to pay for imports. The result was an unfortunate perplexity in the minds of the settlers, who confused the great shortage of funds for long-term capital investment with its result, a scarcity of currency and bank credit. This was no new confusion, but one common to all pioneer countries. The effects were unfortunate: a vicious antagonism toward the East and other sources of capital; a hearty dislike for creditors and the Money Power; a constant demand for fiat money, easy money, and free silver; and popular approval of lax banking laws and of the existence of many small banks and of the loaning of commercial funds for capital and speculative investment.

Despite these unfortunate symptoms, the situation was not all bad, for it contained its own specifics. The demand for capital was strong primarily because of the profitable opportunities available for investment. Annual profits of 30, 60, and 100 per cent were not uncommon, and business men tended to retain their profits, plowing them back into their business. Operating profits were but one phase of capital accumulation. More important was capital gain, or speculative profit. Until 1915 this was an almost certain development, for the growing population, the widening scope of business, the increasing operating profits, and the accumulating capital funds, all caused property to mount in value. Optimistic entrepreneurs forged ahead, building railroads, mills, and factories, and laying out farms. This over-all development, plus a constant influx of settlers desirous of making a fortune, caused values to rise steadily. To a large extent the movement generated its own power.

The period of settlement in the Northwest was the fabled age for the petty capitalist of bold and optimistic spirit. In order to gain fame and fortune, only two qualities were essential — an aggressive disposition and longevity. If a man entered business with determination, operated on borrowed capital, made a living on an operating basis, held on, and lived long enough, the secular growth of values brought him a rich reward. The era compensated the aggressive, the venturesome, and the dogged. It was more important to be venturesome than to be capable; the two qualities combined produced an empire-builder.

The Central Northwest made prodigious capital improvements in the space of a few years. The cuts and fills and tunnels of the railroads, the highways, the factories, farms, houses, apartments and office buildings, the power systems, the streets with their paving, curbs, and sidewalks, and the sewer and water systems represented projects to stagger the imagination. Only a small portion of all this was paid for out of eastern capital. Most of it was created by the system itself. It was the product of an economy so efficient that a small proportion of the workers could supply enough consumer goods for all, and the energies of the remainder could be concentrated on capital improvements. Urged on by the lure of high profits, the system devoted itself to capital creation with amazing success. The constant absorption of capital by physical improvements acted as a forced draught on the engine of physical production. By about 1915 the Northwest was relatively mature; and, although much remained undone, the goal was in sight.

THE DEVELOPMENT OF A LOCAL BANKING ORGANIZATION, 1851–1929

Since there was need for capital to finance local enterprises and ingenious entrepreneurs organized banks to supply the necessary money, the banking system in the Central Northwest seemed to arise out of the local situation.

In the field of origins, there are two schools of thought: the effusionist and the diffusionist. According to the effusionist school, institutions arise out of the local situation, rise, fall and rise again, with but little copying from earlier systems. The diffusionist school believes that ideas and practices flow from one area to another, there is little originality, and much copying. To me, the effusionist idea is much the more pertinent, yet it must be admitted that some of the banks in the Central Northwest closely resembled types which had been developed in far countries during earlier times.

An interesting illustration is the loan bank, examples of which are the Bank of St. George, established in Genoa in 1407 or earlier; the Bank of England, founded in London in 1694; and the Bank of North America, founded in Philadelphia in 1781. These were creditor banks, they had ample capital funds, accepted deposits, made loans, and dealt in domestic and foreign exchange. They were specialized, managed by professional bankers with the primary objective of employing their capital safely and making a profit from a specialized banking business. The most outstanding example of this type in the Central Northwest was the First National Bank of St. Paul. From its establishment, it fitted into this classification.

The merchant banker, who had been of great importance historically, ordinarily had originated as a successful merchant who, when he acquired wealth, abandoned merchandising for banking. There are many illustrations of this in the Central Northwest; probably the best illustration is the Harrison family, which left business and invested its capital in the Security Bank of Minneapolis. To be sure, this bank eventually became an outstanding example of a specialized, commercial (loan) bank.

It might be argued with some success that the overwhelming majority of early northwestern banks were merchant banks. The argument would be that they were not organized by bankers but by merchants, or dealers; they were managed by merchants; they were organized not to find safe employment for abundant capital but to find abundant capital for their needy owners. While admitting the factual accuracy of these contentions, I do not feel that they would justify classifying these banks as merchant banks. They were a hybrid form, developed to meet the current needs; the successful eventually evolved into specialized, commercial (loan) banks.

It is interesting to note the types of banks which, while well known in history, did not develop in the Central Northwest. There are no illustrations of the deposit and transfer banks such as those of Barcelona and Amsterdam. Probably the reason for this is that the commercial banks carried on this business as an adjunct to their other lines. Then, too, there are no prominent illustrations of Jewish money lenders or pawnbrokers developing into bankers. Another omission is the land bank which had been developed in colonial times to finance owners of real estate by issuing bank notes in exchange for their mortgages. This type of operation in the Central Northwest was effectively stopped by the various State constitutions and by the national banking laws. While lack of these types is not mystifying, it is surprising that banks of the type of the *crédit agricole* did not come into existence. This type had been well developed, was well known, and would have filled the demand for long-term capital; yet it never became of any importance. To be sure, there were some attempts in this direction, but these attempts did not occur until after the need for long-term capital had been to a great extent answered by the local banks utilizing short-term capital for this purpose. This method was surprisingly successful, it readily supplied capital, and it financed the rapid development of the Central Northwest.

The first banker in St. Paul commenced business in 1851, devoting himself to commercial banking and the buying of drafts and bills of exchange. Other bankers appeared within a short time. Some had capital and some had none, but all planned to do a business in dealing in exchange and making commercial loans. Many banks, like those on all frontiers, were organized by business men to provide loans on inadequate collateral; others were formed to finance real-estate and timber speculation.

Each field of business was developed by petty capitalists, even though the potential volume of effort lay far beyond their abilities to finance. These business small fry crowded the lobbies of the banks, seeking funds to finance their projects. The thriving commercial and industrial background of the Twin Cities provided a growing demand for genuine commercial loans.

The demand for long-time capital loans was also strong. Funds were needed to finance the construction of mills, elevators, factory buildings, and machinery and for semi-permanent working-capital purposes. The growing business and the increasing population caused a more or less steady appreciation in the value of real estate and local property. Seeing this, every optimistic business man wished to buy as much as he could and made every effort to borrow money to do so. Thus, there was always a large demand for loans. These varied all the way from self-liquidating loans to the wildest speculations.

Many business men retained their earnings for working-capital purposes, so that year by year the working capital of Twin City business increased in volume. As a result of high profits, which fostered the increase of working capital, and the general growth of local liquid capital, the total deposits of Twin City banks gradually increased. Local deposits began to meet the rising demand for local loans, lessening the dependence of the Cities on outside capital. By the close of the nineteenth century the deposits of local business firms were so large that, except for temporary peaks, the banks were able to finance the demand for bona fide commercial loans from local commercial deposits. A conservative bank could restrict its business to commercial loans, employ only local deposits, and make a good profit.

Primarily for convenience and economy, most banks in the area early developed the practice of handling their exchange through one of the large Twin City banks. Their only complaint was that the Twin City banks did not have sufficient funds to extend them a full line of credit, often forcing them to borrow in Chicago or even in New York. By the late 'eighties, however, the Twin City banks commenced to a moderate extent to take care of country banks, and this business tended to grow. As local deposits mounted and capital funds were built up, the Twin City banks were able to extend greater accommodations to the country banks. Their ability declined during the 'nineties, but increased steadily after 1900. By 1920 the Twin City institutions were the bankers' banks for the area. They had correspondent relationships with nearly every bank in the trade territory, clearing their checks, holding their balances, and making them loans. From 1900 onward, this business gained in importance until the great banks regarded themselves as bankers' banks. This business was a small percentage of the total, but it was important.

Panics and Survival in the Northwest, 1873–1929

Although the Twin Cities and southeastern and central Minnesota were fairly well developed by 1873, there had been no great inflation in real-estate values, and the areas were still in a phase of strong growth. The depression of 1873 dealt lightly with them, causing little banking trouble. From 1882 to 1892, however, the Twin Cities grew rapidly, their expansion finally culminating in a real-estate boom. Banks were created in numbers, and institutions which originally had been conservative began to finance real-estate speculation. The Panic of 1893, which was felt through 1897, was destructive in over-expanded areas like Minneapolis and St. Paul; it caused a large number of banks to fail. Even those which survived did so only with the greatest difficulty, and at times it appeared as though they too would go under. It was every man for himself; no one gave aid or expected it. Areas which had not experienced the boom felt only a state of depression; it was the sections which had prospered that felt the collapse. One by one the city banks closed, and those in the older farming areas, too, until there remained only a handful of the strongest. These were indeed strong or they would not have survived the panic and the depression. Their officers had an excellent opportunity to study the results of optimistic management as competitors failed on every side.

The period from 1900 to 1920 was one of uneven prosperity for the entire region. The national secular trend was upward; the area was increasing in population; local values were rising; and from 1917 to 1920 the war boom carried all values to unprecedented highs. The agricultural collapse which started in 1920 was catastrophic: agricultural prices dropped below the cost of production, real-estate values crashed, farm mortgages defaulted, and the pyramid of credit based on agriculture tottered. The entire rural area was depressed, and much of the rural banking structure failed. Again only a few of the strongest country banks survived that long, grinding depression.

The Twin Cities, during the years 1920 and 1921, felt the depression just as severely as did the country. However, they suffered no similar banking collapse. Some Twin Cities banks had restricted themselves to good, self-liquidating commercial loans; one of the first effects of the depression was the repayment of these loans, and as they were repaid the banks became increasingly liquid. The big city banks, which held an overwhelming proportion of the deposits of the area, having survived the depression of the 'nineties, had learned conservatism. A few banks in the Twin Cities did fail, but they were all small. The banks were helped by the strong business revival which started in the cities in 1922, bringing a period of urban prosperity and boom. It was not until 1929 that they commenced to feel the full effect of the secular downswing.

The history of banking in the Northwest is that of a fluid system, created to supply local loans. Banks were easily organized, but approximately two out of every three failed eventually with heavy losses to depositors. There were 3,875 banks in the Ninth Federal Reserve District in 1920; twenty years later, in 1940, this number had been reduced to 1,288. From 1920 to the end of 1934 there were 2,322 definite failures. Then, too, there were innumerable reorganizations in which depositors waived a part of their deposits and stockholders paid in new capital; or stock was sold to new purchasers in order to rebuild capital. These banks have been included in the number which remained open.

What was actually behind failures in a substantial majority of cases was not lack of earnings, not dishonesty, not runs, not the slow draining away of deposits, but genuine insolvency. It was not lack of liquidity that caused the trouble, but poor loans. The bankers, being optimistic, made loans and kept renewing them for a period of years, only to discover finally that the debtor could not pay and that the collateral, if any, was not sufficient to indemnify the bank.

The passage of time cured one basic weakness — the lack of local capital. Sufficient funds accumulated gradually, freeing the banking system from its dependence upon outside deposits. This slow accretion was hastened by the gradual completion of permanent capital improvements, which reduced the demand for funds. Moreover, many existing capital improvements had either been paid for by the owners or had come to settlement through the media of forced sale, foreclosure, or bankruptcy. Capital indebtedness was scaled down to the capacity to pay. As the demand for local investment capital declined, capital loans became more and more a matter of refinancing, much of which was done through government institutions and through agencies other than banks.

Probably the most constructive development was the tendency of the territory's banking business to accumulate in the older banks, which had survived recurring depressions and given proof of capable, conservative management. Of course, after each series of failures new banks were organized in the course of time, but there was a period of some years after each collapse during which only the strong banks were in operation. During that time all the business in the locality went to these banks. Weak banks, often under pressure from banking authorities, requested some strong local bank to take over their deposits. There was a feeling on the part of depositors, too, a desire to do business with a bank which had survived at least one major depression, which gave the older banks an advantage. For a number of reasons, then, there was a steady tendency of deposits toward the sound, strong banks.

Thus, the passage of time and the survival of the fittest tended to strengthen the banking structure by allowing the conservative banks to acquire most of the banking resources without infringing upon the right of anyone to be a banker. While this was constructive, it did not remedy the weakness of most small agricultural communities — an insufficient demand for bona fide commercial loans to justify the operation of a commercial bank. Many of the bankers who survived the depression of the 'twenties resolved not to make capital loans; they commenced to buy bonds with excess local deposits, a policy which had much to justify it if the banker understood bonds and bought good ones. Most country bankers, however, knew little about corporate finance, and poor bonds wrecked many a bank.

By the late 'twenties it became evident that though speculative banking might serve the frontier, it had no place in an old and settled area; only conservative, cautious commercial banking could permanently survive in the Ninth Federal Reserve District. Conservative banking not only could survive; over a period of years it could produce substantial profits. Experienced bankers, recognizing that most of the pressure on banks during a depression is exerted by the failure of weak units, began to find not only a personal responsibility but also a personal interest in the spread of conservative banking.

The Organization of Banking Groups, 1929–1930

Many factors contributed to the development of group banking, with which we are largely concerned, during the 'twenties. The conservative bankers, who controlled the largest portion of the territory's banking resources, and for whom the Twin Cities were the metropolitan center, believed that most banking troubles were rooted in weak, inefficient management and could be remedied by replacing poor managers with sound, conservative operators. They recognized that some troubles were inherent in local situations, but believed that capable management with a little foresight could skirt these pitfalls.

Conservative bankers were strong believers in the maxim that in union there is strength. One bank might be weak, but a group of banks spread over an extended area and working in close coöperation was a power to be reckoned with. For many years the conservative banks in the Twin City area, working through their city correspondents, had coöperated with one another during times of emergency. They knew how dependent each was upon the group. These banks had been closely related for a number of years, becoming more interdependent with the passage of time; during the 'twenties they finally realized that they could best survive through coöperation.

There was another factor which undoubtedly leavened developments during the late 'twenties. That was the expansionist feeling in the air. Everyone had plans for expansion. There was a general mania for size which affected the most conservative. The stock market was the leading item of conversation; everyone was concerned with its advance. The marketability of a security constituted its most important attribute, and its chances of appreciation were of great interest. Local bank stocks had little marketability and very little chance of market appreciation; they were therefore of little interest, and most holders wished they had something with more speculative appeal.

There was nothing simple in the organization of the new bank groups. Even the motives were diverse and complex, and any attempt to simplify them shows a lack of perception. There is little doubt that one strong force was the belief that group banks could make important market profits — not, it should be noted, profits to the group from the issuance and sale of stock, but profits to the stockholders, who would receive a stock with a broad, listed market in exchange for stocks of country banks. Any stock with a good market was popularly believed to sell at a premium because of its broad demand; it was thought, therefore, that the market value of a group-bank stock should be greater than the aggregate book value of the component stocks. Thus, everyone who thought about the matter at all concluded that the organization of a group-banking company should prove profitable to those who exchanged their country-bank stocks for the stock of the holding company. Moreover, the stock would surely advance to new highs in the market, and the fortunate purchasers of early issues would, if they sold in due course, make substantial profits. Even those who purchased the stock at high prices probably would benefit substantially, for the stock would pay a steady dividend. The holders of country-bank stocks became eager for an exchange.

Another motive behind group development was competition with other centers, which had become steadily more severe as country-bank balances gained in importance to the great Twin City banks. As competition grew hotter, rumors spread that certain New York and Chicago banks were preparing to buy banks in order to obtain business in this territory. There were actually a few instances in which outside interests attempted to acquire local banks, and, of course, rumor made the most of them.

When one Twin City bank began to expand by allying itself with its correspondents and with other banks, it precipitated matters. The other bankers' banks thought that they had to do likewise. This might have been only a plausible argument; perhaps the wiser and more profitable course for competitive banks to pursue would have been to remain independent. Its original impetus might carry a group bank a long way, but its very success would alienate many former friends and customers, who would deliberately turn to banks which remained to champion and protect the independent unit. The general belief among bankers was growing that the group system was destined to replace the unit system, and that the individual bank could survive only if it organized or joined a group.

The most immediate result of the attempt to acquire group members was a complete change in the banking alignment of the territory. The old uneasy balance of four great groups was upset. In acquiring Twin City banks the First Bank Stock group was the more successful; it merged three of the old groups, the First National Bank of St. Paul, the First National Bank of Minneapolis, and the Merchants National Bank of St. Paul, to form the First Bank

Stock Corporation. Then it acquired a group of banks in rural regions, but there the Northwest Bancorporation scored its success. Although the Bancorporation lost in St. Paul, it gathered in an outstanding group of outlying banks, representing an important cross section of regional banking. The movement toward group banking resulted in the formation of two groups, each a closely knit financial organization.

The amazing aspect of the entire development was its spontaneity. Once started, it gathered momentum as it went. Everything combined to facilitate its rapid strides. Country bankers were not too well pleased with their experiences and earnings during the 'twenties; times had been hard and earnings low. They had survived innumerable scares and now were looking for some means of balancing their precarious position. They sincerely believed that group banking would provide a strength upon which they could rely if conditions turned for the worse. The possibilities of profits made the joining with a group very enticing to the stockholders of country banks, who had seen few dividends in years and who were often unable to sell their stock at any reasonable price. The group plan offered stockholders steady dividends, perhaps some cash, and the probability of market appreciation.

Far from avoiding the groups, country banks sent representatives to Minneapolis to open negotiations. At times the offices of the two groups were crowded with them. There was no need to seek out members. The bankers, pursuing their own interests, sought admission; the leaders of the groups had only to pick and choose. They preferred the older, larger banks, and, while they acquired only a small percentage of the total number of banks in the area, they obtained a much larger proportion of total deposits. By the end of 1930 the groups had acquired only about 10 per cent of the banks in the Northwest (222 out of 2,118), but these banks had over 40 per cent of total deposits. By 1940, after the innumerable bank closings of the 'thirties, the groups had about 13 per cent of the number of banks in operation (163 out of 1,288) and 55 per cent of total deposits.

Group banking spread over the Northwest like a prairie fire because it was based on both the self-interest of local bankers and the strengthening of the banking system. It had all the advantages of unit operation, retaining the former local operating officials to transact local business and make contacts with local citizens. The officers of the member banks liked the new system because it preserved their position, their work, their salaries, and their prestige. At the same time, they were part of a coöperative movement designed to strengthen the banking structure. Everywhere local interests would be protected, local citizens better served, and local profits augmented, for each unit was now part of a mighty bulwark. Thus, group banking expanded in the Northwest. It was the logical product of the evolution of conservative unit banking.

ORDEAL AND SURVIVAL OF GROUP BANKS, 1930–1935

While the general stock-market crash in the fall of 1929 did not directly affect the groups, it ended any possibility of issuing more of their stock for cash. The general collapse carried the newly issued stock of the group banks downward, killing public desire for it and destroying one of the major forces of expansion. When the stock was not going up, country-bank stockholders preferred to retain their own stock; and the fact that the groups could not replenish their cash from the sale of stock on the general market made them cautious about paying cash. Since the public did not want group stock, and the groups could not pay cash for new banks, expansion ceased.

One exception should be noted. The progress of the depression was so alarming to some country bankers that they sought shelter. In many instances they stopped haggling over terms of acquisition and made concessions so that the groups would assume responsibility. Since the groups were not particularly perturbed during the first two years of the depression, they were still willing to acquire banks. This expansion, however, was encouraged for reasons diametrically opposite those for earlier growth. Finally, the continued advance of the depression made both groups refuse new banks even as gifts. By that time they had troubles enough without acquiring any more.

The first effect of the depression upon the group banks was a moderate increase in deposits, accompanied with a constant inflow of money as self-liquidating loans were repaid. Eventually there was a decline in deposits as depositors withdrew funds to meet living expenses and operating deficits, and it became increasingly hard to obtain repayments on loans. Though for the groups as a whole the decline in deposits was not serious, it would have been embarrassing to certain individual banks, had they been forced to rely on themselves. For instance, in banks in the copper-mining regions, deposits shrank 55 per cent. Banks in drought-stricken areas showed comparable declines. In the mixed-farming sections the decline seldom exceeded 35 per cent over a three-year period (1930–1933), and in the Cities the decline was only 17 per cent. For the groups as a whole, declines over the three-year period amounted to about 27 per cent.

In the group banks it was not so much the decline in deposits which caused trouble as the losses, both actual and unrealized, on capital assets. The greatest source of trouble was the loans made for permanent working-capital purposes. To be sure, the bulk of these loans was repaid in due course, but not without losses.

While most bank loans were in good condition and were promptly paid, there was a fringe of questionable loans which defaulted and were written down. Losses were greatly aggravated by over-optimism. The bankers, both in the city and in the country, kept hoping that conditions would improve and they could avoid taking losses. They refrained from selling bonds early in the depression, and rather than admit a loss on a loan, they attempted to renew it.

Next to these loans the major source of trouble for the group banks lay in their bond portfolios. Bonds had been purchased to provide a ready source of cash during an emergency, but many of the issues were of poor quality. Eventually many bonds defaulted and became involved in lengthy reorganizations.

In many banks the government examiners forced the recognition of losses; the examiners for the group banks were more severe, requiring member banks to admit potential losses and to write down assets to conservative figures. As a result, the individual banks in each group made substantial charge-offs. At first these losses were charged to surplus; however, in instance after instance the unit banks were so weakened by recurring losses that they were unable to stand further charge-offs. Then the group organization contributed whatever cash was necessary to avoid impairing capital funds. Sometimes the groups purchased poor assets from their unit banks at book value.

At the beginning of the depression the two corporations had substantial funds in their treasuries derived from the cash sale of stock to the public. They also continued to receive cash dividends from the strongest member banks, using them to replenish assets. As time dragged on, however, the treasury funds of the groups neared exhaustion, and their managements commenced to worry over the possible duration of the depression.

Despite all their tribulations, every member of each group was open for unrestricted business at the time of the bank holiday, and as soon as the holiday was over, every group bank immediately reopened for unrestricted withdrawal. In this respect, group banking had met the test.

With the passing of the depression's low point, conditions changed for the better in the banks. Bonds recovered in value, and debtors paid many loans already charged off. At the same time, operating earnings improved. There was one rule which both groups observed: under normal, recurring circumstances a bank had to earn operating costs, charge-offs, a reserve for losses, and some return on capital funds. Unless these conditions could be met, the bank was either merged or liquidated. In most cases drastic action was not necessary, but every bank survived only on an earnings basis.

The managements of the groups did not wish to be caught again unprepared for trouble. They used most of their income to build reserves and capital funds, and dividends were either non-existent or nominal. The groups were cautious and conservative in making loans; in buying bonds they restricted themselves in most cases to United States and short-term municipal obligations.

The principal beneficiary of the development of group banking has been the general public. It has received an excellent type of banking service offered by banks which remained open during the depression. Depositors of each unit bank have always received one hundred cents on the dollar, regardless of the effect on the bank, and they have always had an opportunity of getting loans. Bank employees come second among those benefiting from group banking. They have had steady employment with only nominal salary adjustments during the depression, cuts which usually were restored with the return to even a semblance of normal conditions. Moreover, employees enjoy liberal insurance and pension plans. The elimination of officers and employees who have failed to measure up to group standards has given younger men opportunities.

The one who has paid for all this service has been the stockholder, who has seen the market price and the book value of his stock drop, earnings fall, and dividends shrink. Group banking was not to blame for the adverse developments which caused the tremendous market decline common to all stocks. The decline in book value, earnings, and dividends was inherent in the banking system and existed before the groups were formed. Had the groups not been created, however, the depression would have bankrupted many present group members. It seems obvious, therefore, that the great majority of stockholders, those who received their stock in exchange for bank stocks, have much for which to be grateful; had they not made the exchange, they might easily have been wiped out in bankruptcy, and in many cases they would have been doubly liable. They still have a stock of value, paying a moderate dividend and possessing good chances of improvement.

The stockholders who actually suffered were those who during the boom bought and paid cash for their stock. There is no denying their loss. The only reply possible is that 1929, when the stock was originally purchased, was an abnormal year; they might have bought something else in which their loss would have been just as great. At least, they have the dubious satisfaction of knowing that their money helped to write off losses in the banking system and helped to keep the financial mechanism of the Northwest solvent during the depression.

Federal Deposit Insurance Corporation, 1934–1940

The banks which survived until the bank holiday were hard-bitten veterans, yet they too were in serious condition, many of them actually insolvent. After the holiday, those which were still solvent as to deposits opened as soon as they had been examined. Others were allowed to reopen only after they had been reorganized and placed on a sound basis.

The Federal Deposit Insurance Corporation went into operation in 1934. Its protection was given a great deal of publicity both by the government and by many banks — the general public had to be convinced that the guarantee was sound and that money in a guaranteed bank was perfectly safe. This campaign generated confidence in the system as a whole. Now, the average depositor gives little thought to the solvency of his bank; he is satisfied if the bank is covered by FDIC insurance. Of course, about the only way the public can determine the solvency of a bank is by trial and error. Perhaps the general public should not be criticized for its inability to recognize sound banks and good banking. Even among capable bankers there is a difference of opinion as to what constitutes good banking: the liberal banker thinks it is the free and easy supplying of credit; the conservative banker thinks it is the cautious advancing of money where he believes there is no great risk. In order to obtain riskless loans, the conservative banker is forced to cut his interest charges to a nominal figure; this reduces his income, but it also minimizes his losses and strengthens his chances of survival. If a banker can pursue a policy of little risk and, because of large deposits and low operating costs, produce satisfactory earnings, he is in a strong position indeed.

Only after a depression is over, the damage appraised, and the survivors counted, can it be determined which bank was in the right. Banking cannot be criticized on the basis of a few months or years; its results must be judged by an entire secular trend, beginning with depression and passing through recovery, prosperity, boom, and collapse to another depression, and on through succeeding business cycles. Only then can it be known whether the extra income of a liberal bank was sufficient to exceed the extra losses or whether the losses dragged the bank down to bankruptcy, disgraced its management, and wiped out its stockholders. Did the conservative bank actually earn more than the liberal bank? Did it serve the community best by standing as a pillar during the depression and acting as a brake during prosperity? Under the old system of banking, history gives a definite answer: the intelligently conservative bank stayed open, earned something for its stockholders, supplied work for its employees, and served society by protecting the working capital and savings of the people, keeping them always available, even in times of trouble. The liberal bank collapsed during the depression. Eventually it was liquidated; and its loans, deposits, and customers went to the banks which remained open.

Under the present situation the Federal Deposit Insurance Corporation stands the losses on deposits up to $5,000, making deposits immediately available to their owners. As a matter of practice, however, it seldom allows an insolvent bank to close. When it finds that a bank is insolvent, it often asks some solvent bank in the same community to assume the deposits, the FDIC guaranteeing the solvent bank against loss. Where such a practice is followed, the FDIC works in favor of conservative banking. It not only avoids the scares and complications engendered by failures, but it also eliminates the liberal management, adding the deposits to those of a conservative bank. Under such circumstances it does not interfere with the survival of the fittest; it aids and abets it.

The fact that, as a practical matter, a bank cannot operate successfully without FDIC coverage gives the FDIC a great deal of authority. It can, to all practical purposes, regulate the number of banks coming into existence, thus keeping excessive competition from developing and preventing a resurgence of wildcat banking. By restricting the creation of new banks, great progress can be made in strengthening the banking structure. Then, too, the FDIC can exert pressure on banks which are pursuing dangerous policies. Whenever a bank gets into trouble, it can force a merger and eliminate the old management. These powers make it capable of extensive regulation.

A potential danger is the FDIC's exposure to political pressure and popular whim, for during good times poor banking is popular. Though the FDIC has powers to enforce good banking, it may not always use them; it could just as easily devote itself to saving liberal banks in the name of democracy and the theory that every man has the right to be a banker. If that is done, the policy may succeed for years, but the inevitable collapse will be seriously aggravated and the day of reckoning will indeed be severe.

Conclusion

The development of banking in the territory economically tributary to the Twin Cities was marked by a ready adaptability to economic needs. The numerous poorly managed, weakly financed banks with neither local deposits nor genuine local commercial loans were bound to have trouble during the recurring panics and depressions. Their difficulties were softened as long as the locality was in a phase of strong growth. When the territory became mature, the collapses were long, severe, and murderous as far as the incompetent banks were concerned. Despite their seriousness, these depressions and panics were beneficial. They forced banks to fight for survival, and only the basically sound were able to meet the test. Thus, the weak banks were eliminated, while the conservative survived and grew in strength.

Group banking was a logical, evolutionary step in the development of unit banks in the Ninth Federal Reserve District. The larger, more conservative banks which survived from one depression to the next knew each other well and maintained definitely friendly relations. They realized their interdependence and recognized the strength of coöperation. Individual bankers, though they would not consider selling their banks, were not averse to joining a federation if they could retain their authority, work, and income. They were willing to delegate many functions to a regional office, but they had to preserve their local autonomy and prestige. Once started, group banking spread like a rumor. The territory was ripe for it; it afforded remarkable advantages and solved many problems. It started with vigor, promising to absorb every large bank in the area. However, the depression followed closely upon its advent and within a short time checked its headlong advance. While banks were still willing and eager to join, the groups began to have troubles enough without taking in new members. The group executives had not had sufficient time to overhaul the assets of newly acquired banks, a misfortune which at times threatened to bankrupt them. They had all they could do to survive, but survive they did.

On the heels of the depression came the New Deal with its banking legislation regulating holding companies and separating commercial from investment banking. Banks had to dispose of their investment units, but the new regulations for bank holding companies required no important changes in either group.

As the depression waned, both groups began to repair the ravages, restoring capital funds, building up reserves for losses, writing off real estate and bank buildings, and establishing conservative policies in regard to loans and investments. Yet despite caution and conservatism, there are moderate profits. The groups are deliberate in this policy of conservatism. They believe that cautious management is a blessing to bank stockholders. Moreover, it may be that, if the Federal Deposit Insurance Corporation pursues constructive policies, it eventually will close the more liberal banks, and conservative institutions will inherit their deposits. If the FDIC abandons conservatism and subsidizes liberal banks, the groups will need strength to withstand the eventual crash. No matter what the circumstances, the groups are convinced that their stockholders will benefit from conservative policies and practices.

It takes a bold man to speak with certainty of the future, but in the financial history of the area surrounding the Twin Cities certain significant developments are plainly visible. One is the fact that throughout the territory most capital improvements have been made; those that remain seem to be insignificant in comparison with those already completed and can easily be financed from depreciation funds and current income. The territory will probably never again be so largely dependent upon outside capital for permanent improvements. Then, too, barring confiscatory federal taxation, we may expect that industry, commerce, and farming will continue to produce substantial profits; and that capital, especially commercial and investment capital, will continue to accumulate in the territory. The slackening of local demand and the amassing of a local surplus will widen further the cleft between creditor and debtor systems of banking.

There is no doubt that conservative banks will grow in size and probably in the percentage of total banking assets which they hold. Eventually the group banks will reach their goal in reserves and capital funds. They will cease to dispose of banks and, in more auspicious days, may again pursue a policy of expansion — not, to be sure, the mad snatching of 1929, but a quiet acquisition within the trade territory. There will be no shortage of funds for this purpose, for by that time the groups will have ample capital and generous reserves. The stockholders, unaccustomed to liberal dividends, will not object to a diversion of earnings if they are assured that it is in the best interests of the groups. It does not seem likely that expansion will be extensive territorially, but it might be intensive within the trade area.

The Twin Cities have come a long way since 1851 when they were two raw villages of log cabins and muddy streets, one at the head of navigation on the Mississippi, the other a few miles upstream at the mighty Falls of St. Anthony. Then the territory was a wilderness inhabited only by the wild Indian, the equally wild trapper, the buffalo, and the prairie dog. Now the two villages have fused into one metropolitan center serving a relatively mature era. The region has been developed physically; capital has been accumulated in plenty; a strong financial organization has been forged. Banking has done its best to supply the demands made upon it by farming, industry, and commerce. Its history, a record of efforts to meet these needs, forms but one segment of the general economic and business history of the Northwest.

APPENDICES

APPENDIX 1

THE FIRST NATIONAL BANK OF ST. PAUL

Balance Sheets, 1864 and 1940

APRIL 1, 1864

Loans and Discounts		$ 91,678.65
Indebtedness of the Directors		.00
Overdrafts		19,492.66
Due from Banks and Bankers		15,559.31
Due from National Banks		.00
Specie and other lawful money of the U. S.		95,409.64
Cash Items and Revenue Stamps		26,289.97
Bills of Solvent Banks		1,600.00
Remittances		24,600.03
U. S. Bonds deposited with T. U. S. Circulation		131,000.00
" " " " " " " " other purposes		64,000.00
U. S. Bonds 7/30 Notes and Certfs. of kind on hand		11,041.94
Bills of Suspended Banks		.00
Real Estate		.00
Furniture & Fixtures (Not yet adjusted)		.00
Expense a/c		1,414.64
		$ 482,086.84
Capital [Stock paid in]		$ 184,400.00
Circulating Notes received from Comp't.	$50,000.00	50,000.00
Less circulating notes on hand	13,100.00	
Notes Outstanding	$36,900.00	
Profit & Loss		2,566.50
Due to Banks and Bankers		48,594.31
Due to Individuals & Corporations other than banks		73,983.35
Due to Treasurer of U. S.		26,432.50
Due Deposits on demand		96,110.18
Amount due not included under either of the above heads		.00
		$ 482,086.84

JULY 4, 1864

Loans and Discounts	$ 143,020.16
Current Expenses	2,621.28

APPENDIX 1 (*Continued*)

Remittances and other Cash Items	3,304.47
Due from First National Bank, Milwaukee	2,778.56
" " " " ", Pittsburgh	8.68
" " Fourth " ", New York	15,546.66
" " Second " ", Chicago	239.68
" " Bank of State of Minnesota	3,931.36
" " P. M. Myers & Co., N. Y.	70,769.13
" " Other Banks and Bankers	6,044.71
U. S. Bonds with U. S. Treas. for Cir.	183,000.00
" " " " U. S. Deposits	134,000.00
" " " on hand	77,144.44
Other U. S. Securities	32,270.03
Cash on hand notes of this bank	46,120.00
" " " Other Nat. Banks	820.00
" " " State Banks	10,116.00
Specie	17,140.35
Other lawful money	406,858.07
	$ 1,155,743.58

Capital Stock paid in	$ 250,000.00
Circulating Notes Rec'd from Compt.	164,000.00
Individual Deposits	404,223.66
U. S. Deposits	307,525.90
Due State Banks, Sundry Small Items	2,744.48
" Bank of Stillwater	8,001.19
" Thorne's Bank	4,822.05
" Minneapolis Bank	1,495.63
" Interest	12,930.67
	$ 1,155,743.58

DECEMBER 31, 1940

Cash on hand and Due from Banks	$ 81,803,571.77
U. S. Government Securities	21,157,809.66
Bonds and Securities	4,420,652.63
Loans and Discounts	57,214,326.16
Interest Earned but not Collected	203,552.69
Customers' Liability on Account of Acceptances, Letters of Credit and Foreign Bills	67,098.50
Stock in Federal Reserve Bank	360,000.00
Bank and Office Building	3,000,000.00
	$168,227,011.41

APPENDIX 1 (*Continued*)

Capital Stock	$ 6,000,000.00
Surplus	6,000,000.00
Undivided Profits	1,542,132.72
Unallocated Reserves for Losses	813,575.81
Reserve for Accrued Taxes, Interest and Expenses	621,275.07
Reserve of Manufacturers and Others on Notes purchased from them	573,725.02
Discounts Collected but not Earned	77,921.55
Acceptances, Letters of Credit and Foreign Bills	67,098.50
Deposits	152,531,282.74
	$168,227,011.41

Total money contributed by stockholders through 1940	$ 10,500,000.00
Total dividends paid through 1940	$ 20,337,094.07

APPENDIX 2

THE FIRST NATIONAL BANK OF MINNEAPOLIS

BALANCE SHEETS, 1865, 1872, AND 1940

JANUARY 23, 1865

Resources

Cash on Hand and Due from Banks	$	28,745.47
U. S. Government Bonds		1,500.00
U. S. Government Bonds Deposited with U. S. Treasury		35,000.00
Bond Premium Account		.00
Loans and Discounts		55.00
Bank Building & Other Real Estate		.00
Furniture and Fixtures		.00
Interest Account		772.75
Capital Stock Subscribed but not Paid		6,000.00
Other Assets		27.70
	$	72,100.92

Liabilities

Capital Stock	$	50,000.00
Surplus		.00
Undivided Profits		.96
Circulation Account		.00
Other Liabilities		.00
Deposits		22,099.96
Total Liabilities	$	72,100.92

DECEMBER 31, 1872

Resources

Cash on Hand and Due from Banks	$	119,930.58
U. S. Government Bonds		5,850.00
U. S. Government Bonds Deposited with U. S. Treasury		100,000.00
Bond Premium Account		6,302.91
Loans and Discounts		570,191.48
Bank Building & Other Real Estate		21,608.99
Furniture and Fixtures		3,719.47
Interest Account		.00
Capital Stock Subscribed but not Paid		.00
Other Assets		1,234.51
	$	828,837.94

APPENDIX 2 (*Continued*)

Liabilities

Capital Stock	$ 100,000.00
Surplus	15,585.96
Undivided Profits	26,195.52
Circulation Account	89,500.00
Other Liabilities	.00
Deposits	597,556.46
	$ 828,837.94

DECEMBER 31, 1940

Resources

Cash on Hand and Due from Banks	$ 73,383,077.65
U. S. Government Bonds (Direct or Fully Guaranteed)	51,783,000.00
Guaranty Fund (U. S. Bonds with Commissioner of Banks)	600,000.00
Loans and Discounts	42,598,889.06
Other Bonds and Securities	7,436,357.08
Overdrafts	10,208.30
Bank Buildings	648,633.68
Customers' Acceptance Liability	648,873.25
Bankers' Acceptances Purchased	384,000.00
Interest Earned but not Collected	364,780.43
Total Resources	$177,857,819.45

Liabilities

Capital Stock	$ 6,000,000.00
Surplus	6,000,000.00
Undivided Profits	2,725,473.27
Reserve for Interest, Expenses, Taxes, Etc.	1,039,903.31
Interest Collected but not Earned	169,480.14
Letters of Credit and Acceptances	648,873.25
Deposits	161,274,089.48
Total Liabilities	$177,857,819.45

Total money contributed by stockholders through 1940	$ 11,773,000.00
Total Dividends paid through 1940	$ 24,013,300.84

APPENDIX 3

THE NORTHWESTERN NATIONAL BANK OF MINNEAPOLIS

Balance Sheets, 1872 and 1940

SEPTEMBER 7, 1872

Resources

Cash on Hand	$ 113,200.71
Due from Banks (Jay Cooke & Co., Phila., Pa.)	2,065.33
U. S. Bonds	50,000.00
Bank Building	24,080.22
Furniture & Fixtures	1,881.63
Bond Premium Account	6,437.50
Expense Account	2,299.61
	$ 199,965.00

Liabilities

Capital	$ 152,650.00
Circulation	45,000.00
Individual Deposits	2,315.00
	$ 199,965.00

List of Individual Deposits as of September 7, 1872

William H. Dunwoody	$ 2,315.00

DECEMBER 31, 1940

Resources

Cash and Due from Federal Reserve and other Banks	$ 54,353,267.47
U. S. Government Securities, direct and fully guaranteed	*44,766,628.43
Other Bonds	*11,618,956.66
Loans and Discounts	48,466,135.24
Stock in Federal Reserve Bank in Minneapolis	300,000.00
Customers' Liability on Letters of Credit and Acceptances	38,717.98
Interest Earned but not Collected	336,484.70
Banking House	4,288,000.00
Furniture and Fixtures	.00
Real Estate Owned Other than Banking House	.00
Other Resources	51,613.01
Total Resources	$164,219,803.49

APPENDIX 3 (*Continued*)

Liabilities

Capital Stock — Common	$ 5,000,000.00
Surplus	5,000,000.00
Undivided Profits	954,310.73
Reserve for Contingencies	655,744.64
Total Capital Accounts	$ 11,610,055.37
Reserve for Interest, Taxes and Other Expense	542,363.37
Interest Collected but not Earned	316,467.76
Letters of Credit and Acceptances	38,717.98
Deposits	151,712,199.01
Total Liabilities	$164,219,803.49
Total Dividends paid through 1940	$ 7,237,500.00
Total money contributed by stockholders through 1940	$ 15,114,000.00

* United States Government and other securities carried at $21,841,367.68 are pledged to secure public and trust deposits and for other purposes as required or permitted by law.

APPENDIX 4

THE NORTHWEST BANCORPORATION

Comparative Consolidated Balance Sheets, 1930–1940

(000's omitted)

Assets of Affiliated Banks	*1940*	*1939*	*1938*	*1937*
Cash and Due from Banks	$146,267	$133,495	$127,420	$110,523
U. S. Govt. Obligations	116,947	117,335	114,438	111,230
Other Bonds and Securities	46,151	50,922	47,249	44,669
Stock of Federal Reserve Bank	996	1,007	1,005	......
Loans and Discounts	160,807	147,010	118,768	130,135
Commercial Paper	4,582	4,463	5,141	......
Overdrafts	64	62	56	58
Customer Liability on Accpt.	13	33	24	38
Bank Premises	10,636	10,156	10,255	10,246
Other Real Estate	462	666	1,289	1,358
Int. Earned but not Collected	1,742	1,743	1,570	1,496
Other Assets	268	312	278	382
Assets of Other Companies	893	1,058	1,284	1,286
Assets of Northwest Banco	600	335	275	134
Totals	$490,431	$468,600	$429,053	$411,556
Liabilities				
Demand Deposits	$342,779	$316,968	$280,187	$260,072
Time Deposits	101,251	104,515	104,552	107,144
Total Deposits	444,030	421,483	384,739	367,217
Circulation	......	......	......	......
Letter of Credit	13	33	24	39
Int. Collected but not Earned	1,256	1,078	828	1,040
Other Liabilities	199	590	488	260
Reserve for Taxes, Interest and Expense	1,416	1,245	1,318	1,351
Reserve for Contingencies:				
Banks	1,740	1,559	1,517	1,330
Bancorporation	3,081	2,801	3,220	3,794
Preferred Stock & Debentures	......	5,462	6,085	8,713
Minority Interest	1,472	1,451	1,481	1,460
Capital & Surplus	37,224	32,896	29,353	26,352
Totals	$490,431	$468,600	$429,053	$411,556

APPENDIX 4 (*Continued*)

1936	*1935*	*1934*	*1933*	*1932*	*1931*	*1930*
$111,773	$123,867	$117,783	$ 94,131	$ 70,511	$ 73,971	$110,756
136,636	111,192	131,808	65,615	44,536	46,361	39,850
50,847	45,568	49,657	62,466	72,292	81,254	82,604
......	......	......	......	......	......	......
123,312	112,599	106,599	117,833	147,552	193,939	222,905
......	......	......	......	......	......	......
52	59	45	53	62	156	181
143	260	244	137	185	878	1,007
11,706	11,632	11,162	11,128	12,364	12,030	10,777
......	......	......	......	......	......	......
......	......	......	......	......	......	......
1,967	2,151	3,023	3,293	4,135	4,808	3,785
2,064	2,269	2,083	2,798	932	......	12,775
137	110	199	213	294	5,324	9,843
$438,638	$409,709	$422,604	$357,668	$352,864	$418,721	$494,485
$285,826	$256,574	$248,670	$181,049	$161,221	$198,441	$253,624
107,504	103,807	110,064	109,233	128,989	143,956	156,344
393,331	360,381	358,734	290,282	290,210	342,398	409,965
......	......	7,192	10,555	10,437	6,152	5,900
145	264	250	141	198	882	......
......	......	......	......	......	......	......
1,246	1,299	962	795	4,587	11,803	6,168
2,081	1,821	1,726	1,725	1,601	1,982	2,390
7,200	8,287	15,347	16,774	14,231	3,038	1,136
......	......	......	......	......	......	......
10,048	16,970	24,979	25,534	......	......	......
1,598	1,532	1,565	1,541	2,341	2,611	2,500
22,988	19,155	11,849	10,319	29,259	49,854	66,423
$438,638	$409,709	$422,604	$357,667	$352,864	$418,721	$494,485

APPENDIX 5

THE NORTHWEST BANCORPORATION

Dividends and Market Range of Its Stock, 1929–1940 (Per Share)

Year	*Dividend*	*Market Range*
1940	$ .20	12 – 7¾
1939	.10	11 – 6½
1938	....	8¾– 5
1937	....	16½– 5½
1936	....	14 – 7⅝
1935	....	10¾– 3½
1934	....	6½– 3
1933	....	14 – 3⅛
1932	.80	21⅞– 7
1931	1.80	36⅞–20⅝
1930	1.80	55½–30¾
1929	1.80	100 –50.35

APPENDIX 6

THE FIRST BANK STOCK CORPORATION

COMPARATIVE COMBINED BALANCE SHEETS OF THE MEMBER BANKS, 1930–1940

(000's omitted)

Resources	*1940*	*1939*	*1938*	*1937*
Cash	$189,047	$173,361	$131,541	$114,583
United States Governments	126,430	130,660	145,600	145,329
Other Bonds	24,145	24,890	27,252	29,658
Loans and Discounts	141,066	122,544	104,709	112,174
Overdrafts	45	39	34	54
Customer Liability on Accept.	721	990	890	1,018
Bank Buildings	6,338	7,045	7,900	8,636
Int. Earned but not Collected	1,353	1,314	1,289	1,297
Other Resources	59	84	99	152
Total Resources	$489,205	$460,928	$419,316	$412,899
Liabilities				
Capital	$ 20,295	$ 20,345	$ 20,370	$ 20,550
Surplus	16,224	16,199	16,270	16,197
Undivided Profits	6,719	6,269	5,661	5,028
Preferred Stocks	......	......	......	......
Totals	43,238	42,813	42,301	41,775
Reserves for Contingencies	1,642	1,277	1,129	1,232
Reserves of Man. on Notes	574	590	828	1,032
Accruals	2,031	1,736	1,876	1,870
Deposits	440,981	413,506	372,276	365,954
Letters of Credit & Accept.	721	990	890	1,018
Other Liabilities	18	16	16	18
Circulation	......	......	......	......
Total Liabilities	$489,205	$460,928	$419,316	$412,899

APPENDIX 6 (*Continued*)

1936	*1935*	*1934*	*1933*	*1932*	*1931*	*1930*
$133,906	$112,998	$ 91,726	$ 69,863	$ 69,947	$ 72,084	$ 96,487
159,508	128,474	121,007	80,314	42,722	40,599	57,407
35,671	35,437	53,769	53,356	68,706	89,776	89,289
107,060	137,719	110,170	130,633	145,087	183,803	184,733
41	16	35	22	24	44	72
1,243	2,012	2,812	4,541	1,798	3,635	4,505
9,216	9,810	10,060	11,266	11,446	11,443	8,749
1,493	3,067	3,488	2,301	4,279	......	......
228	377	1,173	568	2,246	5,365	3,596
$448,366	$429,912	$394,239	$352,864	$346,256	$406,747	$444,837
$ 20,640	$ 21,620	$ 20,815	$ 21,305	$ 22,390	$ 22,530	$ 22,960
16,134	15,429	12,081	13,336	14,562	14,810	15,191
4,351	2,794	4,277	2,266	2,469	4,231	4,042
......	250	1,490	......	......	......	......
41,125	40,093	38,663	36,907	39,421	41,571	42,193
1,481	1,122	1,510	1,823	3,122	4,375	4,868
......	......	......	......	......	......	......
1,899	2,916	2,287	2,297	2,613	2,604	2,323
402,524	383,753	337,224	296,325	289,721	348,014	384,814
1,223	2,000	2,709	4,439	1,781	3,661	4,485
115	27	151	43	842	896	737
......	......	11,696	11,030	8,755	5,626	5,417
$448,366	$429,912	$394,239	$352,864	$346,256	$406,747	$444,837

APPENDIX 7

THE FIRST BANK STOCK CORPORATION

Dividends and Market Range of Its Stock, 1929–1940 (Per Share)

Year	*Dividend*	*Market Range*
1940	$ .60	12¾– 9¾
1939	.50	11½– 9⅞
1938	.50	11½– 7¾
1937	.50	17⅛– 9
1936	.45	17 –12
1935	.25	15 – 7⅞
1934	.20	9⅞– 6⅛
1933	.20	14 – 5½
1932	.50	12¾– 6½
1931	1.00	24¼–11⅜
1930	1.00	35½–19¾
1929	1.00[a]	64¾–34¾

[a] Pro forma

APPENDIX 8

THE NORTHWEST BANCORPORATION

List of Members, 1940

Minnesota

Minneapolis:

Northwestern National Bank and Trust Company
(Including Lincoln, North American, and Lake Street Offices)
Second Northwestern State Bank
Third Northwestern National Bank
The Fourth Northwestern National Bank
The Fifth Northwestern National Bank
The Central National Bank
Midland National Bank and Trust Company

Albert Lea: The First National Bank
Appleton: Northwestern State Bank
Austin: Austin State Bank
Dawson: Northwestern State Bank
Dodge Center: Dodge Center State Bank
Duluth: First and American National Bank
Faribault: The Security National Bank and Trust Company
Fergus Falls: Fergus Falls National Bank and Trust Company
Hastings: The Hastings National Bank
Hopkins: Security National Bank
Jordan: Northwestern State Bank
Lake Park: State Bank of Lake Park
Lanesboro: Scanlan-Habberstad Bank and Trust Company
Litchfield: The Northwestern National Bank
Luverne: Rock County Bank
Mankato: The National Citizens Bank
Marshall: The First National Bank
Montevideo: Union State Bank
Moorhead: First National Bank
Northfield: State Bank of Northfield
Ortonville: Northwestern State Bank
Osseo: Farmers State Bank
Owatonna: Security Bank and Trust Company
Red Wing: The First National Bank
St. Paul: The Empire National Bank & Trust Company

APPENDIX 8 (*Continued*)

St. Paul: Northwestern State Bank
Sauk Rapids: Union State Bank
Slayton: The Murray County State Bank
South St. Paul: Stock Yards National Bank
Thief River Falls: Union State Bank
Tracy: Farmers and Merchants State Bank
Two Harbors: First National Bank
Virginia: State Bank of Virginia
Warren: Peoples State Bank
Waterville: The First National Bank
Winona: The First National Bank

North Dakota

Bismarck: The Dakota National Bank and Trust Company
Fargo: The First National Bank and Trust Company
Grafton: The Grafton National Bank
Hillsboro: Northwestern State Bank
Jamestown: The James River National Bank
Maddock: Farmers State Bank
Mandan: The First National Bank
Minot: First National Bank
Napoleon: Stock Growers Bank
Valley City: The American National Bank
Wahpeton: The Citizens National Bank

South Dakota

Aberdeen: First National Bank
(Including branches at Britton, Groton, Milbank, Mobridge, and Redfield)
Rapid City: First National Bank of The Black Hills
(Including branches at Belle Fourche, Deadwood, Hot Springs, Lead, Newell, Spearfish, and Sturgis)
Sioux Falls: Northwest Security National Bank
(Including branches at Brookings, Chamberlain, Dell Rapids, Gregory, Huron, and Madison)
Watertown: The First Citizens National Bank

Montana

Anaconda: Daly Bank and Trust Company
Dillon: The First National Bank

APPENDIX 8 (*Continued*)

GREAT FALLS: The Great Falls National Bank
HARLOWTON: The Continental National Bank
HAVRE: The Hill County State Bank
HELENA: Union Bank and Trust Company
KALISPELL: The First National Bank
LEWISTOWN: Northwestern Bank of Lewistown
MALTA: The First State Bank
ROUNDUP: Miners and Merchants Bank
SHERIDAN: Bank of Sheridan

WISCONSIN

GRANTSBURG: The First National Bank
LA CROSSE: The National Bank of La Crosse
NEW RICHMOND: The First National Bank
PRESCOTT: The First National Bank

NEBRASKA

HASTINGS: The Hastings National Bank
NORFOLK: The National Bank of Norfolk
OMAHA: The United States National Bank
OMAHA: Stock Yards National Bank
OMAHA: The South Omaha Savings Bank

IOWA

DENISON: The First National Bank
DES MOINES: Iowa–Des Moines National Bank and Trust Company
MASON CITY: The First National Bank
MASON CITY: Northwest Savings Bank
SIOUX CITY: The Live Stock National Bank

APPENDIX 9

THE FIRST BANK STOCK CORPORATION

List of Members, 1940

Minnesota

Minneapolis:

- First National Bank and Trust Company
- Bloomington–Lake National Bank
- Hennepin State Bank
- Minnehaha National Bank
- Produce State Bank

Saint Paul:

- First National Bank
- First Trust Company
- Farmers and Merchants State Bank
- First State Bank
- Grand Avenue State Bank
- Security State Bank

Albert Lea: Freeborn County National Bank
Alexandria: Farmers National Bank
Austin: First National Bank
Benson: First State Bank
Blue Earth: First and Farmers National Bank
Brainerd: First National Bank
East Grand Forks: Minnesota National Bank
Fairmont: First National Bank
Graceville: First State Bank
Heron Lake: First National Bank
Ivanhoe: Farmers and Merchants National Bank
Lakefield: Farmers State Bank
Litchfield: State Bank of Litchfield
Little Falls: American National Bank
Luverne: Luverne National Bank
Mankato: First National Bank
Minneota: Farmers and Merchants State Bank
Northfield: Northfield National Bank and Trust Company
Owatonna: First National Bank
Paynesville: First State Bank

APPENDIX 9 (*Continued*)

PIPESTONE: Pipestone National Bank
ROBBINSDALE: Security State Bank
ROCHESTER: First National Bank
SAUK CENTRE: Merchants National Bank
SPRING VALLEY: First National Bank
WASECA: Farmers National Bank
WHEATON: First State Bank
WILLMAR: Security National Bank
WINDOM: First National Bank

MICHIGAN

CALUMET: Branch of National Metals Bank of Hancock
HANCOCK: National Metals Bank
With Branches at Calumet, Ironwood and Laurium
IRONWOOD: Branch of National Metals Bank of Hancock
LAURIUM: Branch of National Metals Bank of Hancock

MONTANA

BILLINGS: Midland National Bank
BOZEMAN: Commercial National Bank
BUTTE: Metals Bank & Trust Company
FORSYTH: Forsyth State Bank
FORT BENTON: Chouteau County Bank
GREAT FALLS: First National Bank
HAVRE: Montana National Bank
HELENA: First National Bank & Trust Company
LEWISTOWN: National Bank of Lewistown
LIVINGSTON: National Park Bank
MILES CITY: First National Bank
MISSOULA: Western Montana National Bank

NORTH DAKOTA

BISMARCK: First National Bank
CANDO: First State Bank
CAVALIER: Merchants and Farmers Bank
COOPERSTOWN: First State Bank
FARGO: Merchants National Bank and Trust Company
GRAND FORKS: Red River National Bank
JAMESTOWN: National Bank of Jamestown
LANGDON: Northwestern Bank

APPENDIX 9 (*Continued*)

LIDGERWOOD: First National Bank
MINOT: Union National Bank
PARK RIVER: First State Bank
ROLLA: Rolette County Bank
VALLEY CITY: First National Bank

SOUTH DAKOTA

ABERDEEN: Aberdeen National Bank & Trust Company
CLARK: Clark County National Bank
GETTYSBURG: Potter County Bank
HIGHMORE: First State Bank
HURON: Branch of National Bank of South Dakota, Sioux Falls
LEMMON: First National Bank
MILLER: First National Bank
SIOUX FALLS: National Bank of South Dakota
With Branches at Huron and Vermillion
VERMILLION: Branch of National Bank of South Dakota, Sioux Falls

APPENDIX 10

THE NINTH FEDERAL RESERVE DISTRICT

Banks, Loans, Investments, Deposits, and Borrowings, 1920–1940

(000's omitted)

Call Dates	*No. of Reporting Banks*	*Loans*	*Investments*	*Deposits*	*Borrowings*
2-28-20	....	$1,492,327	$293,847	$1,855,998	$104,700
5- 4-20	....	1,530,577	277,444	1,825,005	142,743
6-30-20	3,877	1,586,036	263,513	1,785,604	171,420
9- 8-20	....	1,561,632	269,877	1,765,502	189,233
11-15-20	....	1,563,987	274,222	1,748,181	199,768
12-29-20	3,875	1,514,463	270,640	1,654,958	195,985
2-21-21	....	1,435,609	268,565	1,566,217	176,360
4-28-21	....	1,413,662	261,971	1,539,862	174,461
6-30-21	3,856	1,424,790	262,944	1,539,519	188,685
9- 6-21	....	1,401,845	260,072	1,525,713	187,787
12-31-21	3,826	1,356,165	252,446	1,512,229	153,776
3-10-22	....	1,324,987	264,323	1,561,235	130,037
5- 5-22	....	1,319,238	270,807	1,546,997	127,402
6-30-22	3,810	1,326,760	284,037	1,582,414	128,545
9-15-22	....	1,341,324	291,359	1,620,994	123,556
12-29-22	3,793	1,327,665	304,876	1,658,436	105,321
4- 3-23	3,747	1,322,211	322,122	1,711,436	88,173
6-30-23	3,730	1,321,536	332,545	1,687,457	97,407
9-14-23	3,678	1,319,334	329,604	1,689,881	98,730
12-31-23	3,507	1,255,271	342,445	1,666,935	75,445
3-31-24	3,349	1,194,105	342,494	1,629,527	56,134
6-30-24	3,256	1,138,316	337,709	1,593,656	55,601
10-10-24	3,240	1,146,276	371,836	1,715,109	39,895
12-31-24	3,223	1,128,056	428,885	1,781,068	23,617
4- 6-25	3,177	1,099,318	459,221	1,747,722	20,248
6-30-25	3,133	1,090,221	465,642	1,724,747	23,056
9-28-25	3,125	1,098,600	471,625	1,758,985	22,873
12-31-25	3,057	1,066,175	492,148	1,759,718	15,711
4-12-26	2,995	1,044,292	504,208	1,714,930	16,138
6-30-26	2,928	1,026,051	507,503	1,682,203	17,234
12-31-26	2,756	985,950	503,899	1,654,612	14,780
3-23-27	2,720	958,601	528,099	1,620,633	15,858
6-30-27	2,679	948,102	527,289	1,615,216	15,631
10-10-27	2,657	971,308	539,013	1,710,545	11,143
12-31-27	2,613	946,242	580,804	1,700,622	8,009
2-28-28	2,593	939,179	589,833	1,688,042	9,195
6-30-28	2,555	940,212	600,191	1,677,259	14,938
10- 3-28	2,536	949,996	602,265	1,722,114	19,671
12-31-28	2,497	949,594	602,273	1,723,207	9,492

APPENDIX 10 (*Continued*)

Call Dates	*No. of Reporting Banks*	*Loans*	*Investments*	*Deposits*	*Borrowings*
3-27-29	2,468	951,505	608,097	1,670,418	19,110
6-29-29	2,411	944,051	592,318	1,650,800	19,060
10- 4-29	2,383	985,241	591,588	1,678,205	44,656
12-31-29	2,353	934,824	570,361	1,634,204	17,710
3-27-30	2,293	913,506	572,821	1,592,496	7,384
6-30-30	2,247	872,619	580,362	1,598,024	10,635
9-24-30	2,197	855,653	582,271	1,586,524	10,964
12-31-30	2,118	836,291	557,289	1,547,457	10,472
3-25-31	2,089	821,577	561,579	1,538,151	9,104
6-30-31	2,021	799,175	563,669	1,510,387	10,607
9-29-31	1,916	746,955	553,978	1,396,912	10,375
12-31-31	1,816	699,707	520,084	1,309,669	14,262
6-30-32	1,756	628,004	508,172	1,181,157	26,954
9-30-32	1,717	597,599	485,201	1,113,318	31,078
12-31-32	1,658	560,225	451,972	1,088,907	30,479
6-30-33	1,467	462,370	429,638	1,008,911	12,478
10-25-33	1,461	464,895	442,784	993,638	8,845
12-30-33	1,448	437,508	445,098	1,013,257	6,601
3- 5-34	1,449	421,172	480,333	1,051,372	3,993
6-30-34	1,444	405,312	525,963	1,092,725	1,266
10-17-34	1,446	398,794	552,478	1,161,721	625
12-31-34	1,432	375,388	581,847	1,197,718	331
3- 4-35	1,425	371,148	592,028	1,207,657	524
6-29-35	1,416	385,176	572,923	1,244,737	451
11- 1-35	1,407	430,504	569,329	1,284,301	356
12-31-35	1,407	431,997	584,410	1,306,333	179
3- 4-36	1,404	415,925	578,674	1,295,704	217
6-30-36	1,404	397,757	632,242	1,372,005	130
12-31-36	1,387	414,918	680,700	1,425,417	58
3-31-37	1,367	415,092	667,318	1,384,181	65
6-30-37	1,367	431,370	663,731	1,396,861	121
12-31-37	1,360	454,321	637,940	1,375,949	320
3- 7-38	1,348	436,143	649,338	1,363,272	139
6-30-38	1,347	436,806	610,910	1,378,011	208
9-28-38	1,338	442,101	621,649	1,368,213	199
12-31-38	1,327	447,204	630,168	1,403,956	303
3-29-39	1,322	445,496	624,715	1,385,092	124
6-30-39	1,312	462,476	608,479	1,429,293	58
10- 2-39	1,307	503,410	604,437	1,488,198	75
12-30-39	1,305	526,498	590,585	1,519,188	178
3-26-40	1,300	537,039	586,737	1,518,570	37
6-29-40	1,291	543,338	567,573	1,130,100	154
12-31-40	1,288	609,494	565,436	1,628,951	246

APPENDIX 11

THE NINTH FEDERAL RESERVE DISTRICT

Bank Failures, 1920–1940

Year	*Number of Banks*	*Number of Failures*	*Number of Reopenings*
1920	3875	35	1
1921	3826	73	15
1922	3793	64	31
1923	3507	279	19
1924	3223	295	33
1925	3057	168	26
1926	2756	283	55
1927	2613	142	44
1928	2497	94	12
1929	2353	84	7
1930	2118	157	8
1931	1816	271	25
1932	1658	135	14
1933	1448	235	14
1934	1432	7	5
1935	1407	...	3
1936	1387	4	..
1937	1360	16	..
1938	1327	22	..
1939	1305	5	..
1940	1288	3	..

NOTES AND REFERENCES

CHAPTER I

1. Isaac Atwater, *History of the City of Minneapolis* (New York, 1893), pp. 21–22.
2. William Watts Folwell, *Minnesota, The North Star State* (Boston, 1908), p. 90.
3. Marion Daniel Shutter, editor, *History of Minneapolis* (Chicago, 1923), p. 262.
4. Henry A. Castle, *History of St. Paul and Vicinity* (Chicago, 1912), vol. i, p. 61.
5. Shutter, *op. cit.*, p. 85.
6. *Ibid.*, pp. 82–83.
7. *Loc. cit.*
8. *Ibid.*, p. 84.
9. Atwater, *op. cit.*, p. 529.
10. Mildred L. Hartsough, *The Twin Cities as a Metropolitan Market* (Minneapolis, 1925), p. 31.
11. Atwater, *op. cit.*, p. 581.
12. Shutter, *op. cit.*, p. 354.
13. *Ibid.*, p. 362.
14. *Loc. cit.*
15. *Ibid.*, p. 358.
16. Hartsough, *op. cit.*, p. 72.
17. J. F. Williams, *History of St. Paul* (St. Paul, 1876), pp. 44, 173.
18. Hartsough, *op. cit.*, p. 73.
19. *Ibid.*, p. 77.
20. William Watts Folwell, *The Five Million Loan*, Minnesota Historical Society Collections (St. Paul, 1915), vol. xv, p. 190.
21. *Statutes at Large*, II: 195, 197; 34th Congress, 3rd Session, *Senate Journal*, 205, 313 (Serial 873); *House Journal*, 619–625 (Serial 892); *Congressional Globe*, 613, 626, 699, 973, 1068–1069, 1072.
22. Folwell, *The Five Million Loan*, p. 190.
23. William Watts Folwell, *A History of Minnesota* (St. Paul, 1924), vol. ii, p. 41.
24. *Ibid.*, p. 42.
25. *Ibid.*, p. 43.
26. *Constitution of Minn.*, Art. 9, sec. 5, 10.
27. Folwell, *The Five Million Loan*, pp. 195–196.
28. *Ibid.*, p. 196.
29. *Ibid.*, pp. 200, 202.
30. *General Laws* (Minn.), 1858, p. 303.
31. Folwell, *A History of Minnesota*, vol. ii, pp. 52–53.
32. *Ibid.*, p. 58.
33. *General Laws* (Minn.), 1860, p. 297.
34. Folwell, *A History of Minnesota*, vol. ii, pp. 57–58.
35. Colonel William Crooks, *The First Railroad in Minnesota*, Minnesota Historical Society Collections (St. Paul, 1905), vol. x, part 1, p. 448.
36. Joseph A. A. Burnquist, editor, *Minnesota and Its People* (Chicago, 1924), vol. i, p. 544.
37. Hartsough, *op. cit.*, p. 87.

38. Horace B. Hudson, editor, *A Half Century of Minneapolis* (Minneapolis, 1908), pp. 59 ff.

39. Charles Byron Kuhlmann, *The Development of The Flour Milling Industry in the United States* (Boston, 1929), p. 152.

40. Hartsough, *op. cit.*, p. 60.

41. *Loc. cit.*

42. *Ibid.*, p. 55.

43. *Loc. cit.; Minneapolis City Directory*, 1900, p. 1484.

44. *Ibid.*, 1883–1884, pp. 430, 434; 1888–1889, p. 952.

45. Hartsough, *op. cit.*, p. 40.

46. *Thirteenth Census of the United States*, 1910, vol. ix, p. 594.

47. Hartsough, *op. cit.*, p. 69.

48. *St. Paul City Directory*, 1883–1884, p. 703.

49. *Ibid.*, 1889–1890, p. 1309; 1892, p. 1385.

50. Hartsough, *op. cit.*, p. 67.

51. *Ibid.*, p. 52.

52. *The Minneapolis City Directory* of 1901 lists four automobile dealers in its classified section, p. 1440.

53. Folwell, *Minnesota, The North Star State*, p. 98.

54. Edward Van Dyke Robinson, *Early Economic Condition of Agriculture in Minnesota* (Minneapolis, 1915), p. 45.

55. *Loc. cit.*

56. Hartsough, *op. cit.*, p. 173.

57. William H. Budd, *History of Martin County, Minnesota* (Fairmont, 1897), p. 1.

58. Folwell, *A History of Minnesota*, vol. iv, pp. 16–18.

59. *Ibid.*, p. 333.

60. *Loc. cit.*

61. *Thirteenth Census of the United States*, 1910, vol. i, p. 30.

62. Doane Robinson, *A Brief History of South Dakota* (New York, 1905), p. 115.

63. *Ibid.*, p. 220.

64. *Ibid.*, p. 150.

65. *A South Dakota Guide* (Pierre, 1938), pp. 118–119.

66. *Thirteenth Census*, 1910, vol. i, p. 30.

67. Hubert Howe Bancroft, *History of Washington, Idaho and Montana, 1845–1889* (San Francisco, 1890), p. 601.

68. C. A. Lounsberry, *History of Montana*, History of the Great Northwest (Minneapolis, 1901), p. 74.

69. Bancroft, *op. cit.*, p. 616.

70. *Twelfth Census*, 1900, vol. x, p. 139.

71. Bancroft, *op. cit.*, p. 732.

72. *Ibid.*, p. 736.

73. *Ibid.*, p. 753.

74. *Twelfth Census*, 1900, vol. vi, p. 843.

75. *Thirteenth Census*, 1910, vol. v, p. 71.

76. *Fourteenth Census*, 1920, vol. vii, p. 200.

77. *Thirteenth Census*, 1910, vol. i, p. 30.

CHAPTER II

1. Sidney A. Patchin, *The Development of Banking in Minnesota*, Minnesota Historical Society Collection (St. Paul, 1917), vol. ii, p. 116.
2. *Ibid.*, p. 124.
3. *Loc. cit.*
4. St. Paul *Pioneer Press*, Aug. 18, 1875.
5. Castle, *History of St. Paul and Vicinity*, vol. i, p. 289.
6. Pamphlet, *Merchants National Bank* (St. Paul, 1922), p. 17.
7. *Ibid.*, p. 18.
8. Shutter, *History of Minneapolis*, p. 287.
9. *Loc. cit.*
10. General C. C. Andrews, editor, *History of St. Paul, Minnesota* (Syracuse, N. Y., 1890), pp. 374–375.
11. Shutter, *op. cit.*, p. 288.
12. *Loc. cit.*
13. *Loc. cit.*
14. Pamphlet, *75 Years of Service, First National Bank and Trust Company of Minneapolis* (Minneapolis, 1939), p. 4.
15. Ms. Historical Files, First National Bank, Minneapolis. Note on founders of bank, undated.
16. Shutter, *op. cit.*, p. 287.
17. *Ibid.*, p. 288.
18. On Oct. 22, 1857, H. C. Sandford, assignee of Borup and Oakes, ordered filing of proofs of claim. St. Paul *Pioneer and Democrat*, Oct. 24, 1857.
19. Castle, *op. cit.*, p. 291.
20. Hartsough, *The Twin Cities as a Metropolitan Market*, p. 115.
21. *General Laws* (Minn.), 1858, pp. 69, 81.
22. Castle, *op. cit.*, p. 291.
23. *Loc. cit.*
24. Ms. Record Book (in files of the bank). Manual of Progress of the First National Bank of St. Paul.
25. *Loc. cit.*
26. *Loc. cit.*
27. *Loc. cit.*
28. *Loc. cit.*
29. *Loc. cit.*
30. *Loc. cit.*
31. Castle, *op. cit.*, p. 293.
32. *Ibid.*, p. 292.
33. *Loc. cit.*
34. *Loc. cit.*
35. *Merchants National Bank*, p. 18.
36. *Loc. cit.*
37. Shutter, *op. cit.*, p. 288.
38. *75 Years of Service*, p. 5.
39. *Loc. cit.*
40. Ms. Notes, First National Bank, Minneapolis, Dec. 15, 1864.
41. *75 Years of Service*, p. 7.

42. Ms. Historical File, First National Bank, Minneapolis, Statements, Oct. 1, 1877, and July 1, 1885.

43. *Ibid.*, Dividend Record.

44. Shutter, *op. cit.*, p. 297.

45. *Loc. cit.*

46. *Loc. cit.*

47. *The Book of Minnesotans* (Chicago, 1907), p. 303.

48. Ms. Cumulative Record Book, Northwestern National Bank, Minneapolis, p. 2.

49. *Ibid.*, p. 3.

50. *Ibid.*, p. 1.

51. *Loc. cit.*

52. *Loc. cit.*

53. Pamphlet, *Northwestern National Bank, 60 Years as a Citizen of Minneapolis* (Minneapolis, 1932), p. 6.

54. Ms. Cumulative Record Book, Northwestern National Bank, p. 7.

55. Shutter, *op. cit.*, p. 294.

56. Ms. Cumulative Record Book, Northwestern National Bank, p. 8.

57. *Merchants National Bank*, p. 6.

58. *Ibid.*, pp. 8, 12.

59. *Ibid.*, p. 12.

60. *Ibid.*, p. 18.

61. Shutter, *op. cit.*, p. 298.

62. *Loc. cit.*

63. Budd, *History of Martin County, Minnesota*, p. 98.

64. *Ibid.*, p. 100.

65. The writer's grandfather paid 12 per cent on bank loans in Fairmont.

66. Budd, *op. cit.*, p. 106.

67. *Loc. cit.*

68. Information concerning Lidgerwood has been obtained from Miss Mary O. Movius of Lidgerwood.

69. *Report of the Comptroller of the Currency* (Washington, 1901), vol. ii, p. 885.

70. *Loc. cit.*

71. *The Book of Minnesotans*, p. 413.

72. *Loc. cit.*

73. *Loc. cit.*

74. Shutter, *op. cit.*, p. 293.

75. *Ibid.*, p. 294.

76. Pamphlet, *The Security National Bank* (Minneapolis, 1908), p. 1. (In files of First National Bank, Minneapolis.)

77. *Loc. cit.*

78. *Who's Who in America 1940–1941* (Chicago, 1940), p. 546.

79. *Loc. cit.*

80. *Mpls. City Directory*, 1880–1881, p. 87.

81. Shutter, *op. cit.*, p. 299.

82. Ms. Cumulative Record Book, Northwestern National Bank, p. 14.

83. *Ibid.*, p. 16.

84. *Ibid.*, p. 19.

85. *The Book of Minnesotans*, p. 121.

86. *75 Years of Service*, p. 11.

87. Ms. Cumulative Record Book, Northwestern National Bank, p. 21.

88. *Ibid.*, p. 22.

89. Ms. Stockholders Subscription Book. (In files of First National Bank of Minneapolis.)

90. *Ibid.*

91. *75 Years of Service*, p. 9.

92. *Ibid.*, p. 11.

93. Ms. Notes, First National Bank, Minneapolis, July 15, 1894; Apr. 5, 1895.

94. *75 Years of Service*, p. 13.

95. *Ibid.*, p. 26.

96. *Ibid.*, p. 13.

97. Ms. Cumulative Record Book, Northwestern National Bank, p. 37.

98. *Ibid.*, p. 40.

99. *Loc. cit.*

100. *Ibid.*, p. 41.

101. *Ibid.*, p. 43.

102. *Loc. cit.*

103. *Ibid.*, p. 45.

104. Manual of Progress.

105. Joseph Gilpin Pyle, *The Life of James J. Hill* (Garden City, N. Y., 1917), vol. ii, p. 309.

106. *Loc. cit.*

107. Ms. Notes, First National Bank, Minneapolis, Apr. 28, 1913.

108. A trust agreement dated May 5, 1913, placed the Minneapolis Trust Company stock with trustees, and the pro rata interest thereon was endorsed on the stock of the First National Bank.

109. Ms. Notes, First National Bank, Minneapolis, Mar. 19, 1915.

110. *Loc. cit.*

111. Ms. Letter, F. A. Chamberlain to stockholders of Security National Bank, Mar. 20, 1915.

CHAPTER III

1. Pamphlet, *Comparative Bank Deposits, Minnesota, North Dakota, South Dakota and Montana for the Past Twenty Years* (Minneapolis, 1920), p. 2.

2. *Loc. cit.*

3. *Rand McNally Bankers Directory* (Chicago, 1921), pp. 673, 1049, 1301, 849.

4. Pamphlet, Curtis L. Mosher, *The Causes of Banking Failures in the Northwestern States* (Minneapolis, 1930), p. 28.

5. *Loc. cit.*

6. *Rand McNally*, 1921, pp. 1052, 1061.

7. *Ibid.*, p. 1323.

8. *Ibid.*, p. 852.

9. *Report of the Comptroller of the Currency*, 1920, vol. i, p. 246.

10. *Loc. cit.*

11. *Loc. cit.*

12. *Loc. cit.*

13. Federal Reserve Act, Dec. 23, 1913, sect. 24.

14. Ms. Report on Farmers Bank. (All items are found in file in possession of the First National Bank of Minneapolis.)

15. *Loc. cit.*

16. *Ibid.*

17. *Ibid.*

18. *Ibid.*

19. *Ibid.*

20. *Ibid.*

21. *Ibid.*

22. *Ibid.*

23. *Ibid.*

24. *Ibid.*

25. *Ibid.*

26. Ms. Report on the bank in question. (All items are in file in possession of the First National Bank of Minneapolis.)

27. *Loc. cit.*

28. *Loc. cit.*

29. *Idem*, Financial statement, May 30, 1915.

30. *Idem*, List of certificates of deposit, Jan. 18, 1918.

31. *Idem*, Comparative financial statements.

32. *Idem*, letter dated May 7, 1917.

33. *Idem*, letter dated Nov. 16, 1914.

34. *Idem*, letter dated Dec. 14, 1918.

35. *Idem*, letter dated Jan. 18, 1919.

36. *Idem*, Report dated Apr. 30, 1920.

37. *Idem*, Statements, Oct., 1915; Sept., 1916; Sept., 1917; Nov., 1918; Sept., 1919; Dec., 1920; and Oct., 1921.

38. These companies' advertisements appeared in *Commercial West*.

39. Ms. Balance sheet of Ulland, Mealey, Carley Company, dated Sept. 30, 1919.

40. *Ibid.*, Feb. 7, 1920.

41. This is a statement of an officer of the company and is confirmed by an examination of its ledgers.

42. The ledger shows that on Sept. 17, 1921, its bank stocks were disposed of and its notes and accounts receivable increased sharply.

43. Ms. Letter dated Nov. 23, 1931.

44. Ms. Theodore Albrecht, Historical Data Relating to the Union Investment Company (unpublished, dated Apr. 16, 1940), in files of Northwest Bancorporation, p. 1.

45. Statement of Mr. Theodore Albrecht.

46. Albrecht, Historical Data, p. 1.

47. *Loc. cit.*

48. *Ibid.*, p. 4

49. *Ibid.*, p. 5.

50. *Ibid.*, p. 11.

51. *Thirty-Sixth Annual Report of the Chamber of Commerce*, Minneapolis, Dec., 1918, p. 85.

52. The government set a fair price for No. 1 dark Northern wheat in Minneapolis of $2.21 a bushel. It purchased all wheat offered at this price and later sold it. The price was held down but not absolutely fixed. It sold at $3.25 a bushel in Jan., 1920.

53. Ivan Wright, *Bank Credit and Agriculture* (New York, 1922), p. 178.
54. *Yearbook of the U. S. Department of Agriculture* (Washington, D. C., 1919, 1921), 1918, p. 465; 1920, p. 554.
55. *Commercial West*, vol. 37, no. 4 (Jan. 24, 1920), p. 7.
56. *Loc. cit.*
57. *Yearbook of U. S. Dept. of Agric.*, 1918, p. 453; 1920, p. 539.
58. *Statistical Abstract of the United States* (Washington, D. C., 1922), 1921, pp. 144–145.
59. *Ibid.*, p. 148.
60. Mosher, *op. cit.*, p. 29.
61. *Loc. cit.*
62. *Loc. cit.*
63. Statement of Lyman E. Wakefield in *Branch, Chain and Group Banking*, Hearing before the Committee on Banking and Currency, 71st Congress, Second Session, H. R. 141 (Washington, 1930), vol. i, p. 883.
64. *History of Wages in the United States from Colonial Times to 1928*, U. S. Dept. of Labor, Bureau of Labor Statistics, No. 499 (Washington, 1929), pp. 227, 229.
65. Alvin S. Tostlebe, *The Bank of North Dakota: An Experiment in Agrarian Banking* (New York, 1924), p. 20.
66. *Ibid.*, p. 21.
67. Thomas Bruce Robb, *The Guaranty of Bank Deposits* (Boston, 1921), p. 172.
68. *Ibid.*, p. 173.
69. *Ibid.*, p. 174.
70. *Commercial West*, vol. 37, no. 1 (Jan. 3, 1920), p. 49.
71. Robb, *op. cit.*, p. 164.
72. *Ibid.*, p. 163.
73. *Commercial West*, vol. 38, no. 23 (Dec. 11, 1920), p. 41.
74. Tostlebe, *op. cit.*, p. 69.
75. *Commercial West*, vol. 37, no. 8 (Feb. 21, 1920), p. 42.
76. *Loc. cit.*
77. *Loc. cit.*
78. Tostlebe, *op. cit.*, p. 97.
79. *Loc. cit.*
80. *Loc. cit.*
81. *Ibid.*, p. 104.
82. *Ibid.*, p. 139.
83. *Commercial West*, vol. 38, no. 24 (Dec. 11, 1920), p. 40.
84. Tostlebe, *op. cit.*, p. 131.
85. *Loc. cit.*
86. *Ibid.*, p. 132.
87. *Ibid.*, p. 116.
88. *Commercial West*, vol. 37, no. 2 (Jan. 10, 1920), p. 52.
89. *Loc. cit.*
90. U. S. Dept. of Agric., Circular no. 101, Dec., 1929, p. 11.
91. *Commercial West*, vol. 37, no. 2 (Jan. 10, 1920), p. 11.
92. *Ibid.*, vol. 37, no. 1 (Jan. 3, 1920), p. 18.
93. *Ibid.*, vol. 37, no. 2 (Jan. 10, 1920), p. 11.
94. *Ibid.*, no. 3 (Jan. 17, 1920), p. 14.
95. *Ibid.*, no. 5 (Jan. 31, 1920), p. 20.
96. Wakefield, in *Branch, Chain and Group Banking*, p. 884.

97. *Commercial West*, vol. 38, no. 11 (Sept. 11, 1920), p. 18.

98. Federal Reserve Bank of Minneapolis, *Monthly Report of Crop and Business Conditions*, vol. i, no. 62 (Apr., 1920), p. 1.

99. *Ibid.*, no. 60 (Feb., 1920), p. 1.

100. *Ibid.*, no. 62 (Apr., 1920), p. 1.

101. Mosher, *op. cit.*, p. 10.

102. *Commercial West*, vol. 38, no. 11 (Sept. 11, 1920), p. 18.

103. Fed. Res. Bank of Mpls., *Monthly Report*, vol. i, no. 68 (Oct., 1920), p. 3.

104. *Commercial West*, vol. 38, no. 4 (July 24, 1920), p. 7.

105. *Fifty-Seventh Ann. Rep. of Ch. of Com.* (Minneapolis, 1939), p. 18.

106. *Commercial West*, vol. 38, no. 11 (Sept. 11, 1920), p. 51.

107. *Ibid.*, vol. 37, no. 25 (June 19, 1920), p. 55.

108. *Ibid.*, vol. 38, no. 12 (Sept. 18, 1920), p. 48.

109. *Fifty-Seventh Ann. Rep. of Ch. of Com.*, p. 18.

110. Fed. Res. Bank of Mpls., *Monthly Report*, vol. i, no. 69 (Nov., 1920), p. 2.

111. E. A. Goldenweiser, *Federal Reserve System in Operation* (New York, 1925), p. 30.

112. *Ibid.*, p. 5.

113. *Ibid.*, p. 35.

114. Ms. Statements, First National Bank, Minneapolis, Sept. 12, 1919, and Nov. 15, 1920.

115. Ms. Statements, Northwestern National Bank, Minneapolis, Sept. 12, 1919, and Nov. 15, 1920.

116. *Commercial West*, vol. 38, no. 11 (Sept. 11, 1920), p. 18.

117. *Loc. cit.*

118. Goldenweiser, *op. cit.*, p. 4.

119. *Commercial West*, vol. 38, no. 2 (July 10, 1920), p. 11.

120. Mosher, *op. cit.*, p. 30.

121. *Commercial West*, vol. 37, no. 4 (Jan. 24, 1920), p. 14.

122. Ms. Statements, First National Bank, Minneapolis, Sept. 12, 1919, and Nov. 15, 1920.

123. Ms. Statements, Northwestern National Bank, Minneapolis, Sept. 12, 1919, and Nov. 15, 1920.

CHAPTER IV

1. *Commercial West*, vol. 39, no. 1 (Jan. 1, 1921), p. 20.

2. *Ibid.*, vol. 37, no. 25 (June 19, 1920), p. 55.

3. Fed. Res. Bank of Mpls., *Monthly Report*, vol. ii, no. 82 (Nov. 28, 1921), p. 102.

4. *Ibid.*, no. 78 (July 29, 1921), p. 61.

5. *Ibid.*, vol. iii, no. 136 (May 28, 1926), p. 233.

6. *Ibid.*, vol. ii, no. 76 (May 27, 1921), pp. 11–12.

7. *Ibid.*, no. 92 (Sept. 28, 1922), p. 177.

8. *Ibid.*, p. 175.

9. *Ibid.*, no. 105 (Oct. 29, 1923), p. 287.

10. *Ibid.*, no. 84 (Jan. 31, 1922), p. 128; *History of Wages in United States to 1928*, p. 227.

11. Fed. Res. Bank of Mpls., *Monthly Report*, vol. iii, no. 115 (Aug. 28, 1924), p. 57.

12. *Ibid.*, no. 117 (Oct. 28, 1924), p. 81.

13. Ms. Letter dated May 10, 1920. Unless otherwise specified, correspondence between the First National Bank of Minneapolis and country banks has been taken as it appears in their files.

14. *Ibid.*, Aug. 25, 1920.

15. *Ibid.*, Aug. 30, 1920.

16. *Ibid.*, Dec. 1, 1920.

17. *Ibid.*, Dec. 10, 1920.

18. *Ibid.*, Dec. 23, 1920.

19. *Ibid.*, Dec. 27, 1920.

20. Financial statements dated May 4, 1920, and Apr. 15, 1921.

21. Ms. letter dated Aug. 5, 1921.

22. *Ibid.*, Oct. 12, 1921.

23. Memorandum dated Apr. 24, 1922.

24. Ms. Letter dated Nov. 29, 1922.

25. *Ibid.*, Dec. 2, 1922.

26. *Ibid.*, July 30, 1923.

27. *Ibid.*, financial statements dated May 4, 1920, Sept. 6, 1921, and July 30, 1923.

28. Fed. Res. Bank of Mpls., *Monthly Report*, vol. iv, no. 164 (Sept. 29, 1928), p. 164.

29. *Ibid.*, vol. i, no. 69 (Nov. 28, 1920), p. 192.

30. *Commercial West*, vol. 39, no. 25 (June 18, 1921), p. 35.

31. *Ibid.*, vol. 40, no. 3 (July 16, 1921), p. 10.

32. Tostlebe, *The Bank of North Dakota*, p. 203.

33. *Commercial West*, vol. 40, no. 19 (Nov. 5, 1921), p. 7.

34. *Ibid.*, no. 12 (Sept. 17, 1921), p. 32.

35. Fed. Res. Bank of Mpls., *Monthly Report*, vol. ii, no. 82 (Nov. 28, 1921), p. 112.

36. Tostlebe, *op. cit.*, p. 205.

37. *Commercial West*, vol. 40, no. 26 (Dec. 24, 1921), p. 14.

38. *Ibid.*, vol. 39, no. 5 (Jan. 29, 1921), p. 39.

39. *Ibid.*, vol. 40, no. 20 (Nov. 12, 1921), p. 11.

40. *Ibid.*, vol. 44, no. 8 (Aug. 25, 1923), p. 10.

41. Mosher, *The Causes of Banking Failure*, p. 13.

42. Fed. Res. Bank of Mpls., *Monthly Report*, vol. iii, no. 133 (Feb. 27, 1926), p. 209.

43. Tostlebe, *op. cit.*, p. 21.

44. *Commercial West*, vol. 43, no. 10 (Mar. 10, 1923), p. 7.

45. Fed. Res. Bank of Mpls., *Monthly Report*, vol. iii, no. 133 (Feb. 27, 1926), p. 209.

46. *Commercial West*, vol. 45, no. 8 (Feb. 23, 1924), p. 14.

47. *Ibid.*, no. 9 (March 1, 1924), p. 10.

48. *Ibid.*, vol. 47, no. 5 (Jan. 31, 1925), p. 11.

49. Fed. Res. Bank of Mpls., *Monthly Report*, vol. iii, no. 117 (Oct. 28, 1924), p. 85.

50. *Loc. cit.*

51. *Loc. cit.*

52. *Commercial West*, vol. 46, no. 22 (Nov. 29, 1924), p. 10.

53. *Ibid.*, vol. 48, no. 11 (Sept. 12, 1925), p. 10.

54. *Ibid.*, vol. 47, no. 2 (Jan. 10, 1925), p. 8.
55. *Loc. cit.*
56. *Ibid.*, vol. 46, no. 22 (Nov. 29, 1924), p. 10; vol. 49, no. 3 (Jan. 16, 1926), p. 10.
57. Fed. Res. Bank of Mpls., *Monthly Report*, vol. iii, no. 133 (Feb. 27, 1926), p. 209.
58. *Ibid.*, vol. iv, no. 169 (Jan. 29, 1929), p. 194.
59. *Ibid.*, vol. iii, no. 117 (Oct. 28, 1924), p. 85.
60. *Commercial West*, vol. 38, no. 24 (Dec. 11, 1920), p. 41.
61. *Ibid.*, vol. 41, no. 16 (Apr. 22, 1922), p. 36.
62. *Ibid.*, vol. 40, no. 4 (July 23, 1921), p. 36.
63. *Loc. cit.*
64. *Ibid.*, vol. 40, no. 9 (Aug. 27, 1921), p. 38.
65. *Ibid.*, vol. 39, no. 9 (Feb. 26, 1921), p. 38; vol. 42, no. 27 (Dec. 30, 1922), p. 11.
66. *Ibid.*, vol. 45, no. 20 (May 17, 1924), p. 8.
67. *Ibid.*, vol. 43, no. 25 (June 23, 1923), p. 36.
68. *Ibid.*, vol. 45, no. 1 (Jan. 5, 1924), p. 36.
69. *Loc. cit.*
70. *Ibid.*, vol. 46, no. 17 (Oct. 25, 1924), p. 36.
71. *Ibid.*, vol. 48, no. 2 (July 11, 1924), p. 37.
72. *Ibid.*, no. 10 (Sept. 5, 1925), p. 7.
73. *Ibid.*, vol. 50, no. 7 (Aug. 14, 1926), p. 20.
74. *Ibid.*, vol. 48, no. 10 (Sept. 5, 1925), p. 8.
75. *Ibid.*, vol. 56, no. 19 (Nov. 16, 1929), p. 13.
76. *Loc. cit.*
77. *Ibid.*, vol. 48, no. 11 (Sept. 12, 1925), p. 10.
78. Statement of J. Cameron Thomson in *Operation of the National and Federal Reserve Banking System*, Hearings before a Sub-committee of the Committee on Banking and Currency, 71st Congress, 3d Session, S. R. 71 (Washington, D. C., 1931), part 4, p. 563.
79. Russell A. Stevenson, editor, *A Type Study of American Banking* (Minneapolis, 1934), p. 12.
80. Fed. Res. Bank of Mpls., *Monthly Report*, vol. iii, no. 128 (Sept. 29, 1925), p. 165.
81. Mosher, *op. cit.*, p. 14.
82. *Commercial West*, vol. 49, no. 14 (Apr. 3, 1926), p. 9.
83. *Ibid.*, vol. 48, no. 1 (July 4, 1924), p. 8.
84. *Loc. cit.*
85. Fed. Res. Bank of Mpls., *Monthly Report*, vol. iii, no. 141 (Oct. 29, 1926), pp. 272–273.
86. *Ibid.*, vol. iv, no. 159 (Apr. 28, 1928), p. 23.
87. *Ibid.*, vol. v, no. 183 (Mar. 28, 1930), p. 20.
88. Mosher, *op. cit.*, p. 30.

CHAPTER V

1. *Rand McNally Bankers Directory*, 1921, p. 738.
2. Fed. Res. Bank of Mpls., *Monthly Report*, vol. ii, no. 106 (Nov. 28, 1923), p. 4.

3. *Ibid.*, no. 76 (May 27, 1921), p. 10.
4. *Ibid.*, Special Report, Jan. 31, 1922, p. 10.
5. *Loc. cit.*
6. *Loc. cit.*
7. *Loc. cit.*
8. *Loc. cit.*
9. For instance, see Chapter IV.
10. *Commercial West*, vol. 40, no. 18 (Oct. 29, 1921), p. 11.
11. *Loc. cit.*
12. *Loc. cit.*
13. *Ibid.*, vol. 41, no. 12 (Mar. 25, 1922), p. 28.
14. *Ibid.*, no. 16 (Apr. 22, 1922), p. 11.
15. *Ibid.*, no. 19 (May 13, 1922), p. 11.
16. *Ibid.*, vol. 43, no. 24 (June 16, 1923), p. 13.
17. *Ibid.*, vol. 44, no. 24 (Dec. 15, 1923), p. 10.
18. *Ibid.*, no. 21 (Nov. 24, 1923), p. 11.
19. *Ibid.*, vol. 43, no. 7 (Feb. 17, 1923), p. 4.
20. *Ibid.*, vol. 45, no. 25 (June 21, 1924), p. 10.
21. *Ibid.*, vol. 48, no. 10 (Sept. 5, 1925), p. 28.
22. *Ibid.*, vol. 49, no. 8 (Feb. 20, 1926), p. 11.
23. *Ibid.*, vol. 43, no. 7 (Feb. 17, 1923), p. 11.
24. Ms. Record kept by First Service Corporation, St. Paul, of liquidation of closed banks.
25. *Commercial West*, vol. 49, no. 10 (Mar. 6, 1926), p. 10.
26. *Ibid.*, no. 15 (Apr. 10, 1926), p. 28.
27. *Ibid.*, no. 19 (May 8, 1926), p. 28.
28. *Ibid.*, vol. 51, no. 4 (Jan. 22, 1927), p. 28.
29. *Ibid.*, vol. 52, no. 14 (Oct. 1, 1927), p. 42.
30. *Ibid.*, vol. 45, no. 19 (May 10, 1924), p. 10.
31. Manual of Progress of the First National Bank of St. Paul.
32. *Commercial West*, vol. 49, no. 13 (Mar. 27, 1926), p. 28.
33. *Ibid.*, no. 17 (Apr. 24, 1926), p. 28.
34. *Ibid.*, vol. 51, no. 2 (Jan. 8, 1927), p. 28.
35. *Commercial West*, vol. 39, no. 9 (Feb. 26, 1921), p. 10.
36. *Ibid.*, vol. 42, no. 9 (Aug. 26, 1922), p. 7.
37. *Commercial West*, vol. 42, no. 1 (July 1, 1922), p. 10.
38. *Ibid.*, no. 6 (Aug. 5, 1922), p. 11.
39. *Ibid.*, no. 22 (Nov. 25, 1922), p. 8; no. 23 (Dec. 2, 1922), p. 11.
40. *Ibid.*, no. 26 (Dec. 23, 1922), p. 11.
41. *Ibid.*, no. 13 (Sept. 23, 1922), p. 11.
42. *Session Laws of the State of Minnesota*, 1923, chap. 170, sec. 1, p. 194.
43. *Commercial West*, vol. 43, no. 11 (March 17, 1923), p. 28.
44. *Ibid.*, vol. 48, no. 6 (Aug. 8, 1925), p. 28.
45. *Loc. cit.*
46. *Ibid.*, no. 18 (Oct. 31, 1925), p. 28.
47. *Ibid.*, vol. 51, no. 19 (May 7, 1927), p. 28.
48. *Ibid.*, vol. 52, no. 1 (July 2, 1927), p. 9.
49. *Ibid.*, no. 15 (Oct. 8, 1927), p. 19.
50. *Ibid.*, no. 19 (Nov. 5, 1927), p. 10.

51. *Ibid.*, vol. 45, no. 2 (Jan. 12, 1924), p. 9.
52. *Ibid.*, vol. 37, no. 17 (Apr. 24, 1920), p. 36.
53. *Ibid.*, vol. 40, no. 4 (July 23, 1921), p. 28.
54. *Loc. cit.*
55. *Ibid.*, no. 27 (Dec. 31, 1921), p. 28.
56. *Ibid.*, vol. 41, no. 16 (Apr. 22, 1922), p. 10.
57. *Ibid.*, vol. 42, no. 1 (July 1, 1922), p. 11.
58. *Ibid.*, no. 25 (Dec. 16, 1922), p. 10.
59. *Ibid.*, vol. 41, no. 20 (May 20, 1922), p. 11.
60. *Ibid.*, vol. 42, no. 16 (Oct. 14, 1922), p. 11.
61. *Ibid.*, no. 8 (Aug. 19, 1922), p. 28.
62. *Ibid.*, vol. 53, no. 2 (Jan. 14, 1928), p. 15.
63. *Ibid.*, vol. 41, no. 19 (May 13, 1922), p. 10.
64. *Ibid.*, vol. 45, no. 20 (May 17, 1924), p. 21.
65. *Ibid.*, vol. 47, no. 16 (Apr. 18, 1925), p. 10.
66. *Loc. cit.*
67. *Ibid.*, vol. 48, no. 20 (Nov. 14, 1925), p. 11.
68. *Ibid.*, vol. 49, no. 6 (Feb. 6, 1926), p. 28; no. 18 (May 1, 1926), p. 10.
69. *Ibid.*, vol. 50, no. 6 (Aug. 7, 1926), p. 5.
70. *Ibid.*, no. 17 (Oct. 23, 1926), p. 28; vol. 51, no. 19 (May 7, 1927), p. 15.
71. Ms. Letter, First National Bank, Minneapolis, to stockholders, Jan. 27, 1928.
72. *Commercial West*, vol. 53, no. 14 (Apr. 7, 1928), p. 10.
73. *Ibid.*, vol. 54, no. 6 (Aug. 11, 1928), p. 12.
74. Ms. Records, First National Bank, Minneapolis, Jan. 8, 1929.
75. *Loc. cit.*
76. *Commercial West*, vol. 55, no. 2 (Jan. 12, 1929), p. 19.
77. *Ibid.*, vol. 56, no. 16 (Oct. 26, 1929), p. 20.
78. *Ibid.*, no. 18 (Nov. 9, 1929), p. 26.

CHAPTER VI

1. *Rand McNally Bankers Directory*, 1928, p. 900.
2. *Ibid.*, p. 906.
3. *Loc. cit.*
4. Mpls. *Directory*, 1928, p. 2406.
5. *Rand McNally*, 1928, p. 900.
6. *Loc. cit.*
7. *Ibid.*, p. 905.
8. Mpls. *Directory*, 1928, p. 1387.
9. *Commercial West*, vol. 49, no. 5 (Jan. 30, 1926), p. 11.
10. Mpls. *Directory*, 1928, p. 365.
11. *Rand McNally*, 1928, p. 900.
12. *Ibid.*, p. 905.
13. *Best's Life Insurance Reports* (New York, 1928), p. 730.
14. *Rand McNally*, 1928, p. 905.
15. Mpls. *Directory*, 1928, p. 2478.
16. *Ibid.*, p. 1274.
17. *Rand McNally*, 1928, p. 905.
18. *Ibid.*, p. 926.

19. Record Book, *Manual of Progress of the First National Bank of St. Paul.*
20. *Rand McNally*, 1928, p. 926.
21. *Ibid.*, p. 925.
22. *Commercial West*, vol. 49, no. 18 (May 1, 1926), p. 10.
23. *Rand McNally*, 1928, pp. 868 ff., 1052 ff., 1318 ff., and 1622 ff.
24. U. S. Laws, Federal Reserve Act, approved Dec. 23, 1913 (38 Stat. 251, chap. 6), Sec. 7, par. 1–2.
25. *Best's Insurance Reports, Fire and Marine* (New York, 1928), p. 523.
26. *Loc. cit.*
27. *Ibid.*, pp. 360, 428, 585.
28. *Ibid.*, p. 903.
29. N. S. B. Gras and Henrietta M. Larson, *Casebook in American Business History* (New York, 1939), p. 137.
30. *Ibid.*, p. 143.
31. *Best's Life Insurance Reports* (New York, 1928), p. 593.
32. *Ibid.*, p. 730.
33. *Ibid.*, p. 731.
34. *Commercial West*, vol. 55, no. 15 (Apr. 20, 1929), p. 20.
35. Fed. Res. Bank of Mpls., *Monthly Report*, vol. iv, no. 156 (Jan. 28, 1928), p. 97.
36. *Commercial West*, vol. 43, no. 19 (May 12, 1923), p. 10; vol. 52, no. 14 (Oct. 1, 1927), p. 14.
37. *Rand McNally*, 1928, p. 906.
38. *Ibid.*, p. 900.
39. *Ibid.*, p. 926.
40. *Moody's Manual of Investments, Railroad Securities* (New York, 1928), p. 1470.
41. *Ibid.*, p. 1471.
42. *Moody's Manual of Investments, Industrial Securities* (New York, 1928), p. 22.
43. *Commercial West*, vol. 51, no. 19 (May 7, 1927), p. 11.
44. *Ibid.*, vol. 56, no. 2 (July 13, 1929), p. 15.
45. *Ibid.*, vol. 55, no. 6 (Feb. 16, 1929), p. 15.

CHAPTER VII

1. *Commercial West*, vol. 47, no. 12 (Mar. 21, 1925), p. 5.
2. *Ibid.*, vol. 39, no. 16 (Apr. 16, 1921), p. 13.
3. *Ibid.*, vol. 40, no. 26 (Dec. 24, 1921), p. 3.
4. *Loc. cit.*
5. *The New Nicollet Hotel* (pamphlet, privately printed, Minneapolis), p. 2.
6. *Ibid.*, p. 3.
7. *Loc. cit.*
8. *Ibid.*, pp. 5–6.
9. *Ibid.*, p. 6.
10. *Loc. cit.*
11. *Commercial West*, vol. 47, no. 2 (Jan. 10, 1925), p. 4.
12. *Ibid.*, no. 8 (Feb. 21, 1925), p. 11.
13. *Ibid.*, vol. 41, no. 22 (June 3, 1922), p. 52.
14. *Ibid.*, vol. 48, no. 19 (Nov. 7, 1925), p. 5.
15. *Ibid.*, no. 5 (Aug. 1, 1925), p. 27.

16. *Ibid.*, no. 6 (Aug. 8, 1925), p. 5.
17. *Ibid.*, no. 12 (Sept. 19, 1925), p. 11.
18. *Ibid.*, vol. 50, no. 22 (Nov. 27, 1926), p. 10.
19. *Loc. cit.*
20. *Ibid.*, no. 13 (Sept. 25, 1926), p. 30.
21. *Ibid.*, vol. 47, no. 18 (May 2, 1925), p. 11.
22. *Ibid.*, vol. 48, no. 1 (July 4, 1925), p. 52.
23. *Ibid.*, vol. 49, no. 9 (Feb. 27, 1926), p. 11.
24. Ms. Memorandum dated Feb. 23, 1932, Mr. A. C. Regan to officers of the First Securities Corporation.
25. *Commercial West*, vol. 55, no. 6 (Feb. 16, 1929), p. 15.
26. *Ibid.*, vol. 51, no. 1 (Jan. 1, 1927), p. 42.
27. *Loc. cit.*
28. *Ibid.*, no. 2 (Jan. 8, 1927), p. 4.
29. *Ibid.*, no. 1 (Jan. 1, 1927), p. 24.
30. *Ibid.*, no. 3 (Jan. 15, 1927), p. 4.
31. *Ibid.*, no. 6 (Feb. 5, 1927), p. 51.
32. *Ibid.*, no. 12 (Mar. 19, 1927), p. 10.
33. *Ibid.*, no. 16 (Apr. 16, 1927), p. 6.
34. *Ibid.*, no. 15 (Apr. 9, 1927), p. 9.
35. *Ibid.*, no. 19 (May 7, 1927), p. 11.
36. *Ibid.*, no. 23 (June 4, 1927), p. 17.
37. *Ibid.*, vol. 53, no. 10 (Mar. 10, 1928), p. 34.
38. *Ibid.*, no. 12 (Mar. 24, 1928), p. 36.
39. *Loc. cit.*
40. *Ibid.*, no. 14 (Apr. 7, 1928), p. 23.
41. *Ibid.*, no. 26 (June 30, 1928), p. 22.
42. *Ibid.*, no. 24 (June 16, 1928), p. 2.
43. *Ibid.*, vol. 54, no. 4 (July 28, 1928), p. 3.
44. *Ibid.*, no. 21 (Nov. 24, 1928), p. 17.
45. *Ibid.*, no. 25 (Dec. 22, 1928), p. 9.
46. *Ibid.*, vol. 55, no. 7 (Feb. 23, 1929), p. 36.
47. *Ibid.*, p. 31.
48. *Ibid.*, no. 9 (Mar. 9, 1929), p. 36.
49. *Ibid.*, no. 11 (Mar. 23, 1929), p. 14.
50. *Ibid.*, no. 13 (Apr. 6, 1929), p. 44.
51. *Ibid.*, no. 15 (Apr. 20, 1929), p. 20.
52. *Ibid.*, vol. 56, no. 1 (July 6, 1929), p. 19.
53. *Ibid.*, vol. 55, no. 10 (Mar. 16, 1929), p. 17.
54. *Ibid.*, vol. 56, no. 2 (July 13, 1929), p. 15.
55. *Ibid.*, vol. 55, no. 20 (May 25, 1929), p. 36.
56. *Ibid.*, vol. 56, no. 9 (Sept. 7, 1929), p. 20.
57. *Ibid.*, no. 5 (Aug. 10, 1929), p. 4.
58. *Ibid.*, no. 8 (Aug. 31, 1929), p. 4.
59. *Loc. cit.*
60. *Ibid.*, no. 12 (Sept. 28, 1929), p. 11.
61. *Ibid.*, no. 11 (Sept. 21, 1929), p. 20.
62. *Ibid.*, no. 24 (Dec. 21, 1929), p. 11.

63. *Ibid.*, no. 18 (Nov. 9, 1929), p. 26.
64. *Loc. cit.*
65. *Loc. cit.*

CHAPTER VIII

1. Kuhlmann, *Development of the Flour Milling Industry*, p. 173.
2. *Loc. cit.*
3. *Ibid.*, p. 175.
4. *Loc. cit.*
5. *Loc. cit.*
6. *Ibid.*, p. 176.
7. *Loc. cit.*
8. *Ibid.*, p. 166.
9. *Commercial West*, vol. 39, no. 7 (Feb. 12, 1921), p. 35.
10. *Ibid.*, vol. 43, no. 7 (Feb. 17, 1923), p. 30.
11. For instance, F. A. Chamberlain, P. J. Leeman, and Messrs. C. T. Jaffray, L. E. Wakefield, and R. W. Webb.
12. *Moody's Public Utility Securities*, 1921, p. 837.
13. *Ibid.*, 1925, p. 1129.
14. *Commercial West*, vol. 48, no. 19 (Nov. 7, 1925), p. 17.
15. *Ibid.*, vol. 53, no. 18 (May 5, 1928), p. 15.
16. *Moody's Industrial Securities*, 1929, p. 3126.
17. *Ibid.*, p. 1309.
18. *Ibid.*, p. 2951.
19. *Ibid.*, 1923, p. 398.
20. *Ibid.*, p. 1808.
21. *Ibid.*, 1926, p. 2514.
22. *Ibid.*, p. 2065.
23. *Ibid.*, p. 1177.
24. *Ibid.*, 1929, p. 1993.
25. *Loc. cit.*
26. *Loc. cit.*
27. *Commercial West*, vol. 55, no. 13 (Apr. 6, 1929), p. 13.
28. *Ibid.*, vol. 53, no. 1 (Jan. 7, 1928), p. 19.

CHAPTER IX

1. Except where otherwise indicated, this account is obtained from personal conversation with the officers of Northwest Bancorporation.
2. Statement of E. W. Decker in *Branch, Chain and Group Banking*, Hearings before the Committee on Banking and Currency, 71st Cong., 2d Sess., H. R. 141 (Washington, 1930), vol. i, part 8, p. 792.
3. Pamphlet, *Survey of Banking Industry in the Northwest and Record of Northwest Bancorporation as a Holding Company* (Minneapolis, 1938), p. 4.
4. Northwest Bancorporation, Ms. Directors' Minutes, Jan. 30, 1929.
5. *Idem*, *First Annual Report*, Dec. 31, 1929, p. 5.
6. *Commercial West*, vol. 55, no. 2 (Jan. 12, 1929), p. 10.
7. Ms. Memorandum, Mr. Henry Verdelin to officers of First National Bank, Minneapolis, dated Jan. 28, 1929. In files of First National Bank, Minneapolis.

8. *Survey of Banking Industry in the Northwest*, p. 3.
9. Ms. Directors' Minutes, Northwest Bancorporation, Jan. 30, 1929.
10. *Ibid.*, Feb. 19, 1929.
11. *Manual of Progress*, First National Bank, St. Paul.
12. Interview with Mr. Herbert Hallenberg of the Northwest Bancorporation.
13. Ms. Executive Committee Minutes, Northwest Bancorporation, March 30, 1929.
14. Decker, in *Branch, Chain and Group Banking*, vol. i, part 8, p. 791.
15. Statement of Mr. Herbert Hallenberg.
16. Financial Statement, Mar. 28, 1929.
17. Ms. Contract dated Feb. 19, 1929, between the stockholders of the Security National Bank and Trust Company of Faribault and the Northwest Bancorporation.
18. Advertising file, Northwest Bancorporation.
19. Ms. Contract dated Feb. 21, 1929, between the stockholders of the Citizens National Bank, Watertown, South Dakota, and the Northwest Bancorporation; Ms. Contract dated Feb. 20, 1929, between the stockholders of the First National Bank of Watertown, South Dakota, and the Northwest Bancorporation.
20. Ms. Contract dated Apr. 29, 1929, between the stockholders of the Fergus Falls National Bank and the Northwest Bancorporation.
21. Ms. Contract dated Apr. 18, 1929, between the stockholders of the Security National Bank of Sioux Falls, South Dakota, and the Northwest Bancorporation.
22. Ms. Contract dated July 29, 1929, between the stockholders of the James River National Bank of Jamestown, North Dakota, and the Northwest Bancorporation.
23. Ms. Executive Committee Minutes, Northwest Bancorporation, Apr. 15, 1929.
24. *Commercial West*, vol. 55, no. 22 (June 8, 1929), p. 50.
25. Ms. Directors' Minutes, Northwest Bancorporation, June 28, 1929.
26. Decker, in *Branch, Chain and Group Banking*, vol. i, part 8, p. 791.
27. Pamphlet, *The Great Northwest* (Mpls., 1928), p. 26.
28. Ms. Agreement dated June 12, 1929, between the Dakota National Bank of Aberdeen, South Dakota, and the First National Bank of Aberdeen, South Dakota.
29. Ms. Agreement dated June 14, 1929, between the Citizens Trust and Savings Bank of Aberdeen, South Dakota, and the First National Bank of Aberdeen, South Dakota.
30. Ms. Agreement dated June 6, 1929, between the shareholders of the First National Bank of Aberdeen, South Dakota, and the Northwest Bancorporation.
31. *Commercial West*, vol. 56, no. 1 (July 6, 1929), p. 9.
32. *Loc. cit.*
33. Ms. Letter, Mr. E. W. Decker to the stockholders of Northwest Bancorporation, Aug. 15, 1929.
34. *Commercial West*, vol. 56, no. 8 (Aug. 31, 1929), p. 10.
35. *Ibid.*, no. 10 (Sept. 14, 1929), p. 9.
36. *Time*, vol. xiv, no. 8 (Aug. 19, 1929), p. 56.
37. Interview with Mr. W. H. Brenton.
38. Ms. Agreement dated Aug. 21, 1929, between the prospective stockholders of the Iowa–Des Moines National Bank and Trust Company and the Northwest Bancorporation.
39. Ms. Supplement to above agreement, also dated Aug. 21, 1929.
40. Des Moines *Register*, Sept. 13, 1929.
41. *Commercial West*, vol. 56, no. 10 (Sept. 14, 1929), p. 10.
42. Ms. Traders Records, First National Bank and Trust Company, Minneapolis.

43. *Commercial West*, vol. 56, no. 12 (Sept. 28, 1929), p. 8.

44. *Bancorporation News*, vol. i, no. 2 (Dec., 1930), p. 4.

45. *Commercial West*, vol. 56, no. 14 (Oct. 12, 1929), p. 21.

46. *Ibid.*, p. 20.

47. Ms. Agreement dated Sept. 14, 1929, between the stockholders of the Spokane and Eastern Trust Company and the Northwest Bancorporation.

48. Ms. Directors' Minutes, Northwest Bancorporation, Sept. 27, 1929.

49. *Ibid.*, Oct. 10, 1929.

50. Decker, in *Branch, Chain and Group Banking*, vol. i, part 8, p. 830.

51. Ms. Letter, Mr. E. W. Decker to the stockholders of Northwest Bancorporation, Oct. 12, 1929.

52. *Commercial West*, vol. 56, no. 21 (Nov. 30, 1929), p. 8.

53. Northwest Bancorporation, *First Annual Report*, Dec. 31, 1929, p. 3.

54. *Loc. cit.*

55. *Ibid.*, p. 7.

56. *Loc. cit.*

57. Testimony of J. Cameron Thomson in *Operation of the National and Federal Reserve Banking Systems*, part 4, p. 568.

58. Decker, in *Branch, Chain and Group Banking*, vol. i, part 8, p. 831.

59. *Commercial West*, vol. 57, no. 1 (Jan. 4, 1930), p. 10.

60. Ms. Agreement dated Jan. 31, 1930, between the stockholders of the Empire National Bank, St. Paul, and the Northwest Bancorporation.

61. *Commercial West*, vol. 59, no. 19 (May 10, 1930), p. 6.

62. *Bancorporation News*, vol. i, no. 2 (Dec., 1930), p. 4.

63. Thomson, in *Operation of the Nat. and Fed. Res. Banking Systems*, part 4, p. 576.

64. Northwest Bancorporation, *Second Annual Report*, Dec. 31, 1930, p. 8.

65. *Ibid.*, p. 10.

66. Ms. Executive Committee Minutes, Northwest Bancorporation, Dec. 10, 1930.

67. *Ibid.*, Sept. 10, 1930.

68. *Bancorporation News*, vol. ii, no. 2 (June, 1931), p. 2.

69. Northwest Bancorporation, *Third Annual Report*, Dec. 31, 1931, pp. 20–21.

70. *Ibid.*, p. 10.

71. *Ibid.*, p. 16.

72. *Ibid.*, p. 18.

CHAPTER X

1. First National Bank, Minneapolis, *Annual Statements*, 1921–1929, inclusive.

2. Wakefield, in *Operation of the Nat. and Fed. Res. Banking Systems*, part 4, p. 612.

3. Personnel Records, P. J. Leeman, First National Bank, Minneapolis.

4. *Loc. cit.*

5. Statement of Mr. W. A. Volkman, vice-president, First National Bank, Minneapolis.

6. Statement of Mr. Lyman E. Wakefield, president, First National Bank and Trust Company, Minneapolis.

7. This account was given by one of the officers of the First National Bank, Minneapolis.

8. *Loc. cit.*

9. *Commercial West*, vol. 55, no. 12 (Mar. 30, 1929), p. 9.

10. *Ibid.*, no. 15 (Apr. 20, 1929), p. 20.

11. Ms. Contracts between the First Bank Stock Investment Company and the respective banks.

12. *Loc. cit.*

13. Figures taken from the annual statements dated Dec. 31, 1929.

14. Information as to Leeman's reaction has been acquired from conversation with the officers of the First National Bank and Trust Company, Minneapolis.

15. Financial Statement, June 30, 1929.

16. *Commercial West*, vol. 56, no. 8 (Aug. 31, 1929), p. 9.

17. Financial statements dated Dec. 31, 1929.

18. Ms. Circular letter dated Aug. 27, 1929, from First Bank Stock Corporation to stockholders of various banks.

19. *Loc. cit.*

20. Ms. Offering circular dated Sept. 6, 1929, of the First St. Paul Company and the First Minneapolis Company.

21. *Loc. cit.*

22. Statement of Mr. L. B. Hogue, secretary of First Bank Stock Corporation.

23. Ms. Commitment File, First Bank Stock Corporation.

24. *Loc. cit.*

25. Ms. Traders' Records, First National Bank and Trust Company, Minneapolis.

26. First Bank Stock Corporation, Ms. Commitment File.

27. *Idem*, *First Annual Report*, Dec. 31, 1929.

28. *Idem*, Ms. Directors' Minutes, Feb. 18, 1930.

29. *Idem*, *First Annual Report*.

30. Ms. Traders' Records, First National Bank and Trust Company, Minneapolis.

31. *Commercial West*, vol. 56, no. 25 (Dec. 28, 1929), p. 9.

32. *Loc. cit.*

33. Ms. Proceedings, First Annual Conference of the First Bank Stock Corporation (Minneapolis, 1930), p. 125.

34. *Ibid.*, pp. 119 ff.

35. *Ibid.*, pp. 126 ff.

36. *Commercial West*, vol. 56, no. 23 (Dec. 14, 1929), p. 8.

37. *Ibid.*, vol. 57, no. 5 (Feb. 1, 1930), p. 14.

38. *Loc. cit.*

39. *Loc. cit.*

40. *Loc. cit.*

41. Ms. Commitment File, First Bank Stock Corporation.

42. *Commercial West*, vol. 59, no. 11 (Mar. 15, 1930), p. 20.

43. Ms. Commitment File, First Bank Stock Corporation.

44. Ms. Acquisition contracts of the respective banks supply details.

45. Record Book, *Manual of Progress of the First National Bank of St. Paul.*

46. Interview with Mr. Philip L. Ray.

47. Ms. Commitment File, First Bank Stock Corporation.

48. Compiled by Mr. L. B. Hogue, secretary, First Bank Stock Corporation.

49. First Bank Stock Corporation, *Third Annual Report*, Dec. 31, 1931, p. 11.

50. *Idem*, *Fifth Annual Report*, Dec. 31, 1933, p. 13.

CHAPTER XI

1. Mpls. Fed. Res. Bank, *Monthly Report*, vol. v, no. 181 (Jan. 29, 1930), p. 5.
2. *Loc. cit.*
3. E. H. H. Simmons, *The Principal Causes of the Stock Market Crisis of Nineteen Twenty Nine* (New York, 1930), p. 7.
4. *Ibid.*, p. 10.
5. F. Cyril James, *The Growth of Chicago Banks* (New York, 1938), vol. ii, p. 986.
6. *Ibid.*, p. 987.
7. *Ibid.*, p. 988.
8. Ms. Traders' Records, First National Bank and Trust Company, Minneapolis.
9. *Loc. cit.*
10. *Loc. cit.*
11. Mpls. Fed. Res. Bank, *Monthly Report*, vol. vi, no. 221 (May 29, 1933), p. 40.
12. *Idem, Annual Report, 1932* (Minneapolis, 1933), pp. 3–5.
13. *Loc. cit.*
14. *Idem, Monthly Report*, vol. vi, no. 229 (Jan. 29, 1934), p. 101.
15. *Idem, Annual Report, 1932*, p. 4.
16. *Loc. cit.*
17. *Loc. cit.*
18. Ms. Letter dated Dec. 31, 1940, from the Tower Company to its stockholders.
19. Ms. Letter dated Dec. 9, 1930, from W. H. Felson, First National Bank and Trust Company, Minneapolis, to Utah Savings and Trust Company, Salt Lake City.
20. *Loc. cit.*
21. Pamphlet, E. W. Backus, *Save Your Investment in Minnesota and Ontario Paper Company Bonds* (Minneapolis, 1934), p. 25.
22. *Loc. cit.*
23. *Loc. cit.*
24. *Loc. cit.*
25. *Ibid.*, p. 27.
26. *Ibid.*, p. 28.
27. *Ibid.*, p. 35.
28. *Ibid.*, p. 6.
29. Ms. dated Sept. 6, 1935, Memorandum of Mr. H. Verdelin to officers of First National Bank and Trust Company, Minneapolis.
30. Baker Properties, Incorporated, *Annual Report*, 1930.
31. *Loc. cit.*
32. *Ibid.*, 1931, 1932, 1933.
33. Ms. Statistical file on the Baker Properties, Incorporated, in the possession of the First National Bank and Trust Company, Minneapolis.
34. *Loc. cit.*
35. Ms. Memorandum dated April 6, 1935, from Mr. H. Verdelin to officers of the First National Bank and Trust Company, Minneapolis.
36. Ms. Letter dated February 14, 1933, to the stockholders from the Nicollet Hotel, Incorporated.
37. Ms. Memorandum dated Nov. 8, 1935, from Mr. H. Verdelin to the officers of the First National Bank and Trust Company, Minneapolis.
38. *Ibid.*, dated May 13, 1933.

39. *Loc. cit.*
40. Mpls. Fed. Res. Bank, *Monthly Report*, vol. vi, no. 217 (Jan. 28, 1933), p. 4.
41. *Ibid.*, vol. v, no. 206 (Feb. 29, 1932), p. 204.
42. *Loc. cit.*
43. *Ibid.*, vol. vi, no. 229 (Jan. 29, 1934), p. 101.
44. *Loc. cit.*
45. *Idem*, *Annual Report, 1931*, p. 6.
46. Figures supplied by the Minneapolis Federal Reserve Bank.
47. James, *op. cit.*, p. 1026.
48. *Ibid.*, p. 1027.
49. Lawrence Sullivan, *Prelude to Panic* (Washington, 1936), p. 3.
50. *Ibid.*, p. 3.
51. Mpls. Fed. Res. Bank, *Annual Report, 1932*, p. 10.
52. Sullivan, *op. cit.*, pp. 7–8, 10.
53. James, *op. cit.*, p. 1047.
54. *Ibid.*, p. 1053.
55. *Fed. Res. Bulletin*, vol. xix, no. 3 (Mar., 1933), p. 114.
56. *Ibid.*, p. 115.
57. *Ibid.*, p. 118.
58. *Ibid.*, p. 119.
59. *Ibid.*, p. 120.
60. Cyril B. Upham and Edwin Lamke, *Closed and Distressed Banks* (Washington, 1934), p. 258.
61. *Loc. cit.*
62. *Loc. cit.*
63. *Loc. cit.*
64. J. F. T. O'Connor, *Banks Under Roosevelt* (Chicago, 1938), p. 42.
65. *Ibid.*, p. 43.
66. *Ibid.*, p. 46.
67. *Fed. Res. Bulletin*, vol. xix, no. 106 (June, 1933), pp. 385 ff.
68. *Ibid.*, vol. xx, no. 7 (July, 1934), p. 487.
69. *Ibid.*, vol. xxi, no. 9 (Sept., 1935), pp. 603 ff.

CHAPTER XII

1. Ms. Northwest Bancorporation, Plan of Internal Organization, June 1929.
2. *Loc. cit.*
3. *Loc. cit.*
4. *Loc. cit.*
5. *Loc. cit.*
6. *Idem*, *Third Annual Report*, Dec. 31, 1931, p. 10.
7. *Ibid.*, p. 27.
8. *Loc. cit.*
9. *Loc. cit.*
10. *Loc. cit.*
11. *Ibid.*, p. 21.
12. *Idem*, *Second Annual Report*, Dec. 31, 1930, p. 7.
13. *Idem*, *Third Annual Report*, Dec. 31, 1931, p. 19.
14. *Idem*, Ms. Directors' Minutes, Oct. 19, 1931.

15. *Loc. cit.*
16. *Loc. cit.*
17. *Loc. cit.*
18. *Loc. cit.*
19. *Idem, Fourth Annual Report*, Dec. 31, 1932, p. 21.
20. *Loc. cit.*
21. *Loc. cit.*
22. *Ibid.*, p. 15.
23. *Ibid.*, p. 6.
24. *Idem*, Ms. Directors' Minutes, Oct. 19, 1931.
25. *Idem, Fourth Annual Report*, Dec. 31, 1932, p. 21.
26. *Loc. cit.*
27. *Ibid.*, p. 3.
28. *Idem*, Ms. Executive Committee Minutes, Jan. 11, 1933.
29. *Loc. cit.*
30. *Loc. cit.*
31. *Idem*, Ms. Directors' Minutes, Nov. 17, 1932.
32. A description of this run was obtained from an officer of the Northwest Bancorporation.
33. *Loc. cit.*
34. *Loc. cit.*
35. *Loc. cit.*
36. Northwest Bancorporation, Ms. Executive Committee Minutes, July 14, 1933.
37. *Ibid.*, June 21, 1933; Directors' Minutes, June 21, 1933.
38. *Ibid.*, Sept. 14, 1933.
39. *Idem, Fifth Annual Report*, Dec. 31, 1933, p. 8.
40. *Idem*, Ms. Directors' Minutes, June 22, 1933.
41. *Ibid.*, Dec. 27, 1933.
42. *Idem*, Ms. Executive Committee Minutes, July 14, 1933.
43. *Idem*, Ms. Directors' Minutes, Sept. 14, 1933.
44. *Idem*, Ms. Executive Committee Minutes, June 27, 1933.
45. *Idem*, Ms. Directors' Minutes, Jan. 9, 1934.
46. *Ibid.*, Aug. 10, 1933.
47. *Ibid.*, Oct. 23, 1933.
48. *Ibid.*, Sept. 14, 1933.
49. *Loc. cit.*
50. *Ibid.*, Dec. 11, 1933.
51. *Loc. cit.*
52. *Idem, Fifth Annual Report*, Dec. 31, 1933, p. 11.
53. *Ibid.*, p. 6.
54. *Ibid.*, p. 16.
55. Statement of Mr. J. Cameron Thomson, president of Northwest Bancorporation.
56. Ms. Directors' Minutes, Northwest Bancorporation, Oct. 23, 1933.
57. Minneapolis *Tribune*, Nov. 23, 1933, p. 1.
58. *Ibid.*, Dec. 3, 1933, p. 4.
59. *Ibid.*, Dec. 12, 1933, p. 2.
60. *Loc. cit.*
61. St. Paul *Dispatch*, June 30, 1934, p. 1.
62. *Loc. cit.*

63. *Ibid.*, July 25, 1934, p. 1.
64. *Ibid.*, Aug. 2, 1934, p. 7.
65. Minneapolis *Journal*, Sept. 23, 1934, p. 2.
66. *Loc. cit.*
67. New Ulm *Review* (Minnesota), Sept. 27, 1934, p. 2.
68. St. Paul *Pioneer Press*, Sept. 23, 1934, pp. 1–2.
69. St. Paul *Dispatch*, Nov. 10, 1934, p. 6.
70. St. Paul *Pioneer Press*, Sept. 28, 1934, p. 7.
71. Minneapolis *Tribune*, Nov. 14, 1934, p. 1.
72. *Ibid.*, Dec. 8, 1934, p. 6; Dec. 9, 1934, p. 1; Dec. 12, 1934, p. 1.
73. *Ibid.*, Jan. 16, 1935, p. 1.
74. St. Paul *Daily News*, Jan. 24, 1935, p. 1.
75. Minneapolis *Tribune*, Oct. 19, 1935, p. 9.
76. *Loc. cit.*
77. *Ibid.*, Feb. 1, 1936, p. 1.

CHAPTER XIII

1. First Securities Corporation, Offering circulars.
2. Information supplied by officers of First Bank Stock Corporation.
3. Comment of officers of First Service Corporation.
4. *Loc. cit.*
5. Comment of officers of the First National Bank and Trust Company, Minneapolis.
6. Ms. Record of the Reorganization Department, First Service Corporation, Minneapolis.
7. Comment of Mr. Hugh W. Martin, vice-president, First Service Corporation, Minneapolis.
8. *Proceedings, First Annual Conference of the First Bank Stock Corporation* (Minneapolis, 1930), p. 10.
9. *Commercial West*, vol. 60, no. 15 (Oct. 11, 1930), p. 10.
10. *Proceedings, Second Annual Conference of the First Bank Stock Corporation* (Minneapolis, 1931), p. 144.
11. Offering circular of First Securities Corporation describing Frontenac Trust Shares.
12. *Loc. cit.*
13. Trust Agreement dated Feb. 2, 1931, between Frontenac Trust Shares and the Trust Company of New Jersey.
14. *Proceedings, Second Annual Conference of the First Bank Stock Corporation* (Minneapolis, 1931), p. 150.
15. *Loc. cit.*
16. *Loc. cit.* (H. E. Atwood.)
17. First Bank Stock Corporation, *Third Annual Report*, Dec. 31, 1931, p. 5.
18. Comment of officers of First Bank Stock Corporation.
19. *Loc. cit.*; this is borne out by the low loss ratio in commercial loans.
20. *Commercial West*, vol. 63, no. 2 (Jan. 9, 1932), p. 12.
21. Statement of Mr. Henry Verdelin, assistant vice-president, First Service Corporation.

22. Ms. Records of the Reorganization Department, First Service Corporation, Minneapolis.
23. First Bank Stock Corporation, annual statements for the respective years.
24. *Loc. cit.*
25. *Loc. cit.*
26. *Loc. cit.*
27. *Loc. cit.*
28. First Bank Stock Corporation, *Fifth Annual Report*, Dec. 31, 1933, p. 11.
29. These were assumed in full by the merged organization.
30. Ms. Minutes of a special stockholders' meeting held Jan. 24, 1933.
31. First Bank Stock Corporation, *Fifth Annual Report*, Dec. 31, 1933, p. 31.
32. *Idem*, annual reports for the respective years.
33. It employed on an average $30,000,000.
34. First Bank Stock Corporation, *Proceedings of Second Annual Conference* (Minneapolis, 1931), p. 5.
35. *Idem*, annual reports for the respective years.
36. *Commercial West*, vol. 61, no. 18 (May 2, 1931), p. 9.
37. First Bank Stock Corporation, annual reports for the respective years.
38. *Loc. cit.*
39. *Loc. cit.*
40. *Commercial West*, vol. 64, no. 5 (July 30, 1932), p. 33.
41. *Loc. cit.*
42. Statement of Mr. A. H. Kennedy, president of First Bank Stock Corporation.
43. *Loc. cit.*
44. Statement of Mr. F. S. Lytle, vice-president, Western Montana National Bank, Missoula.
45. *Loc. cit.*
46. *Loc. cit.*
47. *Loc. cit.*
48. *Loc. cit.*
49. First National Bank of St. Paul, *Annual Report*, Dec. 31, 1933, p. 40.
50. Statement of Mr. A. H. Kennedy, president of First Bank Stock Corporation.
51. *Loc. cit.*
52. *Loc. cit.*
53. Statement of Mr. L. B. Hogue, secretary, First Bank Stock Corporation.
54. First Bank Stock Corporation, *Fifth Annual Report*, Dec. 31, 1933, p. 9.
55. *Loc. cit.*
56. *Ibid.*, p. 8.
57. *Loc. cit.*
58. *Idem, Sixth Annual Report*, Dec. 31, 1934, p. 4.
59. *Ibid.*, p. 11.
60. *Idem, Seventh Annual Report*, Dec. 31, 1935, p. 11.
61. Ms. Letter dated Nov. 18, 1933, from the First National Bank and Trust Company, Minneapolis, to the shareholders of Frontenac Trust Shares.
62. *Ibid.*, dated Dec. 12, 1933.
63. *Banking Act of 1933*, signed June 16, 1933.
64. The charter was granted May 2, 1922.
65. Ms. Financial statement dated Aug. 31, 1924, sent by Minneapolis Trust-Joint Stock Land Bank to prospective bondholders.

66. Ms. Circular letter dated Nov. 1, 1933, from O. M. Corwin, president, to the bondholders of the Minneapolis Trust-Joint Stock Land Bank.

67. *Loc. cit.*

68. *Loc. cit.*

69. *Loc. cit.*

70. *Ibid.*, dated April 23, 1934.

71. *Ibid.*, dated Sept. 14, 1934.

72. First Bank Stock Corporation, *First Annual Report*, Feb. 18, 1930, p. 2.

73. *Idem*, *Fifth Annual Report*, Dec. 31, 1933, p. 11.

74. *Ibid.*, pp. 15–19.

75. *Loc. cit.*

76. *Idem*, *Third Annual Report*, Dec. 31, 1931, p. 7; and *Fifth Annual Report*, Dec. 31, 1933, p. 6.

CHAPTER XIV

1. Minneapolis Federal Reserve Bank, *Report of the Federal Reserve Agent*, Dec. 31, 1935, p. 5.

2. *Idem*, *Monthly Report*, vol. vii, no. 264 (Dec. 28, 1936), p. 50.

3. *Ibid.*, no. 282 (June 28, 1938), p. 134.

4. *Ibid.*, no. 298 (Oct. 28, 1939), p. 200.

5. First Bank Stock Corporation, *Second Annual Report*, Dec. 31, 1930, p. 8; *Sixth Annual Report*, Dec. 31, 1934, p. 12.

6. *Idem*, *Chronological List of Acquisitions, Consolidations, Sales, and Liquidation of Affiliates.*

7. *Loc. cit.*

8. *Idem*, *Eighth Annual Report*, Dec. 31, 1936, p. 4.

9. Statement of Mr. J. Cameron Thomson, president of the Northwest Bancorporation.

10. Northwest Bancorporation, *Twelfth Annual Report*, Dec. 31, 1933, p. 5.

11. Statement of Mr. J. Cameron Thomson.

12. *Loc. cit.*

13. Northwest Bancorporation, *Twelfth Annual Report*, Dec. 31, 1940, p. 16.

14. Statement of Mr. J. Cameron Thomson.

15. Northwest Bancorporation, annual reports for the respective years.

16. *Loc. cit.*

17. *Idem*, *Twelfth Annual Report*, Dec. 31, 1940, p. 4.

18. See the annual reports of both companies for the respective years.

19. As indicated in previous chapters, all banks suffered from a steady shrinkage of deposits but seldom from runs. This shrinkage was at such a slow rate that solvent banks were able to obtain cash.

20. Statement of Mr. R. W. Webb, vice-president, First National Bank and Trust Company, Minneapolis.

21. Statement of Mr. Ben S. Woodworth, advertising manager, First National Bank and Trust Company, Minneapolis.

22. For instance, Household Finance Corporation.

23. The savings accounts of banks showed only a moderate increase while these increased sharply.

24. Federal Deposit Insurance Corporation, *Annual Report*, Dec. 31, 1939, p. 11.

25. *Ibid.*, p. 23.
26. *Ibid.*, p. 10.
27. Figures supplied by the Minneapolis Federal Reserve Bank.
28. See the annual reports of both groups for the respective years.
29. Decker, in *Branch, Chain and Group Banking*, vols. i and ii, parts 1–5.
30. Banking Act of 1933, approved June 16, 1933.
31. Banking Act of 1935, approved Aug. 23, 1935.

INDEX

INDEX